The Penitent State

The Penitent State

*Exposure, Mourning, and the Biopolitics of
National Healing*

Paul Muldoon

Great Clarendon Street, Oxford, OX2 6DP,
United Kingdom

Oxford University Press is a department of the University of Oxford.
It furthers the University's objective of excellence in research, scholarship,
and education by publishing worldwide. Oxford is a registered trade mark of
Oxford University Press in the UK and in certain other countries

© Paul Muldoon 2023

The moral rights of the author have been asserted

All rights reserved. No part of this publication may be reproduced, stored in
a retrieval system, or transmitted, in any form or by any means, without the
prior permission in writing of Oxford University Press, or as expressly permitted
by law, by licence or under terms agreed with the appropriate reprographics
rights organization. Enquiries concerning reproduction outside the scope of the
above should be sent to the Rights Department, Oxford University Press, at the
address above

You must not circulate this work in any other form
and you must impose this same condition on any acquirer

Published in the United States of America by Oxford University Press
198 Madison Avenue, New York, NY 10016, United States of America

British Library Cataloguing in Publication Data

Data available

Library of Congress Control Number: 2023940187

ISBN 978-0-19-883162-4

DOI: 10.1093/oso/9780198831624.001.0001

Printed and bound in the UK by
Clays Ltd, Elcograf S.p.A.

Links to third party websites are provided by Oxford in good faith and
for information only. Oxford disclaims any responsibility for the materials
contained in any third party website referenced in this work.

Acknowledgements

It takes a village to raise a book—or, at least, it did to raise this one. Looking back, it is not the long solitary hours puzzling over things that stand out in my mind but the people who gave me encouragement or diversion when I needed it. The intellectual debts are, as always, too many to list, but a few cannot pass without mention. An old mentor at Monash University, Michael Janover, who retired before I began this book, was nevertheless an important inspiration for the kind of work that it is or attempts to be. The disregard it shows for disciplinary boundaries is, for better or worse, a legacy of his broadminded approach to the study of politics and its relationship to life. One should follow the question wherever it goes, right Michael? Other colleagues at Monash University, especially Narelle Miragliotta, Michael Ure, and Ben Wellings, were instrumental in helping me maintain my sanity and sense of an academic vocation. I doubt I'd have kept going if it weren't for them.

I am very grateful also to Juliet Rogers who read many (way too many!) drafts along the way and who was unfailingly generous and insightful. I will forever treasure those conversations. Will Kymlicka provided some very helpful advice on the book proposal and Dominic Byatt at Oxford University Press was supportive and helpful. I would also like to thank the two anonymous reviewers who provided just the advice I needed on the first draft of the manuscript. The book is better—I hope!—because they took the time to address the shortcomings of its first iteration. My good friend, Andrew Schaap, was kind enough to read a late version of the Introduction and provide critical suggestions. I didn't want to hear it, but I'm glad I did. I was fortunate too to have won the inaugural manuscript prize of the Melbourne Political, Legal and Social Theory Network and receive dedicated readings of various chapters from Lulu Weis, Benjamin Moffat, Stephanie Collins, Vanessa Barolsky, Terry McDonald, and Juliet Rogers (again!). I thank the organizers of the MPLAST Network, Terry McDonald, Liane Hartnett, and Matteo Bonotti, for this opportunity to reflect and rethink. It made the book better.

I would not have been able to write this book without the family and friends who knew when to ask (and when not to!) and who injected life into those long stretches of alone time. The uncomplicated support and endless antics of the 'Wheezers' were a welcome distraction—long may they ride in their strategically mediocre way. I am grateful too to those friends in 'the hood' (you know who you are!) who have shared so honestly and generously in the ups and downs of life. Thanks for helping me to celebrate the little things along the way (and for finally giving up on asking me to go camping). I was born into a family of five children and consider myself blessed to have siblings who do those things that only sisters and brothers would do. You are a gift and life would be so much poorer without you. My own children, Gus and Gracie, have played no small role in the creation of this book and are a constant reminder of the need for new beginnings. Their regular refrain of 'oh, are you STILL doing that?' has certainly done its bit to expedite the writing process and remind me that I might eventually have to do something else. I can only hope that their assessment of the book as 'completely unreadable' says more about their age than mine (though I will happily concede that J.K. Rowling is better—a bit). I must, finally, thank my beautiful partner, Katie, for being there for the whole bumpy ride. You are the music.

Contents

Introduction: Living by Symbols   1

1. **What Emergency? Damaged Life and the Biopolitics of State Repentance**   37
   - I   A New Species of Trouble: The Half-Life of the Alienated Survivor   44
   - II   Emergency, Defence, and Survival: The Over-Life of the Guilty Sovereign   53
   - III   The Governance of Psychic Life and the Decision on Trauma   63

2. **New Life: The Civil Wound and the Problem of Political Renewal**   79
   - I   From Prohibition to Process   86
   - II   Trauma, Latency, and the Work of Mourning   101
   - III   The Two Cultures of Collective Memory Revisited   110

3. **The Monumentalization of Shame: A Negative Mirror for the People**   127
   - I   A Matter of Identity (and Trauma)   130
   - II   Symbols of Death and Sites of Mourning   141
   - III   Error in Mourning   159

4. **An Exercise of Sovereignty in the Mode of Contrition**   169
   - I   A Rape of the Soul So Profound   175
   - II   Reckoning with Exceptionalism: Political Apology as an Act of Sovereignty   178
   - III   A New Sovereign?   192
   - IV   'A True Renaissance': Apology, Reason of State, and Indigenous Resurgence   198

5. **The Therapy of Reconciliation**   213
   - I   All and Each: The Return of the Pastorate?   220
   - II   For the Sake of the Future: Flushing the Wound and Clearing the Air   234
   - III   The Gift of Sight   243

6. A Different Catharsis? Penance and Purification in the Society of the Spectacle — 265
    I The Presentation of the Wound and the Cathartic Event — 268
    II Proximity and Intimacy — 281
    III Catharsis without Clarification? — 285

Conclusion: Remorseless Penance—Exposure, Falling, and Healing — 297

Bibliography — 313
Index — 325

Introduction

Living by Symbols

> How can nations come to terms with traumatic legacy like genocide, civil war, or political repression? Do nations have psyches like people? Can nations overcome a painful, evil past the way individuals do? Can people overcome collective trauma? If so, what are the steps to achieve national mental health?
>
> Mark Amstutz, The Healing of Nations[1]

On 7 December 1970, the chancellor of West Germany, Willy Brandt, turned his body into compelling proof of the thesis that 'we live by symbols'.[2] After laying a wreath at the foot of the memorial to the Jewish victims of the Warsaw ghetto, Brandt fell to his knees and bowed his head in silence, adopting the posture and demeanour of the true penitent: humble, remorseful, apologetic. Evidently as sincere as it was solemn, this unpremeditated gesture of contrition was remarkable in the true sense of the word: noteworthy simply by virtue of its exceptionality. Cases of subjects falling to their knees before their sovereign, in the manner of a penitent before their God, have long been a staple of history and historical drama. In the great history plays of Shakespeare, kneeling is not just the act of the remorse-filled subject who begs their king for mercy but the very mark of sovereign power: 'how dare you not kneel in my presence?', says Richard II to his would-be usurpers.[3] However, it was not until Brandt's *Kniefall* that history presented us with an instance of the reverse: the sovereign person falling to *his* knees, apologizing for and implicitly begging forgiveness for *his* wrongs. What did it mean? Had the world been turned upside down or was it rather that it had finally been righted?[4]

The enduring fascination exercised by this famous 'apologetic gesture'[5] is not so hard to explain. Even in the society of the spectacle, where the remarkable sustains itself at saturation levels, the image of the sovereign turned suppliant, petitioning forgiveness instead of dispensing mercy, remains as irresistible as it is confounding. Could there be a more exquisite, yet more

2 The Penitent State

baffling, inversion of sovereign power? In a subsequent reflection, Brandt passed off his most memorable act of contrition as self-explanatory, even commonplace: 'under the weight of German history, and carrying the burden of millions who were murdered, I did what people do when words fail them'. Brandt, to be sure, is not the only person to fall speechless in the face of the Shoah. Not even a writer as gifted as Primo Levi could escape the conclusion that 'our language lacks words to express this offence'.[6] As disarming as it first appears, however, the appeal to 'doing what people do' hardly suffices to quiet the manifold questions prompted by the image of a head of state on bended knee. How does a sovereign become burdened by a national history? Before whom does this sovereign fall and on whose behalf do they offer atonement? And what, finally, does this fall (from innocence, from grace, from inviolability?) actually achieve politically speaking?

Although Brandt's visit to Poland formed part of his *Ostpolitik*—a diplomatic initiative designed to normalize relations with 'the East'—his *Kniefall* in Warsaw is commonly regarded as having paved the way for a reconciliation much closer to home. According to John Borneman (and the view is widely shared), Brandt's 'purely symbolic gesture of remorse' did more than simply make the daily headlines; it 'inaugurated a new phase in relations between Germany and the Jews it had persecuted'.[7] Acting as the highest representative of the German people (and hence as a point of symbolic exchange between the physical body and the body politic), the chancellor had managed to pour balm on the deepest of internal wounds by tendering himself as evidence of a penitent state. For Borneman, it was an act of recognition and more. In falling to his knees, he claimed, Brandt had not just affirmed the value of the Jewish 'other' but forever changed the German state by showing that it now accepted, without demur, the need to atone for that diabolical war of extermination waged at home. And is he not right? Received as a hero by the '68ers' (the first generation of Germans to revolt against the Nazi past), that sovereign on his knees remains to this day something of an icon in Germany and beyond. Few things speak more clearly of the significance of the *Kniefall* to the new, self-effacing German state than the fact that this gesture at a memorial has now become one in its own right. 'Today', as Borneman duly notes,

> Brandt's act of remorse has been memorialized as a constitutive act of the German people in the post-unification German Historical Museum in Berlin. Alongside recordings of other famous events in 20th century German history, including the building and the opening of the Berlin Wall, a looped video of Brandt's *Kniefall* plays continuously.[8]

That looped video and those carefully chosen words ought to give us pause. In democratic theory, constitutive acts 'of the people' belong to a very special category. They are the acts that express the core commitments of the political community and establish the basic code of values according to which its members seek to live. Constitutive acts are so-called because they bear upon the 'constitution of the people' in the broad, identity-forming, sense—the sense in which they declare who they are or what they stand for *as a people*. Logically, the first, and most important, constitutive act is that which founds the political community as such by creating a unified body politic out of a disorganized multitude. This, in the liberal tradition, is the fabled moment of the social contract in which every person enters into a covenant with every other person to create that sovereign person which, in the words of Hobbes, is 'the reall Unitie of them all'.[9] However, it would be a mistake to follow Hobbes in assuming that the business of constitution, of the making of the body politic, finishes there. In democratic societies the identity of the state is always a work in progress because the relationship to the constitution is forever being renegotiated. Whenever the day-to-day business of governing is interrupted by constitutive acts undertaken 'in the name of the people', the basic code is altered and, as Mihalia Mihai puts it, 'the contours of the demos itself are redrawn'.[10] If Borneman is correct, the *Kniefall* was one such identity-defining act for the Germans. In expressing the fallibility and humility of sovereign power, Brandt had, it seems, turned himself at once into a living symbol and a symbol to live by.[11]

The memorialization of Brandt's *Kniefall* suggests the passing of time has done little to weaken its symbolic power as a mark of the new, repentant Germany, forever on its knees. The same could not be said, however, about its status as an historical anomaly.[12] Our age, it is now routinely suggested, is an age of remorse or an age of apology—an age in which making amends for the past has become a sufficiently important global preoccupation to justify talk of a new political form: 'the penitent state'.[13] From around the world evidence of the emergence of this penitent state can easily be piled up: truth commissions are held, political apologies are offered, reparation payments are made, bones are returned, monuments are torn down, and atonement rituals are multiplied endlessly. Taken together, these various symbolic manifestations of repentance and redress lend support to the view that a seismic shift has taken place in the orientation of the modern state—a shift away from the celebration of heroes and towards the recognition of victims. In this new, morally sensitized, political milieu, memory—or, to be more precise, the 'memory of wounds'—seems to command a larger share of public attention than ever before. Wounded subjects are encouraged to tell their stories to the civic-body-turned-collective-witness and public recognition (and public funds) are doled out to them in a pitiable attempt to repair the irreparable. Now less the exception than the norm, the proliferation of these scenes of repentance has made it increasingly plausible to say, with John Torpey, that 'we are all Germans now'.[14]

The fact that sovereign acts of repentance and redress are, by now, all too familiar does not mean, however, that they are any less curious.[15] Political societies, as Thomas Spragens once put it, articulate and celebrate their 'overarching purposes' through rituals of all kinds. 'By singing national anthems, pledging allegiance to the flag, and honoring their founding fathers', he wrote, 'the members of a society participate in and express their support of the larger meanings which their society seeks to embody.'[16] For the most part, such rituals belong to the venerable state practice of remembrance that feeds, and is itself fed by, patriotic sentiment—a practice at least as old as Pericles' funeral oration, whose aim is not simply to show citizens *what* it is they belong it but to convince them it is something *worth* belonging to.[17] The *raison d'état* behind such rituals scarcely needs explaining: as well as reflecting glory back upon the state, commemoration of the noble and heroic creates a political culture in which sacrifice, the subordination of private interest to public good, is normalized. But what of rituals of repentance that focus on victims? To the extent that they too relate to the 'larger meanings' that a society seeks to embody, sovereign acts of repentance and redress can also be considered an identity-shaping practice of remembrance. Only, in this case, the *raison d'état* is much more difficult to discern. What possible reasons of state could lay behind the decision to 'be sorry' (*paenitere*) and how could the impact of these acts of 'self-punishment' (*paenitentia*) that recall the shameful past be anything but deleterious to civic pride? As Edmund Burke once put it, '[t]o make us love our country, our country ought to be lovely'.[18]

Exactly what the stakes of this problem are become more evident once we clarify what we are talking about. In *Getting Even*, Jeffrey Murphy defines repentance as

> the remorseful acceptance of responsibility for one's wrongful and harmful actions, the repudiation of the aspects of one's character that generated the actions, the resolve to do one's best to extirpate those aspects of one's character, and the resolve to atone or make amends for the harm that one has done.[19]

If we assume, for the moment, that these conditions can be applied to collectives as well as individuals, we will immediately see that states must meet a very demanding ethical standard in order to be regarded as genuinely or authentically repentant. Beyond taking responsibility for wrongdoing (not something commonly associated with sovereign states), it would be incumbent upon them to eliminate the 'default of character' that enabled such wrongdoing to take place and then do whatever is necessary to make amends for the damage they have caused. Taken seriously, in other words (and how else could they be taken?), sovereign acts of repentance would appear to be an undertaking of constitutional significance—an undertaking in which the political community redefines itself by acknowledging an historical fault in its overarching purposes and commits to corrections in its constitutional structure and political culture. Insofar as it performed as an act of state, therefore, such repentance would appear to mark a radical departure from traditional state practice in which the noble is celebrated and the ignoble is consigned to oblivion. Ought we take the age of apology as evidence of a new kind of state in the making? Perhaps a better, more ethically mature, one whose use of public memory as a form of care shows that it finally understands the legitimate scope of its power?[20]

The answer to that question is not straightforward. Among those who have reflected not simply on this or that expression of sovereign repentance but on the meaning of repentance as a practice of state, opinion remains divided as to whether it constitutes a sign of political maturity or of political malaise. For Elazar Barkan, Martha Minow, Roy Brooks, Elizabeth Kiss, Alan Cairns, Donald Shriver, and Janna Thompson, among many others, our newfound interest in saying sorry and making amends deserves to be celebrated for both extending the reach and deepening the meaning of justice.[21] Typically, such advocates champion the rectification of past wrongs (including the retrospective classification of particular actions *as wrongs*) on the basis that the recognition of wrongdoing is itself a meaningful expression of justice—what now goes by the name of 'restorative justice'—that helps create a more decent, more inclusive society. While none of these advocates assume that official acts of repentance can undo the damage done to peoples (often racially defined) through state violence, they do assume that there is value—both for the victims and the community at large—in having that damage officially acknowledged and, to the extent that it is possible, repaired through symbolic and material forms of amends. Restorative justice, they suggest, greatly expands the range of responses to harm because, unlike retributive justice, which looks only to impose a penalty on the perpetrator, or distributive justice, which looks only to the equalization of life chances, it looks to the affirmation of identity. It is in this spirit that Barkan will suggest that 'the moral economy of restitution' is valuable, not simply because it 'enables the victims to claim a share of the economic pie' but because it aids in 'legitimizing their histories, their stories, and their identities'.[22]

Others have criticized the practice of sovereign repentance on the grounds that it privileges victims over agents, entrenches fractures in the public sphere, and disables transformative politics. The worry for John Torpey (and similar concerns have been raised by Richard Vernon, Charles Maier, Richard Rorty, Wendy Brown, and Pascal Bruckner) is that the belated attention now being granted the 'once neglected suffering of victims' has gone hand in hand with 'the eclipse of visionary modes of imagining the future'.[23] Writing in 2001, he framed the problem in this way: 'we find ourselves in post-socialist and post-utopian condition, which, in the absence of any plausible vision of different and better future society, instead fixes its gaze on the past and seeks to "make whole what has been smashed"'.[24] Torpey, to be fair, is not wholly damning of the politics of repentance and redress, especially in situations where other avenues of political action have been closed down by the rise of the neoliberal hegemony. Yet the phrase with which he concludes speaks volumes about his sense of the essentially quixotic and backward nature of the righting old wrongs project.[25] For Torpey, the problem is not just that no amount of reparation is going to 'make whole what has been smashed'. It is also that our obsession with mending the wounds of the past leaves us, like Klee's angel of history, with our backs to the future. The more our 'consciousness of catastrophe' tightens its grip, he notes, the harder it becomes 'to generate enthusiasm for a transformative politics that speaks to the vast majority, as socialism once attempted to do'.[26]

If we were left to judge matters on the basis of this debate alone, we would be forced to come to the conclusion that what is essentially at stake in state repentance is ideology. Irrespective of whether we see it as a dispute between conservatives and radicals (as Torpey is inclined to) or between the cultural left and the economic left (as Rorty is inclined to), the matter would still ultimately come back to the question not just of *where* one stands in relation to the ideal of progress but *how* one understands progress as an ideal. If one sides with the advocates, state repentance is inherently progressive (even as it seeks to conserve group identities) because it is accepting of difference. In it one finds recognition not simply of the dignity of 'the other' but of the fact that attacks upon difference, launched in the name of some mythical, undifferentiated polity, represent a backward step in civilization. If one sides with the detractors, state repentance is inherently regressive (even as it seeks to progress justice claims) because it orientates politics towards the past rather than the future and diversity rather than unity. Built upon the belief that it is easier to create dystopias than utopias, it places a taboo on bold action and

Introduction 7

gives rise to a politics in which repair is privileged over reform (to say nothing of revolution—the word that can no longer be spoken). But is ideology the only basis upon which one might judge? Could it be that, in applying the old categories of left and right, we force a novel phenomenon into an ideological straitjacket that doesn't quite fit and which may actually disguise what sovereign repentance really is and does?

Arguably, all one needs to do to show up the limitations of these ideological viewpoints is to take note of the word that is forever being invoked in relation to these gestures of repentance and redress: 'healing'. As Minow, Torpey, and many others on both sides of the ideological divide have observed, the effects of collective violence are now commonly cast 'in terms of trauma', and the manifold forms of sovereign repentance—from the public memorial, which places the crime squarely before the people, to the truth commission, which brings buried violations back into the public light—are legitimated in the 'language of healing'. As Minow succinctly puts it: 'the paradigm is health, rather than justice'.[27] That one should find abundant evidence of this paradigm in a book entitled *The Healing of Nations* is not, of course, all that surprising. If the question of 'collective trauma' and 'national healing' did not appear there, it would surely not appear anywhere. But even a brief acquaintance with the literature on restorative justice (whose very name points to the crossing of the medical and the juridical) is enough to show that Mark Amstutz's interest in 'how nations come to terms with traumatic legacy like genocide, civil war, or political repression' is simply one expression of a discourse of healing that is nothing if not post-ideological. 'Politically', writes Roy Brooks,

> remorse improves the national spirit and health. It allows a society to heal and move forward in the wake of an atrocity. This is the central lesson one takes from the people of Germany and South Africa as they have struggled to deal with the aftermath of Nazi crimes and apartheid, respectively.[28]

The 'central lesson' here could not be clearer; between trauma and recovery lies the work of that great healer of the nation: sovereign repentance.

If these claims are true, though, if healing really is both the purpose and the payoff of those sovereign acts of repentance—acts that seemingly punish the polity by forcing it to face up to and make amends for the ugly truth of its past—it may be just as idle to speak of a 'new public morality', in the way of Barkan, as of a 'melancholy absorption in the past', in the way of Torpey. The critical issue, one might hazard, is not whether remorseful acceptance and making amends is radical or conservative, future-orientated or past-orientated, but how it shifts politics onto the terrain of life itself. Thanks largely, it seems, to the infusion of Freudian (or perhaps more broadly psychoanalytic) thought in Western culture, the concepts of trauma and recovery, loss and mourning, have become a staple of our political diet.[29] Where we once might have spoken simply of wrongs and reparation, we now speak of wounds and healing. Doubtless one reason why reconciliation, that ancient and, for the longest time, strictly theological concept, has become politically all-pervasive is because it dovetails so neatly with the therapeutic presumption that it is not enough to simply restore the rule of law; one must also mend the wounded nation. Repentance and forgiveness have risen again because they belong conceptually (and, in the eyes of some, functionally) to the process of healing.[30] And yet, as pervasive as this psychological-cum-theological idea of healing has become, political science still struggles to wean itself from an analytic frame in which everything is either conservative or radical. Might we make more headway in our attempts to understand acts of sovereign repentance and redress if we paid less attention to moral injustice and political progress and more to psychological damage and therapeutic intervention?

This book uses a biopolitical, as opposed to an ideological, lens to look at practices of state repentance and assess their implications for the emancipatory, democratic project. Drawing on the work of Schmitt, Foucault, and Agamben, it asks a deceptively simple question: what are states actually doing when they 'do penance'? How are these penitential gestures—especially the gesture of apology that has become so ubiquitous—performed and what implications do they carry for the way power is exercised? By examining these phenomena in the light cast by political theology, the theory of the state of exception, and the notion of biopower, I seek to show that sovereign repentance is not what, or rather *not all that*, it first appears. If it speaks of a newfound compassion for the suffering of victims and/or a politically futile attempt to make whole what has been smashed, it also works to consolidate state power and license new forms of biopolitical intervention. Concerned as much with the question of life as of legitimacy, acts of sovereign penance consistently blur the line between symbolic form and biological process, gesture of remorse and instrument of catharsis. In them, I argue, one finds evidence not (or not *just*) of a new moral sensibility and not (or not *just*) of the exhaustion of utopian energies but of the way trauma has entered into politics and politics into trauma. With this in mind, I suggest the urgent critical task may not be, as many critics seem to think, to make sure states do penance better but to reveal the link between such acts of penance and the kind of power which, through the use of exceptional institutions, takes hold of life and tries to heal its wounds.

*

Why Schmitt, Foucault, and Agamben? That the name Carl Schmitt is rarely mentioned in discussions of state repentance and restorative justice will come as no surprise.[31] Associated more closely with the abuse of state power than contrition in the aftermath of it, Schmitt seems at first blush an unlikely figure of illumination. Often described, albeit without any fondness, as the Hobbes of the twentieth century, Schmitt is famous for having located the essence of politics, its *differentia specifica*, in the friend–enemy distinction. Like Hobbes (and, interestingly enough, Locke too), who understood the social contract as the moment when *a* group split itself off from the rest of humankind to create a discrete political society, Schmitt took the view that the state and its enemies were born at the same time. War, as he saw it, was an ineliminable threat, created by the distinction between 'us' and 'them' which, at one and the same time, enabled the creation, and established the boundary, of political community. Commonplace since Hobbes, the idea that war is an ever-present possibility in, if not the defining condition of, an international system composed of sovereign states is no longer quite so shocking—even if Schmitt's insistence that it was the existential threat of the enemy that made the political association both superior to and more meaningful than all other associations was. However, as George Schwab has rightly pointed out, it was the 'infusion of the friend-enemy criterion into domestic political struggles' that made Schmitt a figure of suspicion to the liberal pluralists of his own day and of revulsion to the victims of the Nazi regime which he ultimately supported.[32]

It was Schmitt's belief that pluralism was a luxury the state could not afford, least of all in times of crisis, that made his concept of the political so dangerous. Applied to struggles *internal* to the political community, the friend–enemy distinction lent itself only too easily to the disqualification of political opponents and, ultimately, to the state racism of the National Socialists that made every Jew an enemy of the state.[33] In the end, it was left to history to reveal what ought, by then, have already been evident; namely, that the notion of the enemy offered in *The Concept of the Political* was far too susceptible to misapplication.[34] However, there are other aspects of Schmitt's critique of liberal pluralism and the rule of law that cannot be disposed of quite so easily. In his previous book, *Political Theology*, Schmitt drew attention to the fact that the state cannot exist without a sovereign authority. Since it was impossible for every eventuality to be anticipated by the law, no state could do without an agent or actor whose singular role it was to make decisions on the exception.[35] In unprecedented situations—in situations, in other words, where no rule applied—it fell to the sovereign to determine what measures needed to be taken to maintain public safety and safeguard the state. Consistent with his view that all the significant concepts in the modern theory of the state were but secularized theological concepts, Schmitt located the essence of sovereignty in the God-like power of free judgement, going so far as to suggest that the decision in politics was analogous to the miracle in nature in its irregular, undetermined, and wholly eruptive quality.[36]

Implicitly or explicitly, the movement of restorative justice forces us to train a critical eye on this decisionist element in modern state politics—and this for two reasons. The first relates to the way the power to decide on the exception gives licence to violence. Since it is always the sovereign who, acting in the name of the people and on the pretext of an emergency, makes the decision to eliminate an enemy, it is precisely its right to decide on the exception that demands for apology and reparation open up to scrutiny. When the sovereign repents, it is effectively repenting for having abused its power or, more precisely, for having *mis-used* its right to decide on the exception and made enemies where there weren't any. But the issue returns in another guise as well for the simple reason that these sovereign acts of repentance and redress seem, for all intents and purposes, to be expressions of that self-same power to decide on the exception. Incapable of being subsumed under a general rule, the decision to apologize (or to repent in other ways) is precisely the kind of a-legal, transcendent decision that is unthinkable in the absence of sovereignty. The public memorials, political apologies, and truth commissions examined in this book can be fairly described as 'institutions of exception' because they are a manifestation of the power the sovereign enjoys to act outside the law in moments of real or perceived crisis. Regardless of whether he is referenced or not, therefore, the relevance of Schmitt to this area of state practice is difficult to deny and is, implicitly at least, acknowledged all the time. Ironically enough, then, it may in fact be the turn to the concept of biopolitics, as pioneered by Foucault and extended by Agamben, that stands most in need of some preliminary justification.

Foucault, as is now well known, believed modernity had given rise to two new forms of power—disciplinary power (or anatomo-power) and regulatory power (or biopower)—that differed from sovereign power in taking life rather than territory as the object of government. In the case of disciplinary power, the 'life' in question was the life of the individual body. For Foucault, an entire disciplinary technology appeared in the seventeenth and eighteenth centuries that worked to render the body at once efficient and docile; which worked, that is, to maximize its productive utility and minimize its unruly tendencies. Based around spatial separations (what Foucault, with the prison in mind, referred to as 'cellular technologies')[37] and temporal divisions (like the timetable) that allowed each body to be closely observed and precisely directed throughout the day, this disciplinary power appeared first in military barracks in the form of exercises and drills before being extended to, and refined within, a variety of 'micro-institutions': prisons, schools, hospitals, workshops. In the case of regulatory power, the 'life' in question was the life of the social body. Arriving slightly later in historical terms, this regulatory power was intimately bound up with the emergence of statistics (literally the records of the state) which made it possible for the state to 'know' the population as a whole for the first time. Once such statistics had been gathered long enough to be assembled serially in time, it became possible to detect irregularities in various 'life processes'—birth rates, death rates, morbidity rates—and intervene in them as necessary to re-establish equilibrium.[38]

With the advent of these two new forms of power, claimed Foucault, something unprecedented in the history of Western politics took place: 'the biological came under State control'.[39] Unlike sovereign power, whose relationship to life was confined largely to the right to take it away, disciplinary and regulatory power took hold of life as a resource and set out to administer, optimize, and multiply it.[40] Although each operated at a different level, made use of different techniques, and utilized a different institutional framework, they were by no means mutually exclusive. On the contrary, precisely calculated, in their respective fields, to maximize latent forces and energies or, as Foucault put it, 'to optimize a state of life', they complemented each other and dovetailed into each other.[41] Between them, they established a continuous apparatus, extending from the micro to the macro, from 'man-as-body' to 'man-as-species', for the governance of life in relation to what was assumed normal to it. Just as disciplinary power will seek to normalize conduct at the organic or bodily level, regulatory power will seek to normalize life processes at the biological or population level. The aim, in both cases, will be to identify deviations from the norm that diminish or threaten life—'behavioural norms' on the one hand, 'statistical norms' on the other—and then iron them out through precisely targeted disciplinary and regulatory interventions. In simple terms, then, one can define biopower as 'the set of mechanisms through which the basic biological features of the human species became the object of a political strategy'.[42]

For Foucault, one of the clearest markers of this entry of power into life was to be found in the domains and sciences that suddenly became of political significance. The only reason, on his account, that sexuality rose to prominence as a public issue in the nineteenth century was because it existed at the point where body and population, discipline and regularization, meet.[43] As a site, on the one hand, where moral discipline is inscribed and, on the other hand, where biological processes are situated, sexuality connected the life of the individual and the life of the population, making it of enormous strategic importance. If one could control sexuality, he claimed, one could, as it were, 'take possession of life'.[44] Similarly, it was precisely because the organic and the biological were drawn within the domain of security in the course of the nineteenth century that medicine emerged as the great handmaiden of power. 'Medicine', noted Foucault, 'is a power-knowledge that can be applied to both the body and the population, both the organism and biological process, and it will therefore have both disciplinary and regulatory effects.'[45] However, sexuality was not the only domain, and medicine not the only science, that was incorporated into politics. Since the object which now needed to be governed was nothing short of life itself, the 'apparatuses of security', as Foucault called them, had 'a constant tendency to expand'. 'New elements' were, he suggested, 'constantly being integrated' as their character and implications as vital forces began to be understood.[46]

In this book I advance the proposition that practices of sovereign repentance and redress belong to this centripetal movement in which new domains (in this case, trauma) and new sciences (in this case, psychology) are continually drawn into the apparatuses of security. Like sexuality in the nineteenth century, I argue, trauma emerged as a site of strategic importance in the twentieth century because it constituted a point of intersection between the organic and the biological, disciplinary power and regulatory power. As soon as it began to be recognized as a disorder that affects both organic function and biological process, trauma ceased to be something that could be consigned to the private realm or entrusted to the couch. Manifest not just as damage to the individual psyche but as a disruption to collective psychological processes, it posed a threat to life that necessitated its incorporation in politics both as an object of knowledge and a target of power.[47] One advantage, I suggest, of looking at sovereign acts of repentance and redress from a biopolitical perspective is that it allows us to see past the ethical mask such acts characteristically wear and grasp the operations of memory directed *against* trauma that go on behind it. More than simply a vehicle for recognizing wrongdoing and restoring dignity to victims, such acts operate at the disciplinary and the regulatory level, the first through establishing norms of emotional hygiene (expression over repression, forgiveness over resentment) and the second through catalysing forms of social catharsis. Conceived, in other words, not simply as operations of but as operations *upon* memory, sovereign acts of repentance intervene at both the organic and biological level in order to help individuals and societies 'come to terms' not, as is so often said, with that vague thing called 'the past' but rather with those 'lost love objects', as Freud called them, that can never come back and which thereby threaten to turn the past into an eternal present.

It is, perhaps, in relation to 'the past that will not pass'—evoked originally in reference to the Shoah in Germany—that the biopolitical dimension of sovereign repentance and redress becomes most clearly manifest.[48] For, even before one enlists the help of Freud, the phrase points us in the direction of a biological blockage. What is this past that will not pass, this unfinished business, if not a thwarted movement, a stalled process, an intestinal disorder? Freud clarifies the problem by explaining this blockage with reference to the phenomenon of loss. The reason, on his account, the past does not pass is because the 'work of mourning', the work of emotionally/erotically detaching oneself from the 'lost love object', is resisted and hence infinitely prolonged. All 'significant bereavements', he suggested in 'Mourning and Melancholia' (and there are few greater causes of significant bereavement than sovereign violence), lead to 'severe deviations' from normal behaviour. The loss of a beloved person, a precious ideal, a cherished homeland—all are symptomatically associated with a state of profound depression: loss of interest in the outside world, loss of the ability to love, a turning away from anything not related to the memory of the deceased; in short, a loss of desire. But, as he goes on to note, '[w]e rely on it being overcome after a certain period of time, and consider interfering with it to be pointless, or even damaging'.[49] It is only when time proves powerless to correct this severe deviation from normal behaviour and the bereaved subject, in addition to the symptoms noted above, suffers a loss of self-esteem that mourning is revealed as melancholia and the question of therapeutic intervention arises.[50] Acting, Freud tells us, 'like an open wound', the complex of melancholia is, I would suggest, still the best name we have for the past that will not pass.[51] It describes the pathological state of an unending (which is another way of saying 'a failed') mourning—a mourning, in short, that does not produce closure of its own accord and which, as a result, necessitates the kind of quasi-legal, quasi-therapeutic 'institutions of exception' examined in this book.

Although, as we shall see, therapeutic interventions of this nature are always context specific, they conform to the general logic of biopower by operating predominantly upon the 'milieu'—that is, upon the multiplicity of natural and artificial elements which, working together, create a general environment which bears directly upon 'all who live in it'.[52] As Foucault notes, that new 'political personage' called 'population' to which biopower addresses itself is not the collection of juridical individuals commanded by the law but 'a thick natural phenomenon', subject to its own regularities, which cannot simply be ordered to do something. If one wishes to manipulate it to certain ends, one must have an understanding of the many variables within the milieu that impact upon its one invariant element: desire. As Foucault would have it, the surprise that greeted the first theorists of population in the eighteenth century was not that every individual acts out of desire, or that it was nigh on impossible to deter them in their pursuit of their desires, but that the general interest of the population was best served by giving 'free play' to this desire. Although individuals might be deceived about what was truly in their interests, allowing them to pursue those interests in an unrestricted way tended to lead to favourable outcomes for the social body more generally. The art of governing (and here the contrast between the old sovereign power and new biopower becomes marked) was thus not about saying no to this desire but about saying yes to it; about stimulating it, encouraging it, and harnessing it in ways that produced beneficial effects, if not for every individual, then at least for the general population.[53]

The challenge, of course, was to know exactly *how* to say 'yes' to desire. Since this thick natural phenomenon called population had its own regularities—rates of births and deaths, injuries and diseases, production and consumption, which remained relatively constant year in, year out—the challenge of government (a challenge liberalism will take very seriously) was always to know when to leave well enough alone. As Foucault once put it, 'if one governed too much, one did not govern at all' because one disturbed the drivers of desire unnecessarily and provoked results contrary to what one wanted.[54] Ultimately what one was looking to do was to operate, in a highly reflected and calculated way, on the 'surface' which this subterranean (and thus not fully penetrable) phenomenon of population presented to government; namely, the customs and behaviours, opinions and feelings, of individuals. As Foucault sets it out, population is a Janus-faced phenomenon that appears under two different guises: insofar as it concerns humans in their connection with biological processes it is known as 'the species'; insofar as it concerns humans in their connection with government it is known as 'the public'. The two faces are conjoined—conceptually through the concept of population and empirically through the milieu—but it is only by way of the latter ('the public') that power gains access to the former ('the species'). In order to get hold of desire and ensure that the biological processes operating at the level of the species—one of which, I am suggesting, is the process of mourning—function just as they should, one had to go to work upon behaviours and opinions, reshaping the milieu in such a way as to optimize a state of life.

It is because it treats crimes against humanity as an open wound in the social body and sovereign acts of repentance as attempts to reshape the milieu that the concept of biopower is central to this book. However, as will perhaps already be evident through the inclusion of Schmitt and Agamben, it does not follow Foucault in assuming that the powers that take possession of life in the nineteenth century—the powers which make the basic biological features of the human species an object of a political strategy—are either entirely heterogeneous to or completely disconnected from sovereign power.[55] Having associated the latter—sovereign power—with the right to kill, Foucault seems to leave it only one role to play in the new biopolitical apparatus dedicating to 'making live'; namely, that of identifying, isolating, and, if necessary, eliminating the so-called biological danger, the 'diseased' or 'degenerate' groups within the population that pose (or are deemed to pose) a threat to the life of the whole. Proof that sovereign power has been used in this way in the modern age can be found only too easily in the cases of state racism that assume critical importance in this book: the Shoah in Germany, the Stolen Generations in Australia, and Apartheid in South Africa.[56] In each of these cases, the sovereign found a racial justification for withdrawing legal protection from an entire people, turning it into the degenerate life, the 'life unfit for life', which is either infinitely exploitable or wholly superfluous.[57] But it is not clear that this is the only situation in which, or the only conditions under which, sovereign power is mobilized within a biopolitical governmentality. If political apologies and other symbolic acts of penance really can, as Roy Brooks puts it, 'allow a society to heal', a rethinking of the place of the sovereign in the biopolitical apparatus is required.

Returning to Foucault, one quickly discovers that the scope of sovereign power is not limited solely to the right to kill or to take away life. It is, in fact, more generally expressed in the right to deduct, to take away immunities and protections; in short, to expose to risk or danger.[58] As Foucault himself acknowledged, the use of sovereign power in biopolitical projects of racial extermination was something of an exception: 'Nazism alone', he suggested in reference to the Final Solution, 'took the play between the sovereign right to kill and the mechanisms of biopower to this paroxysmal point.'[59] Far more common in the age of biopower was the mobilization of the sovereign right of exception for the purposes of what he called 'indirect murder': 'the fact of *exposing* someone to death, increasing the risk of death for some people, or, quite simply, political death, expulsion, rejection, and so on' (emphasis added).[60] Like other concepts situated at the intersection of sovereign power and biopower (Esposito's concept of immunity quickly comes to mind), that of exposure 'plays' equally well in the legal and medical register. One can increase the risk of death for someone just as surely by withdrawing the legal protections that secure them against abuse as by denying them the welfare measures that sustain their life. To be 'exposed' in this way is, in effect, to be left 'in the open', without any cover or insurance against either the arbitrary exercise of power or the vicissitudes of life. Exposure, one might reasonably conclude, is the privileged means by which sovereign power produces 'unprotected' or 'bare' life.

Arguably, it is in relation to this idea of exposure that Agamben makes his most valuable contribution to Foucault's analysis of biopower. For 'bare life' is the term Agamben famously uses to describe the life which only has a relationship to law through its exclusion from it.[61] As the title of his most renowned book indicates, the classic instance of this is the sacred man of ancient Rome, *Homo sacer*, who can be killed with impunity, not because he lives outside the law but because he has been abandoned by it. Explicitly denied the protection of the law (either human or divine), *Homo sacer* lives as one permanently exposed to death and survives, *if he survives*, only by virtue of the extra-legal, ethical sensibility of those who could, at any moment, take his life without sanction. But, as Agamben makes clear, *Homo sacer* is less a legal curiosity than a cipher for all those members of the political community who have been exposed to death in the 'state of exception' because of their anomalous or unassimilable status. Never fully at one with itself, he suggests, 'the people' has, from the very first, been the subject of a 'biopolitical fracture'—and here Agamben will distinguish 'the People' (upper-case P) who belong to the state from 'the people' (lower-case p) who are deemed a threat to it—that puts those who cannot be fully integrated or who *refuse to be fully integrated* at risk of annihilation.[62] For Agamben, as for Foucault, it is the programme of racial extermination instigated against the Jews in Nazi Germany that best exemplifies this biopolitical project to produce a pure or undivided people.[63] But if the Jews are the representatives par excellence of the bare life that the modern, biopolitical polity creates within itself, they are by no means the only representatives. As Hannah Arendt noted in the *Origins of Totalitarianism* and Achille Mbembe demonstrated in *Necropolitics*, Blacks, Indigenous Nations, and People of Colour have suffered similar fates. Before and after the Shoah, the colonized have been mercilessly exposed to death.[64]

One way of understanding sovereign acts of repentance and redress (at least in the cases of Germany, Australia, and South Africa examined in this book) is as an attempt to make amends for the production of bare life in state racism. Ostensibly, it is the sense of shame the perpetrators are belatedly brought to feel in the face of the stories of abandoned life which drives them to heal that biopolitical fracture and bring the wounded back inside the political community. A destructive, racial biopolitics in which the 'healthy' are differentiated from the 'diseased' gives way to an affirmative, democratic biopolitics in which every life is valued and protected in the same way.[65] On this reading, the age of apology emerges as a moment—truly joyous and hopeful—in which biopower is transformed and attempts to 'cure' the social body by eliminating biological enemies give way to attempts to 'care' for the social body by mourning lost friends; in short, as Esposito puts it, immunity to community.[66] Although, here again, the sovereign addresses itself to a biological danger—in this case, the danger of an 'unfinished mourning'— and here again its capacity to 'optimize a state of life' turns on the exceptional position it occupies in the constitutional order as the 'person' entitled to withdraw legal protections, there is no hint of a destructive 'thanato-politics' of genocide. Quite the contrary. For when the sovereign steps outside the law *this time* it is not to expose others but to expose itself. The figure of 'bare life' makes an uncanny return here, not simply in the bodies of those once abandoned by the law who reappear to tell the truth of their living death but in the body of the sovereign who falls to its knees and abandons *itself* to the contingency of their healing forgiveness.

Clearly there is much that is surprising about the willingness the sovereign has shown in the age of apology to play this peculiar role: exposing itself to disgrace in the present as a form of penance for exposing others to death in the past. But, on closer examination, it is not, in fact, at all inconsistent with the exceptional position it occupies in the constitutional order or the responsibility it must now shoulder, as part of the biopolitical apparatus, for regulating threats to life. As Agamben, building on the work of Schmitt, has rightly pointed out, the sovereign man bears a curious resemblance to the sacred man in the sense that he too occupies a 'zone of indistinction' inside and outside the law—a zone where law slides into violence, human into beast.[67] Just as the sacred man, in being banned from the protection of the law, is not so much returned to the state of nature where all are beasts as singled out *by means of the law* for treatment as a beast, the sovereign man, in exercising the right of the exception, is able *by means of the law* to exempt himself from legal restraint and act in the manner of a beast.[68] Metaphorically speaking, in other words, the sovereign man is no less a hybrid of human and animal, law and lawlessness, than the sacred man. Indeed, as Agamben notes in his reflections on Hobbes' *Leviathan*, the conclusion of that famous social contract does not, in fact, bring an end to the possibility of man acting as a wolf to man. It simply restricts the right to behave as a wolf to the sovereign himself.[69] Even when the state of nature has been left far behind, the exercise of violence remains the prerogative of the sovereign man, his metamorphosis into the wolf an ever-present possibility.

It is this paradoxical position of being at once inside and outside the law—'included', as Agamben puts it, 'only by way of an exclusion'—that makes symbolic gestures of remorse like that of political apology both possible *and* powerful as instruments of healing. For, in these instances, the sovereign man once again makes an appearance as a (lawless) beast, only in this case not to exercise the violence that is his prerogative but to make amends for having previously deployed it against his own subjects. Reduced symbolically (as Brandt was literally) to the penitent on his knees, the sovereign man undergoes a kenosis, an emptying of power, in which his immunity is surrendered and his fate—his redemption as a lawful man—is ironically passed into the hands of those he once excluded from legal protection and exposed to death. Whether he is restored as a figure of justice or condemned as a figure of violence now depends entirely upon the willingness of his victims to extend him the extra-legal, supererogatory 'gift' of forgiveness—the gift that rehumanizes the wolf by prising the doer from the deed, the sovereign from the crime. In the act of repentance, to put the matter simply, it is the sovereign who stands exposed, naked before the truth of his injustice. And what better reparation could there be? No longer invulnerable, that great, all-powerful leviathan is, at last, humiliated and humbled, turned into a deliciously sorrowful spectacle for those who suffered unspeakably as internal enemies in the state of exception. Now it is them who have the right to say: 'how dare you not kneel in our presence?'.

At this point it might reasonably be objected that I have not just rethought the place of the sovereign in the biopolitical apparatus but completely inverted it. For while there are grounds for suggesting the concept of 'bare life' (conceived here as an expression of the power of the sovereign to expose to death) simply fills a missing conceptual space in Foucault's analytics of power, it is harder to reconcile that analytics with a sovereign that voluntarily exposes itself to disgrace and exile; that voluntarily exposes itself, in other words, to a kind of political death. Foucault, a critic might reasonably say, instructed us to 'cut off the king's head', not become seduced by the spectacle of him cutting off his own. But, then, what clearer sign could there be of the emergence of a new system of power than this self-decapitation? If, as Foucault tells us, biopower operates on the principle that it is ultimately society, and not the sovereign, that 'must be defended', there is no logical reason why the sovereign might not, from time to time, be required to make a sacrifice and render himself the object of a 'gloomy festival of punishment' in order to alter the milieu.[70] While symbols are clearly not the be-all and end-all when it comes to regulating the life of 'the species', they are by no means without impact upon the behaviours and opinions of 'the public', especially when the symbol in question is the sovereign himself. How else might one explain the transformative effect, the emotional opening to reconciliation, created by a purely symbolic gesture of remorse from a head of state?[71] Might the 'theatrical representation of pain', once the singular fate of the body of the condemned within the system of sovereign power, have become the singular duty of the body of the sovereign within the biopolitical apparatus—its means of removing the blockage in desire created by an unfinished mourning?[72]

Foucault, to be sure, does not explicitly entertain the possibility.[73] Yet his work is by no means devoid of hints that the symbolic power of the sovereign might be susceptible to appropriation as an instrument of healing within the biopolitical apparatus. In his lecture series at the Collège de France of 1975–6 published as *Society Must Be Defended*, he effectively reaffirmed his attraction to sovereignty as a site of symbolic significance by alluding to the artificially deferred death of General Franco. That this tyrant who had exercised the sovereign right of life and death with great savagery for over forty years should, at the end of his life, have fallen under the sway of a medical regime that kept him alive even after he was technically dead was, for Foucault, an ironic testament to the subordination of sovereign power to biopower. What clearer sign could there be of the ascendance of the biopolitical than the incapacity of this ruthless sovereign to control even his own death?[74] But, of course, as Foucault inadvertently shows through the choice of this example, the advent of biopower seems to do little to diminish the symbolic power of the sovereign figure. It is only because Franco is the sovereign master of death that his loss of mastery over his own acquires its special poignancy and, for Foucault at least, its joyous connotations. Biopower may have won, but the victory only produces the emotional response that it does—in this case, a healing joyfulness—because it is a victory (might one even say a restorative revenge?) over the sovereign person himself.

This book builds on this implicit recognition of the symbolic significance of the sovereign within the milieu by treating it as an important instrument in the governance of life. Despite the overwhelming focus on the so-called killing function in Foucault, Agamben, and Mbembe, I suggest the age of apology actually testifies simultaneously to *two* points of contact between sovereign power and biopower. At the same time that it draws our attention to the tendency of sovereign power to turn genocidal whenever it is repurposed within a biopolitical governmentality (draws our attention, that is, to its historical implication in state racism), it also reveals the importance of its monopoly on the instruments of symbolization in producing certain healing effects. As I seek to show in the analyses that follow, sovereign power has now been integrated into the apparatus of biopower as a site of cathartic healing. By staging itself in the form of 'bare life', exposed and abject before the truth of its violence, the sovereign has not simply gifted its citizens symbols to live by but bolstered their emotional lives by providing them with a means of overcoming the trauma of their exposure to—and, perhaps even more importantly, *their implication in*—crimes against humanity. While the word 'healing' may ultimately prove to be something of a misnomer in this context, the public memorials, political apologies, and truth commissions that expose the sovereign in its violence do seem to facilitate a kind of cathartic release—the flow of suppressed affect—in a way that is inherently difficult to quantify but which is not without an impact upon what is now instructively referred to as the 'emotional climate'.[75] When the sovereign forgoes its immunity in repentance, when it goes down on its knees and begs for forgiveness, the stalled process of mourning starts up again, giving rise to a cathartic discharge that clears the air and makes breathing easier—at least for some.

Whether the victims and perpetrators of state racism enjoy the same experience of healing in the wake of these moments of exposure is debatable, to say the very least. Taken (as it often is) as an expression of the desire to heal the 'biopolitical fracture' that state racism opens up, sovereign repentance lays claim to general support. Far from entrenching fractures in the public sphere, it reconciles, rejoins, and unites by revaluing the 'life unworthy of life' as life worthy of life; as life, in short, that *matters*. The formerly exploitable and expendable 'people' (lower-case p) are recognized as part of the People (upper-case P) allowing the losses they suffered in the state of exception to become the subject of collective mourning—now they too, as Judith Butler puts it, are treated as 'grievable life'.[76] Ironically enough, in other words, the people is only healed, only made whole again, when the leviathan prostrates itself before those it once sought to eradicate in the name of unity. And yet, the true irony, or so I will argue, is that this symbolic reversal from sovereign to suppliant actually works, in accordance with the logic of biopower (where it is always the population as a whole, not particular groups within, that constitutes the 'object of care'), to create a cathartic upheaval that revitalizes the social body. Freed by the act of repentance from the melancholy of the inexpiable, the perpetrators are able to recover their self-esteem and live again, while the victims are left to wrestle with the new challenges that come with the exposure of their 'inner self' in truth telling and the plea for (or expectation of?) forgiveness that comes from the apologetic sovereign body.

*

This book is at once indebted to, and seeks to build upon, the work of scholars who have revealed the ambiguous character of official attempts to repair past injustices and heal the wounded nation. The list of these includes, but is not limited to, those sceptical about the recent entrance of apology and forgiveness into politics; those who worry about the marginalization (if not the pathologization) of 'negative emotions' like anger, resentment, and indignation under the pressure of reconciliation movements; those who recognize the slippery nature of shame and the way it drives perpetrators to reparative gestures which heal their own narcissistic wounds; those who have shown how mourning works not simply as a universal biological process but as a contested political practice; and those who have problematized catharsis as a model of individual and national healing.[77] At the risk of conflating diffuse phenomena, but in the hope of revealing subterranean connections, this book attempts to integrate and reconfigure these critiques around the problem of damaged life and its biopolitical regulation in institutions of exception. Adopting the concept of 'exposure' as its critical instrument, it explores how acts of repentance that seem to strip the sovereign bare in its violence function as therapeutic moments in which the trauma of victims is at once centred and decentred. Ostensibly undertaken in the name of healing and reconciliation—in the name, that is, of a life-enhancing 'restorative justice'—such acts seem, at one and the same time, to assist the biopolitical objective of optimizing a state of life while re-exposing the victims (and everyone else) to state power.

'Healing', as we will discover, is not only an extraordinarily pervasive concept but also a highly permissive one. At once a metaphorical ideal, applied to broken bodies, souls, relationships, and nations, and a medical objective, used in relation to efforts at restoring normal, biological functioning, it has a slippery, elusive quality that makes it an inherently difficult target of analysis. While the concept is encountered at every turn, it is rarely clear what is actually meant by it because the metaphorical and the medical are almost always ambiguously entwined. This study proceeds on the basis that there is something serious at stake in 'healing', even if the term is not always used in a serious (by which I mean literal) way. One of the benefits of taking a biopolitical *perspective* in this context is that it allows us to clarify just what those stakes are without committing to the idea that 'healing' carries the same meaning and implications in every situation. While it does not abandon claims to truth or give up on trying to understand what sovereign repentance is really all about, therefore, the methodological approach taken in this study is more closely allied with what Sergei Prozorov has called 'experimental analytics'.[78] The point of the inquiry is not to prove that acts of sovereign repentance are inherently biopolitical or that there is no other way of understanding them. It is rather to explore what opens up when such acts are viewed from a biopolitical perspective. What new possibilities in thought and action does this perspective make available?

As an attempt to see how things look from a biopolitical perspective, the book delivers three key insights. The first is that acts of sovereign repentance cannot be properly understood from (and may, in fact, be disguised by) ethico-normative perspectives which assume, firstly, that the state is only driven to symbolic acts of remorse through an interest in legitimation and, secondly, that the only role of political theory is to try and ensure it takes wrongs seriously by establishing norms of sincerity. Although it is clearly tempting to treat acts of repentance and redress as expressions of the curtailment of sovereign power in the age of human rights, the adoption of a juridico-political perspective (one that pays due attention to *raison d'état* and with that to the performative dimension of repentance) allows us to see the utility they have for the state as tools of healing and revitalization. As should become clear, the institutions of exception—memorials, apologies, commissions—in which the sovereign exposes the ugly truth of its crimes and attempts to make amends for them are not simply about regaining legitimacy for the self by recognizing the dignity of the other; they are also about repairing the damaged life that sits *on both sides* of the biopolitical fracture. Standing behind or, better still, *infused within* this politics of recognition is a biopolitics of healing that tries to regulate the biological anomaly of the past that will not pass by intervening in the mourning process. The fact that the sovereign must sometimes be dragged—kicking and screaming, as it were—into apologizing for its crimes does not mean that it doesn't also have its (biopolitical) reasons for doing so. Within the institution of exception, it is invariably life as well as legitimacy that is at stake.

The second key insight is that the exposure that takes place in these institutions of exception cuts both ways. In principle, symbolic acts of repentance are a freely undertaken form of self-punishment in which the sovereign exposes itself in its crimes as a way of doing justice to, and healing the trauma of, its former victims. Apology marks the end of the reign of denial (that exemplary expression of the 'immunization paradigm') by revealing the sovereign as the violent beast that it was (and is). Hence the sense of shame that falls upon those incorporated in his person through the social contract. Invariably, however, it is not just the sovereign but life itself that gets exposed when buried truths (and dead bodies) are exhumed. Grounded in the suffering of victims and aimed at the compassion of perpetrators, truth telling has emerged as a royal road to the 'inner life' of subjects. More than simply giving victims an opportunity to tell their stories, it grants access to the hidden chambers of the soul and opens the door to various forms of emotional regulation. To be called to reveal the truth is, in effect, to be called to expose oneself in the agony of loss and it is this 'sharing of private pain in a public way', as Minow puts it, that allows trauma to find its way into the political world and become available for therapeutic treatment. Those who were exposed to violence in the state of exception are thus invariably exposed again in ways that seem to do as much to jeopardize as to recognize their human and civil dignity.

The third, and final, insight is that there appears to be something of an inverse relationship between therapeutic reconciliation and critical reflection. In principle, as Murphy makes clear, there is no greater spur to self-reflection than the act of repentance. If we are honest in what he calls our 'remorseful acceptance of responsibility for our wrongful and harmful actions', we are inevitably led to question what it is about us—what in our character or constitution—that allowed those harmful actions to take place. Repentance for the act and reflection on the self are intertwined and, in fact, hard to imagine in the absence of one another.[79] Ideally speaking, then, repentance in the kind of political contexts under discussion in this book should be accompanied by reflection on the nation-state as a political form and, more precisely, on the friend–enemy distinction that serves as its organizing principle. However, as we will see throughout this study, the subordination of these acts of repentance to the interest of healing tends to undermine whatever potential they carried to spark critical reflection on the problems of the nation-state. Unlike the institution of Greek tragedy which I turn to as a comparison in Chapter 6, our modern institutions of exception seem to present the civil wound in ways that provoke catharsis but which foreclose upon critical reflection about the problem of going wrong in politics.

All these insights build across the work as a whole and rely upon the constant interchange of theoretical elaboration and case study. Thus, while the book dedicates one chapter each to public memorials, political apologies, and truth commissions, it is not easily divided into theoretical elaboration and practical application. Rather, it proceeds on the basis that these new institutional forms in which the sovereign ostensibly 'does penance' by exposing itself in its violence are not just operations of memory but operations *upon* memory whose biopolitical character and ethical implications need to be analysed, as it were, one by one. To the extent, however, that the first two chapters grapple with the emergence of trauma as a matter of state and healing as a reason of state, they do lay important groundwork for the chapters that follow. As will soon become evident, the concept that sits at the core of these two chapters (and the book more generally) is that of 'damaged life'. Symptomatically manifest in a range of neuroses, damaged life is the violence of state racism etched on bodies. It refers, most obviously, to the fragmented half-lives of those who, in Audre Lorde's haunting phrase, 'were never meant to survive'[80]—the victims and descendants of victims whose worlds were ruined by the arbitrary exercise of sovereign power and whose biopolitical struggles have, as a consequence, tended to be organized around a right of existence itself. But it refers also, albeit more controversially, to the lives of those who, even if they did not exercise or even benefit from the power of extermination, feel somehow implicated in (even traumatized by?) the shameful past which belongs to *their* nation-state and which strips *them* of the fantasy of innocence and goodness.[81]

Damaged life, the life from which something irrecoverable has been lost and in which the mourning process stalls, is a genuine psychological phenomenon: the 'open wound' Freud referred to as melancholia. But it is also a political problem. Seen from the perspective of *raison d'état* (which, as I try to show, is increasingly how it is seen), trauma is a signifier of devitalization and danger. It marks the psychic life, both individual and collective, which, in its refusal to let go or its 'inability to mourn', has ceased to function at its optimum level and which, potentially at least, has become a threat to the vitality of the state. Whether because it is regarded as the source of unending cycles of violence (following the formula violence begets trauma and trauma begets violence) or because it is associated with a life-sapping defence against the shameful past, trauma has now found its way into biopolitical calculations of risks to life. Indeed, to the extent that it is conceived, much like a volcano, in terms of latency, trauma has come to occupy the rather unique place of the emergency yet to come. Visible only in its symptoms, it elicits strategies of healing that seek to prevent the psychic eruption that must, at some point, finally arrive. Remorseful acceptance and making amends—in short, repentance—is, on this biopolitical reading, the pre-emptive strike the sovereign launches against the biological anomaly of an unfinished mourning. At once foreshadowing and preparing the analyses that follow, then, the first two chapters examine this political discourse of trauma and the emergence of the collective psyche as an object of government—an object that must be known and treated in the interests of restoring 'normal life'.

In Chapter 1, I try to show what it is about trauma that makes it a matter of state and why gestures of remorse that utilize the symbols of sovereign power have become an important means of healing damaged life. Drawing upon some pioneering works of post-Freudian psychoanalysis, the chapter derives two intimately related figures who, in their mutually constitutive pathology, comprise the complex of 'social trauma': the half-life of the alienated survivor (who dies while living) and the over-life of the guilty sovereign (who lives while dead). Although opposed in law as victim and perpetrator, these two figures are arrestingly mirrored in psychoanalytic discourse because both fall beyond the reach, firstly, of the juridical processes that govern response to harm (compensation and punishment) and, secondly, of the psychological processes that govern recovery from loss (mourning and de-cathexis). As the case of Germany reveals, some crimes do not simply mock legal institutions of compensation and punishment; they exceed the capacity of the psychic mechanism to process loss. Bound together in this 'double excess', or so the psychoanalysts tell us, neither the alienated survivor nor the guilty sovereign can escape their melancholic syndrome, their 'inability to mourn', until the political community is willing to risk self-devaluation by carrying out acts of repentance. Only when the sovereign falls to its knees and takes the people with it in a cathartic upheaval does the melancholy come to an end and the social body regain its health.

In Chapter 2, I seek to reveal how influential this way of thinking about damaged life has now become, not just discursively but also institutionally, by drawing a contrast between the ancients and the moderns in their 'treatment' of civil wounds. Drawing upon Nicole Loraux's seminal study of the divided city of ancient Greece, I identify a decisive historical turn in the methods used to reinvigorate the body politic and begin anew in the wake of civic trauma. Characteristically, I suggest, the ancients took recourse to the institution of oblivion (amnesty) out of a fear that an *endless* mourning would expose the *polis* to a destructive 'grief-wrath'. By contrast, we moderns take recourse to the institutions of repentance (memorials, apologies, commissions) out of a belief that an *unfinished* mourning can be brought to a conclusion by political means. Productive, I argue, of a range of new institutional forms in which truth telling and societal grieving play a key role, this shift from prohibition to process or from oblivion to repentance is entirely consistent with a biopolitical governmentality in its refusal to take life just as it is. Where natural processes—in this case, the process of mourning—have become stalled, the sovereign seems less and less inclined to apply the old-fashioned ban of Pericles (or Creon) that neutralizes the threat of melancholia by forcing it back into the private realm.[82] Instead, it has opted to spend some of its symbolic capital in gestures of remorse which, in acting as a biological catalyst, allow societies to overcome their inability to mourn and 'move on'.

In the following chapters, I turn to three different national cases (Germany, Australia, and South Africa) in order to gain an understanding of how different institutional expressions of repentance—public memorials, political apologies, truth commissions—work simultaneously as expressions of penance and instruments of healing (and instruments of healing *because* they are expressions of penance). In Chapter 3, I examine the case of the Berlin Memorial to the Murdered Jews of Europe in an attempt to reveal the political stakes of consciously reflecting the civil wound back to the body politic. Composed of 2,711 concrete slabs (*stelae*) spread across 19,000 square metres in central Berlin, the Memorial places genocide squarely in public sight in what looks, for all intents and purposes, to be a remorseful acceptance of responsibility by the guilty sovereign. Exactly what effect this (seemingly negative) representation of the civic self has as an operation of—or, to be more precise, *upon*—memory is not, however, altogether clear. *Contra* Habermas, who interprets the Memorial as a manifestly future-orientated sign of a purified, post-national, German identity, I treat it as a site where reflection on the violence inherent to the nation-state as a political form falters. By reading it in relation to the Vietnam Veterans Memorial in Washington, DC—a memorial site *from which* it is distinguished politically but *to which* it is compared aesthetically—I reveal how the cathartic possibilities made available to *all Germans* by the Memorial to the Murdered Jews rest upon a sense of 'similar possibilities' which is not only historically inaccurate but which also serves to deflect attention from the failures of the state. Somewhat perversely, I will suggest, the Memorial offers consolation for (and relief from) the suffocating presence of the Shoah in German life.

In Chapter 4, I examine what is commonly regarded as the foremost expression of the penitent state: the gesture of political apology. Unlike a great deal of work in political philosophy, much of which is focused on how a political apology can be made good (that is, its ethico-normative conditions of sincerity), I investigate how a political apology can be made at all (that is, its juridico-political conditions of possibility). If, following Schmitt, we assume the essence of the sovereign's power consists in its right to 'go beyond the law', its subjection to a Christian ethical code in which wrongdoing necessitates atonement seems tantamount to a profound reshaping of its character and authority. Could it be, I ask, that the age of apology has given birth to a new sovereign, an 'other-orientated' rather than 'self-orientated' power, which has finally learnt to care? Against those who treat apology as an ethical gesture that confirms the humbling of sovereign power in the democratic age, I interrogate it as a biopolitical gesture that leans on the transcendent, God-like character of the sovereign to alleviate a sense of shame. Working with and against Michael Fagenblat's account of the Australian Government's apology to the Stolen Generations as an 'exercise of sovereignty in the mode of contrition', I try to unpack the tension, already foreshadowed in the previous chapter, between sovereignty as a power of self-assertion and contrition as a gesture of self-abasement. Concerned more with the self than the other, I argue, political apologies might be best understood as an inverse coronation ritual in which the discontinuity, rather than the continuity, of sovereign power is staged. In the act of apology, the sovereign splits itself off from the crimes of the past, freeing the people it incorporates as a body politic from the enervating burden of shame. Made new again by this sovereign act of contrition, the post-apology state makes its coercive reappearance in the lives of its victims as something structurally unchanged yet deserving of forgiveness.

In Chapter 5, I seek to show how the institution of the truth commission can operate simultaneously as a means of exposing the hidden crimes of the guilty sovereign and of the hidden lives of the alienated survivors. Concerned, primarily, with clarifying the nature and effect of the South African Truth and Reconciliation Commission (TRC) as a 'healing operation', the chapter sets out to analytically disentangle the two types of biopolitical governance it seemed to manifest: pastoralism and governmentalism, or what Foucault has labelled the *ratio pastoralis* and the *ratio gubernatorial*. If we are willing to take the representations of those in and around the Commission at face value, I suggest, the TRC was an expression of a benevolent, pastoral power whose primary objective was to restore the South African flock as a 'bundle of life' through moral gestures of remorse and forgiveness. Against this ethical conception of the TRC as a work of communal restoration built upon generosity of spirit, I go on to re-present it as an expression of governmental power that purified the 'emotional climate' by staging a collective catharsis. By compressing, intensifying, and personalizing the suffering it put on display, I argue, the TRC ensured that its hearings would have a dramatic impact upon the popular psyche. As private pain was made public property, a cathartic effect was produced which could be diffused widely through the population without requiring any moral transformation. Although celebrated for 'healing the nation', I argue that the cost of the TRC's healing operation was a certain blindness to the structural injustice of Apartheid and an unforgiving exposure of the 'inner life' of its victims.

In Chapter 6, I attempt to get greater critical purchase on these various expressions of sovereign repentance by juxtaposing them with another, albeit much older, 'institution of exception' in which the civil wound is reflected back to the public with cathartic effects: Greek tragedy. Following the classicists, I argue that the capacity of Greek tragedy to contribute to the emotional *and* intellectual edification of the city derived from the fact that it placed the inner ills of the city at a distance from the audience. By dislocating *from* Athens what it staged *for* Athens, tragedy allowed the audience assembled at the annual festival of the Great Dionysia to reflect, in the true sense of the word, on the problem of error in politics. By contrast, our insistence on making the audience confront the past, on bringing them, quite literally, 'face to face' with it, seems only to displace political questions onto the terrain of intimacy where trauma turns into spectacle and reflection into sentimentalism. Allowed to indulge in a grief that shuttles between the singular and the universal, between *the one* that was lost and *all those* who were lost, the citizen-spectators conjoined in mourning through the memorial, the apology, and the commission seem to be perversely relieved of the responsibility to reflect on what happened and, more to the point, on how what happened might be intrinsically connected to the faults of the nation-state as a political form.

Notes

1. M. Amstutz, *The Healing of Nations: The Promise and Limits of Political Forgiveness*, Lanham, MD: Rowman and Littlefield, 2005, p. 24.
2. Justice Holmes quoted in S. Levinson, *Written in Stone: Public Monuments in Changing Societies*, Durham, NC: Duke University Press, p. 106.
3. The full passage reads: 'We are amazed, and thus long have we stood/To watch the fearful bending of thy knee, Because we thought ourself thy lawful king;/And if we be, how dare thy joints forget/To pay their aweful duty to our presence?' W. Shakespeare, *Richard II*, ed. by Cedric Watts, Hertfordshire: Wordsworth, 2012. Act III, Scene III, l. 72-77,
4. Instructively, Vladimir Jankélévitch, renowned for excoriating the Germans as an 'unrepentant people' whose contrition was 'worth nothing', was still sufficiently moved by Brandt's *Kniefall* to describe it as an 'amazing gesture'. See V. Jankélévitch, 'Should We Pardon Them?', *Critical Inquiry*, 22, Spring 1996, pp. 565–566.
5. Although there is some debate as to whether Brandt's silent genuflection meets the conditions of an apology, I follow Borneman (and many, many others) in treating it as an 'apologetic gesture' on the grounds that it has been received and described in this way. See J. Borneman, 'Can Public Apologies Contribute to Peace? An Argument for Retribution', *Anthropology of East Europe Review*, 17(1), 1999, pp. 8–9; M. Gibney and E. Roxstrom, 'The Status of State Apologies', *Human Rights Quarterly*, 2001, 23, p. 928; D. Paez, 'Official or Political Apologies and Improvement of Intergroup Relations: A Neo-Durkheimian

Introduction 29

Approach to Official Apologies as Rituals', *Revista de Psicologia Social*, 25(1), 2010, pp. 1–15; P. Hazan, *Judging War, Judging History: Behind Truth and Reconciliation*, Stanford, CA: Stanford University Press, 2010, p. 21.
6. P. Levi, *Survival in Auschwitz: The Nazi Assault on Humanity*, New York: Touchstone, 1996, p. 26.
7. J. Borneman, 'Political Apologies as Performative Redress', *SAIS Review*, 25(2), 2005, p. 62.
8. Borneman, 'Political Apologies as Performative Redress', p. 62.
9. T. Hobbes, *Leviathan*, London: Penguin Books, 1985, p. 227.
10. M. Mihai, *Negative Emotions and Transitional Justice*, Columbia, MO: Columbia University Press, 2016, p. 36.
11. According to Borneman, Brandt's *Kniefall* 'frequently comes up on television talk shows, especially by members of the first post-war generation, the "68ers", who identify the apology as one of the few times they were actually proud of a German statesman, or, by extension, were themselves proud to be German'. Borneman, 'Can Public Apologies Contribute to Peace?', p. 15.
12. As Mark Gibney has recently noted, perhaps the clearest measure of the growing prominence of political apologies is found less in the fact that they have become common than in the fact that they have become a normative expectation. These days, he notes, it is not the presence of apology but the absence of one that is likely to raise questions. One could also enlist the towering figure of Jacques Derrida in support of this trend. In his essay 'On Forgiveness' from 2001, Derrida was already speaking of the 'proliferation of scenes of repentance' on the geopolitical stage since 'the last war' (meaning World War II). See M. Gibney, 'Introduction to a Symposium on Political Apologies', *Journal of Human Rights*, 20(5), 2021, p. 580; J. Derrida, *On Cosmopolitanism and Forgiveness*, London: Routledge, 2001, p. 28; and D. Celermajer, 'Apology and the Possibility of Ethical Politics', *JCRT*, 9(1), Winter 2008, p. 14.
13. P. Bruckner, *The Tyranny of Guilt: An Essay on Western Masochism*, Princeton, NJ: Princeton University Press, 2010, p. 108. See also B. Forchtner, *Lessons from the Past?*, London: Palgrave Macmillan, 2016, pp. 111–149.
14. The full sentence reads as follows: '"we are all Germans now" in the sense that all countries (and many other entities as well) that wish to be regarded as legitimate confront pressures to make amends for the more sordid aspects of their past and, often, to compensate victims of earlier wrongdoing'. The comment is reminiscent of one offered much earlier by Hannah Arendt: 'For many years now we have met Germans who declare that they are ashamed of being Germans. I have often felt tempted to answer that I am ashamed of being human. This elemental shame, which many people of the most various nationalities share with one another today, is what finally is left of our sense of international solidarity; and it has not yet found an adequate political expression'. See J. Torpey, 'Introduction: Politics and the Past' in J. Torpey (Ed.), *Politics and the Past: On Repairing Historical Injustices*, Lanham, MD: Rowman and Littlefield, 2003, p. 3; H. Arendt, 'Organised Guilt and Universal Responsibility' in H. Arendt, *Essays in Understanding 1930–1954: Formation, Exile and Totalitarianism*, New York: Schocken Books, 1994, p. 131.
15. As Paul Ricoeur noted, 'the spectacle of public penance leaves one puzzled'. P. Ricoeur, *Memory, History, Forgetting*, Chicago, IL: Chicago University Press, 2004, p. 484.
16. T. Spragens, *Understanding Political Theory*, New York: St Martin's Press, 1976, p. 3.

30   The Penitent State

17. Thucydides, *History of the Peloponnesian War*, London: Penguin Books, 1972, sections 34–47. For a brilliant commentary on this speech, see J. Colaiaco, *Socrates against Athens: Philosophy on Trial*, New York: Routledge, 2001, pp. 75–104.
18. E. Burke, *Reflections on the Revolution in France*, New Haven, CT: Yale University Press, 2003, p. 67.
19. J. Murphy, *Getting Even: Forgiveness and Its Limits*, Oxford: Oxford University Press, 2003, p. 41.
20. In abusing or misusing others, according to Murphy, the wrongdoer 'assumes a greater power than is his right to assume'. Repentance would point to the fact that he has come to terms with 'the legitimate scope of his power'. See Murphy, *Getting Even*, p. 47. This sentence also builds on Ricoeur's understanding of memory as a 'figure of care'. 'In memory-as-care', he writes, 'we hold ourselves open to the past, we remain concerned about it'. Ricoeur, *Memory, History, Forgetting*, p. 505.
21. E. Barkan, *The Guilt of Nations: Restitution and Negotiating Historical Injustices*, Baltimore, MD: Johns Hopkins University Press, 2000; M. Minow, *Between Vengeance and Forgiveness*, Boston, MA: Beacon Press, 1998; R.L. Brooks (ed.), *When Sorry Isn't Enough: The Controversy over Apologies and Reparations for Human Injustice*, New York: New York University Press, 1999; E. Kiss, 'Moral Ambition within and beyond Political Constraints: Reflections on Restorative Justice' in R. Rotberg and D. Thompson (eds.), *Truth v Justice*, Princeton, NJ: Princeton University Press, 2000, pp. 68–99; A. Cairns, 'Coming to Terms with the Past' in J. Torpey (ed.), *Politics and the Past*, pp. 63–90; and J. Thompson, *Taking Responsibility for the Past*, Cambridge: Polity, 2002; D. Shriver, *Honest Patriots: Loving a Country Enough to Remember Its Misdeeds*, Oxford: Oxford University Press, 2005.
22. Barkan, *The Guilt of Nations*, p. 348.
23. Torpey, 'Introduction', pp. 1, 26. Nearly a decade before Torpey, Charles Maier was already puzzling to explain why American politics had 'become a competition for enshrining grievances'. In response to the question of why memory now appeared to play a larger role in civic and political life, Maier claimed: 'my own belief is that at the end of the twentieth century western societies have come to the end of a massive collective project. It is not just the project of the communist or even the socialist Left or even of the left tout court, although the end of these agendas is apparent. It is also the end, or at least the interruption, of the capacity to found collective institutions that rest on an aspiration for the future'. 'The surfeit of memory', he went on to argue, 'is a sign not of historical confidence but of a retreat from transformative politics. It testifies to the loss of a future orientation, of progress towards civic enfranchisement and growing equality.' More recently, Pascal Bruckner has referred to the same 'strange inversion': 'the past, which is naturally fragile and doomed to sink into darkness, takes precedence over the present and the future, transforming the living into visitors to cemeteries'. C. Maier, 'A Surfeit of Memory? Reflections on History, Melancholy and Denial', *History and Memory*, 5(2), 1993, pp. 147, 150; and P. Bruckner, *The Tyranny of Guilt*, Princeton, NJ: Princeton University Press, 2010, p. 96. See also R. Vernon, *Historical Redress: Must We Pay for the Past?*, London: Continuum, 2012, p. 8; R. Rorty, *Achieving Our Country: Leftist Thought in the Twentieth Century America*, Cambridge, MA: Harvard University Press, 1997, p. 33; and W. Brown, *States of Injury: Power and Freedom in Late Modernity*, Princeton, NJ: Princeton University Press, 1995, pp. 52–76.

24. J. Torpey, '"Making Whole What Has Been Smashed": Reflections on Reparations', *Journal of Modern History*, June 2001, p. 343.
25. The phrase is, of course, borrowed from Walter Benjamin's analysis of a Paul Klee painting in which the 'Angel of History' is depicted with her back turned to the future, gazing down at the debris left by the storm of progress.
26. Torpey, '"Making Whole What Has Been Smashed"', p. 354.
27. See Minow, *Between Vengeance and Forgiveness*, p. 63. See also pp. 21–22; J. Torpey, *Making Whole What Has Been Smashed: On Reparations Politics*, Cambridge, MA: Harvard University Press, 2006, p. 15; B. Leebaw, 'The Irreconcilable Goals of Transitional Justice', *Human Rights Quarterly*, 30, 2008, p. 116; D. Million, *Therapeutic Nations: Healing in an Age of Indigenous Human Rights*, Tucson, AZ: University of Arizona Press, 2013, p. 23.
28. R.L. Brooks, 'Reflections on Reparation', in Torpey (ed.), *Politics and the Past*, p. 112.
29. Ian Hacking is, perhaps, only exaggerating slightly when he claims 'Freud transformed Western consciousness more surely than the atomic bomb or the welfare state'. One of the most important texts in the popularization of Freud, which Hacking mentions and which I examine at some length in Chapter 1, is J.L. Herman, *Trauma and Recovery*, New York: Basic Books, 1992. See I. Hacking, 'Memoro-Politics, Trauma and the Soul', *History of the Human Sciences*, 7(2), 1994, p. 40.
30. As Dian Million has noted, 'A theory of trauma is embedded in an internationally recognized economy of justice that reconciliation belongs to.' In a similar fashion, Pierre Hazan has noted that a 'restorative' form of justice 'introduces terms, often of a religious or psychoanalytic inspiration and totally foreign to the vocabulary of the Cold War, to the political lexicon: reconciliation, truth, punishment, pardon, repentance, catharsis'. See Million, *Therapeutic Nations*, p. 2; and P. Hazan, *Judging War, Judging History*, p. 10.
31. One important exception to this is A. Schapp, *Political Reconciliation*, London: Routledge, 2005, pp. 15–23.
32. Ironically, according to Schwab, it was precisely in relation to extremist parties like the Nazi Party, intent on subverting the state, that Schmitt applied the concept of 'enemy'. As early as 1932, writes Schwab, he had argued that 'only those parties not intent on subverting the state be granted the right to compete for parliamentary and governmental power'. See G. Schwab, 'Introduction' in C. Schmitt, *The Concept of the Political*, Chicago, IL: University of Chicago Press, 2007, pp. 14–16.
33. On the Jews (and other ethnic groups) being made enemies of the state, see H. Arendt, 'Mankind and Terror' in H. Arendt, *Essays in Understanding 1930–1945*, New York: Schocken Books, 1994, pp. 300–301; and P. Levi, *The Drowned and the Saved*, London: Penguin Books, 1988, p. 38.
34. As Chantal Mouffe, and other advocates of agonistic democracy, have argued, between friend and enemy stand the adversaries who enliven democracy and erode hegemony by pursuing robust contestation within the shared symbolic space of the democratic game. See C. Mouffe, *On the Political*, London: Routledge, 2005 and A. Schaap, *Political Reconciliation*, London: Routledge, 2005, p. 22.
35. As he famously noted in the first line of the book: 'Sovereign is he who decides on the exception.' C. Schmitt, *Political Theology*, Chicago, IL: University of Chicago Press, 2005, p. 5.
36. Schmitt, *Political Theology*, p. 36.

37. M. Foucault, *Discipline and Punish: The Birth of the Prison*, London: Penguin Books, p. 149.
38. Foucault summarizes these insights from his so-called middle period in the final lecture of his 1975-6 series at the Collège de France. However, they appear also in condensed form in the first volume of *The History of Sexuality*. See M. Foucault, *Society Must Be Defended: Lectures at the Collège de France 1975-76*, trans. by David Macey, London: Penguin Books, 2004, pp. 239-253;M. Foucault, *The History of Sexuality: An Introduction*, Harmondsworth: Penguin, 1987, pp. 139-140.
39. Foucault, *Society Must Be Defended*, p. 240.
40. Foucault, *The History of Sexuality*, pp. 136-137. As Dreyfus and Rabinow have noted, in biopolitics 'The individual was of interest exactly insofar as he could contribute to the strength of the state. The lives, deaths, activities, work, miseries, and joys of individuals were important to the extent that these everyday concerns became politically useful.' See H. Dreyfus and P. Rabinow, *Michel Foucault: Beyond Structuralism and Hermeneutics*, Chicago, IL: University of Chicago Press, 1982, p. 139.
41. Foucault, *Society Must Be Defended*, p. 246.
42. Foucault, *Security, Territory, Population: Lectures at the Collège de France 1977-1978*, New York: Picador, 2007, p. 1.
43. Foucault, *The History of Sexuality*, pp. 25-26.
44. See Foucault, *Society Must Be Defended*, pp. 249-253.
45. Foucault, *Society Must Be Defended*, p. 252.
46. M. Foucault, *Security, Territory, Population*, p. 45.
47. Ian Hacking, aping Foucault, has coined the idea of 'memoro-politics' to cover the way the anatomo- and biopolitical aspects of psychology have entered into Western culture. Unlike Hacking, however, who describes 'memoro-politics' as a 'third pole' of modern power, I'm inclined to see it as a simple extension of the anatomo- and biopolitical. See I. Hacking, 'Memoro-Politics, Trauma and the Soul', *History of the Human Sciences*, 7(2), 1994, pp. 29-52.
48. C.S. Maier, *The Unmasterable Past: History, Holocaust, and German National Identity*, Cambridge, MA: Harvard University Press, 1988.
49. S. Freud, 'Mourning and Melancholia' in *On Murder, Mourning and Melancholia*, trans. by Shaun Whiteside, London: Penguin Books, 2005, p. 204.
50. Freud, 'Mourning and Melancholia', p. 204.
51. Freud, 'Mourning and Melancholia', p. 212.
52. For an extended discussion of this concept of the milieu, see Foucault, *Security, Territory, Population*, pp. 20-23.
53. See Foucault, *Security, Territory, Population*, pp. 71-75.
54. M. Foucault, 'Space, Knowledge, Power' in P. Rabinow (ed.), *The Foucault Reader*, Harmondsworth: Penguin Books, 1987, p. 242.
55. As Milchman and Rosenberg note, Foucault's famous claim about our failure to think power outside of the paradigm of the juridical monarchy—'we still have not cut off the head of the king'—essentially meant that 'if we want to analyse modern power relations, we need to extricate ourselves from the theory of sovereignty'. As Foucault himself pithily put it, '[w]e must at the same time conceive of sex without the law, and power without the king'. See Foucault, *The History of Sexuality*, pp. 88-89, 91; and A. Milchman and A.

Rosenberg, 'Michel Foucault: Crises and Problematizations', *The Review of Politics*, 67(2), 2005, p. 339.

56. Foucault makes explicit reference to the first of these cases in the final chapter of the first volume of *The History of Sexuality*. Much of what he says there was, however, already anticipated by Arendt who, as early as the 1950s, saw the intrinsic connection between 'racial politics' and the systematic attempt to 'eliminate what is harmful and unfit for life'. See Foucault, *The History of Sexuality*, pp. 149–150; Arendt, 'Mankind and Terror', p. 306.
57. On this point, see D. Fassin, 'Another Politics of Life Is Possible', *Theory, Culture, Society*, 26(5), 2009, pp. 54–55.
58. The classic instance of this is the condition of war where the sovereign can require his subjects to take part in the defence of the state and, as Foucault puts it, 'expose their life'. Foucault, *The History of Sexuality*, pp. 135–136.
59. Foucault, *Society Must Be Defended*, p. 260.
60. Foucault, *Society Must Be Defended*, p. 256.
61. In the introduction to *Homer Sacer*, Agamben draws the two forms of power Foucault aimed to separate—sovereign power and biopower—back together by suggesting 'the inclusion of bare life in the political realm constitutes the original—if concealed—nucleus of sovereign power. *It can even be said that the production of a biopolitical body is the original activity of sovereign power*'. G. Agamben, *Homo Sacer: Sovereign Power and Bare Life*, Stanford: Stanford University Press, 1998, p. 6.
62. Agamben, *Homo Sacer*, pp. 177–179.
63. Agamben, *Homo Sacer*, p. 179.
64. H. Arendt, *The Origins of Totalitarianism*, San Diego, CA: Harvest, 1979, pp. 158–184; A. Mbembe, *Necropolitics*. Durham, NC: Duke University Press, 2019, pp. 66–92. I should add here that in the colonial case, 'exposure to death' includes both the physical assault upon life and the cultural assault upon Indigeneity. The idea, put forward in the American context, of 'killing the Indian' in order to 'save the man' provides a perfect exemplification of this kind of biocultural death. On this point, see P. Wolfe, 'Settler Colonialism and the Elimination of the Native', *Journal of Genocide Research*, 8(4), 2006, p. 397.
65. See S. Prozorov, *Democratic Biopolitics: Popular Sovereignty and the Power of Life*, Edinburgh: Edinburgh University Press, 2020, pp. 5–9.
66. R. Esposito, 'Community, Immunity, Biopolitics', *Angelaki: Journal of Theoretical Humanities*, 18(3), 2013, pp. 83–90.
67. Agamben, *Homo Sacer*, p. 109.
68. This point is reminiscent of one made by Aristotle in *The Politics*: 'he who bids the law rule may be deemed to bid God and Reason alone rule, but he who bids man rule adds an element of the beast'. Aristotle, *The Politics*, 1287a 29–31.
69. G. Agamben, *Homo Sacer*, pp. 91–111.
70. M. Foucault, *Discipline and Punish*, p. 8.
71. The allusion here is, of course, to Brandt's *Kniefall*, but one might think also of the symbolic significance David Scott assigns to the body of Maurice Bishop, the recovery of which he takes to be critical to the possibility of civil reconciliation in the aftermath of the failed revolution in Grenada. It is the absent dead body of the prime minister, he notes, that stands in the way of the 'reparative mourning that might help relieve the melancholic

burden of that unresolved past'. See D. Scott, *Omens of Adversity: Tragedy, Time, Memory, Justice*, Durham, NC: Duke University Press, 2014, p. 111.
72. This phrase is, once again, taken from *Discipline and Punish*. See Foucault, *Discipline and Punish*, p. 14. As we have just noted, one of the things that differentiates biopower from disciplinary power is that it works less on individual bodies than on the general milieu. Since 'life' inevitably suffers a decline in the absence of movement, 'the circulation of both people and things', the primary objective of the apparatuses of security is always to remove blockages that jeopardize the 'flow' of life—above all, they endeavour to keep people and things in motion. See Foucault, *Security, Territory, Population*, pp. 48–49.
73. He does, however, suggest that 'the judicial institution is increasingly incorporated into a continuum of apparatuses (medical, administrative, and so on) whose function are for the most part regulatory'. Foucault, *The History of Sexuality*, p. 144.
74. Foucault, *Society Must Be Defended*, pp. 248–249.
75. J. De Rivera and D. Páez, 'Emotional Climate, Human Security, and Cultures of Peace', *Journal of Social Issues*, 63(2), 2007, pp. 233–253.
76. The concept is, of course, taken from Judith Butler. J. Butler, *Precarious Life: The Powers of Mourning and Violence*, London: Verso, 2006, p. 20.
77. Some of the key works which have inspired this one include E. Povinelli, 'State of Shame: Australian Multiculturalism and the Crisis of Indigenous Citizenship', *Critical Inquiry*, 24(2), 1998, pp. 575–610; Schaap, *Political Reconciliation*; C. Griswold, *Forgiveness: A Philosophical Exploration*, Cambridge: Cambridge University Press, 2007; T. Brudholm, *Resentment's Virtue: Jean Amery and the Refusal to Forgive*, Philadelphia, PA: Temple University Press, 2008; B. Honig, *Antigone Interrupted*, Cambridge: Cambridge University Press, 2013; Million, *Therapeutic Nations*; S. Ahmed, *The Cultural Politics of Emotion*, Edinburgh: Edinburgh University Press, 2014; S. Chakravarti, *Sing the Rage: Listening to Anger after Mass Violence*, Chicago, IL: University of Chicago Press, 2014; S. Coulthard, *Red Skin, White Masks: Rejecting the Colonial Politics of Recognition*, Minneapolis, MN: University of Minnesota Press, 2014; L. Stevenson, *Life beside Itself: Imagining Care in the Canadian Arctic*, Oakland, CA: University of California Press, 2014; M. Mihai, *Negative Emotions and Transitional Justice*, New York. Columbia University Press, 2016; and K. Maxwell, 'Settler Humanitarianism: Healing the Indigenous Child Victim', *Comparative Studies in Society and History*, 59(4), 2017, pp. 974–1007.
78. S. Prozorov, *Democratic Biopolitics*, pp. 9–14. In a similar fashion, Dreyfus and Rabinow have referred to 'the interpretative grid of bio-power'. See Dreyfus and Rabinow, *Michel Foucault: Beyond Structuralism and Hermeneutics*, p. 140.
79. As Forchtner notes, 'the rhetoric of penance does not result in closure but commits *us* to a continuous process of self-questioning, of self-reflection and self-criticism'. Forchtner, *Lessons From the Past? Memory, Narrativity and Subjectivity*, London: Palgrave MacMillan, 2016, p. 120.
80. A. Lorde, 'A Litany for Survival' in A. Lorde, *The Collected Poems of Audre Lorde*, New York: WW Norton, 1997. I am very grateful to Andrew Schaap for bringing this poem to my attention.
81. As Susannah Radstone has noted, 'an event's traumatic impact may be linked to its *puncturing* of a fantasy that has previously sustained a sense of identity—national, as well as individual'. The fantasy, in this case, is the fantasy of innocence. In a similar vein, Piotr Sztompka has suggested that 'revisionist interpretations of the national heroic tradition'

and 'revealing the truth about the past' can initiate 'cultural trauma'. See S. Radstone, 'The War of the Fathers: Trauma, Fantasy and September 11', *Signs: Journal of Women in Culture and Society*, 28(1), 2002, p. 468; P. Sztomptka, 'Cultural Trauma: The Other Face of Cultural Change', *European Journal of Social Theory*, 3(4), 2000, p. 452.

82. See Thucydides, *History of the Peloponnesian War*, London: Penguin Books, 1972, sections 34-47 and Sophocles, *Antigone*, Oxford: Oxford University Press, 1994, l.20-38.

1
What Emergency?

Damaged Life and the Biopolitics of State Repentance

Conceived as sovereign acts, constitutive of 'the people', the erection of a national memorial, the offer of a political apology, and the institution of a truth commission belong to the exception rather than the norm of politics. Not only are they unrepeatable, 'one-off' events, they also invert the whole convention of retribution by subjecting the state, rather than its outlaws, to a kind of punishment; namely, that of exposure before the 'ugly' or 'shameful' truth.[1] That these various expressions of repentance and redress are politically anomalous is attested by many critics and inherent in the idea that they function as transformative moments in which the sovereign body disavows the violence of the past and affirms (or re-affirms) its commitment to non-repetition: 'never again'. Used, as it were, to mark a change in the way the community understands and will thereafter seek to conduct itself, they are nothing if not institutions of exception.[2] And yet, attempts to explain these various institutions by reference to the political theory of the exception immediately run into a problem: what possible interest could the sovereign have in memorializing error, expressing contrition, and disturbing truths? In Carl Schmitt's well-known account, the sovereign decision on the exception is invariably justified by reference to the concept of necessity. If the constitutional order is suspended and exceptional measures are instituted, it is always with reference to an impending threat to the survival of the state: war, crisis, disaster.[3] But what is the emergency to which a penitential rite like a political apology responds? What is the crisis that necessitates it?

The most common answer given to this question is a 'crisis of legitimacy'.[4] States, it is regularly argued, are put at risk by accusations of injustice, as much by those that relate to the past as to the present, because their legitimacy ultimately rests upon how they measure up against universal standards of human rights. In the emergent global village, or so *this* story goes, states have lost the capacity to treat their own citizens with impunity. Not only are they more heavily scrutinized than ever before, they are also expected to conform to the norms and rules governing an evolving world (rather than simply international) society in which people enjoy rights both as individual human beings and as members of cultural groups.[5] Of course, since this world society still lacks an effective, not to mention legitimate, executive authority, states that breach those norms and rules generally escape punishment or sanction. However, the more human rights norms have emerged as the standard of civilization, the more states risk their moral standing through non-compliance. Those that refuse to acknowledge their wrongdoing are at risk of being exiled from world society, while those that pay their dues to their victims in the currency of recognition are likely to have their 'moral image' restored. Reparations, as John Torpey has noted, 'pay dividends in terms of political legitimacy': 'in the "age of apology" a society's capacity to face up to its past injustices may do much to enhance its legitimacy, both in world opinion and in the eyes of its own members'.[6]

Invoking the concept of legitimacy in this context seems intuitively right and helps to explain why democratic states have been at the forefront of the movement of restorative justice. While no state in the age of globalization is a sovereign fortress, completely insulated from moral rebuke, the normative commitment democratic states make to 'respect for persons' render them especially vulnerable to critique (and thus more deeply invested in the politics of repentance and redress). In part because they are constitutionally devoted to the idea that all people are born free and equal and in part because they stake their authority in world politics upon their accountability to human rights norms, such states are actually more exposed than their authoritarian counterparts to crises of legitimation. When historical violations are unearthed—a phenomenon that has become more and more common as victim groups (and the moral entrepreneurs that act on their behalf) become adept at appealing to human rights norms and exposing state crimes in domestic and international fora—democratic states lose their precious moral authority and find an imperative to atone.[7] Anyone seeking to understand why democratic states are not just more inclined than others to offer apologies, but are in fact the only states that do, ought, it is suggested, look no further than this. As Mihala Mihai notes, acts of apology have become the 'mark' of the liberal democratic state because the power of such states to command the respect of the international community and the loyalty of their citizens hinges on their moral authority.[8]

Perhaps the clearest indication of the monopoly exercised by this way of thinking about acts of sovereign repentance (that is, as gestures driven by, or promoted by, a crisis of legitimacy) has been the funnelling of critical attention towards the issue of 'sincerity'. Whether because of the electoral gains political leaders can make by atoning (or rather feigning to atone) for the past, the strategic and commercial advantages that can be secured globally through 'the politics of contrition',[9] or simply the good international citizenship status that can be acquired by states who embrace the idea of restorative justice, acts of repentance and redress frequently do 'pay dividends' in ways that invite cynicism about motivation and, with that, the likelihood of real change. As Gibney and Roxstrom note: 'the biggest problem with state apologies is that the apologising state wants it both ways: it wants credit for recognizing and acknowledging a wrong against others, but it also wants the world to remain exactly as it had been before the apology was issued'.[10] In order to ensure the perpetrating state earns its legitimacy dividends, therefore, moral philosophers have invested considerable energy in deducing the conditions that it would need to satisfy in order for its expressions of repentance to be regarded as something more than a cynical exercise in reputation management. Inevitably differences of opinion have emerged as to the precise nature of this 'sincerity test' and no one assumes that such a test could ever divest sovereign acts of repentance of all instrumental or reputational motivations.[11] By and large, however, critics have taken the view that normative standards can be held against the state in such a way that it will either be forced to take the wrong seriously or be shown up as a fraud before the domestic and world publics upon whose favourable opinion it relies for its legitimacy.[12]

The value of these efforts to establish a sincerity test against which to measure sovereign acts of repentance does not require a great deal of explaining or defending. Reducing the risk of faux contrition is clearly an important task, not least of all for those whose trust in the state has been abused (at least) once before. For them, as is often pointed out, an insincere expression of repentance may well be worse than no repentance at all because it simply adds insult to injury. Ironically enough, official denial leaves victims in no doubt as to where they stand and thus in no danger of unfulfilled expectations—to be without reason to hope is to be without risk of disappointment. Expressions of contrition, by contrast, pave the way to the renewal of trust and hence to the risk of further betrayal. 'Empty apologies', as Govier and Verwoerd have rightly noted, 'may actually be harmful to victims if they raise their hopes in order later to dash them.'[13] Insincere to the core, they give symbolism a bad name, cementing its association with all things meaningless and hollow. In the end, however, the value of this kind of critical enterprise is really only as good as the suppositions about the state and the 'reasons of state' upon which it is based. Is it safe to assume that legitimacy is the only value or end that is coveted; the only thing that might drive the sovereign to humiliating acts of repentance in which it falls to its knees, if not literally then at least symbolically, before the victims of its own violence? Is it possible that the sovereign has other reasons for departing from the strategy that is generally, but perhaps now a little too thoughtlessly, equated with *raison d'état*; namely forgetting and denial?

A small, but nevertheless telling, clue that 'crisis of legitimacy' might not be the right or, at least, *not the whole* explanation for exceptional measures of repentance and redress can be found in the frequent (one is tempted to say insistent) reappearance of a word that doesn't quite belong to the conceptual world of politics: 'wound'. In many instances, the use of that word seems so clearly metaphorical—as, for instance, when one reads of the 'wounds of nations' or the 'wounds of the past'—that one is inclined to pass over it without comment or reflection. And yet, the frequency and seriousness with which it is deployed give one reason to believe the word should be taken (and was meant to be taken) in all its visceral literalness and power.[14] Doubtless one of the reasons why the concept of 'wound' has managed to insinuate itself so deeply in discussions of state violence and restorative justice is the ease with which it slips registers and breeds associations. Since 'wound' can be figurative or literal, physical or psychical, visible or hidden, individual or collective, open or closed, curable or incurable (and many more things besides), the concept is nothing if not 'good to think with'. Yet it is clearly not just its ambiguity or its polysemicity that attracts. The reason the concept of 'wound' returns incessantly, or so I would argue, is because it is not just the question of legitimacy that is at stake in the politics of repentance and redress but the question of life.

Talk of wounds points in the direction not of tainted institutions but of damaged life. If its use in the literature is not accidental (and insistent uses are rarely accidental), it suggests that a different or, at the very least, *another* kind of politics is in play in the age of apology: a biopolitics addressed not to a crisis of legitimacy but to a crisis of life. But, of course, if this answer helps to resolve one problem (that of *why* states apologize), it also creates another (that of *what* crisis actually means). The history of epidemics and pandemics (old and new) has, to be sure, provided us with clear examples of how it is that life comes to be 'in crisis' and exactly what form the decision on the exception takes. In the face of diseases that pose an abnormally high threat to the life of the population, the sovereign moves quite swiftly to declare a state of emergency. Public space is mapped and ordered, quarantine measures are introduced, exposure sites are listed, and rights are suspended—all with the intent of stopping transmission of the disease through the free movement of bodies. These now all too familiar measures of the *cordon sanitaire* have been widely accepted, even admitted as logical and necessary, because a pandemic is a scientifically knowable and statistically demonstrable 'crisis of life'. For most citizens, the public disclosure of rapidly escalating infection and mortality rates are persuasion enough of the existence of an emergency. But the matter of risks and remedies is clearly not so straightforward when it comes to those suppurating 'wounds of nations'. Exactly what kind of 'crisis of life' is it where it is 'the past' that places the social body at risk and acts of sovereign repentance that are offered up as a cure?

In his critically acclaimed study of the post-war memory politics of Germany and Japan, *The Wages of Guilt*, Ian Buruma offers one, admirably concise, answer to this question: 'ruined cities, ruined people'.[15] For him, it was the reflections of Stephen Spender, recorded during a visit to Cologne in 1945, that best captured the crisis in question: 'The ruin of the city is reflected in the internal ruin of its inhabitants who, instead of being lives that can form a scar over the city's wounds, are parasites sucking at a dead carcase'.[16] That the invisible, unknown, and seemingly unrepresentable 'interior life' of subjects might find a mirror in the rubble of 'exterior life' is a recurring and by no means unfitting theme in the literature on war-torn and unreconciled societies where the past lives on in unresolved grief and guilt.[17] In the rubble of cities one finds as clear, and as vivid, an image as might be possible for the damaged, fragmented psychic world that is commonly taken to be the mark of trauma. Was not Freud himself forced to fall back on an architectural metaphor and describe traumatic events as those which 'shatter the foundations of life'?[18] As poignant and evocative as it may be, though, the idea that life lived among the ruins is also life in ruins does little to clarify the nature of these traumas, how they come to be constituted as a political problem, and why the sovereign might resort to acts of repentance to resolve them. How exactly are we to understand ruination in interior life and what is it about such damaged life that might necessitate exceptional political measures?

Answers to these questions only really start to emerge when discussions of the wounds of nations exchange allusions to internal ruins for analyses of psychological loss. Buruma is, for instance, at his most illuminating when he draws insight into the 'comparable traumas' suffered by Germany and Japan from the grand process of mourning staged in Günter Grass' novel *The Tin Drum*. In that fictional chronicle of the war, the main character, Oskar Matzerath, is a boy who 'decides' to stop growing at the age of three after being gifted his most prized possession: a tin drum (a veritable 'storehouse of memory') which he strikes incessantly and will not allow anyone to remove from his grasp. The pages of the novel are filled with the memories Oskar 'drums up' (and thereby both meticulously records and 'works through') from the cell he occupies in an insane asylum.[19] Described by Buruma as 'the war's most famous literary witness', Oskar recounts his life with an incisive, and at times excruciatingly lurid, matter-of-factness.[20] If the madness that has overtaken him leads us to doubt his reliability, it does not seem to preclude a clear-eyed view of the hypocrisy, impropriety, and criminality of those around him during the war years. With the tin drum serving as his *aide-mémoire*, Oskar bears witness to the rise of Nazism and the coming of the 'Gasman', revealing, partly through his own complicity, how evil gains a foothold in the world and leaves its mark upon life. His distorted development and apparent madness, his damaged, guilt-ridden life, serves as a striking testament to what happens when individuals and communities see too much and process too little.

Buruma's reference to *The Tin Drum* comes in the final chapter of *The Wages of Guilt*, pointedly entitled 'Clearing Up the Ruins'. Two episodes are singled out as exemplary. The first of these bears upon the lopsided growth that a forgetful Germany and Japan undergo after the war—a growth that Buruma captures with the pithy anatomical asymmetry: 'economic giant', 'political dwarf'. 'When the war is lost', Buruma notes, 'Oskar decides to grow. He buries his tin drum in the sand, and grows, but he cannot grow naturally; so he grows into a humpbacked monster.'[21] Although not without its own ambiguity, this allusion to the burial of memory is certainly clear enough to illuminate the pathological effects of forgetting: however heavy the past has become and however much it seems to jeopardize progress, the decision to throw oneself into 'growth' and exempt oneself from the work of mourning is tantamount to a commitment to political immaturity or, worse, political monstrosity. A few pages later, Buruma refers to another episode as a way of illuminating the kind of reckoning with the past the citizens of Germany and Japan must undertake if they are to return to normal life. In this episode Oskar and his fried Klepp, having started a jazz band, are invited to play at an expensive, high-class nightclub called the Onion Cellar. When the club is full, guests are handed a chopping board, a paring knife, and an onion. Buruma, quoting Grass, explains the meaning of this unusual ritual as follows: 'It did what the world and the sorrows of the world could not do: it brought forth a round human tear. It made them cry. At last they were able to cry again. To cry properly, without restraint, to cry like mad.'[22]

As a pre-packaged allegory of Germany's catastrophic aggression, post-war denial, and aberrant mourning, *The Tin Drum* serves Buruma admirably. Few figures in literature reveal the stakes of the unmastered past better than Oskar Matzerath, that stunted child of horror who finally grew, but wrongly, because he buried his memory. If we can infer anything with confidence from his fate, it is that life cannot return to normal while crimes go unacknowledged and losses unmourned. In the absence of the *work* of memory that he belatedly undertakes—in the absence, that is, of a consciously directed, critical interrogation of the past—life takes on a monstrous shape. In this deeply ominous tale, decision is all. By electing to bury the drum instead of processing its contents, Oskar does not so much correct as exaggerate the deformity caused by his earlier decision not to grow. With forgetting, immaturity tips over into the grotesque. Only the artifice of the Onion Cellar (the prototype of the exceptional institution) is capable of jump-starting the mourning process and repairing damaged life. To the extent that he serves as the symbol of a society still struggling with its memory, therefore, Oskar testifies to the necessity of an artificially driven *politics* of coming to terms. To escape the internal ruin, the deformity of life, memories must be drummed up, truths told, and tears shed. Small wonder that *The Tin Drum* should have received such plaudits or that the Nobel Prize-winning Günter Grass later acquired the mantle of 'Germany's conscience'.[23]

For all their richness, however, such literary allusions can in the end only take Buruma (and us) so far. In order to arrive at a better understanding of the sense of damaged life that appears to both inspire and inform the exceptional measures associated with the politics/biopolitics of repentance and redress, it is necessary to turn to some landmark post-Freudian, psychoanalytic works that specifically seek to understand trauma within a political context and as a political problem. Extending beyond the metaphorical, these texts not only allude to the wounds of the past but also provide a theoretical framework that explains how those wounds are inflicted by political action (or inaction); the impact they have upon both the individual and the collective self; and how they might be treated within a psychoanalytically informed political practice. Focused, in particular, on collective experiences of catastrophic loss and the measures needed to facilitate collective mourning, these works place the question of organic life and the biological process at the centre of politics and explain how acts of repentance and redress can be mobilized as tools of healing. Indeed, since they are already working at the threshold between *zoë* and *bios*, animal life and civic life, they are by no means difficult to reconstruct in biopolitical terms. In them, a governmentality of psychic life emerges in which the social body is constituted as a psychological object that can be studied, known, and regulated in accordance with a conception of 'normal life'.

Our inquiry into this governmentality of psychic life begins with two seminal texts from the early 1990s that focused public attention on the traumas suffered by social groups as a result of official negligence or abuses of power: Judith Lewis Herman's *Trauma and Recovery* and Kai Erikson's *A*

New Species of Trouble. We then turn to an older but potentially even more significant text, in which the focus is less victim trauma than perpetrator trauma: Alexander and Margarete Mitscherlichs' classic study of Germany's 'unmastered past', *The Inability to Mourn*.[24] With the aid of these texts, we will derive two distinct but intimately related images of 'damaged life': the half-life of the alienated survivor (who dies while living) and the over-life of the guilty sovereign (who lives while dead). As will shortly become evident, each of these figures is marked by what, following Agamben, might be called a 'double excess'.[25] Beyond the power both of the psychological processes that govern recovery from loss (mourning and de-cathexis) and the juridical processes that govern responses to harm (compensation and punishment), these mirrored expressions of damaged life constitute an unsettling anomaly for which there is no resolution in organic or social law. In excess of the power of both nature *and* society to restore and reintegrate, they are the melancholic remainders of the past who, in their inability to mourn, lay the foundations of what I will call the emergency yet to come. Ultimately, it is the risk posed by their 'festering wounds'—a risk at once unquestionable and unquantifiable—that provides the pretext for the sovereign decision on the exception: a decision whose main effect will be the reinvigoration of the body politic through the activation of processes of common mourning.

I A New Species of Trouble: The Half-Life of the Alienated Survivor

To pinpoint precisely when the concept of trauma opened a portal for the question of life to enter into politics would require a more thorough genealogical analysis than can be provided here. Two influential texts from the early 1990s can, however, be used to map the contours of a new biopolitical discourse—a discourse that had clearly already been brewing for some time—focused on the psychic implications of political violence and the political implications of psychic disturbance: *Trauma and Recovery* by Judith Lewis Herman and *A New Species of Trouble* by Kai Erikson.[26] Although each is concerned with different kinds of events, both see trauma as much as a collective as an individual phenomenon that impresses itself upon the social body (and poses risks for its health) through the disruption of communal bonds and normal attachments. Represented, in both texts, as a double betrayal—a betrayal *by* the sovereign authorities to whom citizens entrust their safety and *of* the illusory (perhaps even exploitative) nature of the social contract—trauma emerges as something that alienates the survivor from the rest of society and brings them into closer communion with the dead than the living.[27] If it makes sense to speak of an emergency in this context, it is thus less a political emergency for the state than a psychic emergency for the survivors whose exposure to death condemns them to what Herman calls a 'diminished life'.[28] To the extent, however, that Herman and Erikson equate psychological trauma with broken attachments, their work also brings the more general, and inescapably political, problem of the fractured community into view. Since, on their reading, damage to individual life is also damage to relational life, trauma fractures the population as a biological continuum, breaking its emotional circulations and flows in ways that put the life *in* the state and, in extreme cases, the life *of* the state at risk.

Although it makes no claim to being a work of political theory, *Trauma and Recovery* operates in a kind of grey zone between discourses where the pathological is revealed as political and the political is revealed as pathological. Structured around a highly arresting parallel between veterans of political combat and survivors of domestic abuse—both of whom are presented as casualties of organized social violence—the text attributes trauma as much to the regular function of social institutions (in this case, the military and the family) as to the unexpected arrival of violent events.[29] While Herman is by no means blind to the fact that the violation of women in private life has been historically disregarded in ways that the sacrifice of soldiers in public life has not, she justifies the analogy on the grounds that soldiers and women are both structurally disempowered in ways that expose them to harm. Violation, on her reading, is not entirely random or accidental. It is disproportionately the fate of the vulnerable or unprotected, the legally and socially uninsured, within the social body. With powerlessness comes exposure to violence and with exposure to violence comes psychic dissolution and social alienation. For Herman (and herein lies what is perhaps her most significant innovation), this alienation from the community, from the world in which everyone else lives, is less as an ancillary effect of psychic dissolution than a constituent feature of the trauma itself:

> The damage to relational life is not a secondary effect of trauma, as originally thought. Traumatic events have primary effects not only on the psychological structures of the self but also on the systems of attachment and meaning that link individual and community.[30]

For Herman, the root cause of this damage to organic and relational life is the loss of 'basic trust' that follows (or is perhaps coterminous with) an experience of violation and betrayal. As she would have it, the basis of 'all systems of relationship and faith' (including, of course, the political system of relationship and faith created by the social contract) is the sense of safety or basic trust acquired in earliest life in relation with the 'first caretaker'. Without that original experience of care and the faith it creates in the reliability of the world, human beings would not be able to participate in any of the wider relationship structures that rely upon trust: family, community, polity. Viewed from her perspective, religion and politics are not so much departures from that original relationship with the caretaker as extensions of its structural form. Like the first caretaker (the parent), God and sovereign are authorities in whom we place our trust and from whom we expect a certain duty of care. Trauma, in this account, arises from a failure of, or betrayal by, those authorities. When individuals are exposed to violence or death, claims Herman, their belief in the 'good parent' and all its surrogates crumbles. Whether because that 'parent' failed to protect them or, as happens in cases of child abuse and state crime, turned out to be a perpetrator, their faith in the caretaker is shattered. A radical form of alienation arises in such situations because it is not just the loss of one relationship that is at issue, but the loss of that basic trust that makes any and every relationship possible.[31] Put simply, and to return to Freud's phrase, a betrayal of this fundamental nature puts survival itself in question because to destroy trust is to 'tear down the foundations of life'.

Although Herman does not include Jews, Blacks, Indigenous Nations, or People of Colour within her study, the application of her general sequence—caretaking, betrayal, alienation—to those abandoned by the law because of their race seems only too evident. At the risk of speaking in euphemisms, 'betrayal by the caretaker' is precisely what is at stake in that sovereign decision on the exception that produces enemies *internal* to the state and turns them into legitimate targets of harassment, exploitation, massacre, torture, and extermination. In such instances—instances in which the violence of the state is directed against the 'biological anomaly' of the racial other—the destruction of lives and cultures goes hand in hand with the destruction of expectations of care and grounds of trust. For those who survive this exposure to violence, the losses are countless and irreparable, but ultimately every single one can be traced back to the loss of that good parent who is the real unity of them all: the sovereign. To the extent that radical alienation (the liminal state between death and life) serves as a marker of *this* loss, the loss behind every other loss, it is a concept that could be readily applied to the survivors of crimes against humanity.[32] As inquiries into the possibility of reconciliation regularly note, loss of trust in their fellow citizens (what is referred to as horizontal trust), in the institutions of the state (what is referred to as vertical trust), and, most profoundly, in the world itself (what is referred to as basic trust) is the lasting fate of those abandoned by the law and the true sign of the depth of their psychic wound.[33] In this, Jean Amery, truth-teller of the Shoah, can perhaps speak for all those banned from, and by, the law: 'everyday anew I lose my trust in the world'.

As Herman is at pains to show, remedy for this kind of radical alienation is not easily found. With the failure of the caretaker comes the loss of something not readily replaced, putting the survivor at risk of what she calls 'impacted grief'.[34] Perversely enough, the instinctive response of the psychic mechanism, triggered in the emergency, is to refuse the loss. Since betrayal by the caretaker undoes the reliability of the world and puts everything in question, survivors are inclined, and precisely for reasons *of survival*, to resist the task of 'working through' their experience.[35] Rather than embark upon the inherently arduous and inherently slow work of mourning—a work that can only be accomplished through a painful confrontation with the reality of the traumatic event—they seek an immediate, if ultimately futile, relief through strategies of denial or fantasies of resolution. Foremost among the latter for Herman are two responses that have long masqueraded as 'private remedies' for wrongdoing: revenge and forgiveness. For her, the attraction of both actions is as obvious as it is dangerous. While revenge and forgiveness promise to exorcise the trauma through defiant acts of hate and love, they are actually incapable of delivering the catharsis the survivor seeks. In order for real healing to occur, she argues, survivors must overcome their own 'resistance to mourning' and this is something that cannot be done without outside help from the therapist, the support group, and, finally, the community of citizens created in law.[36]

This is not to say, however, that law—at least in its conventional forms—comes to the rescue. For if trauma marks the failure of the psychic mechanism in its ability to digest loss, it also marks the limits of the law in its capacity to provide remedy. However much the alienated survivor may want it (and however much they may be entitled to it), suggests Herman, compensation can never restore the *status quo ante* or replace what the victim has lost. Indeed, since the pursuit of compensation functions psychologically as a defence against the reality of irreplaceable loss, it deserves to be regarded more as a symptom *of* trauma than a remedy *for* it—for Herman it is, in fact, but one of the many 'disguises' that 'resistance to mourning' puts on:

> Prolonged, fruitless struggles to wrest compensation from the perpetrator or from others may represent a defense against facing the full reality of what was lost. Mourning is the only way to give due honour to loss; there is no adequate compensation.[37]

In a striking rebuke to traditional legal thought, Herman goes so far as to lump compensation in with revenge and forgiveness (the two classic 'private remedies' for wrongs that the 'public remedies' of retribution and compensation displace and transcend) as simply one more 'fantasy of magical resolution'.[38] Like revenge and forgiveness, both of which hold out the false promise of restoration, Herman treats compensation as a fetish that only serves to divert the survivor from the unfinished work of mourning. The fact that it is 'right' (legally appropriate) for the survivor to want it only makes it a more seductive, and thus even more perilous, fantasy than revenge and forgiveness.[39] Although incapable of delivering satisfaction, obtaining compensation can turn into an endless pursuit, perpetually deferring the only thing that can actually bring healing: the work of mourning.

Marked, then, by the failure of the two mechanisms—the first psychic, the second legal—which ordinarily facilitate the reintegration of the self, whether with itself or with the polity, trauma is correlated symptomatically with a radical kind of alienation: an alienation not just from the living but also from life.[40] Stripped of their trust in the world, according to Herman, victims of trauma do not simply retreat into themselves; they enter a grey zone between life and death in which their status as 'survivors'—as those who have already, as it were, gotten too close to death—becomes definitive of their identity. Traumatized people, she writes, 'feel that they belong more to the dead than to the living'.[41] Subjected to an experience that belongs 'outside the realm of socially validated reality' and which would, if taken seriously as social violence, be a scandal to that reality, they invariably struggle to find a place for themselves (and *their* story) within the world of those who cling to the illusion of a life safeguarded by rights.[42] For Herman, it is, in fact, entirely symptomatic of the rift trauma opens up between the exposed life of the survivor and the protected life of the citizen that the accusations of betrayal issued by the two groups at the centre of her study—veterans of political combat and survivors of domestic abuse—gained little or no purchase on the social order. To the outside looking in, the traumatized have a distorted view of reality. From the inside looking out, by contrast, it is society itself that is distorted in its systemic disregard for, and wilful denial of, exploitation and abuse.[43] Incapable of acknowledging the truth about the caretaker that the experience of trauma reveals (or perhaps simply unwilling to), the social body condemns survivors to their half-life of broken attachment and, in doing so, inevitably exposes itself to the risk of recurrent cycles of violence and unending claims for compensation.

If credit for pioneering the idea of trauma as both a disruption of and a threat to community must be given to Herman, special note ought still be taken of a work published by Kai Erikson in 1994 (two years after *Trauma and Recovery*) that carried the evocative title *A New Species of Trouble*. In many respects, Erikson's account of trauma does not differ very much from Herman's. He too will define trauma as an experience that damages 'the hardest earned and most fragile accomplishment of childhood': 'basic trust'.[44] In trauma, he suggests, our sense of the reliability of the world is destroyed, precipitating an emergency reaction in the psychic mechanism—a reaction in which sensation is, paradoxically, heightened and dulled and protective withdrawal leads to social estrangement.[45] Those who survive traumatic events, he goes on (again echoing Herman), withdraw from life, believing that 'the decencies by which the human world has always been governed are now suspended—or were never active to begin with'.[46] Arguably, however, it is Erikson rather than Herman who reveals trauma in what, to use Foucault's distinctions, might be called its biological (communal) rather than its organic (individual) dimension; that is, as something that spreads and transfers—as something, in other words, that is transmissible in the same way as a virus. More than simply a fate shared by those exposed to violence as a result of their disempowered position in social structures (for Herman, women and warriors), trauma can, he suggests, also strike at the tissues of social life and damage the social organism.

The title of Erikson's book refers specifically to forms of toxic contamination (three of his five case studies relate to pollutants: the contamination of a waterway, the release of vapours from a gasoline spill, the fallout of radiation from a nuclear accident). Yet the implication throughout is that the 'new species of trouble' he alludes to relates just as much to the pollution of the human community as to the contamination of the natural environment.[47] For Erikson, there is evidently a connection—a connection, I would argue, that is more than simply metaphorical—between the way chemicals and trauma spread through their respective ecosystems: nature and society. In both cases, it becomes permissible to speak, firstly, of 'toxic exposure'; that is, of contact with 'things', whether chemicals or experiences, that pollute and contaminate, and secondly, of 'toxic flows'; that is, of the spread of pollutants, whether from one place to the next or one person to the next, until such time as the whole ecosystem becomes fouled. When large-scale catastrophes strike, claims Erikson, they manifest collectively as well as individually—in his terms, either in damage to the 'tissues of social life' or in the emergence of a 'toxic social climate'.[48] In the former case, the social organism withers from a loss of connection between the parts; in the latter case, it suffers a decline of spirit from a want of good air. Either way, however, one receives testimony of the capacity of trauma to spread like a contaminant, to work its way, slowly and insidiously, through a relational ecosystem, until the community ceases to function as it normally would.

For Erikson, it was the appearance of these same symptoms in a number of different case studies that led him to conclude that the concept of trauma could legitimately be applied to collectives, provided it was qualified in two ways. Firstly, he suggested, trauma ought to be taken to refer less to the blow that does the damage than to the damage that ensues. Since it was the presence of symptoms, not the violence of the impact, which betrayed the existence of trauma, the term could not be located anywhere else but in its effects. Secondly, he claimed, trauma should be taken to refer to a chronic condition as well as an acute happening. If the symptoms resulting from prolonged exposure were identical to those arising from a sharp shock, the former had as much claim to the title of trauma as the latter. With these clarifications, claimed Erikson, trauma 'becomes a concept social scientists as well as clinicians can work with'.[49] Since it was the kind of damage done, not the suddenness of impact, which provided the mark of trauma, and since this damage was capable of being done over the long term as well as the short term, there was no reason why one could not conceive of trauma to the 'tissues of community' as one did trauma to the 'tissues of the body'.[50] For Erikson, in short, trauma could manifest not just in organic dysfunction (individual psychic collapse) but also in the prevailing 'mood' or 'temper' of a community exposed to death and devastation. In extreme cases, he suggested, an experience could so dominate the imagery of the group and govern the way its members related to one another that it became reasonable to speak not just of 'assemblies of traumatized persons' but of 'traumatized communities'.[51]

For Erikson, the most visible political manifestation of the traumatized community was the loss of solidarity and the division of the whole into disconnected parts. Disasters of human making, he wrote, 'often seem to force open whatever fault lines once ran silently through the structure of the larger community, dividing it into divisive fragments'.[52] The most general, and arguably the most politically consequential, expression of this phenomenon was the fissure that opened up between those affected by, and those spared by, the disaster. Characteristically, he noted, 'those not touched try to distance themselves from those touched, almost as if they are escaping something spoiled, something contaminated, something polluted'.[53] Looked at from their perspective, the subjects of toxic experiences (even experiences, like poverty or rape, that do not involve chemicals) become a kind of toxic matter themselves, as if their exposure to violence, to death and devastation, made them dangerously contagious.[54] Meanwhile, those affected by the disaster were magnetically drawn together in a fellowship born of an experience only they understood. Such 'gatherings of the wounded' could, according to Erikson, supply a 'human context' and an 'emotional solvent' within which the work of recovery could begin.[55] However, it was just as likely (indeed far more likely) that they would form into isolated pockets of unresolved anger and grief that the broader, unaffected community avoided like the plague. Among survivors of trauma, he notes, '[e]strangement becomes the basis of communality, as if persons without homes or citizenship or any other niche in the larger order of things were invited to gather in a quarter set aside for the disenfranchised, a ghetto for the unattached.'[56]

Acting, then, in the role of sympathetic witnesses and political advocates, Herman and Erikson illuminate the situation of the radically alienated, only half-alive, survivors of political violence and mishap. Neither, however, leave their readers in any doubt that the social body is implicated in and responsible for the fate of those survivors. As stands to reason, the ghetto for the unattached is only a ghetto because it is bounded by a wider public that denies or, in what amounts to the same thing, fears contamination by the experience of betrayal that its members share in common. Unconscious though it may be, collective denial is just another manifestation of the *cordon sanitaire*. As Herman, in particular, goes to some lengths to show, the 'trauma story' (which, for the sake of precision, ought to be understood as a tale that is not yet properly 'storied' in the sense of being sorted in linear time) is the story that cannot be heard or which will not be listened to outside the ghetto. Since it does not belong to socially validated reality (since it is, in fact, a threat to that reality), it is metaphorically, if not literally, 'unspeakable' in mainstream society. Indeed, while Herman does not employ the same metaphors as Erikson, she effectively attributes the 'bad air' of the ghetto to the fact that the trauma story cannot pass over the wall of denial. True, as it were, only for the alienated survivors, the 'war story' and the 'rape story' are condemned to circulate within the same increasingly polluted air. In the absence of witnesses beyond the ghetto—witnesses who, in their willingness to listen, help survivors come to terms with their loss—their only available line of transmission is down through the generations.[57] As well as dividing the community from itself, therefore, denial is inclined to reproduce the ghetto of the unattached over time, creating the phenomenon that is now commonly referred to as intergenerational or transgenerational trauma.

The significance of collective action to the process of recovery now becomes apparent. Since the response of the psychic mechanism to the emergency of betrayal is maladaptive and the compensatory measures available within the law inadequate, it is not surprising that the psychoanalysts should ultimately bring the repair of damaged life back to a political therapy in which the unspeakable is integrated into the speakable by way of a decision on the exception. If the loss of the caretaker is to be mourned successfully, suggested Herman, 'common rituals' needed to be performed in which the trauma story was publicly witnessed and validated. 'Restoration of the breach between the traumatised person and the community', she wrote,

> depends, first, upon public acknowledgment of the traumatic event and, second, upon some form of community action. Once it is publicly recognised that a person has been harmed, the community must take action to assign responsibility for the harm and to repair the injury. These two responses—recognition and restitution—are necessary to rebuild the survivor's sense of order and justice.[58]

Sadly, for Herman, victims of domestic violence were still waiting for this kind of public recognition and restitution. Something of the sort had, however, been achieved for veterans with the construction of the Vietnam Veterans Memorial in Washington, DC. Simply by recording the names of the dead and the dates on which they died, she claimed, the Memorial had become a 'site of common mourning' at which, *and through which*, the veterans of the war and the caretaker that betrayed them could be rejoined.[59] Indeed, far from being just another cenotaph dedicated to sacrifice in war, the Veterans Memorial had, she suggested, become a place of holy pilgrimage. 'People', she wrote, 'come to see the names, to touch the wall. They bring offerings and leave notes for the dead—notes of apology and of gratitude.'[60] In the secular polity, that black wall of names had, in short, become a 'sacramental place'—a place of healing and reconciliation.[61]

We can conclude this section by noting the double connection between politics and trauma traced in outline by these ground-breaking studies: if the body politic is implicated *in* trauma through violence and negligence, it is also disjointed *by* trauma through damage to relational life. Herman and Erikson, not surprisingly, are concerned almost exclusively with the damaged life of victims and victim communities. Both adopt the perspective of the alienated survivors and champion the public recognition of their wounds (or public legitimation of their stories) in the hope that shared mourning will lead to healing and reconciliation. However, all of their work points to the fact that individual and collective are mutually implicated in trauma and as much in the cure as in the cause. Extrapolating from their work, one might reasonably conclude that there are really only two options for the nation that wounds a part of itself through the abuse of power: either the traumatic contagion is held in the ghetto of the unattached by a *cordon sanitaire* (the strategy of forgetting and denial) or it is integrated into the social body through public recognition and restitution (the strategy of mourning and reconciliation). Herman and Erikson, standing on the side of the victims, clearly favour the second strategy, even as they assume that the first is the default mechanism of the state. Either way, however, their work points to the fact that it is not just individuals, but collectives, and not just organic functions, but biological processes, that are at stake in trauma.

II Emergency, Defence, and Survival: The Over-Life of the Guilty Sovereign

Although it never becomes the primary focus in Herman or Erikson, their discussion of trauma as damage to relational life inevitably raises questions about the barriers to recognition and restitution. What is it that holds the trauma story in the ghetto of the unattached? Or, to put matters the other way around, what props up the wall of denial that sustains those divisions in the social body and prevents the resolution of trauma? In *Trauma and Recovery*, Herman claims that the difficulty individuals have in integrating atrocities into consciousness applies just as well to collectivities: '[t]he knowledge of horrible events periodically intrudes into public awareness but is rarely retained for long. Denial, repression, and dissociation operate on a social as well as an individual level'.[62] Precisely why that might be the case (is denial a survival mechanism, an emergency response, for societies too?) and what might account for the passage from a policy of vehement denial to one of remorseful acceptance is, however, left a little unclear. How did that 'site of common mourning' called the Vietnam Veterans Memorial get built? In line with a commonly held view of politics, according to which the state is always and necessarily invested in the suppression of the truth and the denial of its own violence, Herman claims that it is only ever because of the efforts of social movements that those 'horrible events' are brought out into the open and enter into public consciousness.[63] The long struggles commonly involved in getting states to apologize or repent in other ways bear out her claim. But other possibilities deserve to be considered as well. Is it inconceivable that the state might also have an interest in trauma and recovery? Might it not also want to repair the tissues of social life or cleanse a toxic emotional climate?

The possibility that the state might be strategically invested in trauma is not, of course, entirely alien to the political imagination. As studies of collective memory regularly point out, episodes of historical injustice/psychic trauma have played a constitutive role in the formation of national identities and few things seem to provide more powerful cement for civic solidarity than suffering at the hands of outsiders. Histories of colonial oppression; large-scale terrorist attacks; devastation in war; humiliation at the hands of foreign powers—all these have been adopted as 'chosen traumas' and played a central role in national identity creation and consolidation.[64] Characteristically in such cases a trauma caused by *those without* (the enemy) is appropriated for the purposes of sustaining a sense of unity for *those within* (the friend). That the state might have an interest in trauma that is related, but not fully reducible, to these kinds of strategic assertions of the friend–enemy distinction is not, however, often considered. One of the striking features of the study to which we now turn, *The Inability to Mourn*, is the insight it provides into the psychological benefits that can accrue to the social body, firstly from a strategy of denial and secondly from a strategy of mourning, after the friend–enemy criterion became infused into struggles *internal* to the state. Although primarily concerned to explain the failure of German empathy for the victims of the Shoah in the immediate aftermath of World War Two, *The Inability to Mourn* inadvertently reveals the value of a remorseful acceptance of responsibility for the health not just of the alienated survivor but of the entire social body.

First published in 1967, *The Inability to Mourn* anticipates the work of Herman and Erikson in considering trauma as a collective, politically salient, phenomenon. In this instance, however, it is not the wounds of the victims but those of the perpetrators which are in focus. For reasons that I go on to elaborate, the Mitscherlichs represent the fall of the Third Reich as a national trauma that elicited an instinctive reaction of denial among the German people. Since, in their account, the humiliating reality of defeat could neither be assimilated into the conscious nor eliminated from the unconscious, it created a blockage in memory, living on as an as yet uncomprehended guilt and shame. In their explication of this instinctive reaction to the downfall, the Mitscherlichs provide a highly illuminating account of the ambivalent effects created by the psychic mechanism as it sought to defend itself against an indigestible reality.[65] On the one hand, denial, or the avoidance of 'reality testing', as Freud called it, allowed the Germans to ward off a catastrophic collapse of self-worth. On the other hand, it prevented them from undertaking the work of mourning needed to withdraw their libidinal investment in the Führer and the dream of German greatness he represented. Unable to kill off Hitler without killing off their own self-esteem, the Germans kept him alive, psychologically speaking. Post-war Germany was thus shackled to the over-life of a guilty sovereign, beyond the reach not just of the laws of humans but of the laws of nature—a monster if ever there was one.[66]

Read sympathetically, but with a critical eye on its unstated biopolitical implications, *The Inability to Mourn* is simultaneously an attempt to make sense of, and intervene in, the 'psychological emergency' triggered by the downfall of the Third Reich. In their sweeping diagnosis, the Mitscherlichs trace the origins of that emergency back to the narcissistic foundations of Hitler's rise to power (and beyond that, somewhat more spuriously, to a peculiarly German 'way of loving').[67] Hitler, they argue, only emerged as a 'love object' of the Germans (a target of intense 'libidinal cathexes') because he adapted, and pandered, to their infantile fantasies of omnipotence. Embittered by World War One, and even more so by the conditions of the peace, they installed Hitler as their collective ego ideal for no finer reason than that he 'fulfilled the idea of greatness for his subjects'.[68] In line with Freud's analysis of loss in 'Mourning and Melancholia', the Mitscherlichs argue that the narcissistic nature of this object choice, the fact that it arose from a love of the self rather than a love of the other, guaranteed a melancholic reaction to the downfall of the Third Reich—a reaction, in other words, in which the mourner does no simply fall into a depression but suffers 'an extraordinary diminution of self-regard'.[69] Since the Germans had substituted Hitler for their own ego ideal, fully identifying themselves with him, the loss they experienced was not the loss of another but 'the partial loss of the self, as if by amputation'.[70] Object loss became ego loss. More than just confronting from a moral perspective, therefore, the truth posed a serious threat to life: '[H]ad Germans "taken note" of the reality as it actually was, they would have succumbed to mass melancholia.'[71]

The central hypothesis of *The Inability to Mourn* is that the German populace defended itself against this psychological emergency by way of the 'de-realization of loss'; by way, that is, of the tripartite defence of denial, repression, and projection.[72] By refusing to allow reality to penetrate their consciousness fully, by repressing the intense affect associated with (cathexed with) the Nazi leadership and ideology, and by projecting all responsibility for the war and its crimes onto Hitler, the Germans staunched their narcissistic wound and left themselves free to concentrate their libidinal energy in the economic field. At all levels of society, according to the Mitscherlichs, but particularly among those who had occupied positions of leadership, personal responsibility was disavowed and the past treated as a foreign country. 'For the great majority of Germans who lived through the Third Reich', they wrote, 'looking back on the period of National Socialist rule is like looking back on the obtrusion of an infectious disease in childhood.'[73] Rather than the product of fantasies and desires still at work (and dangerously so) in the present, it could be dismissed as an aberration caused by forces beyond their control;

an unfortunate anomaly upon which any further curiosity was wasted. And so, although, 'rationally speaking', claimed the Mitscherlichs,

> it should have been the most burning problem in their minds, Germans have shown a minimum of psychological interest in trying to find out why they became followers of a man who led them into the greatest material and moral catastrophe of their history ... Instead, with a spirit of enterprise that arouses general admiration and envy, they concentrated all their energies on the restoration of what had been destroyed, and on the extension and modernization of their industrial potential—down to, and including, their kitchen utensils.[74]

Post-war Germany was not, of course, sealed off from the rest of the world (and thus from the expectations of a civilized humanity). As the Mitscherlichs themselves noted, as much as the Germans might have wished the Nazi period away, there was 'a world public which has neither forgotten nor is ready to forget what happened under the Third Reich'.[75] In this instance, however, the need to secure life proved much stronger than the need to secure legitimacy. Whatever desire there was within Germany to gain approval in the eyes of this 'world public', it was not powerful enough to overcome the psychic defences erected against the past and turn the nation towards a policy of repentance. True, the 'pressure of opinion' outside Germany had, according to the Mitscherlichs, 'forced Germans to institute legal proceedings against Nazi criminals, to extend the statute of limitations, and to reconstruct the circumstances of mass crimes'.[76] But such measures only served to reveal the impotence of the law in the face of a monstrous offence (what punishment could be proportional to it?) and supply ordinary Germans with a means of evading the guilt they carried as willing participants in a narcissistic delusion. In short, since there could be no repentance without a life-shattering confrontation with reality, repentance was abjured. So powerful did this instinct prove to be that even the small minority, derisively referred to as 'atonement Germans', who resisted the illusion that guilt could be eliminated by denial were treated as if they embodied a kind of masochistic perversion.[77]

The true perversity, of course, was that the collective denial of the past which, in the eyes of the world, only compounded the crisis of legitimacy turned out to be the saviour of German life. With libidinal energy diverted towards the economy, the self-esteem that ought to have crumpled in the face of a crushing humiliation (and which, ideally speaking, should have sought to repair itself by making amends) was instead rebuilt by the economic miracle. In self-reinforcing fashion, the maniacal effort at reconstruction enabled by the de-realization of loss worked to make that loss seem even less real. 'Economic restoration', noted the Mitscherlichs, 'was accompanied by the growth of a characteristic new self-esteem.'[78] However false its character, and however shaky its foundations, an image of a peaceful and industrious country took hold in which Germans were able to take renewed pride. In effect, the economic miracle acted as a lifeline for the narcissistic drives that had been brought to the brink of collapse by the downfall of the Führer and the delusional self-image of the master race he promoted. The further the reconstruction advanced, the less implausible it became to suggest that a victory had been achieved after all. Loss was concealed by gain and the necessary work of mourning was left undone: 'Instead of a political working-through of the past, as a minimal attempt at making amends, the explosive development of German industry began. Hard work and its success soon covered up the open wounds left by the past.'[79]

Although it is clear from the outset that the Mitscherlichs saw no future in this one-sided orientation towards the economy, neither denial nor the associated defences of repression and projection activated in the post-collapse 'state of shock' are treated as cause for reproach. Looked at from a Freudian perspective, the psychological defence mechanisms that secured the Germans against the melancholy impoverishment of the self were simply 'emergency reactions'; that is, 'processes very close to, if not actual psychological correlates of, *biological* survival processes'.[80] In their account—running so closely in parallel to Schmitt's account of the political emergency in other respects—the burden of guilt that the Germans faced after the war 'was so irreconcilable with the self-esteem essential for continued living that (narcissistically wounded as they were) they had to ward of melancholia'.[81] Far from making a decision to forget the past, in other words, the German populace acted in accordance with an unconscious, and thus more or less sovereign-less, survival imperative:

> Here it is pertinent to introduce our working hypothesis: The Federal Republic did not succumb to melancholia; instead, as a group, those who had lost their 'ideal leader', the representative of a commonly shared ego-ideal, managed to avoid self-devaluation by breaking all affective bridges to the immediate past. This withdrawal of affective cathecting energy, of interest, should not be regarded as a decision, as a conscious, deliberate act; it was an unconscious process, with only minimal guidance from the conscious ego. The disappearance from memory of events that had previously been highly stimulating and exciting must be regarded as the result of a self-protective mechanism triggered, so to speak, like a reflex action.[82]

The fact that there was nothing ethically reprehensible in this emergency reaction to the crisis of life did not mean, however, that these manifold defences, instinctively erected by the psychic mechanism, did not come at a price. In order to ward off mass melancholia, according to the Mitscherlichs, the Germans had needed to ensure that only certain fragments of the past were admitted to memory. Events, like the bombing of German cities, which allowed them to assume the identity of the victim could be incorporated into consciousness, while those that implicated them in the needless sacrifice of innocents, like the concentration camp at Auschwitz and the massacre at Lidice, had to be blocked at the gates. Psychic resources expended in warding off the past were, however, psychic resources unavailable for dealing with the present:

> A very considerable expenditure of psychic energy is needed to maintain this separation of acceptable and unacceptable memories; and what is consumed in the defense of a self anxious to protect itself against bitter reproaches of conscience and doubts of its own worth is thus unavailable for mastering the present.[83]

With 'psychic de-realization', in other words, came 'creative stultification'. While the splitting off of acceptable and unacceptable memories had succeeded in preventing a descent into melancholia, it was also 'helping to ward off insights into unresolved or insufficiently understood problems of contemporary German society'.[84] Even in the furious phase of reconstruction, signals discernible from across the 'whole political and social organism' testified to an absence of vitality.

The irony that slowly begins to dawn in the text is that the psychological defence mechanisms triggered in the emergency had left that giant social and political organism sterile.[85] Not only, claimed the Mitscherlichs, did the unconscious fixation on the past rob the Germans of the capacity to respond in a creative way to the trials of reconstruction, it also blocked their path to political maturation. Democracy, already a political form imposed upon Germany from without rather than grown from within, failed to bloom in the post-war period precisely because it carried the obligation of *responsible* self-government. The development of life that did take place was thus of a completely lopsided nature. As the economy boomed, the polity atrophied, with a 'diffuse indifference' to political problems serving as the defining mark of a citizenry that lacked the capacity to engage empathetically with others (not least of all the Jewish victims of their own aggression). For the Mitscherlichs, the contrast between the 'lively interest' the Germans showed in technical problems and the 'general apathy' they displayed in relation to

What Emergency? 59

issues involving basic political rights was entirely symptomatic of the libidinal investment they had made in denying the Nazi period.[86] The effect of keeping the overwhelming burden of humiliation and shame at bay was the inability to engage in processes of communication that required thought *and* feeling. Far from flourishing, therefore, 'German political life' had slowly but surely begun 'to freeze into mere administrative routine', the insecurely fastened democratic foundations having been given up step by step.[87]

In effect, then, the reaction to the psychological emergency, instinctively decided upon by the psychic mechanism, had worked to create a second, seemingly less urgent but potentially no less dangerous, threat to life. As with Oskar Matzerath, the burial of the past needed to survive the crisis of defeat had produced an additional deformity of character: the German populace of the post-war period emerging as the grotesque, hunchbacked monster whose infantile defence against the past had proved too successful for its own political good. So long as self-esteem remained artificially buoyed by the economic miracle, according to the Mitscherlichs, there was little or no incentive for the Germans to fully embrace democracy and expose their view of the recent past to 'the inconvenient questioning of others'.[88] Only a patient whose symptoms cost him more than what he gained through repression, they suggested, would be inclined to relax the 'interior censorship' preventing the return to consciousness of what had been denied, and in this instance the people were, at least materially, much better off than before.[89] However, the imbalance graphically captured by Buruma's 'economic giant'/'political dwarf' image suggested a thoroughly skewed distribution of desire which, according to the Mitscherlichs' analysis of things, was deeply portentous for the future:

> We cannot bring the dead back to life. But until we Germans manage to free ourselves in relation to the living from the stereotyped prejudices embedded in our history (the Third Reich representing only a recent phase of this), we shall remain chained to our psycho-social immobilism, as to an illness involving symptoms of severe paralysis.[90]

The conclusion towards which *The Inability to Mourn* inexorably leads is that the psychic mechanism could not, in this exceptional case, be trusted to work through the past in a satisfactory way on its own. If the fantasy of greatness—the fantasy which had led the Germans into the arms of Hitler and which had been granted a dangerous after-life by the so-called economic miracle—was to be finally overcome, the Germans would be required to take active measures to ensure that the catastrophic losses they had suffered and, even more importantly, inflicted upon others, in their ill-fated attempt to satisfy their narcissistic drives, were brought to consciousness. As much as they conceded the utility of denial as an emergency reaction, therefore, the Mitscherlichs remained certain of the need for a mechanism, other than the psychic mechanism, to pursue measures other than the withdrawal of all libidinal energy from the past. As they repeatedly underlined, at some point a *political* working through of the past had, *of necessity*, to take place in which the Germans accepted responsibility for the past and set about making amends. Since the content of memories, even when accompanied by violent feelings, quickly fades, they noted, 'repetition of inner conflicts and critical analysis are needed to overcome the instinctive and unconscious self-protective forces of forgetting, denying, projecting, and other similar defense mechanisms'.[91]

For our purposes, it is this pivot from the psychological to the political that assumes the greatest significance. For the better part of the Mitscherlichs' analysis, it is the psychic mechanism that takes on the character of a sovereign power, mobilizing its defences to ensure that life is not destroyed in the emergency. Survival is *its* provenance. Ultimately, however, the reader is left in little doubt that this instinctive, reactive, and thus entirely decision-less response to the downfall of the Third Reich must give way to a course of action consciously decided upon by the so-called ego of the polity: the political sovereign. For the Mitscherlichs, all the evidence pointed to the fact that the psychic mechanism was no more able to eliminate the guilt arising from genocidal aggression than it was able to overcome the shame of having lost face as a civilized nation. The best it could do was hold such feelings back from consciousness by an ensemble of defences whose need for constant maintenance sapped the psychic economy of energy.[92] In their account, denial and paralysis walked hand in hand. If normal life, or something resembling normal life, was to be restored, the so-called de-realization of loss could never be anything more than a makeshift solution. Sooner or later (and better sooner than later) a political process—effectively a grieving process—would have to be initiated that cautiously set about rebuilding the 'affective bridges' to the past that the psychic mechanism had torn down in the state of emergency. Without that, without an attempt to work through the loss of Hitler (and, more precisely, the dream of omnipotence he represented), the Germans would remain in the grip of their narcissistic delusion and, as Adorno, well before the Mitscherlichs, noted, fully susceptible to the return of a disastrous politics.[93]

Their characterization of collective denial as an instinctive reaction notwithstanding, then, the Mitscherlichs still found cause to censure the German government for its failure to facilitate civic efforts in recalling and analysing the catastrophic episode of Nazism. 'Official policy', they wrote, remains anchored to nebulous fictions and wishful thinking and has, to this day, failed to make any searching attempt—even if only for the sake of its own political health—to understand the terrifying past and, among other things, the terrifying influence which Nazi promises were able to acquire over the German people.[94]

Singled out for particular disapprobation in this regard was the failure of the education sector to make inroads upon the problem of denial:

Neither the millions of lives lost in the war nor the millions of Jews slaughtered can prevent most Germans from feeling that they have had enough of being reminded of the past. Above all, there is a total lack of any sense that an effort should be made—from kindergarten to the university—to incorporate the disasters of the past into the stock of experience of German young people, not just as a warning, but as a specific challenge to their national society to deal with the brutally aggressive proclivities these disasters revealed.[95]

The only official action of which the Mitscherlichs appear to unequivocally approve (and which they take as evidence of a 'decisive shift' in German consciousness) is Chancellor Willy Brandt's solemn, apologetic *Kniefall* before the memorial to the Jewish victims of the Warsaw ghetto in 1970. In footnotes added to the text after its original publication, Brandt is praised for having, symbolically as it were, put the knife into Hitler and turned the whole nation into atonement Germans.[96]

Ultimately, what *The Inability to Mourn* reveals, then, is a sovereign body that does not just foreclose on the recovery of the victims but undermines its own health by refusing to risk self-devaluation and remove the *cordon sanitaire* erected against the shameful past. According to the Mitscherlichs, as we have seen, the burden of guilt faced by the Germans after the war was so irreconcilable with the self-esteem essential for continued living that they had no choice, psychologically speaking, but to take flight from it. The result was a reign of denial in which Hitler (and the fantasy of greatness he represented) was granted a perverse over-life. Even amidst the rubble of the downfall, the Germans proved themselves not yet willing, or not yet able, to give up the dream of greatness—hence both their ongoing arrogance towards the soviets without and their disregard for the victims within. Yet, as the Mitscherlichs' would have it, the avoidance of one danger to the social body, that of mass melancholia, only led to the creation of another, that of collective paralysis. If the de-realization of loss, working in conjunction with the economic miracle, had worked to cover up the narcissistic wound, it had by no means succeeded in healing it. However much the Germans might find a salve for their humiliation in economic restoration, the failure to prevent defeat, which had led to the political division of the state, and the failure to prevent genocide, which had led to the moral exile of the state, could not be held back from consciousness forever. In the end, there was only one solution to the paralysis arising from that uncomprehended guilt and shame: bring the over-life of the guilty sovereign to an end by taking the conscious decision to confront the truth.

Two points need to be underlined here by way of a conclusion. The first concerns the intrinsic relationship established between repentance and healing, the acknowledgement of guilt and the completion of mourning.[97] Perhaps the key point to emerge from the Mitscherlichs' analysis was that the catastrophic loss of self-worth suffered by the Germans in the downfall was not going to take care of itself (the economic miracle notwithstanding). Since it was in the nature of trauma to create a blockage in memory that becomes maladaptive over time (a threat to the life it initially served to protect), some kind of external intervention was needed to restore those affective bridges to the past and catalyse the mourning process. Like Gauss' 'Onion Cellar', with its seclusion from workaday life and its techniques for soliciting tears, political institutions had to be contrived that would allow citizens to confront reality, accept their guilt, and mourn their losses. As far as the Mitscherlichs were concerned, little of this 'working through' by way of 'making amends' had thus far been done. Yet their brief reflections on Brandt's *Kniefall* suggest it provided an exemplary instance. There, in the face of the victims of its aggression, the head of state had performed an exceptional gesture of contrition that forced the entire German nation to acknowledge its guilt. With the performance of this sacred gesture, the Mitscherlichs dared imagine, the defences that had prevented the Germans from coming to terms with the narcissistic wound of the downfall had finally been breached. Although much remained to be done, in other words, the *Kniefall* marked the first effort at truth telling, the first concession to 'reality as it actually was', without which the Germans would never be able to recover from their guilt and shame and return to normal life.

The second point concerns the twin justifications the Mitscherlichs offer for these attempts at making amends: moral duty and social health. In a way, *The Inability to Mourn* anticipates *Trauma and Recovery* in its ethical concern with public recognition and common mourning. For the Mitscherlichs, there was never any question that the Germans had a 'moral duty to share in mourning for the victims of their ideological aims'.[98] Without that, without the willingness to recognize and to grieve, the alienated survivors stood no chance of overcoming the trauma of their betrayal and returning to the civic community as full citizens. However, this confrontation with reality is, at the same time, a means of restoring health to a social body whose psychological defence against the past imperils *its* future. Part of the problem in this regard is that the refusal of the downfall manifests symptomatically as a loss of vitality. The paralysis, if not the sterility, of the social and political organism is represented as a dire problem that would never be overcome until the Germans rebuilt those 'affective bridges' to the past and allowed their guilt and shame to make their way into consciousness. But part of the problem also is that a failure to deal with the 'aggressive proclivities' revealed by the National Socialist experiment puts the German nation at risk of repeating the catastrophe. Until such time as Hitler was beheaded in the political imagination, claimed the Mitscherlichs, there was every chance the population would fall under the sway of yet another delusional image of its power and destroy itself all over again. Remembering and working through was deemed to be beneficial, in other words, not just because it would allow the Germans to reconcile with the victims of their ideological aims but because it promised to secure them against their repetitive, if not compulsive, 'susceptibility to unbridled aggressive adventures'.[99] Only, in short, with a political working through of the past could they avert the emergency yet to come.

III The Governance of Psychic Life and the Decision on Trauma

Although they range across very different situations, the studies examined in the previous two sections allow us to make some general observations about the 'crisis of life' we are exploring. As will perhaps already be evident, the Mitscherlichs' analysis of collective trauma in no way contradicts that provided by Herman and Erikson—it simply examines the same phenomenon from a different perspective. At stake for all is the question of what happens, psychologically speaking, when citizens are exposed to violence in the state of exception. Herman, as we have seen, conceives betrayal by the sovereign in terms of the loss of 'the caretaker' and treats its primary effect as radical alienation. Unable to come to terms with a loss so profound (the caretaker being the foundation stone of all trust-based relationships), the survivor is condemned to a half-life of broken attachment until such time as the sovereign catalyses the mourning process by acknowledging the wrong and attempting to make amends ('recognition and restitution'). However, as Herman intimates and the Mitscherlichs demonstrate, it is not just the lives of the victims that are damaged when the sovereign takes recourse to violence—the life of the social body is damaged as well. When the sovereign person is exposed in his failings and his crimes (as Hitler was in his downfall), the collective for whom he functions as an 'ego ideal' can suffer a loss of self-esteem so profound it is placed at risk of psychic collapse. Like the alienated survivor, the guilty sovereign will defend itself against this psychological emergency through various defence mechanisms and suffer the effects of an unfinished mourning, only in this case the primary symptom will not be alienation but paralysis.

As it turns out, then, the half-life of the alienated survivor and the over-life of the guilty sovereign are but two manifestations of the same melancholic syndrome. Neither can escape the past because neither can overcome an increasingly maladaptive resistance to the mourning process. Just as the relationally wounded survivors are sustained in their alienation by their inability to mourn the loss of the caretaker, the narcissistically wounded sovereign is sustained in its guilt by its inability to mourn the loss of self-esteem. Both are in flight from reality. To say that there are parallels—at least at the level of the syndrome—between the one who is wounded (the alienated survivor) and the one who wounds (the sovereign body) is not to say, however, that they are in exactly the same position with respect to the advancement of recovery. Since progress in the work of mourning hinges in both cases upon the public recognition of the injury (that is, upon some official confrontation with, and expression of contrition in relation to, the truth of betrayal), it is ultimately up to the sovereign to begin the healing process *for both parties* by risking self-devaluation. As symptoms of an unfinished mourning, alienation and paralysis find their common remedy in the confrontation of the state with its (violent) self. Healing comes, if it comes at all, when the sovereign steps away from the strategy of denial and engages in that rarest of all political practices: the exposure of the self in gestures of repentance and redress.

One of the most striking features of the analyses examined in the previous two sections is their convergence on this idea of sovereign repentance and common mourning. Notwithstanding the fact that they come at the problem of damaged life from opposite directions (the first from the perspective of the victims, the second from the perspective of the perpetrators), both Herman and the Mitscherlichs arrive at precisely the same solution to the psychological emergency: an artificially contrived work of common mourning based upon the acceptance of collective responsibility for wrongdoing. For Herman, as we have seen, this takes the form of a public memorial; for the Mitscherlichs, it takes the form of a political apology. What is clear in both cases, however, is that the problem of unfinished mourning is only overcome because the sovereign does something exceptional—something, that is, beyond regular law. With the benefit of these analyses it becomes much easier to understand why Elazar Barkan should insist that exceptional institutions of repentance and redress—under whose banner he includes truth telling, restitution, reparation, apology, and memorialization—are needed to 'transform the trauma into mourning'.[100] It is because no law—organic or juridical—answers to the problem of social trauma that the sovereign is compelled to take it into the exception and catalyse the process of mourning by publicly atoning for the injury.

For Herman, this kind of public recognition of the injury is invariably hard won. Were it not for victims' groups and social movements, organized around the right to live, the state would never take any action at all. It may, however, be naive to think that it is always trauma that forces itself upon the state rather than the state that forces itself upon trauma. Against the common presumption that crises simply impose themselves upon the political domain, we should heed the advice of Carl Schmitt (at least on this matter) and acknowledge that no event ever comes pre-packed as a political crisis or a social trauma—it has to be adjudged as such and always, of course, by the legal entity with the authority to do so: the bearer of the sovereign person.[101] Put differently, before the sovereign exercises its prerogative over the exception and decides to make a therapeutic intervention into the life of the population, it must first make a judgement as to type—a judgement that cannot be made in the absence of some understanding of the line dividing a non-traumatic situation from a traumatic one or, as Liz Philipose astutely puts it, a pain that can be 'lived through' from a pain that 'inhibits living'.[102] Unfinished mourning, one might conclude, only becomes the object of a political strategy, a therapy based in repentance and redress, when the sovereign judges it a threat to the vitality of the state.[103]

Of course, as Foucault has shown, it is not necessary for the state to know psychology or psychology to know the state for knowledge and power to become interwoven in this way. As his historical studies of the social sciences have revealed—psychiatry in *Madness and Civilisation*, medicine in *The Birth of the Clinic*, and criminology in *Discipline and Punish*—knowledge can enter into power and power into knowledge in a range of institutional settings and through a variety of different channels.[104] Far from being insulated from political power, he notes, knowledge production—especially that which assumes the form of a scientific discourse—is 'subject to constant economic and political incitement' and 'capable of immense diffusion and consumption'.[105] For Foucault, no biopolitical operation would be possible in the absence of those knowledge systems that monitor the health of the social body and instruct in the regulation of contagions. Of particular significance for him in this context are those essentially physiological sciences—medicine, epidemiology, eugenics—without which the state apparatus would know nothing of organic life or how to protect it. At no point, however, does he exclude psychology—which is, after all, also a science of organic life—from this kind of political function. On the contrary, there are numerous hints in his work that psychoanalysis, despite the 'liberating role' it has played in certain contexts, is also responsible for creating effects 'which fall within the function of control and normalization'.[106]

For evidence of this, one need look no further than the studies we have reviewed in this chapter. Far from being connected to the state (and its biopolitical interests), Herman, Erikson, and the Mitscherlichs write from the perspective of the lives it damages. And yet, one only needs to abstract from the particular case histories examined in their work to uncover a knowledge bearing precisely the three features Foucault took to be distinctive of the biopolitical model of governmentality.[107] Firstly, and most obviously, it is a macro rather than a micro knowledge; a knowledge, that is, of the psychological processes and pathologies that operate at the level of the population rather than at the level of the individual. While the idea of the 'damaged self', so central to Freud, does not lose any of its importance in these studies, the isolated monad is no longer the only, or perhaps even the primary, consideration. Of greater concern is the state of the social body that is revealed when a broad collection of case histories or a wide variety of signs are assembled into a single portrait. In the case of the Mitscherlichs, this population-as-object appears in its most simplified form; namely, as a single organism writ large.[108] With Herman and Erikson, it appears in relation to the fractures and cleavages that cut through it and which divide the republic of the unknowing from the ghetto for the unattached. In both cases, however, a *systemic* perspective is provided in which the population becomes cognizable (and thus, of course, governable) as a psychological object—an object in which the parts are connected by a network of invisible tissues or general climatic conditions (hence the common conduct, collective moods, repetitive imagery) and subject to forms of psychic blockage and contagion.

Secondly, it is a knowledge of processes relating to the 'species life' of the population as they are revealed over time. Although Herman and Erikson centre on the victims of organized social violence and the Mitscherlichs on the perpetrators of that violence, it is not the legal system, with its payments and penalties of just measure, but the psychic economy, with its expenditures and withdrawals of libidinal energy, which is the focus for both. On this front, the Mitscherlichs are, in fact, quite explicit: for them, collective denial, the withdrawal of all psychic energy from the past, is nothing if not nature taking its course. The only law that is relevant to it is the biological law of survival. Herman and Erikson, assuming the role of rights advocates, are slightly less clear about the phenomenon they have under examination. Since both link trauma to betrayed hopes of care, law sits in the background of their analyses as one of the sources of authority that shapes expectations of protection and, of course, heightens the sense of betrayal. Yet trauma remains, for all that, a phenomenon of organic life which reveals itself symptomatically through an instinctual resistance to the work of mourning. For both, distrust in, and disconnection from, the world is an entirely natural (and indeed entirely sensible) response of the psychological mechanism to the loss of the caretaker—albeit a response which, once again operating in the manner of a biological survival mechanism, is inclined to become maladaptive over time.

Finally, and perhaps most importantly, it is a knowledge linked to governing. For both Herman and the Mitscherlichs, the value of knowing the ways of the psychic economy lies in being able to manipulate them in the interests of political life or, more precisely, in being able to redress the shortcomings of species life for social life. Like the regular economy, with its laws of supply and demand, the psychic economy has its laws of cathexis and de-cathexis that keep things in balance. Like the former too, however, it is not immune to shocks. Ideally speaking, as Freud noted, the loss of a 'love object' gives rise to a work of mourning. Faced with the reality of death or disappearance, the ego withdraws the libidinal energy it had tied up in the object, detaching itself piece by piece, until it finally becomes 'free and uninhibited' again.[109] Success in mourning returns the quantum of desire ready for expenditure to its original level. However, in certain exceptional cases, the psychic mechanism proves incapable of completing the mourning process on its own. Whether because of the narcissistic nature of the object choice or because of the overwhelming significance of its death (or perhaps both), the loss in question is in excess of what that psyche is able to process, triggering the emergency defence mechanisms of denial, disassociation, and projection.[110] One of the things that all the works on trauma examined in this chapter make clear is that the instinctive reaction of the psychic mechanism to loss, while serving an immediate utility in the moment of crisis, can become counter-productive in the longer term. In such cases, an imperative is created for the sovereign to intervene in the psychic economy, to make a decision on trauma, so that an unfinished mourning can be finished and normal life can be restored.

Under the auspices of post-Freudian psychoanalysis, then, an understanding of collective psychological processes has emerged which, without being statistically verifiable in the manner of infection curves and mortality rates, suffices for the purpose of identifying crises of life and mobilizing interventions against them. At the heart of this understanding are two general processes that are, at once, autonomously carried out by the psychic mechanism and capable of misfiring in ways that demand remedial intervention: denial and mourning. Denial, as we saw, is, in essence, a phenomenon of blockage. It names the refusal to allow things to enter into consciousness and is, for that reason, one of the most reliable signs psychoanalysis has of overload or shock; that is, of psychic emergency. It is from the denial of the reality of loss, which is another way of saying from the melancholic refusal to let dead things go, that trauma makes itself known. Mourning, by contrast, is the psychic correlate of the digestive function. In mourning, the subject submits to reality and accepts the 'love object' will not return. Insofar as it has the character of a process, it begins with the recognition that what is lost is truly lost, and no act of revenge, forgiveness, retribution, or compensation will bring it back. Mourning, as Freud noted, is best described as 'work' or a 'task' because the withdrawal of libidinal energy (de-cathexes) is a painful activity that cannot be accomplished all at once. Although it provides the only means to truly escaping the past, the process of detaching oneself from the lost love object is often strongly resisted—Freud will speak in this connection of a 'psychical revolt against grief'[111]—and only ever capable of being completed piecemeal.

As with other forms of biopolitical regulation, then, strategic interventions in the psychic life of the population are tied up with the problem of trying to govern something which already, as it were, governs itself. In such cases, as Foucault noted, the risk was not simply of failing to intervene at the crucial time but of intervening when there was no need: recall his suggestion that 'if one governed too much, one did not govern at all' because one would simply 'provoke results contrary to those one desired'.[112] In principle, therefore, the function of the biopolitical apparatus is simply to aid and abet nature by subtly redirecting it when its own processes fail to activate or outlive their utility. Of central concern here, as the studies examined in this chapter have shown, are *political* acts of recognition and restitution, repentance and redress, that break down the wall of denial and allow an unfinished mourning process to move towards its natural conclusion. In resisting the exposure of the shameful truth, the sovereign simply props up those defence mechanisms whose utility as emergency reactions are quickly exhausted. In effect, refusal to publicly bear witness to the trauma story amounts to the same kind of stop-gap measure, the same kind of *cordon sanitaire*, that the political community uses to prevent the transmission of a deadly disease. Designed to defend society against unspeakable truths, it only works in the long run to sustain both the alienated victims and guilty sovereign in a melancholic state. Only when it removes the *cordon sanitaire* and rebuilds affective bridges to the past by engaging in acts of repentance and redress does the sovereign allow the mourning process to resume its natural course and free its citizens from the weight of the past.

Do we have any reason to fear this kind of intervention? The psychoanalytic works examined in this chapter encourage us to see the decision on trauma that leads to sovereign repentance as a critical vehicle of healing and reconciliation. The reason the memorials, the apologies, and the truth commissions are celebrated as expressions of a *restorative* (which is to say a 'healing') justice is because they end the reign of denial that blocks the mourning process. With the exposure of the crimes of the sovereign, the wall dividing acceptable from unacceptable memories is brought down and the natural movement of psychic digestion is restored. One might legitimately wonder, however, whether that decision on trauma can be credited with all the positive effects that are often claimed for it. Located at the intersection of sovereign power and biopower, the institutions of sovereign repentance—memorials, apologies, commissions—operate as zones of indistinction between law and therapy, recognition and mourning, where political power enjoys a level of control over species life unseen outside of totalitarian regimes. As Agamben points out, one of the features of biopolitics more generally is that it has no clear stopping point. Once the walls of the *oikos* are breached and organic life is drawn into the *polis*, basic biological functions are opened up to observation and regulation.[113] Where does the valuation of life end and the manipulation of life begin? As sites where power takes control of subjects insofar as they have a capacity to heal and rouses them to recovery, exceptional institutions form an especially troubling instance of biopower. In these hybrid institutions, where to do justice is to heal and to heal is to do justice, life is not permitted to remain hidden or keep its feelings to itself. On the contrary, it must display itself, objectify its pain in story, and submit to a catharsis that purifies through tears. In short, when 'mourning becomes the law', to appropriate Gillian Rose's memorable phrase, life is exposed to power in a way that is both politically novel and disturbingly familiar.[114]

In adopting a biopolitical perspective, we come to recognize that it is not simply, and perhaps not even primarily, the moral demands of the 'world public' that drives the sovereign to acts of repentance and redress, recognition, and restitution. The need to manage risks to the life it governs (the life of the population which serves as its foremost resource) provides it with reason enough to create those rituals and sites of common mourning that bring healing/reconciliation. Even if there were only the alienated survivors to consider, the state would still need to manage those enduring temptations of revenge and compensation which are not only more attractive (because less arduous) to the victim than the work of mourning but also more unquenchable. As Herman makes abundantly clear, for those betrayed by the caretaker, no blood or money is ever enough because none of it returns what they lost. Less dramatically, but just as saliently from a biopolitical perspective, there is that division between 'those affected' and 'those spared', those exposed to and those protected from, the trauma that undermines the ability of the body politic to story itself as one community and requires great expenditures of psychic energy to maintain and police. As the Mitscherlichs demonstrate, denial is not without its costs *for the perpetrating community*. While the derealization of loss can help ward off mass melancholia in the moment of the psychological emergency, it paralyses the body politic and does nothing to free it of the narcissistic delusion that led it into disaster in the first place. Although difficult to countenance, engaging in a shared work of mourning with the victims of aggression was likely to contribute its bit to preventing the emergency yet to come. As Derrida has remarked: '[i]t is always the same concern: to see to it that the nation survives its discords, that the traumatisations give way to the work of mourning, and that the Nation-State not be overcome by paralysis'.[115]

Psychoanalytic discourse, by and large, encourages us to look favourably upon these kinds of interventions and treat them as instances of an affirmative biopolitics; a belated, but still critical, caring for life. The judgement is attractive, but it may be premature. As has already been intimated above, and as I will develop more fully in the chapters that follow, sovereign acts of repentance and redress that facilitate healing and reconciliation do not just pay dividends, they impose costs. In them, one continually encounters the same kind of demand: the demand that life offer itself up to the collective, that it 'gift itself' to society, as it were, so that *everyone* (and not just the alienated survivors) can overcome the inability to mourn and move on. The gift that the sovereign makes of itself through the exposure of its crimes is easily the most spectacular (and thus the most inclined to blind) of these gifts. But it is by no means the only one. Alongside those purely symbolic gifts of remorse that the sovereign body offers up to the wounded, we will encounter myriad more humble, though arguably much more painful, demands upon life: that of the truth-tellers who must expose their wounds in public; that of the witnesses who must bear the burdens of vicarious trauma; and finally that of the survivors who are called upon to join with their former oppressors in a spirit of reconciliation and give away their grieving once and for all. Only after tracing these manifold 'gifts' will it be possible to finally decide on the biopolitics of repentance and the true price of healing.

Notes

1. As Bronwyn Leebaw has noted, 'transitional justice institutions are extraordinary, temporary, responses to past abuses which places them in tension with core principles associated with rule of law'. I also follow Andrew Escobedo in the view that 'the uncomfortable experience of apologetic remorse amounts to a kind of voluntary self-punishment. This self-punishment affirms the confessive implication that the offender believes he deserves punishment, and thus he administers it himself'. See B. Leebaw, 'The Irreconcilable Goals of Transitional Justice', *Human Rights Quarterly*, 30(1), 2008, p. 110; and A. Escobedo, 'On Sincere Apologies: Saying "Sorry" in *Hamlet*', *Philosophy and Literature*, 41(1A), 2017, p. A165.
2. To quote just one example: 'The period of transitional justice may include war crimes trials, truth commissions, reparations, lustration, and memorials, among other initiatives, and it is a unique moment in political life because the social contract is in the process of being redrawn (and because political obligation is reconsidered); as part of this process the community must respond to the most serious crimes on a large scale, a task more overwhelming than the work of everyday politics'. S. Chakravarti, *Sing the Rage: Listening to Anger after Mass Violence*, Chicago, IL: University of Chicago Press, 2014, p. 3. Although, for the sake of convenience, I refer to these rituals and practices as 'institutions of exception', their classification as institutions is itself questionable given their indeterminate nature.
3. C. Schmitt, *Political Theology*, Chicago, IL: University of Chicago Press, 2005, p. 6.
4. According to Duncan Bell, for instance, 'perceptions of the past are essential in both de-legitimating previous regimes—often through a process of excavating and confronting their crimes, or alternatively in attempting to airbrush them from the history books— and in grounding new claims to political legitimacy'. D. Bell, 'Introduction' in D. Bell (ed.), *Memory, Trauma and World Politics*, London: Palgrave Macmillan, 2006, p. 20.
5. Elazar Barkan refers to this incorporation of group rights within the general category of human rights as a 'neo-enlightenment morality'. See E. Barkan, *The Guilt of Nations: Restitution and Negotiating Historical Injustices*, Baltimore, MD: Johns Hopkins University Press, 2000, p. xx.
6. J. Torpey, *Making Whole What Has Been Smashed: On Reparations Politics*, Cambridge, MA: Harvard University Press, 2006, p. 94. In a similar vein, Elazar Barkan speaks of a 'new world opinion in which appearing compassionate and holding the moral high ground has become a good investment' and Pierre Hazan talks of 'acquiring the "certificate of respectability" in the international community through reparations and big gestures'. See E. Barkan, *The Guilt of Nations*, p. xvi; and P. Hazan, *Judging War, Judging History: Behind Truth and Reconciliation*, Stanford, CA: Stanford University Press, 2010, p. 22. The argument about legitimacy has also been made in relation to apologies offered between states. See T. Bentley, 'The Sorrow of Empire', *Review of International Studies*, 41(3), 2015, p. 629.

7. As Coicaud and Jonsson have noted, 'victims, families or representatives of victims have increasingly called upon norms of human rights to challenge states nationally and internationally'. Coicaud and Jonsson, 'Elements of a Road Map for a Politics of Apology' in M. Gibney, R.E. Howard-Hassman, J. Coicaud, and N. Steiner (eds.), *The Age of Apology: Facing Up to the Past*, Philadelphia, PA: University of Pennsylvania Press, 2008, p. 77.
8. M. Mihai, 'When the State Says "Sorry": State Apologies as Exemplary Political Judgements', *The Journal of Political Philosophy*, 21(2), 2013, pp. 206-207. See also J. Borneman, 'Can Public Apologies Contribute to Peace? An Argument for Retribution', *Anthropology of East Europe Review*, 17(1), 1999, p. 7.
9. The phrase is borrowed from R. Weyeneth, 'The Power of Apology and the Process of Historical Reconciliation', *The Public Historian*, 23(3), 2001, p. 36.
10. M. Gibney and E. Roxstrom, 'The Status of State Apologies', *Human Rights Quarterly*, 23, 2001, p. 936.
11. As Charles Griswold has suggested, 'some level of hypocrisy is no doubt intrinsic to the expression of political apology (for narrowly self-interested motivations are ineliminable when the agent is a political entity)'. C. Griswold, *Forgiveness: A Philosophical Exploration*, Cambridge: Cambridge University Press, 2007, p. 151. For similar views about the risk of insincerity of political apologies, see M. Cunningham, '"Saying Sorry": The Politics of Apology', *The Political Quarterly*, 70(3), 1999, pp. 287-288; R. Joyce, 'Apologising', *Public Affairs Quarterly*, 13(2), 1999, pp. 159-160; T. Govier and W. Verwoerd, 'The Promise and Pitfalls of Apology', *Journal of Social Philosophy*, 33(1), 2002, pp. 144-147; J. Thompson, 'Apology, Justice and Respect: A Critical Defense of Political Apology' in *The Age of Apology*, pp. 34-38; Gibney and Roxstrom 'The Status of State Apologies', pp. 912-914; R. Verdeja, 'Official Apologies in the Aftermath of Political Violence', *Metaphilosophy*, 41(4), 2010, p. 568; Z. Kampf and N. Löwenheim, 'Rituals of Apology in the Global Arena', *Security Dialogue*, 43(1), 2012., pp 43-60; and M. Thaler, 'Just Pretending: Political Apologies for Historical Injustice and Vice's Tribute to Virtue', *Critical Review of International Social and Political Philosophy*, 15(3), 2012, p. 260.
12. See, for instance, Govier and Verwoerd, 'Taking Wrongs Seriously: A Qualified Defence of Public Apologies', *Saskatchewan Law Review*, 65, 2002, pp. 139-162; Verdeja, 'Official Apologies', pp. 563-581; and Thaler, 'Just Pretending', pp. 259-278.
13. Govier and Verwoerd, 'Taking Wrongs Seriously', p. 158.
14. See D. Tutu, *No Future without Forgiveness*, London: Rider/Random House, 1999, p. 29; P. Hazan, *Judging War, Judging History*, p. 26; D. Philpott, 'Beyond Politics as Usual' in D. Philpott (ed.), *The Politics of Past Evil: Religion, Reconciliation and the Dilemmas of Transitional Justice*, Notre Dame, IN: University of Notre Dame Press, 2006, p. 16.
15. I. Buruma, *The Wages of Guilt: Memories of War in Germany and Japan*, London: Atlantic Books, 2009, p. xv.
16. Buruma, *The Wages of Guilt*, p. 49.
17. In 1950, Hannah Arendt too would find a parallel between the external and the internal worlds of the Germans, suggesting 'the indifference with which they walk through the rubble has its exact counterpart in the absence of mourning for the dead'—with the destruction of the city had come the destruction of emotional life. Significantly Arendt, like the Mitscherlichs (whose work we will examine in more depth in this chapter), will attribute this 'lack of emotion' to 'a deep-rooted, stubborn, and at times vicious refusal to face and come to terms with what really happened'. H. Arendt, 'The Aftermath of Nazi

Rule: Report from Germany' in H. Arendt, *Essays in Understanding 1930–1954*, New York: Schocken Books, 1994, p. 249.
18. S. Freud, 'Fixation to Traumas—The Unconscious' in S. Freud, *Introductory Lectures on Psychoanalysis*, trans. by James Strachey, Harmondsworth: Pelican, 1986, p. 316.
19. In the chapter named after the ever-tearful 'Niobe', Oskar declares that objects have much better memories than human beings and serve as the 'unforgetting witness to our every deed'. See G. Grass, *The Tin Drum*, London: Penguin, 2010, p. 177.
20. Buruma, *The Wages of Guilt*, p. 292.
21. Buruma, *The Wages of Guilt*, p. 293.
22. Buruma, *The Wages of Guilt*, pp. 293, 303.
23. See. M. Zehfuss, *Wounds of Memory: The Politics of War in Germany*, Cambridge: Cambridge University Press, 2007, p. xiii.
24. See Buruma, *The Wages of Guilt*, p. 56; T.G. Ash, 'The Truth about Dictatorship', *New York Review of Books*, February 1998, p. 2.
25. G. Agamben, *Homo Sacer: Sovereign Power and Bare Life*, trans. by Daniel Heller-Roazen, Stanford, CA: Stanford University Press, 1998, p. 86.
26. J.L. Herman, *Trauma and Recovery*, New York: Basic Books, 1992; and K. Erikson, *A New Species of Trouble: Explorations in Disaster, Trauma, and Community*, New York: W. W. Norton and Co., 1994.
27. On this idea of trauma as a double betrayal, see also J. Edkins, *Trauma and the Memory of Politics*, Cambridge: Cambridge University Press, 2003, pp. 4, 8, 11; and J. Edkins, 'Remembering Relationality: Trauma Time and Politics' in D. Bell, *Memory, Trauma and World Politics*, London: Palgrave, 2006, p. 109.
28. See Herman, *Trauma and Recovery*, p. 49.
29. Herman describes rape and combat as 'complementary social rites of initiation into the coercive violence at the foundation of adult society'. See Herman, *Trauma and Recovery*, p. 61.
30. Herman, *Trauma and Recovery*, p. 51.
31. 'Traumatic losses', she writes, 'rupture the ordinary sequence of generations and defy the ordinary social conventions of bereavement'. Herman, *Trauma and Recovery*, p. 188.
32. On the liminal state of the survivor, see B. Hamber and R. Wilson, 'Symbolic Closure through Memory, Reparation and Revenge in Post-Conflict Societies', *Journal of Human Rights*, 1(1), 2010, pp. 35–53.
33. See P. De Grieff, 'The Role of Apologies in National Reconciliation Processes' in M. Gibney et al. (eds.), *The Age of Apology*, p. 126; T. Govier and W. Verwoerd, 'Trust and the Problem of National Reconciliation', *Philosophy and the Social Sciences*, 32(2), 2002, pp. 178–205; and Herman, *Trauma and Recovery*, p. 51.
34. Herman, *Trauma and Recovery*, p. 69.
35. 'The descent into mourning', writes Herman, 'is at once the most necessary and the most dreaded task of this stage of recovery'. Herman, *Trauma and Recovery*, p. 188.
36. Herman, *Trauma and Recovery*, pp. 188–190.
37. Herman, *Trauma and Recovery*, p. 190.
38. Herman, *Trauma and Recovery*, p. 190.
39. Herman, *Trauma and Recovery*, p. 190.

40. 'Thereafter', writes Herman, 'a sense of alienation, of disconnection, pervades every relationship, from the most intimate familial bonds to the most abstract affiliations of community and religion.' Herman, *Trauma and Recovery*, p. 52.
41. Herman, *Trauma and Recovery*, p. 52. In a precise echo of this view, Martha Minow has suggested, 'survivors of mass atrocity often feel as though they themselves died, or are living among the dead'. It is perhaps worth mentioning in this regard that the two defining symptoms of melancholia for Freud are a reduction in the sense of self and 'an overcoming of the instinct which compels every living thing to cling to life'. See M. Minow, 'What Hope for Healing?' in R. Rotberg and D. Thompson (eds.), *Truth v Justice: The Morality of Truth Commissions*, Princeton, NJ: Princeton University Press, p. 242; S. Freud, 'Mourning and Melancholia' in *The Standard Edition of the Complete Works of Sigmund Freud*, vol. XIV, ed. by James Strachey, London: Vintage, p. 246.
42. Herman, *Trauma and Recovery*, p. 8.
43. As Herman notes, the classic instance of this in Freud relates to his repudiation of the idea that hysteria is caused by 'premature sexual experience'—that is, by child abuse—because it pointed to the clearly intolerable idea that 'perverted acts against children' were endemic among the good parents of the respectable bourgeoisie. Herman, *Trauma and Recovery*, p. 14.
44. K. Erikson, 'Notes on Trauma and Community', *American Imago*, 48(4), 1991, p. 470.
45. Erikson, 'Notes on Trauma and Community', p. 457.
46. Erikson, *A New Species of Trouble*, p. 240.
47. While most of the book addresses corporate failures to manage the environmental impact of their operations, governmental failures are also very much in the picture. In the epilogue, Erikson even goes so far as to suggest that the age of this 'new species of trouble' began with the Holocaust—an event in which toxic gas played a major, and far from accidental, role in the destruction of a community. Erikson, *A New Species of Trouble*, p. 240.
48. Erikson, *A New Species of Trouble*, p. 237.
49. Erikson, *A New Species of Trouble*, p. 230. See also Erikson, 'Notes on Trauma and Community', p. 457.
50. Erikson, *A New Species of Trouble*, p. 230.
51. See Erikson, *A New Species of Trouble*, p. 230; Erikson, 'Notes on Trauma and Community', p. 461.
52. Erikson, *A New Species of Trouble*, p. 236.
53. Erikson, *A New Species of Trouble*, p. 236.
54. It is worth noting in this context that Herman also describes trauma as 'contagious'—all it takes to spread is a witness. Those who listen to the trauma story, she claims (and there are always some who are willing to bear witness), are inclined to become 'infected' with the same sense of hopelessness, guilt, or rage as the victim in a psychic phenomenon known as 'vicarious traumatization'. Herman, *Trauma and Recovery*, pp. 140, 144–145.
55. Erikson, *A New Species of Trouble*, p. 232.
56. Erikson, *A New Species of Trouble*, p. 232.
57. 'The war story', Herman notes, 'is closely kept among men of a particular era, disconnected from the broader society that includes two sexes and many generations. Thus the fixation on the trauma—the sense of a moment frozen in time—may be perpetuated by

social customs that foster the segregation of warriors from the rest of society'. Herman, *Trauma and Recovery*, p. 67. In *Affective Communities*, Emma Hutchinson echoes Herman in suggesting that incompletion of the mourning process forces grief to become 'complicated' or 'frozen' and that this gives rise to various pathological symptoms including paranoia and revenge. See E. Hutchinson, *Affective Communities in World Politics*, Cambridge: Cambridge University Press, 2016, p. 231.
58. Herman, *Trauma and Recovery*, p. 70. Although Erikson does not attend to the issue of healing with the same assiduity as Herman, he too implies recovery hinges on public recognition and restitution. Survivors, he notes, readily distinguish between traumatic events that issue from the hand of God and those caused by their fellow human beings. They know when someone is to blame and expect responsibility to be taken and amends to be made. As Erikson would have it, this kind of recognition and restitution 'is so elementary a feature of social life that its absence becomes inhuman'. And while his focus is corporate failure, it is hard to see why the points he makes in the following passage would not, *mutatis mutandis*, be applicable to governments as well: 'it can be profoundly painful when the people in charge of a company at the time of a severe mishap deny responsibility, offer no apology, express no regrets, and crouch out of sight behind that wall of lawyers and legalisms'. In such cases, he suggests, survivors are inclined to become infuriated and pursue precisely the kind of legal action the corporation feared. However, as he goes on to note, once again in concord with Herman, this is 'rarely a healing anger'. Having already been exposed in their vulnerability through their exposure to trauma, the survivors now learn that the world is, at best, indifferent and, at worst, hostile to their fate. See Erikson, 'Notes on Trauma and Community', pp. 464–465.
59. Herman, *Trauma and Recovery*, p. 71. While the construction of the Vietnam Veterans Memorial in Washington, DC had delivered combat veterans the 'site of common mourning' they had long needed, according to Herman, victims of domestic violence had been given no choice but to create their own 'living monument' through demands for social change. Herman, *Trauma and Recovery*, pp. 70–73.
60. Herman, *Trauma and Recovery*, p. 71.
61. Herman, *Trauma and Recovery*, p. 71.
62. Herman, *Trauma and Recovery*, p. 2.
63. Having decisively linked recovery to recognition, Herman's greatest lament in *Trauma and Recovery* is the failure of the state to give public recognition to the injury. Rather than accede to the view, endorsed by clinicians and championed by the anti-war and feminist movements, respectively, that two of the key institutions of modern social life—the military and the family—were responsible for producing mass trauma, it challenged the symptoms and refused the diagnosis. What clinical practitioners and advocates took as signs of trauma, it took as signs of manipulation. Thus soldiers were accused of faking their neuroses and women of fabricating their rapes. In the narrative of *Trauma and Recovery*, public recognition had to wait for the emergence of social movements that challenged the sacrifice of young men in foreign wars and the subordination of women in private homes. Only a political movement powerful enough to legitimate an alliance between investigators and patients, claimed Herman, proved sufficient to 'counteract the ordinary social processes of silencing and denial'. Even that, however, failed to produce a permanent shift in public consciousness, particularly with regards to the trauma of domestic violence. 'In spite of a vast literature documenting the phenomenon

of psychological trauma', she noted, 'debate still centres on the basic question of whether these phenomena are credible and real.' Herman, *Trauma and Recovery*, p. 8.
64. See, for instance, W. James Booth, 'Kashmir Road: Some Reflections on Memory and Violence', *Millennium: Journal of International Studies*, 38(2), 2009, pp. 361–377; J. Subotić, 'Narrative, Ontological Security, and Foreign Policy Change', *Foreign Policy Analysis*, 12, 2016, pp. 617–618; and Hutchinson, *Affective Communities*, pp. 214–221.
65. A. and M. Mitscherlich, *The Inability to Mourn*, trans. by Beverley R. Placzek, New York: Grove Press, 1975, p. 11.
66. As Adorno had already noted in a lecture from 1959, 'National Socialism lives on, and to this day we don't know whether it is only as the ghost of what was so monstrous that it didn't even die off with its own death, or whether it never died in the first place'. T. Adorno, 'What Does Coming to Terms with the Past Mean?' in Geoffrey Hartman (ed.), *Bitburg in Moral and Political Perspective*, Bloomington, IN: Indiana University Press, 1986, p. 115.
67. All of the analysis hinges on the idea of narcissistic love. '[S]usceptibility to this form of love', claim the Mitscherlichs, 'is one of the German people's collective character traits'. Mitscherlichs, *The Inability to Mourn*, p. 63.
68. Mitscherlichs, *The Inability to Mourn*, pp. 28, 23.
69. Mitscherlichs, *The Inability to Mourn*, p. 26. According to Freud, two things differentiate melancholia from mourning: (i) some aspect of the loss remains unknown or is withdrawn from conscious and (ii) the patient suffers an extraordinary reduction in self-esteem. See Freud, 'On Mourning and Melancholia' in *On Metapsychology: The Theory of Psychoanalysis*, Pelican Freud Library, vol. 11, Harmondsworth, Penguin, 1987, p. 205.
70. Mitscherlichs, *The Inability to Mourn*, p. 63.
71. Mitscherlichs, *The Inability to Mourn*, p. 44.
72. Mitscherlichs, *The Inability to Mourn*, pp. 24, 28.
73. Mitscherlichs, *The Inability to Mourn*, p. 15.
74. Mitscherlichs, *The Inability to Mourn*, p. 9.
75. Mitscherlichs, *The Inability to Mourn*, p. 29.
76. Mitscherlichs, *The Inability to Mourn*, p. 29.
77. Mitscherlichs, *The Inability to Mourn*, p. 29.
78. Mitscherlichs, *The Inability to Mourn*, p. 13.
79. Mitscherlichs, *The Inability to Mourn*, p. 13.
80. Mitscherlichs, *The Inability to Mourn*, p. 24.
81. Mitscherlichs, *The Inability to Mourn*, p. 44.
82. Mitscherlichs, *The Inability to Mourn*, p. 26.
83. Mitscherlichs, *The Inability to Mourn*, p. 16.
84. Mitscherlichs, *The Inability to Mourn*, p. 7.
85. Mitscherlichs, *The Inability to Mourn*, p. 13.
86. Mitscherlichs, *The Inability to Mourn*, p. 7.
87. Mitscherlichs, *The Inability to Mourn*, pp. 8, 9.
88. Mitscherlichs, *The Inability to Mourn*, p. 15.
89. Mitscherlichs, *The Inability to Mourn*, p. 15.
90. Mitscherlichs, *The Inability to Mourn*, p. 66 (see also p. 14).
91. Mitscherlichs, *The Inability to Mourn*, pp. 14–15.

92. Mitscherlichs, *The Inability to Mourn*, pp. 65–66.
93. Adorno, 'What Does Coming to Terms with the Past Mean?', pp. 122–123.
94. Mitscherlichs, *The Inability to Mourn*, p. 10.
95. Mitscherlichs, *The Inability to Mourn*, p. 13.
96. Mitscherlichs, *The Inability to Mourn*, pp. 7, 14. The Mitscherlichs' assessment of the significance of Brandt's action has been widely endorsed. According to Barkan, for instance, 'We may mark the beginning of the contemporary attitude to the Holocaust at German Chancellor Willy Brandt's recognition of the Nazi crimes during his visit to Warsaw, which also marked the first rupture in the Cold War.' Similarly, Pierre Hazan has written, 'Brandt's silent kneeling changed the perception of Germany more effectively than any number of speeches. The fact that Willy Brandt himself opposed Nazism during wartime strengthened the symbolism of the act. This silent kneeling coming from such a man struck many and foreshadowed the public apologies that would be pronounced by heads of state and government in the post-Cold War era.' And finally, we can cite John Borneman's comments on Brandt's *Kniefall*: 'It frequently comes up on television talk shows, especially by members of the first post-war generation, the "68ers", who identify the apology as one of the few times they were actually proud of a German statesman, or, by extension, were themselves proud to be German.' See Barkan, *The Guilt of Nations*, p. 11; Hazan, *Judging War, Judging History*, p. 21; and J. Borneman, 'Political Apology as Performative Redress', *SAIS Review*, 25(2), 2005, p. 15.
97. Mitscherlichs, *The Inability to Mourn*, p. 50.
98. Mitscherlichs, *The Inability to Mourn*, p. 24.
99. Mitscherlichs, *The Inability to Mourn*, p. 50.
100. Barkan, *The Guilt of Nations*, p. 345.
101. As Tracy B. Strong notes in the introduction to *Political Theology*, 'Schmitt is saying that it is the essence of sovereignty *both* to decide what is an exception *and* to make the decisions appropriate to that exception, indeed that one without the other makes no sense at all.' See T.B. Strong, 'Foreword' in Schmitt, *Political Theology*, p. xii.
102. L. Philipose, 'The Politics of Pain', *International Feminist Journal of Politics*, 9(1), 2007, p. 62. Arguably there is more is at stake in this judgement than first meets the eye. If the sovereign is to know where that line should be drawn (to know, that is, when life really is at risk), it must 'know' trauma in a comprehensive way: in relation to its causes and aggravations, its acute and chronic forms, its cures and therapies. If, in other words, it is to safeguard the social body against that which 'inhibits living', it will need an understanding of psychic functioning so as to know what is normal and abnormal; ways of assessing the psychological resilience (or distress) of a population so as to make risk assessments; and a knowledge of therapeutic techniques so as to know how to intervene in the psychic life of the population and restore it to health.
103. It is in this sense, I think, that James Brasset and Nick Vaughan-Williams are right in suggesting that 'traumatic events are always already "governed" or known'. See J. Brasset and N. Vaughan-Williams, 'Governing Traumatic Events', *Alternatives: Global, Local, Political*, 37(3), 2012, p. 183.
104. See M. Foucault, 'Truth and Power' in *Power/Knowledge: Selected Interviews and Other Writings 1972-1977*, ed. by Colin Gordon, New York: Pantheon Books, 1980, pp. 109–133.
105. Foucault, 'Truth and Power', p. 131.

78 The Penitent State

106. M. Foucault, 'Body/Power' in *Power/Knowledge*, pp. 60–61. See also M. Foucault, *The History of Sexuality*, vol. 1, London: Penguin Books, 1987, p. 5.
107. These three elements are laid out, *inter alia*, in the final lecture of *Society Must Be Defended*. See M. Foucault, *Society Must Be Defended: Lectures at the Collège de France 1975–76*, trans. by David Macey, London: Penguin Books, 2003, pp. 245–247.
108. While admitting that the choice of examples they used to illustrate their thesis could 'seem arbitrary', the Mitscherlichs were confident that any example would confirm the same thing: '[i]n all of them we cannot fail to note the same inhibition, the same blockage of social imagination, the same tangible lack of social creativity'. Mitscherlichs, *The Inability to Mourn*, p. 13.
109. Freud, 'Mourning and Melancholia'.
110. In lecture 18 of his *Introductory Lectures on Psychoanalysis*, 'Fixation to Traumas—the Unconscious', Freud wrote as follows: 'Indeed the term "traumatic" has no other sense than an economic one. We apply it to an experience which within a short period of time presents the mind with an increase of stimulus too powerful to be dealt with or worked off in the normal way, and this must result in permanent disturbances of the manner in which the energy operates.' See S. Freud, *Introductory Lectures on Psychoanalysis 1*, trans. by J. Strachey, Harmondsworth: Penguin Books, 1981, p. 315.
111. S. Freud, *On Murder, Mourning and Melancholia*, London: Penguin Classics, p. 198.
112. M. Foucault, 'Space, Knowledge and Power' in P. Rabinow (ed.), *The Foucault Reader*, Harmondsworth: Penguin Books, 1984, p. 242.
113. Agamben, *Homo Sacer*, p. 131.
114. G. Rose, *Mourning Becomes the Law: Philosophy and Representation*, Cambridge: Cambridge University Press, 1997.
115. J. Derrida, *On Cosmopolitanism and Forgiveness*, London: Routledge, 2001, p. 41.

2
New Life
The Civil Wound and the Problem of Political Renewal

Was there ever a time when damaged life was not an abiding political preoccupation? A time when healing was of no concern to sovereigns? Readers of political theory will immediately recall the 'exhortation' that concludes *The Prince*, where Machiavelli surprises his readers by offering a tearful lament for the 'despoiled' and 'torn' Italian body politic. Having endured 'every kind of desolation', he tells us, the one-time, beating heart of the civilized world, birthplace of the magnificent Roman Empire, has been 'left lifeless', awaiting a redeemer who can 'heal her wounds ... and cleanse those sores which have now been festering for so long'.[1] As if out of nowhere, the language of political realism is abandoned in favour of religious zeal, the rule of principalities in favour of the renewal of nations, and the art of war in favour of the art of medicine.[2] If Maurizio Viroli is right and this chapter genuinely belongs in *The Prince*, it insinuates that the scope of 'the political'—that field of human activity that Machiavelli did so much to revive as an autonomous domain—is not exhausted by the strategic calculus that every prince must master if he is to survive the swings of fortune and hold on to the state.[3] As well as knowing how to overpower and deceive, the prince must also, it seems, know how to reconcile and unify, to heal wounds and restore life. Machiavelli, as is well known, had his sights set on the 'illustrious' Lorenzo de' Medici and tried to seduce him into playing the role of Italy's redeemer/healer with the promise of everlasting glory. But if it is possible to look past the flattery, the exhortation might plausibly be reduced to a more general plea: is there a doctor in the house?

Although it arrives late in *The Prince*, the recognition that 'healing'—the ability to reconcile and unify a political family that has become divided against itself—is a vital political skill is by no means a late invention. One index of the significance it has always assumed in Western thought is the prominent place assigned to it in that political art par excellence: tragic drama. Among the poets of ancient Greece, the recovery of the city after its division into warring factions, what they called *stasis*, is a constant focus and it returns again just as forcefully in that honorary Greek (or, perhaps more accurately, honorary Roman) of the Elizabethan period who clearly knew a little bit about Machiavelli: William Shakespeare. As C.V. Wedgewood has noted, 'it is obvious how much the shadow of the past civil wars and the fear and horror of internecine conflict inspire the history plays of Shakespeare. The division of the country against itself is the ultimate disaster'.[4] The theme of 'civil wounds'—the wounds city-states and nation-states inflict upon themselves through internal war—recurs in a host of the tragic and historical plays, but in marking the end of the Wars of the Roses *Richard III* emerges as something of a special case in this regard—not least perhaps for Shakespeare.[5] At the end of that play, after the murderous Richard of Gloucester, has been pronounced dead, Richmond, the newly crowned king of England, reflects back on the horror of civil discord and looks forward to a golden age of civil peace:

> England hath long been mad and scarred herself:
> The brother blindly shed the brother's blood,
> The father rashly slaughtered his own son,
> The son, compelled, been butcher to the sire.
> All this divided York and Lancaster,
> Deformed, in their dire division.
> O now let Richmond and Elizabeth,
> The true succeeders of each royal house,
> By God's fair ordinance conjoin together,
> And let their heirs, God, if they will be so,
> Enrich the time to come with smooth-faced peace,
> With smiling plenty, and fair, prosperous days!
> Abate the edge of traitors, gracious Lord,
> That would reduce these bloody days again
> And make poor England weep in streams of blood.
> Let them not live to taste this land's increase.
> That would with treason wound this fair land's peace.
> Now civil wounds are stopped, peace lives again.
> That she may long live here, God say 'Amen'.[6]

As is befitting of the moment of transition, the imagery in this passage centres on the grand themes of death and birth, the horror of slaughter and the promise of new life. In sympathy with the political thought of classical Greece, Shakespeare represents civil discord as the worst, because the most perverse, of all forms of violence: the violence one does to oneself. Echoing Thucydides' reflections upon the ill-fated city-state of Corcyra in *The History of the*

Peloponnesian War, he equates civil war with the murder of citizen-brother by citizen-brother and locates its most disturbing expression in the slaughter of son by father.[7] For him, as for the Greeks, civil war is the *ares emphulios*, the 'war within the family', that rips it open and tears it apart, such that the city or state itself becomes an object of mourning: if the Earl of Richmond grieves, he grieves for the lost family of England.[8] With victory over Richard, the madness of this dire division is brought to an end: the 'civil wounds are stopped' and 'peace lives again'. As essential as it is, however, the end of the killing is not the end of the affair—Richmond, who as Henry VII becomes the first of the Tudor kings, cannot settle for a mere *modus vivendi*. If England is not simply to be at peace but to thrive, if it is to enjoy 'smiling plenty' and 'fair prosperous days', it will still have to reckon with its past in some way. The madness that pitted brother against brother, the madness that has made enemies out of friends, must be treated so that the subjects of the realm will once again look upon one another as family.

The problem that confronts Richmond after the death of the 'bloody dog' (and his bloody regime) is the problem that confronts every new ruler in transitional settings: how does one create unity in a house once divided or heal the wounds of a nation that has been at war with itself? Part of the solution to this problem clearly lies in constitutional change. If the wrongs of the past are not to be carried forward, sovereign power must either be placed in a different pair of hands or exercised according to a different set of rules. There can be no new beginning unless a break is made with a broken law. However, as Shakespeare clearly understood, and as his history plays themselves bear witness, the memory of civil war, with its 'streams of blood', does not vanish simply because the crown changes heads. Since England does not cease to be England when sovereignty passes from the (morally/physically) deformed Richard to the (morally/physically) upstanding Richmond, one cannot speak of a radical rupture or a clean slate.[9] The name and the bloody deeds forever connected with the name are carried across the transition in memory, defeating hope of a completely fresh start. To call up a phrase from W. James Booth: 'there is no absolution through constitutional change'.[10] As important as it is, in other words, the transference of sovereign power that restores the rule of law never fully succeeds in 'stopping' the civil wounds (or, as we might say today, healing the nation). Some other operation, an operation of memory, is also necessary.

Shakespeare's historical plays are themselves, of course, an operation of memory that takes the audience, step by step, through the making of the Tudor monarchy out of the chaos of the Wars of the Roses.[11] While it is entirely possible to view them individually as dramatic tales about (or psychological studies of) the various kings and their courts, together they narrate the epic story of England's dismembering and remembering of itself. Whether Shakespeare saw himself as an educator of the civic forum or a doctor of collective memory, he clearly attached some importance to re-playing history in such a way that the audience could grasp the fateful effects of civil discord and the necessity of becoming united under a single sovereign.[12] As with Greek tragedy (to which we will have cause to turn our attention later), the history plays hold up a critical mirror to the state, recalling the 'shameful conquest' the all-conquering nation 'hath made of itself' as a way of bolstering unity and rebuilding hope.[13] 'In an age when religious zeal turned brother against brother', notes Greer, Shakespeare's epic 'sought to reunite the people and raise public morale'.[14] About the role of the bard in shaping the collective memory (and collective feelings) of the English much more could, of course, be said, not least of all in regard to what he excluded from the narrative.[15] Here, however, I want to leave the operation of memory Shakespeare performs for the English people in the Globe, and return to the operation of memory the newly crowned Richmond performs for the English people in *Richard III*.

Richmond's 'memory politics', the means he deploys to prevent the wounds of the past from opening up again in the present, take two different forms, the disparate character and effects of which are the primary focus of this book. The first part of the strategy is cultural in nature. Just before the passage cited earlier, Richmond asks Stanley 'what men of name are slain on either side?' and instructs him to 'inter their bodies as becomes their births'. Immediately after that, he tells him to 'proclaim a pardon to the soldiers fled'.[16] Thus the sacrifices of *all* the nobles will remembered, and the misdeeds of *all* the soldiers forgotten, as if the 'dire division' never existed. Burial honours the dead, pardon exculpates the living, with the recognition of their common humanity (in all its dignity and deficiency) working to dissolve the distinction between the winning and losing factions and prevent the past coming back. The second, and arguably more radical, part of the strategy is biological in nature. By taking Elizabeth as his bride and beginning a new family, Richmond does not simply bring the two houses under a single roof; he mixes up the blood of the two roses. Thanks to this union, a line of heirs will be created who, being neither York nor Lancaster but a mixture of both, cannot take sides or even be of a side. Composed of both houses at the level of their very being, they are the gift of new life that brings new life to England by overcoming the dire division at its root. When they eventually take the throne, York and Lancaster will not just be united, they will be indistinguishable, two lines of blood mixed together in the very body of the sovereign—political regeneration indeed.

Where do we stand in relation to these two strategies today? The first of these operations of memory is immediately recognizable and finds many contemporary analogies. By now we are well accustomed to the idea of collective memory as a cultural construct (one objectified in monuments, rituals, festivals, narratives, and the like), which, in bearing upon the self-image of the political community, is actively shaped by the sovereign authority.[17] As the site, in Jan Assman's formulation, where distinctions are made 'between what appertains to oneself and what is foreign',[18] collective memory is always of interest to government but never more so perhaps than in the aftermath of civil breakdown when doubt exists as to whether there is just one self. At that moment, the ability of the sovereign to mobilize remembrance in ways that make the warring factions forget their differences is more imperative than ever. (And how much smarter does Richmond show himself than Creon when he insists nobles on both sides of the civil conflict be given a burial that befits their birth?) The second of these operations, while also immediately recognizable, appears, at first blush, thoroughly antiquated. To the extent that the marriage between Richmond and Elizabeth remains within the domain of cultural forms, it is not very far removed from our current symbolic politics of reconciliation (which are political marriages in their own way). But the mobilization of biological processes, in this case reproduction, for the purpose of restoring unity and life to the body politic seems to have no contemporary analogy. Since we no longer invest the body of the sovereign with a mystical aura, it does not serve as a site where civil wounds are healed.

We ought not, however, be too quick to assume that we have overcome this division between the cultural and the natural, symbolic expressions of reconciliation and biological processes of regeneration. Since the pioneering work of Maurice Halbwachs, collective memory has tended to be conceived in exclusively cultural terms, as the selective appropriation of past events for the purposes of creating a flattering self-image. The idea that it has anything to do with biology is generally regarded as utter nonsense for the very good reason that there is no collective mind.[19] And yet, as we saw in Chapter 1, there is a species of memory that is held to be applicable to collectives and which is still understood in largely biological terms; I am referring here, of course, to trauma.[20] Although originally deployed by Freud to designate an overload of the individual psychic mechanism (the collapse of its 'digestive processes' in the face of excess stimuli), the concept of trauma is now commonly used in relation to entire populations exposed to violence, not least of all the violence to which they expose themselves in civil war.[21] Thus, to take just two examples, we read that 'France is traumatised by its past, still unable to finish digesting the "strange defeat of 1940" and the wounds wrought by French collaboration' and that the shameful conquest South Africa made of itself in Apartheid has left behind 'a traumatised and deeply divided people'.[22] So pervasive has the notion of collective trauma become, in fact, that a scholar as rigorous as John Torpey could feel excused of the need to supply evidence of it: 'the explosion of the use of the notion of trauma to describe collective historical events—and its ubiquitous antidote, "healing"—would scarcely seem to need documenting'.[23] How, one wonders, has the emergence of trauma as a collective phenomenon, a chronic affliction of the social body, impacted the ancient political art of reconciliation and regeneration? How might it have changed our sense of what is needed to heal the civil wound?

On this matter it is only too easy to be led astray by metaphors. Political philosophers have, for the longest time, drawn analogies between the body and the state, with the despoiling and deformation of the one serving as a correlate for the corruption and disorder of the other. In Machiavelli's Italy, as much as in Shakespeare's England, corporeal defect and deformity (wounds and scars, disfigurement and mutilation) are the privileged symbols of a body politic that lacks unity and vitality, which is 'torn' and 'lifeless'. Shakespeare uses the humpback Richard of Gloucester in precisely the same way in *Richard III* that Grass uses the humpback Oskar Matzerath in *The Tin Drum*; namely, as a potent symbol of a state gone wrong—for only when there is something morally amiss do things not grow right (at least in literature). It is, however, characteristic of all such analogies that they do as much to hold things apart as they do to bring them together. If the image of the deformed body makes the corruption of the state vivid, there is never a suggestion that the problem is actually of a biological nature or that it needs to be resolved by a therapeutic procedure. The conceptual couples 'war/reconciliation' and 'wound/healing' remain as distinct at the level of practice as they are interchangeable at the level of analogy. Not even the reconciliation by reproduction Richmond hopes to achieve by putting the seeds of the two roses into the one garden bed is really an instance of biopolitical intervention, for its 'healing' power is entirely derived from the old idea of royal lines where it is the symbolics of blood, not the biology of sex, that matters.[24] But can the same be said after the explosion of the use of trauma in relation to collective historical events? Is it possible that the creation of new life, the regeneration of the body politic, is now not simply a matter of metaphor but genuinely linked to biological processes—not reproduction, but mourning?

In his seminal discussion of the 'two cultures' of collective memory, Jeffrey Olick makes some offhand, but for our purposes heuristically useful, remarks about the ambiguous character of trauma as a form of collective memory and, implicitly, about the strategies needed to heal it. Evidently reluctant to fall back upon some mystical idea of a collective mind, he suggests that there are really only two senses in which trauma might be said to be 'collective': the first is as the aggregate of the 'multitudinous individual traumas' caused by social violence (he calls this 'collected traumas'); the second is as the single national trauma caused when eruptive historical events such as the civil war in America and the Shoah in Germany create an 'unassimilable breach in the national narrative' (he calls this 'collective trauma').[25] Olick's solution to the problem of trauma is, in other words, to turn it into two radically different kinds of phenomenon: when it is a matter of the individual, trauma is natural/biological; when it is a matter of the collective, it is cultural/symbolic. To talk about 'healing' in the context of the 'civil wound' is thus to still talk about two very different things. For the multitudinous individuals traumatized by their exposure to violence, 'healing' (understood as the restoration of psychic equilibrium) entails attempts, private and clinical, to facilitate reconciliation with loss by therapeutically stimulating the process of mourning. For the collectives traumatized by the breach in their national narrative, 'healing' (understood as the restoration of political unity) entails attempts, public and cultural, to facilitate reconciliation with others by symbolically assimilating the previously unassimilable episode back into the national story.

The 'solution' is elegant and, judging from the repetition of its assumptions in many other contexts, widely shared. Whether it succeeds in eliminating all slippage between the biological and the cultural is nevertheless doubtful. In principle, the problem of 'collected traumas' bears upon the health of the individual; that of 'collective trauma' bears upon the identity of the state. The more, however, one subjects it to scrutiny, the more the boundary between individual health and collective identity begins to blur. Since, as we saw in Chapter 1, unassimilable breaches in the national narrative are impossible to disassociate from the psychic disorders of individuals, and since attempts to assimilate those breaches back into the national story aid (or are assumed to aid) those individuals in their psychological recovery, the cultural and biological, the public and private, are by no means easily separable.[26] Taking a lead from Kim Wale, one might hazard that the two forms of trauma (and, with that, the two modes of healing) are, in fact, thoroughly 'knotted'.[27] Once collective trauma becomes the conceptual frame for thinking about civil disorder, there is no easy way to disentangle the 'healing as biological regeneration' that comes through the regulation of organic processes, like mourning and catharsis, and the 'healing as political reconciliation' that comes through the use of symbolic forms, like memorials and apologies.[28] In contemporary treatments of the 'civil wound', identity meets health and symbolic form meets biological process in a way that recalls the fusion of the two roses in the 'blood' of the offspring. The only difference is that now the healing sought by the operation of memory is the healing of the social body rather than the sovereign body.[29]

The aim of this chapter is to show just how profound an impact the discourse of collective trauma has had upon the memory practices and institutional forms now used by states to heal civil wounds. Despite being extolled by the Greeks, and celebrated long thereafter, as the best means of bringing the troubles of the past to a full stop, amnesty, or what is sometimes called 'institutionalized forgetting', is now discredited as a tool of healing and reconciliation.[30] If one can speak of a 'new doxa' in the field of political transition, it is most definitely against prohibition and in favour of process, against forgetting and in favour of mourning. Unlike the ancient Greeks, I argue, we moderns no longer believe that the civil wound can be 'stopped' through forgetting (or, as it is now instructively characterized, 'denial'). Since, or so we now assume, trauma always returns, inciting cyclical violence or inhibiting social development, the only viable option is to confront it 'face to face'. Thus the *lethe* (forgetting) of the Greeks has been displaced by the *a-lethia* (truth) of the moderns, and the old institution of erasure and restraint (amnesty) by new institutions of memory and mourning (public memorials, political apologies, truth commissions). The change is pronounced and, I will suggest, has far-reaching consequences. The more trauma has emerged as a matter of state, the more identity-shaping operations *of* memory have turned into, or become overlaid by, life-enhancing operations *upon* memory, giving the idea of 'healing' a rather different meaning from that assigned to it in the political tradition that begins with the Greeks and runs up to Machiavelli. In the new institutions of the new restorative justice, reconciliation and healing are not simply conjoined in analogy; they are integrated in practice.

I From Prohibition to Process

One of the things that can be safely inferred from the interest political thought and tragic drama has shown in civil wounds is that they are not easily 'stopped'. Since they do not just reflect disagreement but bring the identity of the state into question, they cannot simply be left to the fabled healing powers of time. Some operation of memory is required that addresses itself directly to the wound and which seeks to make the state and the individuals within it whole again. As we will go on to discover, the general tendency now is to figure this operation in terms of an act of re-narration or narrative reintegration. Just as the healing of individual trauma is meant to come through the integration of an experience which, in falling outside the range of normal life, has become 'split off' from consciousness, the healing of collective trauma is supposed to come through the assimilation of a previously unassimilable event into the national story.[31] Shakespeare, one might argue, anticipated the insights of the burgeoning field of ontological security studies by showing how the devastation of the Wars of the Roses could be overcome through its incorporation into a redemptive narrative in which the English family is finally restored to itself.[32] Something similar, as we shall see, also seems to have been achieved by the placement of the Memorial to the Murdered Jews of Europe in the centre of the newly unified German capital of Berlin. However, the more common response, historically speaking, has been the deletion of the unassimilable event from the story altogether. In the pardon Richmond offers the 'soldiers fled' lies the kernel of an institutionalized forgetting that has been used again and again as a means of erasing those offending chapters of dire division.

The archetype of all such attempts at institutionalized forgetting is doubtless the Athenian Amnesty of 403 BCE that was instituted by the victorious democrats in the wake of the brief, but thoroughly murderous, rule of the Thirty Tyrants (the oligarchs who took hold of the city, with support from Sparta, after the Athenians capitulated in the Peloponnesian War). Having come back from exile and recaptured the city, the 'returning democrats' led by Thrasybulus set about resolving the tensions between the oligarchic and the democratic factions of Athens upon a double mechanism of forgetting. As well as issuing a ban that carried a penalty of death (it is forbidden to recall the misfortunes/evils of the past), the democrats insisted that each citizen take an oath ('I shall not recall the misfortunes/evils of the past'). To the disincentive against 'recalling' created by the threat of punishment was thus added a freely undertaken and hence, it is generally assumed, powerfully binding pledge from each and every citizen.[33] If the classical sources can be trusted, that combination of instruments proved a runaway success: 'After we came together and exchanged the solemn pledges', claimed Isocrates, 'we have lived so uprightly and so like citizens of one country that it seemed as if *no misfortune had ever befallen us*.'[34] In no time at all, it would appear, enemies had been turned back into friends and the division of the city was all but forgotten.[35] A new life had begun.

Imposed upon one of the direst divisions in Athenian political life, the Amnesty of 403 BCE is best seen as a politics *in extremis*—a politics, in other words, that takes recourse to the institution of the exception because no ordinary response measures up to the magnitude of the crisis. In principle, amnesty simply means no indictments and no reparations; that is, no criminal or civil suits where one citizen recalls *against* another or, as Nicole Loraux puts it in her brilliant study of the divided city of ancient Greece, 'wields a memory like a weapon'.[36] And yet, in 403 BCE a connection is forged between amnesty (oblivion in law) and amnesia (oblivion in culture) that is less than complete identity, but more than simply etymological. Among the Greeks, suggests Loraux, amnesty was principally a subtractive operation whose essence lay in taking away any reminders of the fact that the city had once cut itself in two. Enjoined, by means of the ban and the oath, to forget the 'open wound of the dictatorship', the citizens of Athens effectively resumed politics as if the continuity of democratic rule had never been broken.[37] The years 405–403 BCE, marked by that traumatic *ares emphulios*—that 'war within the family'—was simply erased from memory, as if the city had never been lost (or, to be more precise, had never lost its sense of who or what it was). To institute the Amnesty was, in short, to 'purge [the] oligarchic interlude'.[38]

In line with the power all things Greek have exercised over the political imagination in the West, the Athenian Amnesty of 403 BCE has long been regarded, if not as the default method for dealing with civil wounds in politics, as least as a most instructive example. Precisely what it is instructive of may not, however, be as straightforward as first appears. For some, the Amnesty simply serves as the first iteration of a politics of institutionalized forgetting whose formula, while never precisely copied, will reverberate for centuries to come as a prototype of civil peacemaking.[39] For others, it offers an instance of political learning from which we might also learn, the Athenian democrats of 403 BCE having discovered the hard way that retributive measures (specifically those imposed in response to the oligarchic coup of 411 BCE) were inclined to be counterproductive.[40] In what follows, I will make a somewhat different claim about the Amnesty of 403 BCE by treating it as a reflection (and, in fact, an enactment) of a 'politics of life' that is now thoroughly discredited. Drawing primarily upon Loraux's work in *The Divided City*, I argue that what is most instructive about the Amnesty of 403 BCE is the assumption that inspires it: that mourning is an intrinsically destructive force, an enemy of all rational politics, which must be exiled from the city. The reason, I will go on to suggest, amnesty is no longer revered and a new set of exceptional institutions has taken its place is that this assumption has now been decisively rejected.

One way to unearth the 'politics of life' at work in the Amnesty of 403 BCE is to ask what it was exactly that prompted the Athenians to forbid the recalling of misfortunes: against what force was the force of the ban directed? At first blush, the answer to that question seems deceptively simple: the force against which the ban worked was none other than the force of memory. However, as Loraux is at pains to show, such a formulation does as much to mask as to reveal the problem addressed by the ban. In order to truly understand what it targets, she suggests, one is required to go back further still, seeking instruction from the Greece of the anthropologists (the masters of myths and the imaginary) as well as that of the historians (the masters of decisions and events). By rejoining, in this way, what disciplinary boundaries have driven apart, Loraux locates crucial points of contact between the so-called two cities of Athens—the temporal city of the historians and the atemporal city of the anthropologists—and, in so doing, succeeds in revealing the intrinsic value of forgetting as a prophylaxis against the intrusion of organic life and, more specifically, that most perilous *process* of mourning, into political life. One such point of contact, significant for our purposes, is between the Amnesty of 403 BCE and another Athenian ban on memory, dating from the beginning, rather than the end, of the century of democracy: a ban on the performance of Phrynichus' play, *The Capture of Miletus*.

At the time of its performance (around 492 BCE), the background to this play would have been well known to its audience. A colony of Athens dear to the mother city and leader of the Ionian revolt against the foreign tyrants, Miletus was besieged with such violence by the Persians in 494 BCE it was left 'empty of Milesians'. Unlike other cities that prospered under Persian rule even after the Ionian revolt, Miletus never recovered from the wounds inflicted by this war of dispossession/extermination, making it an especially sensitive topic for the Greeks in general and the Athenians in particular (the latter being inclined to see Miletus as part of *their* family). Whether Phrynichus, a slightly older contemporary of Aeschylus, misread the extent of that sensitivity or the conventions of the theatre, he clearly misjudged his audience in reminding them of *their* misfortunes. Although doubtless well intended, notes Loraux, the playwright had brought an action (*drâma*) into the theatre that was 'nothing but suffering for the Athenians'; a drama, in other words, about the wounding of the family and the city, and the city *as a* family. Upon the performance of this play, Herodotus records, 'the whole theatre broke into tears', Phrynichus was fined a thousand drachmae, and the order was given by the Assembly that no one should ever exhibit it again.[41] Here then, as if for the 'first time', notes Loraux, the Athenians were awakened 'to the dangers of recollection when the object of memory is a source of mourning for the civic self'.[42]

The idea that the 'civic self'—for the Greeks, the city; for us, the state—can be wounded underpins the entire discourse about collective trauma and the healing of nations. Few incidents, however, illuminate the nature (or the stakes) of the problem more clearly than this tale of a tale. When the Persians capture Miletus, they burn its sanctuaries and empty it of people, rupturing the sacred bond between people and place. The problem is thus not just that many of the Milesians lose their lives, but that all of the Milesians lose their city: the thing that has, until then, bound them together, physically and affectively, and allowed them to identify as a collective. This break in the continuity of identity, this loss of wholeness, constitutes a social trauma in which every citizen, regardless of what happened to them personally, partakes because they take part in (and are themselves a part of) the city: hence their tearful (over-)reaction to its return in the form of a representation. Similarly, what is most disturbing about the civil war of 405–403 BCE in Athens is the break it introduces in identity. Although, in this case, the citizens were not fully displaced from their homeland (with the friends of the tyrants and the other so-called quiet ones having remained behind), the civil war still split the Athenian family and dismembered the body politic, such that the city ceased to be whole. For Loraux, the grief associated with this loss of continuity in civic identity, this strangely *public* grief which marks a permissive crossing of *oikos* and *polis*, feminine and masculine, *zoë* and *bios*, represents a special kind of danger for the Greeks—a danger so great, in fact, that it will leave a permanent mark on the genre of tragedy. Through the ban placed on *The Capture of Miletus*, she writes, the 'Athenian people make it known that they will not tolerate the staging of anything that affects them painfully'. 'The tragedians', she continues, 'learn the lesson and find ways of avoiding too-current events, unless those events are a source of mourning for others.'[43]

A lesson learnt, to be sure: henceforth tragedy will make its misfortunes fall upon other people in other times, sparing the Athenians the need to mourn the loss of their own city.[44] This is not to say, however, that interest in the civil wound abates in the Greek imagination—if anything, in fact, it seems to intensify.[45] In the long history of ancient Greece stretching from the archaic to the classical, aesthetic forms, as is well known, change. Yet, in their manner of staging misfortunes, the tragedians forged an alliance with Homer, never ceasing to remind the Athenians of just how powerful a force (and just how destructive to the political world of the city) grief could be.[46] In this, according to Loraux, we touch on something very profound—at least for the Greeks. From epic to tragedy, from Achilles to Electra, the same stalking horse appears, confirming, if only by its cultural durability, the fearful place it occupied in the Greek imaginary. This, in the words of the classicist (whose words are always Greek), is the 'extreme grief' or, better still, the 'grief-wrath' (*alastein*) that cannot be forgotten, that does not actually *want* to be forgotten, and which, as a result, is frequently equated with non-oblivion itself.[47] As Loraux notes, the Greek root *alast-* gives many clues as to the enduring, unassuageable nature of this affect: *alesta* refers to deeds that will forever be remembered; *alastōr* is 'the name of the criminal insofar as he has committed unforgettable acts'; *alaston* is 'a ghostly presence that occupies the subject and does not leave'.[48] However, there is one conjunction that appears especially fitting in the current context: *álaston pénthos*—'mourning that refuses to accomplish itself'.[49]

If the work of the poets serves as a cultural radar, the Greeks clearly saw this mourning that refuses to accomplish itself as a serious threat not just to the integrity of the self but to the integrity of the city. In epic, *álaston pénthos* is associated with the kind of irreparable loss—a disappearance or a death—which, being beyond restitution, 'makes the past into an eternal present'.[50] *Álaston pénthos* is the concept that covers the empty time of Penelope's weaving as she grieves for her disappeared (Odysseus) and Menelaus' insomnia as he grieves for his (Helen)—the time when action is confounded and nothing moves forward. In tragedy, not surprisingly, it assumes an even more prominent place, with Electra emerging as the 'perfect incarnation' of the petrified Niobe who 'weeps eternally ... with tears unceasing'.[51] The nub of the problem, in all these cases, is the tendency mourning has to colonize the interiority of subjects and crowd out their capacity for action. As Loraux notes, the ancients were firmly of the view that the 'worst enemy of politics' was the 'anger as mourning [that] causes the ills it assiduously cultivates to "grow"'.[52] If Electra cannot get respite from her sorrows, it is because her sorrows and her have become one and the same thing. Her entire being, as Simon Critchley puts it, is but 'a vast wound of grief'.[53] Once this colonization of the interior happens, political subjectivity—understood here, in Arendtian terms, as the capacity to engage with plural others in speech and action—collapses. The only thing about which those consumed by grief can 'speak' is their own trauma and the only 'action' they can take (which, as Arendt made clear, is no action at all) is vengeance against the one they hold responsible for it.[54]

Akin, as it were, to an uncontainable force, more powerful even than time, this grief-wrath is at its most dangerous when it touches on the question of the city (and in Greek tragedy, of course, it always does).[55] In Sophocles' version of the play, Electra is chastised by the Chorus for being so obsessive in her mourning for her murdered father that she neglects her own life: 'yours is a grief beyond the common measure, a grief that knows no ending, consuming your own life, and all in vain'.[56] Ragged in appearance, neglectful of hygiene, she cleaves so closely to the dead that her relation to the living (and indeed to life itself) remains tenuous at best—a bit like Antigone in this regard, she is, as William Junker puts it, 'dead to life *in* life'.[57] Electra's excessive grief does not, however, simply jeopardize her own life, it jeopardizes the life of the city. The problem with Electra is not simply that she refuses to engage in dialogue and open herself up to the democratic art of persuasion, or that her desire to avenge her father overrides any prudent concern with the political order (though those clearly are significant problems); it is rather, or also, that her mourning 'beyond the common measure' leaves her powerless to act and, as the tutor puts it, 'make an end'.[58] So incapable is she of parting from her grief and entering the artifice of politics, even her desire for revenge goes unfulfilled. Upon receiving news of Orestes' death, Electra, in desperation, rashly determines to take matters into her own hands and kill Clytemnestra and Aegisthus. But had the story not been a ruse and Orestes had truly died, one suspects nothing would ever have happened—Electra and the city would have remained immobilized, locked in an interminable, life-sapping stasis without a future.[59]

Phrynichus' critical mistake, then, was to stir up this person-destroying, city-destroying grief-wrath by making a public representation of an *Athenian* civic trauma. As the citizens look on, a bitterness, at once angry and mournful, returns over a lost homeland and a broken identity. Someone needs to pay. And yet, *The Capture of Miletus* still has one saving grace: it *unites* the citizens in grief. Memories of the reign of the Thirty do no such thing. In this instance, the Athenians have no one to blame for the loss of life and city except each other. Where else can their grief-wrath be directed except back home? The problem that effectively confronted the Greeks in 403 BCE was thus how to contain the toxic fallout of a war within the family. How is one to protect the city in situations where the factional bond has proved more powerful than the familial bond and it is not just a father or a son who has been murdered by an enemy but rather the father and the son who have become enemies to each other?[60] As Loraux would have it, the Greeks saw only one answer to the threat of grief-wrath in such situations. Against this most formidable of all forms of memory, this memory that would rather tear the city to the ground than let its angry grieving go, nothing works save for its direct opposite: the natural oblivion that comes in the form of a drug or the artificial oblivion that comes in the form of a decree.

Predictably, the contact between the two cities of Athens—that of myth and that of history—is broken here. Although allied in their sense of grief as an eternal, unassuageable force, the poets and the politicians part company when it comes to the matter of a cure. In the tales of the poets, as is perhaps to be expected, it is often the *phármakon* that works the magic, relieving the heroes of the most extraordinary ills.[61] Thus Homer will speak of a drug that inures the drinker against grief for a day: no tears will he shed, 'not if his mother died and his father died, not if men murdered a brother or a beloved son in his presence with the bronze, and he with his own eyes saw it'.[62] However, as Loraux makes clear, the Greeks were hardly insensitive to the fact that the 'sweet oblivion' that 'comes from elsewhere', whether as a gift of the Muses or the gift of the grape, only ever brings temporary relief from 'grief-wrath'. For them, the charm that briefly dispels mourning cannot compare to a ban in which the citizen not only submits himself to the authority of the city but 'also asserts that he will maintain control over himself as a subject'.[63] Since it comes from the inside, as a pure exercise of the will, emotional self-discipline (*sophronein*) proves immeasurably more powerful than any *phármakon* in keeping the past at bay: 'I *will not* recall the misfortunes', says the disciplined Athenian citizen, holding himself to a promise that lasts not just for one day but forever.

In the ban of 403 BCE, as in the ban of 492 BCE, then, excess is pitted against excess, oblivion against mourning, in an attempt to erase the trauma of internal war and the loss of continuity in the civic identity. However, as should now be clear, these remarkable events, favourites of the historians, are but instances of a politics of life in which human and animal, civic life and biological life, are set in opposition to each other.[64] If Loraux's reading of the Greeks is faithful, the life of the city, the life exclusive to men, is a rational life that is not just assumed to be superior to organic life but premised on keeping it at bay. For the man to be 'political' (*politikos*), it is not enough, as one learns from reading Arendt, that he be able to move freely outside the space of necessity (*oikos*).[65] He must also be able to control what is needful, what imposes itself with the force of nature, *in himself*; namely, that terrible, all-consuming grief-wrath sparked by personal and civic loss.[66] In this sense, the exclusion of mourning and the exclusion of women in Greek politics are all of a piece—if there is something to which the public must not be exposed, it is not so much the woman in mourning as the mourning *in* woman and, of course, since he too has an organic, instinctual life, the mourning in man.[67] Amnesty is one of the vehicles by which that mourning within is held at arm's length from the public domain. In amnesty, as Loraux notes, one does not simply agree to forget the bad deeds of others, one agrees to 'forget one's own anger, so that the bond of life in the city may be renewed'.[68]

Precisely how important this emotional self-discipline, this cauterization of loss and its associated resentments, was to the life of the city is revealed in another point of contact between the mythological and the historical that Loraux unearths: a text by Plutarch that refers to a factional dispute among the gods and its reception among men. In this mythical tale about the beginnings of Athens, Plutarch praises Poseidon for being 'more political' than Thrasybulus (the leader of the returning democrats in 403 BCE) for showing no resentment after Athena defeats him in their battle for possession of the city. The implication of the additive 'more' in this context is quite straightforward: if Thrasybulus was 'political' for renouncing his resentment (towards the Thirty) in victory, how much 'more political' was Poseidon for renouncing his resentment (towards Athena) in defeat. To be 'political' in this context is to *not* mourn one's losses—even when, *especially when*, one has not enjoyed the compensation of victory. One measure of the significance the Athenians attached to this act of 'divine clemency', according to Loraux, is found in the fact that they marked it twice over: first 'by subtracting the anniversary of the conflict, a grievous memory for the god, from the calendar' and, second, 'by raising an altar to Lethe, Oblivion, in the Erechtheion' (an ancient Greek temple on the north side of the Acropolis dedicated to Athena and Poseidon). For Loraux, the symbolism of placing oblivion on the Acropolis, 'the very place', as she puts it, 'the Athenians like to call the "City"', is unmistakeable: if there is to be *a* city, a city at one with itself, factional disputes must be forgotten. Indeed, since the story of Poseidon and Athena shows that it is conflict, not harmony, which is primary in politics, forgetting does not just restore a unity once broken, it is the condition of possibility of that unity. Oblivion, as Loraux economically puts it, is the very 'basis of life in the city'.[69]

With this we begin to see the full importance of the institution of amnesty to the life of the city (and with that, of course, to the life *in* the city that relies upon its invigorating institutions and protective shield). Always already wounded, as it were, the city emerges as the most precarious 'life' of all because it is a life perpetually put at risk by what is, in fact, congenital to it: divisional strife. From the origin story of Poseidon and Athena the following sequence can be derived: with politics comes factions (the division of the city into 'parties', often the rich and the poor, whose original opposition to each other is uncomfortably returned to the light every time debate seeking consensus is forced back upon the procedure of the vote);[70] with these factions comes a contest (*agon*) for control of the city; with that contest comes the risk of internal war; with internal war comes the loss of the city; and with the loss of the city comes that mourning for the civic self that runs endlessly into the future and plants the seeds of an eternal (or, at least, an eternally recurring) war. The challenge of politics, if one can speak in such terms, is thus to enable constructive factional dispute while preventing destructive internal war.[71] If the semantic range of the concept of *stasis* tells us anything, however, it is that the Greeks had great difficulty, imaginatively and practically, in keeping those two things apart.[72] At once a signifier of taking a position, of aligning oneself with a faction *and* of intestinal disorder, civil war, the concept of stasis speaks of a city that is perpetually at risk of losing itself in the contest of the factions.[73] Lack of unity, the absence of any primordial wholeness or identity in the city, emerges here as something like the original trauma of politics—a trauma which, on Loraux's reading, endlessly repeats: 'in the beginning was the conflict; then came the *polis* … And amnesty would then endlessly reinstitute the city against recent misfortunes'.[74]

Ultimately, for Loraux, there is no more profound expression of the unspeakable, unassimilable nature of this trauma for the Greeks than their attempt to displace civil war from the activity of politics and the space of the city altogether. Among them, she notes, stasis was given two contradictory aetiologies. On the first account, the one, according to her, for which they displayed a distinct preference, stasis comes from the outside. According to this version, civil war is akin to a natural catastrophe that 'rains down' on human societies like 'a plague, an epidemic, a tempest'—a catastrophe, in other words, that arrives from elsewhere and which the fighting city, fighting against itself, but also for itself, has to force back beyond the gates in order to survive. There is, however, another account, 'rarely expressed', according to Loraux, because of the 'dreadful feeling' to which it gives rise, that '*stasis* is born from within the city'.[75] According to this version, stasis 'sleeps within the polis and is always ready to stir' because the *polis* is, by its very nature, rent by factions that seek victory over each other.[76] For Loraux, it is precisely because it gets too close to the truth that this image of the conflict-ridden *polis* must be held under erasure. If forgetting is the *sine qua non* of politics, it is because it is the only mechanism capable of shielding the city from the unspeakable truth of its congenital divisiveness; from the fact, in other words, that it is never really one city at all.[77]

What, then, are we to make of this 'politics of life' that forestalls mourning for the civic self by reburying the ugly truth of disunity and division each time it is exhumed by the factions? That the Greeks should seek to secure political life through the exclusion of grief, a classically female trait, or, as they would have it, failing, should perhaps come as no surprise.[78] Built upon the strict spatial separation of *oikos* and *polis*, the necessities of life and the freedom of action, Greek politics was hardly inclined to let speaking (that most rational art of man) be subverted by crying (that most animal expression of woman).[79] A great deal is revealed about the gendered nature of the Greek imaginary when Sophocles assimilates Electra to the 'sorrowing nightingale' that 'mourns her young unceasingly'.[80] Close to nature, if not, in fact, part of it, woman is least able to control what the experience of loss stirs within.

Indeed, were it not for Achilles' endless weeping and wailing, according to Loraux, that 'worst enemy of politics' would very clearly announce itself as a 'female model of memory'—one which the city does its best to 'confine within the anti- (or ante-) political sphere'.[81] Achilles, at least at first glance, confounds the distinction by drawing grief-wrath into the very centre of the warrior circle. Yet even Achilles disappears as an exception if we accept, as Loraux seems tempted to, that his famous *mênis*, the driving force behind what Henry Staten calls Homer's 'great poem of mourning',[82] is in fact the displaced grief-wrath of his mother, Thetis, over the predestined loss of her demi-god son.[83] Whatever the case with epic, it is very clear that by the time we get to tragedy it is invariably the mothers, the daughters, and, since one can hardly leave out Antigone, the sisters who are consumed by a mourning that slides so readily between grief and wrath that the distinction between the two concepts loses all meaning.[84]

As ever with the Greeks, however, one must be careful not to jump to the wrong conclusions. If the Amnesty of 403 BCE tells us anything, it is that this gendered view of mourning ought to be read politically, not ontologically. Like the misfortunes the tragedians displaced onto other cities, grief-wrath is too consistently excluded from the political sphere of the *andres* not to belong to it in some essential, if unavowable, way. If anything, in fact, the insistence with which mourning is associated with the female speaks of just how much the citizen-brothers feared it in themselves.[85] Are we to assume that the ban the Athenians imposed upon *The Capture of Miletus* had nothing to do with the way it unmanned them? Was this not part of what made this play (and, for Plato, *all* plays) so disturbing? Antigone's laments are only to be expected, but what is a man to do when Creon starts wailing? Plato's notorious objection to representations—whether in epic or tragedy—of 'famous men mourning' rests on his belief that they will disturb the moral equilibrium of the guardians and lead them to assume that chanting laments and dirges even for trivial things is appropriate. Better, he says, to let women do that, provided, he adds, they are not 'admirable women' (or, worse still, perhaps, men dressed as them).[86] In strange alignment with the amnesic tendencies of the democratic state he maligned, Plato codes masculinity in terms of emotional discipline precisely so that men will know to rein in their grief and not recall their misfortunes. For him, as Simon Critchley has recently noted, the whole trouble with tragedy is that 'its endless displays of female grief, wailing, and lamentation ... turns the men who watch it into women'.[87]

For Plato, of course, the ban on famous men mourning is all about protecting the eternal 'republic', the ideal state that is no longer susceptible to the problems of states, from the risk of femininity. But it is possible, as

Holst-Warhaft has argued, that the risk of men turning into women was of particular concern to democratic Athens. In *Dangerous Voices*, she argues that the 'natural' connection drawn between mourning and women was actually an invention of classical Greece which arose from the new demands placed upon the citizen-soldier as a member of a collective.[88] Intent on curtailing the power of the aristocratic families and the ethos of heroic individuality, democratic Athens outlawed excessive funeral rites (often an avenue for lavish displays of wealth and power); insisted that various parts of the mourning process be conducted either indoors or in darkness; and, through the new institution of the funeral oration (made forever famous by Pericles), appropriated public mourning for the glory of the state. Once integral to all stages of ritualized lamentation, women suddenly found themselves cast as the very embodiment of the wrong type of mourning; namely, the endless, unrestrained, vengeful one that either holds the city in a state of suspension or turns it against itself. And yet, if one goes back to the *Iliad*, notes Holst-Warhaft, 'it is the men, rather than the women, who must be enjoined to stop weeping lest they become morbid or dangerous'.[89] Before Electra turned it into a women's problem, it was the greatest hero of all, the matchless Achilles, who was unable to finish his mourning and 'make an end'.

In a way, however, all of this simply reinforces the relation between mourning and danger, forgetting and security. Whether typically female or not, typically aristocratic or not, the mourning that refuses to accomplish itself remains an enemy of politics; a force which one should fear, even more, it seems, than the Persians, because it has no respect for the city. Electra and Antigone may well be mad for grief as their sisters suggest, but it is precisely the madness of their grief, the madness that *is* grief, that makes them a danger to the democratic *polis*. Consumed by mourning, they are unable to bend or yield, to think or act, as the public realm of persuasion and prudence demands. If citizens allow themselves to become like them, if they too succumb to a mourning that refuses to accomplish itself, the city is lost. The key fruit, then, at least for our purposes, of Loraux's investigation into the Greek imaginary is that the animal life of man—a life classical Greece will declare to be acutely manifest in the more or less unchosen, more or less uncontainable, mourning of woman—cannot be allowed to enter the public domain. As soon as this kind of grief escapes the confines of the *oikos* and flows into the *polis*, it makes for disaster. One Achilles (the hero turned mourner) or one Antigone (the mourner turned hero) is enough to disrupt the temporal order of politics and bring the city undone. In the face of such excess grief, politics becomes either inoperable, suspended in a moment of melancholic irresolution, or perverted, destroyed by a violence that turns the city against itself in an endless cycle of revenge.[90]

For the sake of the city, then, mourning—that species of memory that never lets go and which keeps the wound forever green—must be subject to a ban. To be forbidden to recall the misfortunes is to be forbidden to dwell on the losses one suffers when that never-ending factional fight for possession of the city degenerates into internal war and exhumes the congenital divisiveness of the city. This, to be sure, appears very much like biopolitics. For as soon as it is made the target of a ban, the biological process ceases to be wholly external to the political process. Instead, to use Agamben's formulation, it is included in it by way of its exclusion from it. Mourning and forgetting, *oikos* and *polis*, would, on this reading of things, be but the expressions of a biopolitical fracture between the female (denizen) and male (citizen) that has to be forcibly re-imposed like a *cordon sanitaire* every time the city, having torn itself apart, needs to begin anew. In amnesty, the free men make a solemn promise not to be needful women and give in to an endless mourning. And yet, if the ban on recalling misfortunes deserves to be counted as a biopolitics, it is a biopolitics marked by a certain resignation in the face of the unruly power of organic life. Assuming Loraux is correct, the reason mourning must be confined to the anti-political sphere is because nothing can really be done with it. As a force of nature against which even time is powerless, it is simply not amenable to political manipulation. The only option one has in relation to it, and it is by no means a fool-proof one, is displacement. The women in mourning (played, of course, by men) who make their covert return to the public space of appearances in tragedy can thus be regarded as the bearers of a force or energy the democratic *polis* had no means to control and did not think it could withstand. In drama—and especially in that drama called *Antigone*—displacement (to the private realm) is revealed as the mechanism by which mourning is made safe and women made dangerous.[91]

Sophocles' *Antigone* gives us one intimation that this attempt to protect civic life through the exclusion of organic life was not without its sceptics (or its costs). The fact that Creon's ban on the burial of Polynices (his 'emergency decree' against lamentation and mourning) misfired so badly is suggestive of the limits of emotional discipline and the strategy of displacement.[92] Perhaps under normal conditions, when the contest of the factions did not lead to any deaths or disappearances, the cauterization of grief-wrath that was definitive of the citizen under oath sufficed. But could the force of mourning really be held back after the devastation of that traumatic war within the family? Staged in the aftermath of yet another battle over the city by warring factions (here represented by the twin brothers Eteocles and Polynices),

Antigone points, among other things, to the permeability of the boundary between *oikos* and *polis* and the potential for excess grief to become politicized or, rather, politicized *in another way*.[93] Like Polynices' body, Creon wants it out of the city; Antigone wants it in.[94] Creon's breakdown marks Antigone's victory—though it is clearly a pyrrhic one. Was the historical ban in Athens likely to be any more redoubtable than the mythical one in Thebes? Loraux plainly has her doubts. 'One could wager', she writes of the Amnesty of 403, 'that no operation of memory was successful in closing the wound, so deep was the gash made in the city by the conflict.'[95] And the nearer she gets to her conclusion, the more adamant her position becomes: '"Please forget": this utterance is about as viable as the "please ignore" implicit in the subtraction of a contentious date from the Athenian calendar, or the "please keep your eyes closed" in Freud's famous dream.'[96] Amnesty, yes, but total amnesia? Surely not. That which is repressed always returns.

Exactly where the Greeks stop and the classicist begins is not, however, entirely evident here. In her conclusion to *The Divided City*, Loraux makes it clear that she believes collectivities, like individuals, *should* know the 'slow work of mourning—which is the incorporation of a painful or conflictual past, not a rejection or distancing of it'.[97] Had she felt the need to elicit support for this proposition from among the Greeks, she could no doubt have found it in the exceptional institution of the Great Dionysia and the tragic plays it staged for Greek citizens (a point I come back to in Chapter 6). Yet it is hard to suppress the suspicion that here, if only briefly, Loraux, the studious classicist, abandons the restraint she has shown throughout her study of the divided city of ancient Greece to allow a very modern, post-Freudian thought to slip into an altogether different world. 'Whoever speaks of mourning', she writes, 'does not speak of forgetting.'[98] No doubt. But is it not precisely in our insistence on speaking of mourning rather than forgetting that we depart from the ancient Greeks? Is it not here, in our confidence in stimulating and directing (as opposed to simply blocking or displacing) the mourning process through public forms of truth telling that our radically different sense of where politics stands in relation to life is revealed?[99]

Although it involves a jump of many centuries, it does not seem inappropriate to return here to the German example I alluded to at the beginning of this section. In the centre of Berlin, the city which, since the advent of national unification in 1871, the Germans have regarded as their true capital and seat of sovereignty, now stands the imposing Memorial to the Murdered Jews of Europe. Situated on the site of the Berlin Wall (the so-called death strip that once divided the city and the state in two), but erected in memory of a much deeper internal cut, the memorial appears to function in much the same way as the Erechtheion did on the ancient Acropolis; namely, as a site where unity is recovered from division.[100] A temple in the modern style, the Memorial to the Murdered Jews has all the hallmarks of the sacred, only in this case one would have to speak of an altar raised to mourning, not oblivion. Composed of nearly 3,000 concrete slabs (*stelae*) that resemble nothing so much as headstones in an enormous graveyard, the Memorial creates a series of long, straight alleyways that invite citizens to walk (and work) their way through. Under the ground, not far from the site of Hitler's bunker, is an information centre that holds the names of nearly 3 million Jewish Holocaust victims like an enormous repository of bones. The symbolism of all this, once again, seems unmistakeable: in the centre of the city torn asunder by a war both external and internal, in the place the Germans are once again pleased to locate the state, stands a temple of pathways, every one of which passes through the truth of genocide. Have we arrived at the point where we could say it is now mourning, not forgetting, that serves as the basis of life in the state?

Perhaps. Judging from the ever-multiplying scenes of sovereign repentance and societal grieving that have appeared around the world, it is now the male, rather than the female, 'model of memory' that is the worst enemy of politics. Reflected in all the truth commissions and political apologies, the memorial projects and calendric markings is the rise of mourning and coming to terms as a political imperative. What the Greeks buried, we exhume; what they deleted from the calendar, we mark upon it in bold type. For the sake of political life, the violence unleashed against the brother is now placed at the very heart of the state so that it can be remembered and worked through.[101] Indeed, in a striking reversal—one formally announced by the Mitscherlichs—the inability to *start* mourning has, in fact, come to occupy the same place among the moderns as the inability to *stop* mourning once did among the ancients; namely, the place of antinomy and violence, the place where civic selfhood breaks down and the state begins to tear at itself. National examples of this phenomenon could be called up *ad infinitum*. But perhaps the most striking indication of how pervasive this connection between mourning and wholeness has become is provided by the fact that the United Nations General Assembly, the site where the world is simultaneously marked in its unity and division, set aside 27 January (the anniversary of the liberation of Auschwitz-Birkenau) as International Holocaust Memorial Day. Universal grieving over the crime humanity committed against itself is now the condition upon which the world community emerges in its singularity as a political subject; as something greater, that is, than the sum of its national parts.

It would, of course, be wrong (as we shall see in section II) to assume that modern states have completely given up on the institution of amnesty or that 'pacts of forgetting' are entirely without supporters in contemporary political debates. And yet, the shift from the forgetting to mourning is unmistakeable both in theory and in practice. Where the ancient Greeks did everything to bury the memory of division, we moderns draw attention to it as if the exposure of the civil wound was the only means of healing it once and for all. In section II, I seek to simultaneously reveal and explain this turn from forgetting to mourning, prohibition to process. Against the tendency, common to a great deal of commentary, to attribute the disregard in which forgetting is now held to its ethical deficiencies, I argue that the more telling factor, politically speaking, has been its functional deficiencies. The more, I will suggest, that civil wounds have been conceived as social trauma, the more forgetting has come to be associated with a policy of denial which, in foreclosing on psychological recovery, works against the biopolitical interest of the state in optimizing the health and vitality of the population. Increasingly, in short, the regeneration of political life is seen to hinge on a work *of* memory, rather than a ban *on* memory, giving licence to a quite different politics of life—a politics in which the biological processes of mourning (and its cathartic effect) become the target of political regulation.[102]

II Trauma, Latency, and the Work of Mourning

Modern states, needless to say, have not entirely given up on placing bans on memory in the hope of putting an end to intestinal disorder. Although keen to resist what she calls the 'demon of analogy', Loraux herself is by no means deaf to the parallels between the 'family war' that tore ancient Athens apart in 405 BCE and the so-called *guerre franco-française* that plagued her native France in the wake of World War Two—parallels which, in her words, more than once 'whispered to me'.[103] As it had done in the wake of the Revolution (with Louis XVIII declaring a new era of 'union and forgetting' upon ascending the throne),[104] post-war France did its best to stop the 'collabos' and the 'resistants' wielding memory as a weapon in the courts through the amnesty laws (*oubli juridique*) of 1947, 1951, and 1953.[105] These legal amnesties were, however, but a component of a broader cultural amnesia, similar to that of the ancient Greeks, whose single purpose was to cover the 'open wound' of Vichy.[106] In his path-breaking work *The Vichy Syndrome*, Henri Rousso argues quite persuasively that the twelve-year ban imposed on Marcel Ophul's documentary film *The Sorrow and the Pity*—an exposé of

French collaboration with the Nazis (including its anti-Semitic programme) during the Vichy period—was but an instance of a wider, if generally unspoken, policy of censoring the past in the name of the state. Intent on erasing the memory of internal division, post-war France re-founded itself on the myth of universal resistance and did everything in its power to purge the 'Vichy interlude'.[107]

Although it is not surprising Loraux should find an analogy for the Amnesty of 403 BCE so close to home, frequent references to the 'Spanish model' in the literature suggest that the paradigmatic case of a memory ban in the post-war period is not the French erasure of Vichy but the *pacto del olvido* (pact of forgetting) informally instituted in Spain after the death of Franco in 1975.[108] Applied to both the period of the Republican uprising (1936-9) and the vicious thirty-six-year dictatorship that followed (1939-75), the *pacto del olvido* can once again be understood as a conscious strategy to erase a dire division and forestall mourning for the civic self. Seen from an institutional perspective, the centrepiece of this 'pact' was the two-way Amnesty Law of 1977 that simultaneously secured the release of all political prisoners arrested during the dictatorship and prevented the prosecution of Francoist repressors. Truly an amnesty, as one moderate politician put it, 'from everybody to everybody'.[109] And yet, as Paloma Aguilar argues in her magisterial work *Memory and Amnesia*, there is more than enough evidence to suggest that this largely unspoken pact of forgetting fell quietly upon the culture as a whole, once again blurring the distinction between amnesty and amnesia.[110] Aversion to the return of civil war, she noted, led to a kind of tacit self-censorship in relation to anything that threatened to reopen old wounds. 'The absence of measures of political justice and even of public debate about such measures cannot be explained', she noted, 'without taking into account social and political perceptions strongly affected by the traumatic memory of a fratricidal conflict, and an obsessive desire to avoid its repetition.'[111]

Such pacts of forgetting, it is important to note, are not without friends in contemporary debates over the politics of memory. While Timothy Garton Ash, for one, ultimately comes down in favour of truth telling (or, as he puts it, 'history lessons') in his reflections on coming to terms in the eastern European states after communism, he could not help but note that 'the ancient case for forgetting is much stronger than it is quite comfortable for historians to recall'.[112] Others have gone even further in acknowledging the wisdom of the ancients. In his recent polemics *Against Remembrance* and *In Praise of Forgetting* (the latter an expanded version of the former), David Rieff casts doubt on the political merits of remembering when it comes to the dire divisions of the past. As a witness to the civil wars that memory can spark and, on his reckoning, continually renew, Rieff inclines to the Greek (or, as is now often said, Spanish) view that commanded forgetting, whatever its ethical deficiencies, delivers vital benefits to the political community.[113] 'What if', he asks (clearly already more than half-convinced of the answer), 'instead of being the herald of meaninglessness, it is a decent measure of communal forgetting that is the *sine qua non* of a peaceful and decent society?'[114] To this provocation we might also add Pascal Bruckner's recent impassioned defence of forgetting as a prophylaxis against the so-called tyranny of guilt that has us forever mourning our losses and renewing our hatreds. 'There comes a time', he notes,

> when we have to let the dead bury the dead, taking with them their dissensions and their woes. Focusing on what separates us rather than on what unites us is always dangerous. Oblivion is what makes room for the living, for newcomers who want to wipe away the obligations of the past and not bear the burden of ancient resentments. It is a power of beginning again for future generations.[115]

Exactly when that time comes and how the dead are supposed to bury themselves are, to be sure, matters of some equivocation, if not matters of some evasion. Rieff and Bruckner both agree that the 'biological duration' must be respected. So long as there are victims of the crimes still living among us, we are obliged to honour their suffering as best we can. However, both are firmly of the view that there is a point at which remembrance becomes 'hostile to life' in the double sense of both keeping the wounds of the past perpetually open and of closing us off from the fecundity of the future. 'The reality, however, unpalatable', notes Rieff,

> is that collective remembrance has not always been a salutary goad to peace and reconciliation, nor has the failure to remember ... an injustice that a particular group has suffered been toxic to their societies. On the contrary, at numerous times and in numerous places, remembrance has provided the toxic adhesive that was needed to cement old grudges and conflicting martyrologies, as it did in Northern Ireland and in the Balkans for generations, if not for centuries.[116]

Although Rieff's immediate inspiration for this praise of forgetting is Nietzsche's second untimely meditation, his sense of memory as a 'toxic adhesive', binding the factions ever more tightly in their opposition to each other, carries clear echoes of the ancient Greeks. Like them, he remains supremely wary of the power of memory as 'resentment' or 'grudges' to run on endlessly—'for generations, if not for centuries'. And while he does not deny that memory is, or at least *can* be, an ally of justice, he remains deeply sceptical of the view that 'justice is trumps'. In the end, he suggests, peace is the supreme value and peace, as the Greeks knew only too well, is built upon the power of institutionalized forgetting.[117]

The pragmatic merit of this praise of forgetting is in many ways no less compelling now than it was among the Greeks. Yet the argument that it invariably runs up against (and in relation to which it is now always required to take its measure) is precisely the one Electra offered for her intransigence: to forget is to betray the memory of the dead and become complicit in injustice. Powerful even among the Greeks, that argument has taken on such profound significance in the wake of the Shoah as to have become virtually unassailable. Since the Nazi attempt to annihilate an entire people and then erase all traces of the crime, institutionalized forgetting has almost invariably been understood not just as an obstacle to the pursuit of justice but as an extension of the original offence.[118] Where forgetting is not violently denounced on the grounds that it cheats victims out of 'the one thing', as Theodore Adorno put it, 'that our powerlessness can grant them', it is deemed more or less of a piece with the original crime itself.[119] To fail to remember, claimed Paul Ricoeur, is to 'kill the victims twice'—the implication being that advocates of forgetting were guilty not just of being accessories to the original crime (which their forgetfulness completes) but of symbolically repeating it.[120] Through the act of forgetting, the body of the victim is, as it were, incinerated again, only this time without leaving even that trace of the crime upon which a form of public instruction and a practice of public mourning might be built. In short, then, to forget is to conspire and injure. Whether done consciously or unconsciously, it leaves the dead in the very 'holes of oblivion' (this being the name Hannah Arendt gave to the concentration camps) to which the perpetrators consigned them and from which there can now be no rescue other than the rescue of memory.[121]

Heavily indebted to Walter Benjamin's concept of 'anamnestic solidarity'—which might be glossed as the affirmation *in memory* of a brotherhood denied *in history*—this strain of ethical thought stands steadfastly opposed to any operation of memory that attempts to simply draw a line under the past. As its most prominent contemporary public exponent, Jürgen Habermas, argued through his public interventions into the German *Historikerstreit*, in the face of crimes against humanity, the only ethically defensible stance a political community could take was a critical/reflexive one.[122] Against those who would try to leap over the Shoah or erase it as part of the Nazi interlude, Habermas has insisted on keeping the memory alive both out of respect for the victims (for whom the 'weak anamnestic power of solidarity' serves as a form of belated recognition)[123] and as an insurance against the return of a dangerous nationalism. For him (as will be discussed in more detail in Chapter 3), the risks of remembrance, at least in Germany, had been vastly and self-servingly exaggerated out of a narcissistic desire to protect the national self-image. Rather than seek to forget what offends their sense of collective pride, he argued, the Germans were obliged to follow Adorno in 'mercilessly reflecting on a humiliating past that confronts us with a self different than the one we would like to be and think we are'.[124] By avoiding this 'merciless reflection' through their policy of forgetting, the Germans were merely inhibiting self-understanding and, with that, any chance of progressing towards a fully just political community.[125]

Given the highly contextual nature of the discussion and the strong claims on both sides, it is doubtful whether this debate between forgetting and remembrance will ever give rise to a universally applicable moral imperative. Having sensibly conceded merit in both positions, critics have, by and large, been inclined to try and parse it through one of two strategies. The first, premised on the old Aristotelian idea of the happy medium, is to chart a path in collective memory between 'too much' and 'too little'.[126] According to this view, each divided society must, as Donald Shriver puts it, try to 'strike a balance between burying the gruesome past and burying themselves in the memory of it'.[127] The second, rather more sophisticated, strategy (also vaguely indebted to Aristotle) is premised on the idea that decisions about collective memory ultimately come down to the question of what best serves the needs of the present. Rather than assume there is some happy medium to strive for, this approach proceeds on the basis that remembrance and forgetting actually serve different imperatives—enlightenment and justice on the one hand, peace and stability on the other—the merits of which need to be carefully weighed in each instance. Premised on the idea that we cannot always have every morally good thing we want—in this instance, both justice *and* peace— it suggests we have little choice but to exercise our practical wisdom and make difficult choices about what social goal we consider more important or more feasible *in the particular case*. The fact that justice is, in some cases, far too readily sacrificed in the name of peace does not mean there are no instances in which peace really would be jeopardized by an insistence on the claims of memory.[128]

Contextually sensitive (and far less vague than the 'happy medium' approach), the practical wisdom approach seems hard to fault politically or philosophically. And yet, in accepting the terms of the debate exactly as they have been set out—forgetting equates to peace, remembrance to justice— even it fails to take cognizance of what is perhaps the clearest lesson to come out of case studies of divided societies like those of France and Spain; namely, that the ethical objection is not the only—or perhaps the most closely heeded—objection to pacts of forgetting. There is now a functional one too in which forgetting is found wanting not because it breaches some ethical duty of memory but because it is not capable of combating or, more precisely, of completing the psychic processes triggered by the trauma of civil discord. Across a large range of texts and with reference to a large number of cases, one finds the same proposition repeated over and over: contrary to conventional wisdom, pacts of forgetting do not actually secure peace—or, at least, not in the long term—because they leave the mourning process unfinished and invite the past back. Booth effectively sums up the new psychological doxa when he suggests there is really only one lesson that can be drawn from the 'failures of virtually all the national exercises in amnesia': institutionalized forgetting is inherently unstable because 'the past has a habit of returning involuntarily'.[129] Support for this proposition could now be found almost anywhere, but for the sake of brevity we will have to make do with a brief return to the two cases of amnesty/amnesia with which we began this section: France and Spain.

It is obviously not for nothing that the seminal work on memory politics in post-war France carries the title *The Vichy Syndrome*. For Rousso, the reappearance of Vichy as a problem for France to come to terms with in the 1960s only went to show that the trauma of civil discord (and the process of mourning needed to truly overcome it) could not be denied indefinitely. True, after the initial explosion of violence in the *epuration*, the French state had succeeded in staunching the civil wound by turning the resistance into an abstract idea, equivalent to the French identity. In the figure of Charles de Gaulle, resistance and nation were at once conjoined and equated, allowing the memory of the fratricidal conflict to be erased and a 'sacred and edifying history of the Resistance' (what Rousso calls 'resistancialism') to emerge as a myth of foundation.[130] As Rousso would have it, this 'repression' largely held sway until that fateful moment when *The Sorrow and the Pity* 'exhumed the memory of "German France"'. Yet there, in both the 'silences and slips' of the interviewees and the intense emotional reactions of the public, came the proof that 'the foreign war [had] left fewer scars than the civil war'.[131] As a cultural object and site of public reflection, *The Sorrow and the Pity* testified to a 'national neurosis', proving, in its own way, that the return of Vichy had always been something of an inevitability, psychologically speaking:

> Unfinished mourning? Insuperable political contradictions halted the mourning process before it was over. Constant calls to forgive, to reconcile, even to forget the

past clashed with an urgent need to deal with the spontaneous return of repressed material. Even with all the ceremonies and all the trials, old memories simply could not be contained; old wounds re-opened and the dead were hauled into court.[132]

Ultimately, for Rousso, this 'national neurosis' proved incapable of resolution until the trial of Klaus Barbie which, in taking on the character of a public exercise in truth telling about the past, provided France with 'a climax and a catharsis'.[133]

Students of our other contemporary example of amnesty/amnesia, the *pacto del olvido* in Spain, tell a remarkably similar story. According to Madeleine Davis, for instance, the unspoken pact of forgetting began to unravel around the turn of the century as a result of certain 'impulses towards a fuller truth'.[134] This 'belated memory politics' has taken a variety of forms, but its most striking manifestation has been the exhumation, quite literally this time, of Spain's Francoist past. In the year 2000, a non-governmental organization known as the Association for the Recovery of Historical Memory was founded with the twin objectives of coordinating exhumations of the 'Republican disappeared' (estimated to be around 30,000 people) and gathering the stories of those who lost their relatives but were forbidden from mourning them. In this context, the idea of buried memory and the return of the repressed takes on a double significance. In the exhumation of the Republican disappeared, symbolic gesture and biological process are once again conjoined as the body subjected to political repression and the memory subjected to psychological repression return, conjointly and irrepressibly, to the light. Writing in 2005, Davis declared that the reworking of the Spanish national story (away from the narrative of 'shared guilt' that underpinned the amnesty of 1977) was 'a controversial yet cathartic process' that could 'no longer be avoided'.[135] For her, the unravelling of the *pacto del olvido* had simply confirmed the view, long held by analysts of democratization, 'that a society cannot indefinitely avoid coming face to face with past trauma'.[136]

Arguably the most important concept to emerge in the context of this new 'politics of life' is that of latency. As the emergent psychological wisdom would have it, the weakness inherent in amnesty (which is now assimilated to denial) is that it simply places everything in a holding pattern. In amnesty the force of the law is used to bring mourning to a full stop—its tendency towards the interminable, so feared by the Greeks, neutralized. But, as we are told again and again, to deprive grief of oxygen is to prevent reconciliation with loss: nothing can be resolved and hence everything remains latent—ready, when the time is ripe, to come again.[137] Amnesty, writes Rebecca Comay, underlining (and reflecting) this new doxa, is like 'a stasis supervening upon a previous stasis—a kind of shock administered to an inert or emptily gyrating body politic'.[138] In amnesty, everything is arrested in order that it can start up again. But this artificial block upon memory, this 'deep freeze', undoes its own interest in renewal by preserving, in cold storage, precisely what it wished to consign to oblivion. The question is not *whether* memory will thaw but *when* it will thaw. Hence the need for mourning. If one wants to be genuinely free of the past—or, more accurately, of the risk the ghostly over-life which that past poses to real life in the present—one has no choice but to confront it and process it. As the now ubiquitous mantra holds: to avoid an 'acting out', one must engage in a 'working through'.[139]

The significance of this turn from prohibition to process ought not be underestimated. Thanks largely, it would seem, to the widespread diffusion of psychoanalytic insights in contemporary Western culture (and, more precisely, to the transformation of Freud's thesis about 'the return of the repressed' into a political axiom), a great gulf has now opened up between the ancients and the moderns on the merits of recalling misfortunes and exposing the truth of division.[140] If the ancient Greeks were of the view that memory was dangerous and had to be banned, we (post-Freudian) moderns appear to be of the view that few things are more dangerous than placing a ban on memory. 'Experience worldwide', noted Desmond Tutu, here reflecting upon yet another 'house divided against itself', 'shows that if you do not deal with a dark past such as ours, effectively look the beast in the eye, that beast is not going to lie down quietly; it is going, as sure as anything, to come back and haunt you horrendously.'[141] To us, the idea that a political community, formerly at odds with itself, might then simply go on, as Isocrates put it, 'as if no misfortune had happened' seems, quite literally, incredible.[142] For the most part, the best thing we are able to say about such pacts of forgetting is that they keep resentments temporarily at bay; the worst, that they amplify such resentments, redoubling them in their bitterness and potency, effectively planting the seeds for a new wave of violence—the emergency yet to come.[143]

Nowhere, perhaps, is the so-called triumph of the therapeutic more clearly manifest in contemporary politics than in this insistence that there can be no new life without a confrontation with, and digestion of, the past.[144] In stark contrast to the ancient Greeks, it is now forgetting that is equated with repetition, remembrance with renewal.[145] While the former, construed as denial, leads backwards to the cycle of violence, the latter, construed as mourning, leads forwards to the regeneration of politics. 'To be unable to mourn', noted Lifton in his preface to the Mitscherlichs' seminal text, *The Inability to Mourn* (the text discussed at length in Chapter 1), 'is to be unable to enter into the great human cycle of death and re-birth—to be unable, that is, to "live again'".[146] And it is in the name of this 'living again', this living free of the traumatic past, that every political community divided by its own history is now treated as if it was engaged, or *ought* to be engaged, in a process of regeneration centred upon truth telling and societal mourning. The remarkable rise of the 'transitional society' as a political phenomenon or, more accurately, as a category of political thought is, in fact, but one of the more visible signs of the current conviction that there is no escape from process, from a 'working through'. In these societies in process with their 'transitional institutions' and their 'transitional justice', institutionalized forgetting is abandoned in favour of a civic mourning that moves through truth to the promise of new life.[147] The point is not just, to quote Tzvetan Todorov, that 'mourning constitutes another way of disabling memory', it is that it constitutes a better, more effective, way.[148]

To this unassailable consensus surrounding the latency of social trauma and the importance of truth telling to the healing of the nation can be attributed the emergence and the celebration of those new institutions of exception that will be discussed in greater detail in subsequent chapters: the public memorial, the political apology, and the truth commission. Each has been championed over more conventional mechanisms (such as criminal trials) for their capacity to break long-held silences and engage with psychological trauma, facilitating precisely those shared processes of mourning that are now deemed indispensable to breaking the cycles of violence.[149] Yet perhaps the clearest sign of the power of the new discourse of wounds and healing, trauma and recovery is the mark it has left on the very old institution against which it never ceases to rail: amnesty itself. Amnesty, it is important to note, has by no means been completely sidelined as an instrument of renewal within 'transitional' or 'divided' societies. However, as quickly becomes evident, it no longer functions in quite the same way it did for the ancients because its association with amnesia has been decisively cut. Amnesty, as Claire Moon has noted, now sits at the very core of the 'therapeutic order' that conjoins truth, catharsis, healing, and reconciliation.[150] If it was once a means of burying the past, it is now a vehicle for uncovering it, and if it was once justified with reference to the goal of peace, it is now justified with reference to the goal of healing. Offered as an incentive for disclosure within the broader process of truth telling, amnesty now trades justice for truth (as opposed to justice for peace) in the hope that revelations about the past will catalyse the mourning process and facilitate political renewal.[151] In a manner completely foreign to the Greeks, in other words, amnesty is now used to exhume the dead and the disappeared—instead of putting a stop to mourning, it helps to stimulate it.

III The Two Cultures of Collective Memory Revisited

The preceding analysis suggests it might be more profitable to understand the 'two cultures' of collective memory in terms of variations in *operations* (forgetting versus mourning) rather than in terms of variations in *form* (collected versus collective). As operations upon memory, both forgetting and mourning criss-cross the individual and collective levels, creating complex symbolic/psychological circuits which blur the distinction between health and identity, the multitudinous individual traumas and the unassimilable breach in the national narrative. In forgetting, the subtraction of the offending chapter of civil history goes hand in hand with emotional discipline and the refusal of loss. In mourning, the integration of the offending chapter of civil history goes hand in hand with emotional disclosure and the recognition of loss. In both instances, 'healing' hinges upon the creation of a mutually reinforcing relation in which the individual aids the collective in managing its past (either by silencing or expressing their grief) and the collective aids individuals in managing their past (either by denying or acknowledging their loss). Only in the latter case, however, is an effort made to direct, rather than simply contain, the life process. In forgetting, life is held at a distance from politics through the displacement of grief to the anti-political sphere. In mourning, by contrast, life is brought inside the political domain and an effort made to direct the biological process by finishing the unfinished work of mourning.

The shift from prohibition to process, from forgetting to mourning, in our current institutions of exception is thus indicative not just of a newfound interest in the suffering of victims but of that profound re-articulation of the relationship between politics and life that Foucault took to be definitive of modernity (the age of biopolitics). The practice of 'truth telling'—a practice that serves as a kind of subterranean connection linking the various institutions of exception examined in this book—has become the privileged means by which power gains access to psychic life. Reflective of a uniquely post-Freudian understanding of the levers that need to be pulled to restore those 'affective bridges' to the past that allow mourning to occur, truth telling is, at one and the same time, the means by which power gains access to damaged life and the instrument of its cathartic restoration. Although varied as institutions, memorials, apologies, and commissions all endeavour to bring citizens 'face to face' with the wrongs of the past (those famously 'unpalatable truths') in the hope that recognizing what was done will catalyse a collective, societal grieving for what was lost. The 'new life' they promise is thus not just the metaphorical rebirth of the state which Machiavelli invokes in his famous exhortation but the real renewal of individual and collective life (its release from the traumas of the past) through the completion of the mourning process.

The reasons one might offer for resisting this infusion of life into politics were established some time ago. Well before Foucault began to worry about the biopolitical regulation of populations and its insidious 'animalization of man', Hannah Arendt was already raising concerns about the 'rise of the social' and the blurring of boundaries that takes place when the life process intrudes into politics and politics into the life process. In sympathy with the ancient Greeks and their insistence upon a 'strict division' between the activities 'related to the common world' (constitutive of the *polis*) and those 'related to the maintenance of life' (constitutive of the *oikos*), she warned of the tendency biological processes have to impose themselves with the force of necessity. Since the demands of life can neither be set aside nor made the object of choice, they deprive public life of its autonomous character and reduce the political actor to a 'behaving animal'.[152] For Arendt (as for the Greeks), the very distinction of politics (and, with that, of the pre-eminent place of 'action' within the *vita activa*) was tied to the fact that 'it was no longer bound to the biological life process'.[153] The only two ways, on her readings of things, that mourning might legitimately make an entry into public life was through official commemoration (which had more to do with valuing than grieving) and protest movements. The reason she was happy to refer to the black-clad Hungarian women 'mourning their dead in public' as 'the last political gesture of the revolution' was because it constituted a form of mourning as action, not mourning as behaviour. Far from succumbing to a life process that was out of their control, these black-clad women had consciously politicized their grief in order to stage one last act of defiance against the death of freedom in Russian-occupied Budapest.[154]

However, as Loraux's highly suggestive reference to mourning as a 'female model of memory' alerts us, it is not self-evident that the life process by which we come to terms with loss has no place in the 'common world'. In more recent times, feminist scholars as diverse as Martha Nussbaum, Judith Butler, and Jenny Edkins have wilfully transgressed that 'strict division' between public and private by treating mourning as an untapped resource for reconstituting and regenerating political community.[155] Despite their differences, all share a sense of the value of the work of mourning, firstly, in restraining reactive attempts to seek a false healing through forms of violent pay back and, secondly, in expanding the circle of concern beyond those within our own communities. Following Freud in his view of mourning as a process in which the grieving subject finally 'faces up' to the reality of loss, they have argued that public grieving might actually help secure citizens against masculine fantasies of magical resolution (especially the fantasy of revenge) that are premised on the refusal or de-realization of loss. Moreover, since mourning arises from an experience of loss that is common to all vulnerable humans, it has the potential, they suggest, to open people up in compassionate identification to the lives of others within and beyond the borders of the nation-state. If, as Mark Sanders conjectured, state racism (Apartheid by another name) is a 'proscription on the mourning of the other', the institutions of exception that facilitate public grieving for abandoned life would seem to provide its perfect political antidote.[156] Does not this affirmative (and dare one say feminized?) biopolitics of care mark a progressive turning towards formerly denigrated life?

Arendt's fears about the perversion of the common world under the pressure of the life process notwithstanding, then, one does not lack reasons for seeing the turn from prohibition to process as a positive development. In her recent book, *Affective Communities in World Politics*, Emma Hutchinson bolsters the case for process over prohibition by mounting a thorough (and, on the face of things, thoroughly compelling) case for 'societal grieving'. Since, as she would have it, the trauma of civil discord does not simply resolve itself, a great deal hinges on the way in which the political community responds, discursively and institutionally, to the violence that turns inwards and leaves the political family divided in itself. When communities fail to create a time and space to work through trauma or, worse still, use trauma in an instrumental fashion to cement friend–enemy antagonisms, the likelihood of further violence significantly increases. By contrast, when the polity seizes the opportunity to 'properly mourn' its losses as, she claims, South Africa did with the institution of the Truth and Reconciliation Commission, individual and collective wounds are given a genuine chance to heal. On her reading, the 'task of uniting South Africa' necessitated something more than the restoration of the rule of law and the repudiation of apartheid policy: 'individuals and the community as a whole required catharsis'.[157] As complex and subtle as it is in its elaboration, then, her message in the end is admirably clear and succinct: 'less antagonistic and more reflective and regenerative communal configurations depend upon the ability of traumatized communities to confront, grieve and work through trauma'.[158]

At this point, however, it would be judicious to sound a note of caution. By virtue of its enormous cultural cache (not to mention the numbing attraction of anodyne slogans like 'revealing is healing'), the psychoanalytic discourse that simultaneously encircles and legitimates the 'healing of nations' has conspired to present the shift from forgetting to mourning in a thoroughly positive light. With the promise of communal regeneration, of new life, this discourse desensitizes us to the distortions that take place when techniques of truth telling, originally developed in the context of pastoral and therapeutic relations (and even there by no means innocently or unproblematically), are redeployed in political contexts with the aid of the mass media. Loraux's reflections on *The Capture of Miletus* (not unlike Rousso's reflections on *The Sorrow and the Pity*) speak to the political investment that the sovereign body has historically made in controlling mourning by deciding which (or whose) traumas can be rendered as public spectacles. After the disaster of Phrynichus' *Miletus*, tragedy is forced to hold trauma at a distance, allowing mourning only insofar as it arises from the inner ills of *other* cities.[159] But it should not be supposed that such political investment is absent simply because we have now decided to bring our trauma home and confront it 'face to face'. The appearance of an open flow of previously repressed trauma stories notwithstanding, states have hardly ceased to stage the truth of themselves in accordance with principles of *raison d'état*. The only difference this time is that the power of representation, of the dramatic spectacle, is harnessed precisely in order to make the entire audience burst into tears.

In the following three chapters, I focus on the most prominent of the new institutions of exception—public memorials, political apologies, and truth commissions—in order to assess the merits of steering the life process of mourning through acts of sovereign repentance. Although by no means insensitive to the progressive character of shared mourning as a revaluation of the life of 'the other', I try to show how the *imperative* to work through, however beneficial it proves in private, therapeutic settings becomes personally and politically hazardous once it is brought into the public domain and extended through mediatization.[160] As we have seen throughout this chapter, sovereigns that abandon the policy of denial and take on the task of mourning are now commonly considered to be doing the right thing. When Hutchinson argues it is 'highly desirable' for states to work through trauma, she is but confirming the normative view.[161] Yet, in seeking to direct or catalyse the mourning process, the state does something more (and, I would suggest, something much more hazardous) than simply manipulate symbolic forms to recreate unity; it intervenes into a biological process for its own strategic ends. No longer simply an individual pathology, 'unfinished mourning' has entered into political discourse as a threat to vitality and thus as something that needs to be regulated by the apparatuses of security. The desirability of any kind of politically directed 'societal grieving' is thus double-edged. At once a means of acknowledging the loss suffered by the victims of sovereign violence and a means by which the sovereign optimizes a state of life, mourning would seem to have acquired an affinity with forgetting as a technology by which states 'disable memory', stripping it of whatever political potential it held to constitute the political world differently.

Notes

1. N. Machiavelli, *The Prince*, London: Penguin, 2003, p. 82.
2. In chapter 14 of *The Prince*, Machiavelli famously claims that 'the art of war is all that is expected of a ruler'. In one sense, the exhortation reinforces this one-dimensional view by linking the renewal of the country to the creation of the new military system of the citizen army. However, the criss-crossed medical/religious metaphors which speak of wounds and healing, redemption and salvation suggest that is not simply the art of war but the art of medicine that is expected of the ruler; or, even more radically, that war (like the surgeon's knife) is but one tool the prince might employ to achieve healing. See Machiavelli, *The Prince*, pp. 47, 82–84.
3. M. Viroli, *Redeeming the Prince: The Meaning of Machiavelli's Masterpiece*, Princeton, NJ: Princeton University Press, 2014.
4. C.V. Wedgewood, *History and Hope: The Collected Essays of C.V. Wedgewood*, London: Fontana Press, 1987, p. 390.
5. For a discussion of the 'civil wound' in Shakespeare, see M. Neill, 'Shakespeare's Tragedies' in M. de Grazia and S. Wells (eds.), *The New Cambridge Companion to Shakespeare*, Cambridge: Cambridge University Press, 2010, pp. 124–126.
6. W. Shakespeare, *Richard III*, edited by John Jowett, Oxford: Oxford University Press, 2000. Act 5, Scene 7: 23–41.
7. Thucydides, *History of the Peloponnesian War*, London: Penguin Books, 1972, p. 241.
8. In this context it is perhaps worth noting that Hobbes famously claimed that the *Leviathan* had been inspired by 'grief for the present calamities of my country'. See M. Oakeshott, *Hobbes: On Civil Association*, Oxford: Basil Blackwell, 1975, p. 6.
9. On this point, see W.J. Booth, 'Communities of Memory: On Identity, Memory, and Debt', *American Political Science Review*, 93(2), 1999, p. 250.
10. Booth, 'Communities of Memory', p. 260.
11. G. Greer, *Shakespeare*, Oxford: Oxford University Press, 1996, p. 76.
12. As E.M.W. Tillyard has noted, Shakespeare was one of the 'select few who saw a dramatic and philosophical sweep in this part of history'. E.M.W. Tillyard, *Shakespeare's History Plays*, London: Penguin Books, 1991, pp. 65–70.
13. See Shakespeare, *Richard III*, Act 2, Scene 1: 65–66.
14. Greer, *Shakespeare*, p. 77.
15. See, for instance, T. Hoenselaars, "Shakespeare's English History Plays' in de Grazia and Wells (eds.), *The New Cambridge Companion to Shakespeare*, pp. 137–151.
16. Shakespeare, *Richard III*, Act 5, Scene 7: 12–20.
17. The *locus classicus* of this view is J. Assman, 'Collective Memory and Cultural Identity', *New German Critique*, 65, 1995, pp. 125–133. In saying that the sovereign exercises authority over collective memory, I do not wish to imply that it always gets things its own way. If collective memory represents the conjunction of memory and power, it is not just

the power of the sovereign but the power of social actors that determine its contours. Collective memory is always a site of contest, such that the power of the sovereign is generally limited to the temporary stabilization of what is remembered (and what forgotten), what is honoured (and what dishonoured).
18. Assman, 'Collective Memory and Cultural Identity', p. 130.
19. See M. Halbwachs, *On Collective Memory*, Chicago, IL: University of Chicago Press, 1992 and Assman, 'Collective Memory and Cultural Identity', p. 125. Duncan Bell sums up the standard view when he writes: 'Collective memory ... refers, again in a general sense, to widely shared perceptions of the past. It shapes the story that groups of people tell about themselves, linking past, present and future in a simplified narrative. It is what keeps the past—or at least a highly selective image of it—alive in the present.' D. Bell, 'Introduction' in D. Bell (ed.), *Memory, Trauma, and World Politics: Reflections on the Relationship between Past and Present*, London: Palgrave Macmillan, 2006, p. 2.
20. See J. Olick, 'Collective Memory: The Two Cultures', *Sociological Theory*, 17(3), 1999, pp. 345–348.
21. See C. Moon, 'Healing Past Violence: Traumatic Assumptions and Therapeutic Interventions in War and Reconciliation', *Journal of Human Rights*, 8(1), 2009, p. 72.
22. H. Rousso, *The Haunting Past: History, Memory, and Justice in Contemporary France*, Philadelphia, PA: University of Pennsylvanian Press, 1998, p. xix; D. Tutu, *No Future without Forgiveness*, London: Rider/Random House, 1999, p. x.
23. J. Torpey, '"Making Whole What Has Been Smashed": Reflections on Reparations', *Journal of Modern History*, 73(2), 2001, p. 15.
24. On this point, see M. Foucault, *The History of Sexuality: An Introduction*, Harmondsworth: Penguin, 1978, p. 147.
25. Olick, 'Collective Memory', p. 345.
26. Thus when Donald Shriver tell us that 'what poisons the inner life of persons also poisons the inner life of societies', one can no longer assume he is just speaking metaphorically. As one text puts it, 'Because individuals are the fundamental elements in society, pervasive trauma throughout the population can impede the reconstruction of the nation at every other level. In other words, good national health depends on individual healing. It is incumbent on new governments, then, to foster individual reconciliation when personal trauma is widespread; failure to do so can impede national reconciliation and reconstruction.' See D. Shriver, 'Where and When in Political Life Is Justice Served by Forgiveness?' in N. Biggar (ed.), *Burying the Past: Making Peace and Doing Justice after Civil Conflict*, Washington, DC: Georgetown University Press, p. 31; and N.R. Anzola, *Reconciliation in Divided Societies*, Philadelphia, PA: University of Pennsylvania Press, 2011, pp. 44–45.
27. K. Wale, 'Knotted Memories of a Betrayed Sacrifice: Rethinking Trauma and Hope in South Africa', *Memory Studies*, 2022, p. 4. On this interweaving of the personal and the political, the biological and symbolic, see also D. Scott, *Omens of Adversity: Tragedy, Time, Memory, Justice*, Durham, NC: Duke University Press, 2014, pp. 107–109.
28. As Andrew Schaap notes, 'widespread state violence is often understood to result in collective trauma. The traumatic wounds inflicted on individuals can combine to manifest a pathological mood within a community that is more than the sum of private wounds'. Similarly, 'through public narration and acknowledgment of the stories of survivors, it is hoped that a [collective] catharsis might be brought about'. A. Schaap, *Political Reconciliation*, London: Routledge, 2005, p. 19.

29. As Foucault notes, in the seventeenth century, 'the King's body wasn't a metaphor, but a political reality. Its physical presence was necessary for the functioning of the monarchy'. By the nineteenth century, however, it is no longer the king's body but the 'social body which needs to be protected, in a quasi-medical sense'. M. Foucault, 'Body/Power' in M. Foucault, *Power/Knowledge: Selected Interviews and Writings 1972–1977*, edited by Colin Gordon, New York: Pantheon Books, 1980, p. 55.
30. Elster, *Closing the Books*, Cambridge: Cambridge University Press, p. 61. See also W. James Booth, 'The Unforgotten: Memories of Justice', *American Political Science Review*, 95(4), 2001, p. 784.
31. See, for instance, Charles Griswold's discussion of the civil discord caused by the Vietnam War and the importance of creating a 'shared narrative' in civic reconciliation. I return to this example in Chapter 3. C. Griswold, *Forgiveness: A Philosophical Exploration*, Cambridge: Cambridge University Press, 2007, pp. 195–196.
32. The basic premise of the field of ontological security is that states create (and then selectively mobilize) narratives about themselves as a way of stabilizing their identity and legitimating their policy decisions. Just as, to resort the idiom employed in this book, collective memory serves to differentiate between self and other and thus guide state action, narratives establish a kind of 'autobiographical continuity' that allows states to differentiate between policies that are consistent or inconsistent with their sense of self. Revelations about past wrongdoing have a tendency to undermine the ontological security of the state precisely because they threaten this autobiographical continuity. In the face of such revelations, states invariably embark upon a process of re-narration in which the wrongdoing is neutralized as an ontological threat through a story of reconciliation. See C. Kinnval, 'Globalization and Religious Nationalism: Self, Identity and the Search for Ontological Security', *Political Psychology*, 25(5), 2004, pp. 741–767; and J. Subotić, 'Narrative, Ontological Security, and Foreign Policy Change', *Foreign Policy Analysis*, 12, 2016, pp. 610–627.
33. Loraux, *The Divided City: On Memory and Forgetting in Ancient Athens*, New York. Zone Books, 2006, p. 149.
34. Cited in Loraux, *The Divided City*, p. 153.
35. Loraux, *The Divided City*, p. 148.
36. Loraux, *The Divided City*, p. 149. On this point, see also D. Cohen, 'The Rhetoric of Justice: Strategies of Reconciliation and Revenge in the Restoration of Athenian democracy in 403 BC', *European Journal of Sociology*, 42(2), 2001, p. 399.
37. Loraux, *The Divided City*, p. 150.
38. Loraux, *The Divided City*, p. 150. According to David Cohen, Loraux's sense of the Amnesty of 403 BCE as a moment of cultural as well as juridical oblivion is misconceived because actions subsequently taken by the democrats showed that they continued to recall the misfortunes and found other, non-legal, means of exacting their 'revenge'. Cohen's comments do not, however, damage Loraux's broader analysis about the role of forgetting as an antidote to mourning in the life of the city. See Cohen, 'The Rhetoric of Justice', p. 338.
39. P. Ricoeur, *Memory, History, Forgetting*, Chicago, IL: University of Chicago Press, 2004, pp. 453–456.
40. Elster, *Closing the Books*, pp. 3–23.
41. Loraux, *The Divided City*, p. 147.

New Life   117

42. Loraux, *The Divided City*, p. 148.
43. Loraux, *The Divided City*, p. 148.
44. The writing of the tragedy of Athens will, of course, be left to Thucydides.
45. For the Greeks, as M.I. Finley famously noted, 'Faction (stasis) is the greatest evil and the most common danger'. M.I. Finley, 'Athenian Demagogues', *Past and Present*, 21, 1962, p. 6.
46. Tragedy, according to Loraux, 'borrows' this notion of grief-wrath from 'the most ancient poetic tradition, and particularly from epic, which from the first word of the *Iliad* names this active affect mēnis. Wrath of Achilles and, later, wrath of mourning mothers, from Demeter to Cyltemnestra'. See Loraux, *The Divided City*, p. 160.
47. The intimate connection between grief and wrath has been recently been reiterated by Anne Carson in *Grief Lessons*: 'Why does tragedy exist? Because you are full of rage. Why are you full of rage? Because you are full of grief.' And it is precisely because it is tied to grief, to the loss that cannot be replaced, that this rage is so hard to rein in or cast into oblivion. As Loraux points out, Electra does not just say, 'I do not forget my anger'; she says, 'my anger does not forget me'. See A. Carson, *Grief Lessons: Four Plays by Euripides*, New York: New York Review of Books, 2006, p. 7; and Loraux, *The Divided City*, p. 160.
48. Loraux, *The Divided City*, p. 162.
49. In *The Divided City* the translation reads: 'this mourning that refuses to be carried out'. Loraux, *The Divided City*, p. 161. I have adopted the phrasing from a subsequent translation here instead because it seems to give a more accurate rendering of the concept at stake. See N. Loraux, 'Of Amnesty and Its Opposite' in N. Loraux, *Mothers in Mourning*, Ithaca, NY: Cornell University Press, 1998, p. 99.
50. Loraux, *The Divided City*, p. 162.
51. 'A dull fool', she intones against the Chorus, 'might forget a father's miserable death.' Her way, by contrast, is that of Niobe: 'The inconsolable, entombed in stone, Weeping eternally. With tears unceasing.' Electra's personification of grief is exemplary in tragedy, but, as Loraux points out, this mourning without end is there already in that famous *mēnis* of Achilles, at the beginning of a story, at the beginning of ancient Greece. See Sophocles, *Electra and Other Plays*, London: Penguin, 1953, lines 146–153; and Loraux, *The Divided City*, p. 160.
52. Loraux, *The Divided City*, p. 160.
53. S. Critchley, *Tragedy, the Greeks and Us*, London: Profile Books, 2019, p. 140.
54. As Critchley notes, in Sophocles' version of the play, Electra talks only of her own grief and barely moves: 'From the moment she enters, around 100 lines in, until the end of the play some 1400 lines later, Electra simply stands in the doorway of the palace and laments excessively.' With her identity reduced to the outpouring of grief alone, she is effectively 'actionless'. Of course, this dichotomy between 'mourning' and 'action' is, like every dichotomy, open to deconstruction. Not only, as Bonnie Honig has pointed out in relation to Antigone, is mourning sometimes a form of action, a way of lodging a protest or speaking in favour of a rival form of life, it is invariably also the case that something is happening even when nothing appears to be happening. Indeed, in many instances, it is precisely because it forces an interruption or break in the flow of action that mourning takes on significance within the political domain. Mourning becomes an action to the extent that it forces politics to wait. However, as I seek to show in this book, mourning can also become a tool of a state that has tired of waiting, a state that seeks to catalyse the

mourning process within the body politic precisely in order that civic trauma does not remain a source of ongoing stasis or paralysis. See Critchley, *Tragedy, the Greeks and Us*, pp. 53–54; and B. Honig, *Antigone Interrupted*, Cambridge: Cambridge University Press, 2013, pp. 19–20.

55. On this point, see G. Agamben, *Stasis: Civil War as a Political Paradigm*, Stanford, CA: Stanford University Press, 2015, p. 8.
56. Sophocles, *Electra* in *Antigone, Oedipus, Electra* trans. by H.D.F. Kitto, Oxford: Oxford University Press, 1998, ll. 140–143.
57. W. Junker, 'Past's Weight, Future's Promise: Reading *Electra*', *Philosophy and Literature*, 27(2), 2003, p. 410. As Junker points out, it is really Orestes, not her accommodating sister Chrysothemis, who is most vividly contrasted with Electra, for while the latter scarcely lives at all, the former lives twice, fabricating a story of his own death so he can create a space for action.
58. Electra's resistance to persuasion and lack of prudence emerge in her exchange with her sister Chrysothemis. Sophocles, *Electra* in *Antigone, Oedipus, Electra*, ll. 327–405.
59. Electra's futureless life without life finds its parallel in Clytemenstra who lives in such fear of the past she too barely lives at all. 'And her!', she yells at Electra. 'She was the worse affliction; she lived with me, draining me of life.' Electra's refusal to forget her grief effectively means that everyone is stuck.
60. Thucydides, *History of the Peloponnesian War*, London: Penguin Books, 1972, p. 241.
61. Thus, at the beginning of *Antigone* after the armies of Argos have retreated, the Chorus declares: 'Now let us win oblivion from the wars, thronging the temples of the gods in singing, dancing choirs through the night!' See Sophocles, *Antigone* in *The Three Theban Plays*, trans. by Robert Fagles, London: Penguin, 1984, l. 168; and Loraux, 'Of Amnesty and Its Opposite', p. 95.
62. This reference, from the *Odyssey*, is cited by Loraux, *The Divided City*, pp. 157–158.
63. Loraux, *The Divided City*, p. 158.
64. This distinction between animal life and political life is, of course, partly confounded by Aristotle's rendering of man as a 'political animal'. As he famously observed, *polis* life is what is natural for *this* animal. Given, however, that *polis* life, even on Aristotle's rendering, represents the *full* development of the human animal (its *telos*), it is still premised upon the mastery of the instinctive, animal urges. As he states clearly at the outset of *The Politics*, biological processes such as reproduction are 'not a matter of *choice*, but … due to the *natural* urge, which exists in the other animals too'. Hence, if the life of the *polis* is what nature *intended* for man, it can only be realized through the transcendence of the natural urges he shares with other animals through the exercise of that 'master artificer' know as *logos* or reason. A man who mourns like a woman would, on Aristotle's account, have succumbed to the natural urge—he has not filled his natural *telos as a man* because he remains a slave to his instincts or appetites. See Aristotle, *The Politics*, London: Penguin Books, 1992, Book I, 1252a 24.
65. H. Arendt, *The Promise of Politics*, New York: Schocken Books, 2005, pp. 121–122. See also H. Arendt, *The Human Condition*, Chicago, IL: University of Chicago Press, 1958, p. 32.
66. This idea is, to be sure, still entirely consistent with Arendt's claim that mastering the necessities of life in the household was the condition for freedom in the *polis*. Arendt, *The Human Condition*, pp. 30–31.

New Life   119

67. As Charles Segal notes in his discussion of Sophocles' *Antigone*, 'it is Antigone the woman—or perhaps, at another level, the woman in him—that Creon must subdue or, in one of his favourite metaphors, must yoke'. C. Segal, *Interpreting Greek Tragedy: Myth, Poetry, Text*, Ithaca, NY: Cornell University Press, 1986, p. 148.
68. Loraux, *The Divided City*, p. 157.
69. Loraux, *The Divided City*, pp. 153–154.
70. Loraux, *The Divided City*, p. 101.
71. The thinking of that tension now goes by the name of agonistic democracy. See, for instance, C. Mouffe, *On the Political*, London: Routledge, 2005.
72. Loraux, *The Divided* City, pp. 10, 64, 104–108. See also M.I. Finley, 'Athenian Demagogues', *Past and Present*, 21, 1962, p. 6.
73. According to Finley, Athens was something of an exception among the Greek city-states in this regard, having only succumbed to civil war in 508, 411, and 404 BCE. Yet, as he goes on to note, even Athenian politics had an 'all or nothing quality' to it: 'the objective on each side was not merely to defeat the opposition but to crush it, to behead it by destroying its leaders'. Finley, *Athenian Demagogues*, p. 21.
74. Loraux, *The Divided City*, p. 155.
75. Loraux, *The Divided City*, p. 65.
76. See Loraux, *The Divided City*, p. 40.
77. This thesis about forgetting being the foundation of the political is developed at length in *The Divided City* and neatly glossed by Ricoeur: 'The decree, accredited by oath, ordering that "the evils not be recalled" claims to do no less than to hide the reality of *stasis*, of the civil war, the city approving only external war. The body politic is declared to be foreign to conflict in its very being.' Ricoeur, *Memory, History, Forgetting*, p. 500.
78. As Charles Segal notes, 'For the Greeks after Homer, even more sharply than for us, tears were a gendered category. Although men wept, tears were particularly characteristic of women. Women's "love of lamentation" and "love of tears" were a commonplace of Greek thought, often reiterated in tragedy. Like all intense emotions, weeping was associated with the female and with irrationality, and thus required social regulation.' C. Segal, *Euripides and the Poetics of Sorrow: Art, Gender and Commemoration in Alcestis, Hippolytus and Hecuba*, Durham, NC: Duke University Press, 1993, p. 63. For an extended discussion of the gendered nature of the Greek imaginary in which the female is associated with earth and emotion, the male with culture and reason, see the pioneering work of Genevieve Lloyd, *The Man of Reason: 'Male' and 'Female' in Western Philosophy*, London: Routledge, 1984, pp. 1–10.
79. This sense of the radical division of Greek society between household economy and political community, the necessities of life and the freedom of action, is derived primarily from Arendt. '*Polis* life', on her reading, began where the non-negotiable demands of biological necessity, the 'urgency of life', ended. Indeed, on her account, the very distinction of politics as an activity lay in the fact that 'it was no longer bound to the biological life process'. However, Arendt is hardly the only one to remark upon it or to note the enormous significance that speech assumed in the *polis*. As Jean Pierre Vernant has noted, one indication of how important speech was to the life of the *polis* can be found in the fact that the Greeks made it into a divinity, *Peitho*, persuasion. It is also worth recalling in this context that Sophocles likens Antigone's unrestrained mourning for her

brother Polynices, conducted in defiance of yet another ban on memory, to a bird crying over an empty nest. See Arendt, *The Human Condition*, pp. 22–38; J.P. Vernant, *The Origins of Greek Thought*, Ithaca, NY: Cornell University Press, 1982, p. 49; and Sophocles, *The Three Theban Plays*, trans. by Robert Fagles, London: Penguin Books, 1984, ll. 423–425.
80. Sophocles, *Electra*, ll. 107–108.
81. Loraux, 'Of Amnesty and Its Opposite', p. 98.
82. H. Staten, *Eros in Mourning: Homer to Lacan*, Baltimore, MD: Johns Hopkins University Press, 1995, p. 8.
83. Loraux, 'Of Amnesty and Its Opposite', p. 98.
84. Thus Electra, that figure of mourning personified, will, in one and the same breath, cry bitter tears that 'shall never end' and cry out to the gods of the underworld ('Hades, Persephone, Hermes, steward of death, Eternal Wrath and Furies') to avenge the murder of her lost father. Sophocles, *Electra and Other Plays*, trans. by E.F. Watling, London: Penguin Books, 1953, ll. 106–120.
85. See G. Holst-Warhaft, *Dangerous Voices: Women's Laments in Greek Literature*, Florence: Taylor and Francis, 1992, p. 20.
86. Plato, *The Republic*, trans. by Robin Waterfield, Oxford: Oxford University Press, 1998, 387e–388e.
87. Critchley, *Tragedy, the Greeks and Us*, p. 186.
88. Holst-Warhaft, *Dangerous Voices*, pp. 90, 100.
89. As Holst-Warhaft has also noted, almost from its inception, the *polis* found it necessary to legislate against the traditional behaviour of women in festivals related to mourning and in lamentation at funerals. Holst-Warhaft, *Dangerous Voices*, pp. 85–86. On this point, see also O. Taxidou, *Tragedy, Modernity and Mourning*, Edinburgh: Edinburgh University Press, pp. 175–176.
90. There are clear echoes here of what Jenny Edkins calls 'trauma time'—the time that 'destabilises any production of linearity'. J. Edkins, *Trauma and the Memory of Politics*, Cambridge: Cambridge University Press, 2003, p. 16. Whether an authentic feminist politics is to be found in resisting the absorption of mourning into the political domain (thereby preserving the radical difference of Antigone) or in remaking the political domain such that it becomes compatible with it (thereby making a radically different Creon) is a matter of ongoing debate in reception studies. For an excellent discussion of this question, see B. Holmes, *Gender: Antiquity and Its Legacy*, Oxford: Oxford University Press, 2012. If I could summarize the argument of the current book in one sentence, it would be that mourning *has* been brought into the public domain, but without creating a radically different Creon.
91. By associating mourning with femininity, classical Greece inevitably made woman the repository of all that was dangerous in it: the emphasis upon individuality, the keen sense of personal loss, the desire for vengeance. All of this, as Holst-Warhaft rightly notes, comes to the fore in tragedy. 'In the tragedies of Aeschylus, Sophocles and Euripides', she writes, 'we see the last vestiges of a world where women controlled the mourning of the dead.' See Holst-Warhaft, *Dangerous Voices*, p. 103; and Taxidou, *Tragedy, Modernity and Mourning*, p. 9.
92. Sophocles, *Antigone*, l. 9 in Sophocles, *The Three Theban Plays*, trans. by Robert Fagles, London. Penguin Classics, 1984.

New Life   121

93. Since the exclusion of mourning from the *polis*, its privatization or de-politicization, is itself a political act, its return at the hands of Antigone is perhaps best seen less as a politicization than a politicization of a different kind.
94. 'What Antigone demands', according to Charles Segal, 'is that the state take into itself the sanctity of blood relations, the value of affection and emotional ties, the uniqueness of the individual.' In like fashion, Bonnie Honig has suggested that the conflict between Antigone and Creon has its foundation in a contest between excessive, aristocratic mourning which celebrates the individual (Antigone) and restrained, democratic mourning which glorifies the collective (Creon). See Segal, *Interpreting Greek Tragedy*, p. 158; Honig, *Antigone Interrupted*, pp. 95–120.
95. Here again I have given preference to the translation offered in *Mothers in Mourning*. See Loraux, *Mothers in Mourning*, pp. 88–89. The comparable passage in *The Divided City* appears at p. 150. On this point, at least, David Cohen seems to be in broad agreement with Loraux. 'No reconciliation, however successful', he writes, 'can completely wash away all resentment and suspicion.' Prevented from using memory like a weapon in the courts, the democrats found other ways to satisfy their grudge against the aristocratic families who lent their support to the Thirty. Cohen, 'The Rhetoric of Justice', pp. 341–342.
96. Loraux, *The Divided City*, p. 261.
97. Loraux, *The Divided City*, p. 264.
98. Loraux, *The Divided City*, p. 264.
99. As Cohen points out, 'the argument that the victims have a right to know the truth plays no role in the Athenian context. The justification for prosecution focus only on exacting revenge and deterring future would be oligarchs'. Cohen, 'The Rhetoric of Justice', p. 350.
100. Of the place of the Nazi past in a reunified Germany, Irene Misselwitz wrote as follows: 'The common trauma had to re-enter consciousness again after reunification along with a head-on confrontation with our damaged ethnic identity'. I. Misselwitz quoted in B. Gook, *Divided Subjects, Invisible Borders: Re-unified Germany after 1989*, London: Rowman and Littlefield, 2015, pp. 35–36.
101. As Pierre Hazan has rightly noted, the ambition of transitional justice 'is not to erase the past but, on the contrary, to integrate the stain of the crime into the heart of society'. See P. Hazan, *Judging War, Judging History: Behind Truth and Reconciliation*, Stanford, CA: Stanford University Press, 2010, p. 9.
102. Although I am focused exclusively on the phenomenon of public grief here, the prominence of psychoanalysis as a behavioural science and the entry of the mourning process into political consideration is entirely consistent with Arendt's views about the 'rise of the social' in the modern period, the principal effect of which has been to channel the life process itself into the public realm. Arendt, *The Human Condition*, p. 45.
103. Instructively, the text Loraux cites here is Henri Rousso's *The Vichy Syndrome*. See Loraux, *The Divided City*, p. 154. Both Jon Elster and David Cohen draw similar parallels between the rule of the Thirty, installed by Sparta, and the Vichy regime, installed by Germany. See Elster, *Closing the Books*, p. 10 and Cohen, 'The Rhetoric of Justice', pp. 341, 356.
104. See B. Vivian, *Public Forgetting: The Rhetoric and Politics of Beginning Again*, University Park, PA: Penn State University Press, 2010, p. 43.
105. See H. Rousso, *The Vichy Syndrome, The Vichy Syndrome: History and Memory in France since 1944*, Cambridge, MA: Harvard University Press, 1991, pp. 49–54.
106. Rousso, *The Vichy Syndrome*, p. 113.

122 The Penitent State

107. As a former resistant argued before a Senate committee on cultural affairs in 1971, the film 'destroys myths that the people of France still need'. For a discussion of this episode, see Rousso, *The Vichy Syndrome* (the quote above appears at p. 110); and D. Rieff, *In Praise of Forgetting: Historical Memory and Its Ironies*, New Haven, CT: Yale University Press, 2016, p. 85.
108. As Paloma Aguilar has noted, the pact of forgetting quickly established itself as a paradigm, with amnesty often being referred to simply as the 'Spanish model'. See P. Aguilar, 'Justice, Politics and Memory in the Spanish Transition' in A. Barahona de Brito, C. Enriquez, and P. Aguilar (eds.), *The Politics of Memory: Transitional Justice in Democratising Societies*, Oxford: Oxford University Press, 2001, p. 93; T.G. Ash, 'The Truth about Dictatorship', *The New York Review of Books*, February 1998, pp. 3–5; and Rieff, *In Praise of Forgetting*, pp. 122–126.
109. Aguilar, 'Justice, Politics and Memory in the Spanish Transition', p. 103.
110. As Aguilar writes in the conclusion to her book, 'It was a question of forgetting the resentments of the past, of "wiping the slate clean" for all, of retaining the lessons of history without stirring up the past, in order to be able to build a future of democratic peace and harmony together.' P. Aguilar, *Memory and Amnesia: The Role of the Spanish Civil War in the Transition to Democracy*, trans. by Mark Oakley, New York: Berghahn Books, 2002, p. 269.
111. Aguilar, 'Justice, Politics and Memory in the Spanish Transition', p. 97.
112. Ash, in fact, comes down in favour of truth telling or what he calls 'history lessons' as the best way of dealing with a troubled past (a point I return to later in this chapter). See Ash, 'The Truth about Dictatorship', p. 15.
113. D. Rieff, *Against Remembrance*, Carlton: Melbourne University Press, 2011, p. 127.
114. Rieff, *Against Remembrance*, p. 46.
115. P. Bruckner, *The Tyranny of Guilt: An Essay on Western Masochism*, Princeton, NJ: Princeton University Press, 2010, pp. 162–163.
116. Rieff, *In Praise of Forgetting*, p. 87.
117. Rieff, *In Praise of Forgetting*, p. 122.
118. According to Primo Levi, 'The failure to divulge the truth about the Lagers represents one of the major collective crimes of the German people.' He goes on to suggest that 'the entire history of the brief "millennial Reich" can be reread as a war against memory'. P. Levi, *The Drowned and the Saved*, London: Penguin Books, 1988, pp. 4, 18.
119. T. Adorno, 'What Does Coming to Terms with the Past Mean?' in G. Hartmann, *Bitburg in Moral and Political Perspective*, Bloomington, IN: Indiana University Press, 1986, p. 117.
120. P. Ricoeur, *Figuring the Sacred: Religion, Narrative, Imagination*, Minneapolis, MN: Fortress Press, 1995, p. 290. The same point has recently been reiterated by Sara Ahmed. See S. Ahmed, *The Cultural Politics of Emotion*, Edinburgh: Edinburgh University Press, p. 33.
121. H. Arendt, *The Origins of Totalitarianism*, San Diego, CA: Harcourt Brace, 1976, p. 459. Bradford Vivian can be taken as representative of contemporary ethics when he notes that 'Twenty-first-century liberal democratic societies rightly pride themselves for their informed aversion to such totalitarian rites of collective forgetting.' See B. Vivian, *Public Forgetting: The Rhetoric and Politics of Beginning Again*, University Park, PA: Penn State University Press, 2010, p. 63.

New Life   123

122. Habermas' two key interventions into the *Historikerstreit* were later collected in a special edition of *New German Critique*. See J. Habermas, 'A Kind of Settlement of Damages', *New German Critique*, 44, 1988, pp. 25–40; and J. Habermas, 'Concerning the Public Use of History', *New German Critique*, 44, 1988, pp. 40–51. For a summary of this debate, see R.C. Holub, *Jurgen Habermas: Critic in the Public Sphere*, London: Routledge, 1991, pp. 162–189.
123. Habermas, 'Concerning the Public Use of History', p. 44.
124. Habermas, *A Berlin Republic: Writings on Germany*, trans. by Steven Rendall, Cambridge: Polity Press, 1998, p. 17.
125. Whether that is what forgetting does *in every instance* is up for debate. As Bradford Vivian has noted, erasure of unpalatable truths is not the only form public forgetting can take. Political communities can also enlist forgetting in the name of counter-histories. In this vein one might, for instance, call for a forgetting of Shakespeare's epic history so that other narratives, less focused on the seat of sovereignty, can find a place in the collective memory. See Vivian, *Public Forgetting*, pp. 46–60.
126. As Martha Minow writes, 'A common formulation posits the two dangers of wallowing in the past and forgetting it. Too much memory or not enough; too much enshrinement of victimhood or insufficient memorialization of victims and survivors; too much past or too little acknowledgement of the past's staging of the present; these joined dangers accompany not just societies emerging from mass violence, but also individuals recovering from trauma.' M. Minow, *Between Vengeance and Forgiveness*, Boston, MA: Beacon Press, 1998, p. 2.
127. D. Shriver, 'Where and When in Political Life is Justice Served by Forgiveness?', p. 31.
128. 'Is memory necessarily a good thing?', questions Tzvetan Todorov, 'Is forgetting always a curse?' The answer, as can perhaps already be anticipated from the way the questions are framed, is no. 'Memory', as he later affirms, 'is neither good nor bad in itself'—everything depends upon 'the uses we make of the past' and the 'manner in which we reminisce'. T. Todorov, *Hope and Memory*, London: Atlantic Books, 2005, pp. 3, 160–161.
129. Booth, 'Communities of Memory', p. 259.
130. Rousso, *The Vichy Syndrome*, p. 100.
131. Rousso, *The Vichy Syndrome*, p. 104.
132. Rousso, *The Vichy Syndrome*, p. 58. In a similar vein, Timothy Garton Ash has noted 'successful democracies such as postwar France have been built on a conscious policy of forgetting, although at a cost, which often has not shown up until a generation later' and Mark Amstutz has claimed 'France's failure to confront the collaboration of the Vichy government with the Nazis in the aftermath of World War II has left a festering wound in the French nation that has still not healed'. See Ash, 'The Truth about Dictatorship', p. 15; and Amstutz, *The Healing of Nations: The Promise and Limits of Political Forgiveness*, Lanham, MD: Rowman and Littlefield, 2005, p. 21.
133. Rousso, *The Vichy Syndrome*, p. 133.
134. M. Davis, 'Is Spain Recovering Its Memory? Breaking the *Pacto del Olvido*', *Human Rights Quarterly*, 27(3), 2005, p. 867.
135. Davis, 'Is Spain Recovering Its Memory?', p. 879.
136. Davis, 'Is Spain Recovering Its Memory?', p. 880. See also Ignacio Fernández de Mata, 'Sin Carries the Penance: The Spanish Civil War's Conflicts of Guilt and Justice' in K.

Chainoglou, B. Collins, M. Phillips, and J. Strawson (eds.), *Injustice, Memory and Faith in Human Rights*, London: Routledge, 2018, p. 89.
137. Thus Edkins: 'What has been forgotten—subjugated knowledges—like the memory of past traumas, returns to haunt the structures of power that instigated the violence in the first place. Trauma is that which refuses to take its place in history as done and finished with.' Edkins, *Trauma and the Memory of Politics*, p. 59.
138. R. Comay, 'Resistance and Repetition: Freud and Hegel', *Research in Phenomenology*, Spring 2015.
139. See D. La Capra, *Writing History, Writing Trauma*, Baltimore, MD: The Johns Hopkins University Press, 2001, p. 21.
140. See, for instance, M. Amstutz, *The Healing of Nations*, p. viii.
141. D. Tutu, 'Interview', *Index on Censorship*, 5, 1996, p. 39. His reference to South Africa as 'a house divided against itself' appears in Tutu, *No Future without Forgiveness*, pp. 155–156.
142. In the sentence that proceeds the one just quoted, Tutu responds to the suggestion of a national amnesia by saying 'you have to keep saying to those people that to pretend that nothing happened, to not acknowledge that something horrendous did happen to them, is to victimize the victims yet again'. Tutu, 'Interview', p. 39.
143. 'The ordinary response to atrocities', claimed Judith Lewis Herman, 'is to banish them from consciousness.' Yet, as she goes on to note, atrocities 'refuse to be buried': '[e]qually as powerful as the desire to deny atrocities is the conviction that denial does not work'. Herman, *Trauma and Recovery*, New York: Basic Books, 1992, p. 1. Later in the text she writes: 'At some point the memory of the trauma is bound to return, demanding attention' (p. 174).
144. The allusion is to P. Rieff, *The Triumph of the Therapeutic: Uses of Faith after Freud*, New York: Harper and Row, 1966.
145. This is, of course, the central message of one of Freud's most famous essays. See S. Freud, 'Remembering, Repeating and Working-Through', *Collected Works*, standard edition, pp. 147–156.
146. Lifton, 'Introduction' in Mitscherlichs, *The Inability to Mourn*, trans. by B.R. Placzek. New York: Grove Press, 1975, p. vii.
147. The 'will have to' in the following quote from Amstutz is indicative: 'If the deep political cleavages of society are to be healed and if enemies are to move towards reconciliation, the injuries, crimes, and injustices of the past will have to be confronted through truth telling and acknowledgment.' Amstutz, *The Healing of Nations*, p. 221. It is also perhaps worth noting here that mourning has long been associated with the state of transition, particularly that between death and life. See Holst-Warhaft, *Dangerous Voices*, p. 21.
148. Todorov, *Hope and Memory*, p. 172.
149. Thus, to cite just a few examples, Kaitlin Murphy will champion memorials for their ability to engage viewers 'in a shared process of learning, remembering, mourning and healing'; and Sonali Chakravarti will champion truth commissions on the basis that they 'provide greater opportunities for engaging with traumatic experiences in a politically significant way.' See K.M. Murphy, 'Fear and Loathing in Monuments: Rethinking the Politics and Practices of Monumentality and Monumentalization', *Memory Studies*, 14(6), 2021, pp. 1150, 1152, 1154; Chakravarti, *Sing the Rage: Listening to Anger after Mass Violence*, Chicago, IL: University of Chicago Press, 2014, pp. 49, 50, 55.

150. C. Moon, 'Healing Past Violence: Traumatic Assumption and Therapeutic Interventions in War and Reconciliation', *Journal of Human Rights*, 8, 2009, pp. 71–72.
151. As Minow noted more than twenty years ago, amnesty has been 'wrested from political necessity' and adopted as a 'mechanism for advancing the truth-finding process'. Minow, *Between Vengeance and Forgiveness*, p. 57.
152. Arendt, *The Human Condition*, pp. 28–33, 43–45.
153. Arendt, *The Human Condition*, p. 37.
154. H. Arendt, 'Totalitarian Imperialism: Reflections on the Hungarian Revolution', *The Journal of Politics*, 20(1), 1958, p. 5.
155. See M. Nussbaum, *Political Emotions: Why Love Matters for Justice*, Cambridge, MA: The Belknap Press, 2013, pp. 257–295; J. Butler, *Precarious Life: The Powers of Mourning and Violence*, London: Verso, 2006, pp. 29–30; Edkins, *Trauma and the Memory of Politics*; T. Rosenberg, *The Haunted Land: Facing Europe's Ghosts after Communism*, New York: Random House, 1995; and E. Hutchinson, *Affective Communities in World Politics*, Cambridge: Cambridge University Press, 2016.
156. As he goes on to note, 'Though by no means adequately understood by the Commission or its commentators and critics, the implication was clear: in order to overcome the divisions of the past, in order to make reparation for the violations of the apartheid era, an equally massive joining in mourning would have to take place. Mourning will make good for the violations of the apartheid era. As a system of social separation, apartheid would be undone through condolence.' M. Sanders, 'Remembering Apartheid', *Diacritics*, 32(3/4), 2002, pp. 60, 72.
157. Hutchinson, *Affective Communities in World Politics*, p. 248.
158. Hutchinson, *Affective Communities in World Politics*, p. 229.
159. As Honig has recently noted, the ban imposed upon Phrynichus' *The Capture of Miletus* 'puts some pressure on the common notion that Athenians shed tears at the theatre that they were not allowed to shed elsewhere. Instead, the episode suggests, tragic theatre, this new institution of exception, was also a regulated, disciplined domain within which some subversion was tolerated. Permitted, approved, if still also transgressive, tragic theatre was a relatively safe venue that allowed and even occasioned emotions like, but not the same as, the emotions once solicited by female mourners, some of whom were "professionals", not unlike the actors who performed in dramas'. Honig, *Antigone Interrupted*, p. 103.
160. As Rieff notes, 'it is a psychological truism that an individual's effort to recover his or her memories, whether readily available or repressed, when done properly and seriously in a therapeutic context (Freud's *Durcharbeiten*) can be healing. Unfortunately, this has led to the psychological pop-culture commonplace that to be able to remember a traumatic experience is the necessary first step in coming to terms with it. And the same is now thought to be the case with the collective memories of social groups'. Rieff, *In Praise of Forgetting*, pp. 105–106.
161. Hutchinson, *Affective Communities in World Politics*, p. 245.

3
The Monumentalization of Shame

A Negative Mirror for the People

One of the ways in which political communities establish their identities is through what they put on public display. More than simply sites where honour and glory are bestowed, monuments, memorials, parades, and rituals are places where the polity 'narrates itself', giving expression to where it came from, what it holds dear, and who it imagines itself to be. In them, as in many other forms of public media, remembrance is used not just as a marker of value but as a tool of self-understanding—in effect, the maker of the monuments 'makes the collective' by showing (quite literally) what the people stand for and who they think they are. That all such attempts to reflect the collective back to itself are expressions of power practically goes without saying. Since every allocation of public space or time involves a decision about what to mark as significant, collective memory is always selective memory. Almost without exception (though, as we shall see, there are some notable exceptions), the noble is illumined and the ignoble elided, testifying to the pithy truth that there is no revealing that is not also a concealing, no remembering that is not also a forgetting.[1] Exactly what citizens see and learn about themselves as they wander around the urban landscape is thus far from politically disinterested or historically objective. By and large, the image reflected back to them is a narcissistic one; an image to admire and applaud; a fantasy of innocence and achievement. But, as ever in politics, there are complications aplenty.

Monuments to the nation are built to endure, but they rarely do.[2] Erected at a certain historical moment in honour of 'the best'—the founders, the explorers, the political leaders, the heroic soldiers, and the sporting heroes—they are ever in danger of falling victim to the senseless longevity of rock. Like stone-age men frozen in ice, they remain physically intact long after they have become culturally untimely. Revolutions bring death to monuments in double-quick time because they overturn the table of values used to differentiate the best from the worst, the heroes from the villains. But social evolution can easily do a number on them as well. Unmoved by the changes going on

The Penitent State. Paul Muldoon, Oxford University Press. © Paul Muldoon (2023).
DOI: 10.1093/oso/9780198831624.003.0004

around them, monuments almost invariably reach a point where they lag so far behind social norms they cease to represent (all of) 'the people'. Time strips them of the invisibility enjoyed by everything that fits comfortably into the mainstream and they find themselves standing out once again—only, this time, for all the wrong reasons. None of this, of course, is *necessarily* the fault of the monument, the people who erected it, or the figure(s) it celebrates. Politicized anew for being 'out of time', such monuments can find themselves at the centre of culture wars for the simple reason that the people has become something or *wants to become something* that was not anticipated when they were erected. Monuments that fall (or which are quietly disappeared) are often just the collateral damage of these attempts to reconstitute the people.

That we are currently in the throes of one of these culture wars is only too evident.[3] In the last twenty years or so, social movements arising out of the claims of different identity groups for recognition have politicized the symbols of the nation in a variety of locations, calling attention to their shortcomings as a mirror for the people. Part of the problem from their perspective is the woefully unrepresentative nature of what has been monumentalized. As they rightly point out, looking around the capital cities of Western countries, one could be forgiven for thinking that the people was composed solely of white men or that they were the only ones who had ever done anything worthy of remembrance.[4] Civic recognition does not reflect civic contribution, pointing to a certain shallowness in the process of democratization and an indifference to the detrimental effects of non-recognition.[5] But there is another, perhaps even more psychologically significant, aspect to the problem as well: implicitly or explicitly, it is suggested, many of the existing monuments to the nation provide symbolic endorsements of misogyny, racism, slavery, and colonial appropriation, perpetuating the trauma of groups who have suffered historically from abuses of power.[6] The issue for them, in other words, is not simply that they never see themselves reflected in the pantheon of national heroes; it is also that the injustices committed against them (and the losses they sustained because of them) are nowhere publicly affirmed. At once inconsistent with, and destructive of, the narcissistic fantasy of national innocence and achievement, their experience of persecution and exposure is never, in Sanford Levinson's memorable phrase, 'written in stone'.[7] On the contrary, the reality of their suffering is denied and the trauma of betrayal repeats.

One should hardly wonder, then, at the so-called aesthetics of rage that has inspired the recent 'Rhodes Must Fall' campaign in South Africa, the 'Cook Must Fall' campaign in Australia, and numerous other acts of resistance against the authorized symbols of the nation: the burning of flags, the graffitiing of statues, the disputes over contentious dates, and the campaigns to rename (streets, buildings, districts, festivals, and even entire nations).[8] Assuming that what the psychoanalysts say is true, and the recovery of the survivors hinges on their experience of betrayal being confirmed through public recognition, tearing down the symbols of oppression might be one way to prevent the trauma from perpetually repeating itself. An urban landscape denuded of public tributes to the rapists, the anti-Semites, the slave traders, and the colonizers would at least be a landscape in which the wronged are not confronted daily with the indifference of mainstream society to their suffering. For the victims, or so it would seem, each 'fall' marks a step towards recovery. And yet, there is also a sense in which the removal of those reminders of indifference is only that: a first step. As Herman and other trauma specialists have noted, a truly *restorative* justice, one that rebuilds the survivors' sense of order and willingness to trust, would be one in which the political community actively recognizes the wounds inflicted by the wrong (and goes some way towards healing them) by creating sites where the victims and the perpetrators can come together in shared mourning.

It is in this context that I propose to examine one of those exceptions alluded to earlier that display the ignoble rather than the noble: the Berlin Memorial to the Murdered Jews of Europe which was opened to the public in 2005 after ten years of rancorous debate and two project competitions. Designed by Peter Eisenman (with the assistance of the artist Richard Serra), the Memorial is a physically imposing, vaguely ominous assembly of black pillars (*stelae*) occupying 19,000 square metres in the centre of the city. Overflowing with pathos, it looks, on first impressions, to have dealt sensitively and successfully with what Henry Pickford has called the 'unique complications' that attend a nation's attempt to erect 'a memorial to a people its earlier government had sought to eradicate'.[9] Symbolically located in the restored capital after the reunification of East and West, the Memorial effectively declares to all that the great crime of the German nation, the crime from which its critics say it has been perpetually in flight, will be hidden no more.[10] What more by way of repentance could be asked of it? As powerful as it may be, however, the temptation to simply celebrate the Memorial as 'united Germany's ultimate apology for the Holocaust'[11] needs to be tempered by an analysis of the way it functions as yet one more attempt at coming to terms. At once a declaration of responsibility for the future ('never again Auschwitz') and a site of mourning about the past, the Memorial both signifies politically *and* intervenes biopolitically. The judgement we pass upon it is thus at least in part dependent upon the work we take it to be doing not just as an operation *of* but also as an operation *upon* memory. Does the field of *stelae* create a space for mourning and reflection, giving rise, as Eisenman hoped, to an experience 'that cannot be psychologically assimilated with ease', or is it rather, as one commentator suggested, 'a band aid for the open wound of the Holocaust'?[12]

I A Matter of Identity (and Trauma)

Memorials to the war dead are, of course, nothing new. They are one of the most common ways in which nations ground their identity and foster a sense of loyalty and devotion among citizens. Almost without exception, however, they are erected in honour of those courageous soldiers who embody the spirit of the collective by making the ultimate sacrifice for their country: the heroes/victims of war. The Memorial to the Murdered Jews breaks this time-honoured mould by exposing and 'centring' (symbolically and geographically) one of the greatest injustices ever committed by a sovereign people—an injustice so diabolical that the concept of crimes against humanity is now forever associated with it. In principle, as Dominic La Capra has noted, there is no decisive reason why a 'negative event' cannot be 'sacralized and turned into the basis of an identity'.[13] But for obvious reasons, injustices (and especially injustices on the scale of the Shoah) are more easily sacralized by victims than they are by perpetrators.[14] Inhuman in their aspiration to erase from the earth, wars of extermination are always bad wars and never more so than when they are waged at home against innocent people. Who would stake their identity upon them? It should come as no great surprise, then, that a conservative like Martin Wasler should have decried the erection of the Memorial, declaring it a 'nightmare the size of a football field' dedicated to the 'monumentalisation of our shame'.[15]

Putting aside for the moment the issue of whether it is right for the Germans to speak of nightmares, an obvious question imposes itself: what possible interest is served by forcing a nation to confront the unspeakable truth of its crime against humanity every day anew? For the victims the matter appears, at least on first impressions, fairly straightforward: with political recognition comes ontological security or at least the promise of it. If Jean Amery speaks for all survivors, it is an open question whether the Jews will ever feel safe in Germany again: 'nothing', he wrote, 'can again lull me into the slumber of security from which I awoke in 1935'.[16] In the wake of such an egregious betrayal, the only protection he felt able to rely upon was the amour of resentment.[17] But that is not to say survivors see no value in public gestures that confront the truth and make public declarations of 'never again'.[18] After the assault upon Jewish life that culminated in the Final Solution, the silence of the German community could only resound in one of two ways: either as indifference or threat. Speaking out is the bare minimum the perpetrating community could do by way of reassurance and the *stelae* field speaks all the more loudly for speaking in the same terms as another survivor of the Shoah, Bruno Bettelheim, once did: 'the Nazis murdered the Jews of Europe'.[19] Without that solemn declaration of a monstrous crime, the alienated remainders of the genocide might fairly conclude that their lives mattered no more now than they did then. What would there be to say they wouldn't do it again?

For the perpetrating community, though, the effect would appear to be quite the opposite: diminished self-regard and an enduring sense of shame. Defending the national honour is, to be sure, the business of conservatives, so it is little wonder that they should have offered endless variations on the same basic theme: 'one can't erect a monument to one's own shame'.[20] But that does not mean references to the Memorial as an instance of 'negative nationalism' were without justification or wider endorsement.[21] A point made by Christian Maier in the context of the Bitburg controversy would appear to be equally applicable here: one does not need to be an ageing war veteran or unrepentant party comrade 'to believe *Mea Culpa* [is] unbecoming as a national motto'.[22] *Mea culpa* would, however, appear to be precisely the motto the Bundestag had in mind when it passed its official resolution on 25 June 1999:

> with the memorial we intend to honour the murdered victims, keep alive the memory of those inconceivable events in German history, and admonish all future generations never again to violate human rights, to defend the democratic constitutional state at all times, to secure equality before the law for all people and to resist all forms of dictatorship and regimes based on violence.[23]

It is not necessary to reject the proposition that 'we are all Germans now' to see this as a singularly powerful expression of that reorientation in public memory according to which the celebration of heroes gives way to the recognition of victims. Indeed, if memorials really are like mirrors, reflecting the nation back to itself, that to the murdered Jews deserves to be counted as one of the most arresting of all because the only image it seems to offer the Germans is that of murderer. Little wonder that some citizens baulked at the idea of having to look into it forevermore. Does not that giant *stelae* field permanently foreclose on the possibility of redemption by taking that unassimilable breach in the national narrative and writing it in stone?

Maybe. But we ought not be too quick to conclude that it offers nothing by way of healing and/or reconciliation. In his remarkable essay 'The

Finger of Blame'—an essay so fecund as to warrant extensive analysis—Jürgen Habermas again takes issue with conservative resentment towards the commemoration of the Shoah, defending the Memorial to the Murdered Jews as a necessary gesture of collective repentance.[24] As difficult to swallow (or digest) as it may be, he argues, the Germans had no choice but to accept the break in their national tradition that the Memorial acknowledges and, in effect, enshrines if they wished to recover their political legitimacy. As we will soon discover, however, the value of this essay does not simply lie in its defence of the *stelae* field as a symbolic marker of a disastrous turn in German history and the responsibility that turn places on citizens to reject atavistic forms of nationalism and embrace the cosmopolitan ethos of human rights. It consists also in its articulation of a communally regenerative politics of mourning. Although Habermas can scarcely be regarded as a theorist of biopolitics, 'The Finger of Blame' clearly situates the Memorial to the Murdered Jews (and acts of collective memory more generally) in relation to life as well as legitimacy. In it, public gestures of remembrance emerge not simply as declarations of identity written solemnly in stone but as acts of solidarity performed expressively in mourning. Without perhaps intending to, in other words, Habermas sketches a biopolitics worthy of endorsement in which the shared life of the new, cosmopolitan community is built upon a shared grief for its old national victims. Later in the chapter we will look more closely at the emotional/psychological effects engendered by the Memorial in order to ascertain whether it really does contribute to the new, post-national, form of life Habermas envisages. To begin with, however, we need to come to an understanding of how he figures its significance as a both a form of political communication and a site of collective mourning.

One of the things to which Habermas clearly takes exception in 'The Finger of Blame' is the idea that the Memorial represents the German people in an unbecoming way. For him, there was nothing in it that was suggestive of self-loathing. The only reason why the Bundestag had, yet again, decided to expose the Germans to their shameful history was to announce a break with the past and redefine the civic self in a more inclusive, more cosmopolitan, way. Only, he suggested, by not hiding the truth or, to be more precise, hiding *from* the truth could citizens make it clear to the world and themselves that the reunited Germany was not (and had no intention of becoming) that kind of country again. The Memorial to the Murdered Jews was, in that sense, no different from the countless other measures taken by the Germans in the post-war period, beginning with the Basic Law of 1949, which testified to the fact that they had not shirked the responsibility of 'never again Auschwitz'. If it acquired a special significance for Habermas as a public gesture of atonement, it was simply because its physical location and material presence within the new capital turned it into 'a *permanent* source of disquiet and admonition' (emphasis added).[25] By writing the genocide in stone and placing it in the heart of Berlin, the *stelae* field would forever remove the possibility of 'looking away'. Indeed, built on such a scale and located in such a position that no one could pretend not to see, it deserved, in his view, to be regarded as a 'manifestly future-oriented sign of a purified German collective identity'.[26]

Inevitably anyone who evokes the concept of purification in this context runs the risk of raising fears of an undeserved redemption (measured against what criteria and granted by what authority?). But Habermas is not saying, or, at least, I do not take him to be saying, that the Memorial to the Murdered Jews cleanses Germany of its sins. His point is rather that it reflects a conscious commitment to purge itself of the underlying *cause* of those sins: the insular nationalism of the Nazi period that saw the political community divided into racial friends and enemies. Understood properly, he suggested, the *stelae* field was but the latest expression of the bond the German *Kulturnation* had begun to forge with 'universalistic constitutional principles' as a result of its 'long-delayed public reflection on the systematic exclusion and expulsion of all those officially stigmatized as "internal enemies"'.[27] By recognizing (and in the most emphatic way) that systematic exclusion and expulsion as an injustice, the Memorial helped to 'reaffirm the identity of a nation committed to civil rights in a version appropriate to [its] history'.[28] In contrast to his conservative interlocutors, in other words, Habermas assumes the *stelae* field looks forwards rather than backwards. If it returned the political community to the crimes of the past, it was not in order to mire it in shame but to consolidate its legitimacy by making an emphatic statement about what it now is or would like to become. The community it addressed itself to or which, better still, it sought to elicit was not the old national one based upon racial difference but a new cosmopolitan one based upon universal rights.[29]

Habermas' support for the Memorial is thus based less on its aesthetic merits (though he does not disparage those either) than on what he takes it to be 'saying' about the German national identity. Without labouring the symbolic echo between the *stelae* field and a graveyard or making the logical inference that it functions as a site of national mourning, his argument about its politically transformative message implicitly encourages us to 'read' it in relation not simply to one but to two 'deaths'. Firstly, and most obviously, it marks the death of those who were abandoned by the law and exposed to sovereign violence as 'internal enemies'. Unique, according to Habermas, among the many tributes paid in stone to the 'war dead', that to the murdered Jews honours those who fell victim to a domestic killing machine rather than a foreign war machine. Part tribute, part accusation, it commemorates those who died for nothing and, in doing so, admonishes those who killed them for nothing. To think of the Memorial as a form of political communication in the way that Habermas suggests is, however, to recognize that another passing is being signified as well. At the same time that it marks the unhappy death of countless victims of sovereign aggression, it marks the happy death of a civic self founded upon the principles of 'blood and soil', the *jus sanguineous* and the *jus soli*.[30] As a demonstration of a commitment to universalistic constitutional principles (that is, to the natural rights of *all*), the Memorial effectively lays down a new, post-unification dividing line in Germany—no longer that between East and West but that between the 'conventional' (insular) and the 'post-conventional' (universal) nation. Simply by virtue of its presence in the capital, it testified to an insight into the destructive potential of the nation-state and the need to check its tendency towards reductive friend–enemy distinctions—an insight, Habermas hoped, the Germans would never again lose sight of.[31]

That Habermas should take such a position on the Memorial to the Murdered Jews is entirely to be expected. Building on the seminal work of Karl Jaspers and Theodor Adorno, he has long insisted that the task of 'working off' a politically compromised past carries obligations at three different levels: the existential, the legal, and the ethical-political. Alongside the duty which falls to every individual to work through their moral guilt, and to the institutions of the state to prosecute punishable acts, the citizens of the political community are required to collectively answer for their violations of human dignity.[32] Although it does little more than distinguish between individual and collective agents, the critical effect of this tripartite framework is to extend (and potentially without limit) the time frame for 'coming to terms'; for, while the first and second dimensions of this 'working off' relate to conscience and law, respectively, limiting accountability to acts and omissions done at the time, the third is a matter of identity and thus something for which *every* citizen, regardless of whether they were 'early' or 'late' born, is responsible.[33] The merit of the Memorial in this context for Habermas lay precisely in the fact that it testified to the willingness on the part of the current generation (the later-born or *Nachgeborenen*) to take on this ethical-political task and fulfil the requirements of 'working off' despite the fact they had not been personally involved in Nazi crimes. Indicative, in his view, of an ethical desire to take responsibility for the darkest chapter of their history and reconstitute the political order accordingly, the *stelae* field gave proof that they understood the burden laid upon them by the past and were not afraid to discharge it by giving public expression to an honest collective self-understanding.[34]

To read the Memorial in the way that Habermas suggests (namely, as 'a matter of identity') is, then, to make agency, intention, and message the critical issues. As he is at pains to explain to those concerned about the artificiality of the work, no such statement about the cosmopolitan turn in the German *Kulturnation* could have been delivered simply by the preservation of those putatively more authentic sites such as Bergen-Belsen and Auschwitz that the Nazis inadvertently left behind. Although clearly significant in their own right as sites of memory, the concentration camps were more like (unintentional) historical deposits than (intentional) cultural objects. 'Only a memorial', he wrote, 'can attest to the will and message of its sponsors. And only an uncompromising form of art can provide it with an appropriate language.'[35] Akin, in other words, to Brandt's *Kniefall*, only this time collectively endorsed through the Bundestag, the Memorial to the Murdered Jews not only enabled but was itself also an expression of coming to terms because it deliberately brought back the guilty sovereign and set it before the world in an aesthetic medium (in this case, that of the 'plastic arts') in order to make a very public declaration about the fact that the Germans had no intention of exploiting the moment of reunification to bury their history. If it turned to the abstract, formal language of modern art, it was not, according to Habermas (here in complete agreement with James Young and Peter Eisenman), because they wanted to evade the horror of the Shoah but because abstraction provided 'the best protection against embarrassing trivialization'.[36]

Habermas can hardly be faulted for treating the Memorial as a matter of identity. For how could this mirror not reflect the way the German people know themselves and want others to know them? And yet, the more closely one reads the 'The Finger of Blame', the more apparent it becomes that there is more at stake in the *stelae* field than just self-understanding. Somewhat inevitably, the problem of trauma intrudes into the discussion, drawing our attention to the fact the issue at stake is not only what the Memorial says about the German national identity but what it does to (or perhaps for) the German national psyche. One trauma that scarcely needs to be mentioned here because it provides the inspiration for the Memorial is, of course, the trauma of those 'stigmatized as internal enemies' and turned into targets of 'exclusion and expulsion'. That is the unspeakable trauma for which there really are no words and that Habermas, out of respect, dares only allude to. But there is another one too which Habermas, his lack of sympathy for it notwithstanding, is unable to ignore: the trauma of a broken civic tradition, 'inflicted' upon the Germans by the fact that the Shoah refuses to fade in memory. In a revealing allusion to the alimentary metaphor Nietzsche uses in his musings on memory as illness, Habermas describes conservative resentment towards the Memorial as 'the gasses of an undigested past which emanate periodically from the stomach of the Federal Republic'.[37] As in Nietzsche's *Genealogy of Morals*, trauma is figured here as that which cannot be processed or worked through, as that which is, in other words, psychically indigestible. Like it or not, he notes, there are Germans who simply cannot stomach the Shoah.

Habermas' discussion of the Memorial follows the same logic that informs all of his work on the German question by indicating that civic memory can (and ought to) do some work in relation to each of these traumas. Thus a new register, one relating more to health than identity, emerges in which memorialization is revealed in what might be fairly described as its 'biopolitical dimension'. As readers of his interventions into the German history wars (*Historikerstreit*) will know, Habermas has long insisted upon a duty of memory/mourning as both an unconditional moral responsibility (a weak, though still vital, way of showing solidarity with the victims of German aggression) *and* a means by which to make the life context of Germany 'liveable' for the Jews. 'Is it not possible to say in general terms', he once wrote, 'the less communality such a collective life-context allowed internally and the more it maintained itself by usurping and destroying the lives of others, the greater then is the burden of reconciliation, task of mourning, and the self-critical scrutiny of subsequent generations.'[38] 'The Finger of Blame' preserves this imperative, with the Memorial receiving Habermas' endorsement in part because of its positive impact upon the 'collective life context'. Self-evidently an attempt to take on the 'burden of reconciliation', fulfil the 'task of mourning', and engage in 'self-critical scrutiny', he adjudges it as one of those rare exercises in civic memory which, in his words, 'make a shared life possible, even bearable, for the other side'.[39] Habermas, to his credit, never claims that the Memorial will (or should) be healing for the Jews. But the distinction he draws between the bearable and the unbearable life points to his longstanding belief that acts of public memory can have a critical impact not just on the political identity of the nation but on the psychic lives of its citizens. Indeed, by making shared grief the condition of a shared life, he reinforces an earlier claim about the power of public memory to impact survivors at the most basic biological level of all; namely, their ability to breathe:

> There is an obligation we in Germany have—even if no one else is prepared to take it upon themselves any longer—to keep alive the memory of the suffering of those murdered at the hands of Germans, and we must keep this memory alive quite openly and not just in our minds. These dead have above all a claim to the weak anamnestic power of solidarity which those born after can now only practice

The Monumentalization of Shame   137

through the medium of memory which is always being renewed, which may often be desperate, but which is at any rate active and circulating. If we disregard this Benjaminian legacy, Jewish fellow citizens and certainly the sons, the daughters and the grandchildren of the murdered victims would no longer be able to breathe in our country.[40]

With regards to that other trauma, caused by the enduring legacy of the Shoah and the loss of continuity in the German national tradition that it entails, Habermas takes a rather different position. 'The Finger of Blame' is, to be sure, by no means lacking in appreciation of just how traumatic it is for the Germans (or at least some of them) that the Shoah refuses to disappear.[41] Just as in Nietzsche, where indigestion is, archetypically, the disorder that afflicts the 'man of *ressentiment*'—the man who, being too impotent to either exact his revenge or forget his insults, suffers from a memory in the mind as one would a stone in the belly—Habermas ties opposition to the Memorial and its 'monumentalisation of shame' back to a deep-seated resentment about the fact that the past refuses to pass and the old German *Kulturnation*, with its venerable traditions, remains an object of perennial suspicion. And yet, consistent with his entire corpus of work on coming to terms, Habermas insists no quarter be given to those who assume the role of government is to alleviate a burdensome historical consciousness by 'reestablishing German continuities' and 'laundering' the past.[42] Seen from his perspective, the Germans had no choice but to accept their disturbing political responsibility 'as an element of a fractured national identity'.[43] 'The break in the continuity of our sustaining traditions', he maintained, 'is the precondition for recovering our self-respect.'[44]

It would not be unreasonable to conclude from this that Habermas' support for the Memorial is built as much upon the way it denies healing for the wounded narcissism of the perpetrators as it provides it for the wounded faith of the victims. Built to stand in perpetuity, the stelae field effectively ensures that the 'open wound of the Holocaust' will remain forever open, denying the 'man of *ressentiment*', the man, in this case, aggrieved by the loss of national honour, the palliative of forgetting. Denial of comfort is, it seems, the one kind of denial to which Habermas happily gives his blessing. Resentment among the Germans is, on his account, simply one of 'the sentiments we wish to overcome' and for which the Memorial, as an uncompromising statement of an unpalatable truth, can 'serve as a barometer'.[45] While acutely conscious of the fact that it had traditionally been in the nature of state symbolism to mollify, he was of the view that in *this* instance (the erection of *Neue Wache* being an altogether different matter) a confrontation with the past had been staged that prevented defensive displacement. Unlike the triumphalist war monuments of old that 'directed the visitor's gaze to the nation's dead', he suggested, the Memorial to the Murdered Jews would focus the public's attention on those it had 'turned into aliens', 'repudiated as enemies', and 'humiliated as subhumans'.[46] Its explicit purpose was not to placate or redeem but to reproach and admonish. However much it was to be expected, therefore, resentment in the face of it would only prove how far the Germans had yet to travel before they arrived at that honest self-understanding needed to join the other in mourning and build a shared life.

On closer examination, however, it becomes evident that Habermas assigns the Memorial a far greater role in the psychic life of the Germans than simply the denial of their ease and comfort. As damning as he is of the desire for normalization (that is, of the 'defusing' or 'laundering' of the past), he sketches more or less the same relationship between uncovering and recovering, the exposure of the crime and the restoration of the self, as the Mitscherlichs. In truth, he notes in 'The Finger of Blame', it is only those concerned with the image *others* form of the Germans who worry about the 'mark of shame'. In their resentment towards the Memorial, they testified to the narcissism of the insecure nationalist whose love of country always looks elsewhere for reassurance. By contrast, those interested in the image German citizens retrospectively formed *of themselves* were able to accept the Memorial as something 'which enable[d] them to look each other in the face'.[47] For Habermas, in other words, it was not the 'looking at' but rather the 'looking away from' the crime that was responsible for the lingering sense of discomfort German citizens felt in each other's presence. Only, he implied, when the offence was always in view (which is another way of saying only when no attempt was made to displace it) would they cease to feel the need to wander around with downcast eyes. The *sotto voce* psychological message here is hard to miss: now consciously in charge of their own history, the Germans would no longer be paralysed by the inner conflict created when their self-image remained dependent upon keeping the skeletons hidden in the closet. Regardless of what others saw, they would understand that the image being reflected back to them was not that of 'murderers' but that of 'murderers no more'.

Without being explicitly biopolitical, then, Habermas' analysis of the Memorial is irreducibly hybrid in the way it criss-crosses the juridical and medical registers. Coming to terms is shown to be as much a psychological de-cathecting process as it is an identity re-forming process, as much about recreating the conditions of a shared life through a process of collective mourning as it is about regaining political legitimacy through a commitment to universal principles. For the survivors, there is the belated recognition of their life as grievable—a recognition that reduces fears of repetition and makes it possible to breathe easier. To them, the Memorial does not just say you were unlawfully harmed; it says your existence is no less valuable, no less deserving of lamentation in death and protection in life than any other existence. You will never be abandoned by the law again and suffer what Bettelheim, prefiguring Habermas, called the 'cutting off of Jewish breathing space'.[48] For the perpetrators there is the public admission of their actions as criminal—an admission that alleviates the paralysis of intra-psychic conflict and makes it possible to sleep easier. With them, the incorporation of the Memorial into Berlin becomes symbolic of the incorporation of the Shoah into consciousness. Finally brought into the open and exposed to the light of day, the crime against humanity is rendered available for reflection and integration, depriving it of the ability to trouble the Germans quite so much at night. Paradoxically enough, in other words, it is the erection of the Memorial that allows the Germans to escape the unconscious hold of the Shoah, freeing them of precisely that sense of shame conservatives feared it would set in cement.

The fear that inevitably arises here is that the Memorial does much more by way of healing for the Germans than it does for the Jews. Are they not the ultimate beneficiaries of this clearing of the air? Is it not them, rather than the Jews, who are freed of their nightmares? The answer, as we will see in section II, is quite possibly yes. However, if we follow Habermas in his reading of things, the Memorial to the Murdered Jews would still seem, *in principle*, to qualify as an expression of an affirmative biopolitics because it marks a break from the Germany that maintained itself by usurping and destroying the lives of others. If he is right about what the *stelae* field communicates, the condition upon which it becomes life-enhancing for the Jews and Germans alike is the condition of repentance. As his remarks on the transformation of the *Kulturnation* underline, it is only because the Memorial symbolizes a remorseful acceptance of responsibility and a commitment to cosmopolitan reconstitution—a commitment, that is, to a wholesale re-evaluation of the friend–enemy distinction which lead to the Shoah—that it clears the way for the shared mourning that founds the shared life. Had it not testified to this political rupture, or, as Habermas once put it, to a decisive break from the 'traditions and forms of existence which have been poisoned by inexpressible crimes',[49] there would have been no real assurance of 'never again' and its value as a harbinger of a new, cosmopolitan form of existence in which the Jews can breathe freely would have been dramatically undercut. In short, the mourning that the Memorial enables can be regarded as affirmative in a biopolitical sense because it entails a reflection upon (and a letting go of) those national traditions that inhibit solidarity.

A crucial question thus arises: how confident can we be that the Memorial will contribute to that kind of emotional/reflective experience? Will it induce a mourning process in which German citizens not only express their unconditional solidarity with the victims by grieving for their loss but also withdraw their libidinal investment in the *Kulturnation* that sustained itself by usurping and destroying the lives of others? Will it, in other words, focus sufficient critical attention on the friend–enemy distinction to build the cosmopolitan form of life that would allow the Jews (and all those others once deemed unworthy of life) the space to breathe? It is important to recall here that Habermas' conclusions about the political import of the Memorial are based largely upon his assessment of the intentions behind it, rather than the reactions engendered by it. In his Kantian-inflected analysis, reason and purpose dominate experience and aesthetics. In a post-traditional society like Germany, where collective memory has been 'drawn into the current of reflection', the effect a memorial has on its national audience will, he suggests, ultimately depend upon the 'reservoir of reasons that led to its erection'.[50] Put simply, understanding and affect, dislodged from tradition, have become dependent on knowing why.[51] However, even Habermas concedes that there is an affective, non-rational surplus to every symbolic representation that bears upon the cultural memory of the nation. Indeed, in speaking of the 'pathos of the negative' in the 'stelae field', he implicitly acknowledges what others have also observed: the capacity of such memorials to be powerfully affecting.[52] The issue that his essay leaves open, therefore, is how this pathos impacts upon the critical intent of the Memorial in encouraging the Germans to withdraw the psychic investment they have made in the insular nation-state and reinvest it in constitutional patriotism. Will the Memorial induce the reflective experience that Habermas assumes, guiding visitors to a post-conventional identity, or will it rather induce a psychologically easing, but politically sterile, emotional discharge?

In 2003, several years before the Memorial to the Murdered Jews was opened, Alison Lewis was already posing the question of its effect on the 'psychic life of the nation': 'will the monument encourage memory and remorse, or will it facilitate a form of collective catharsis?'[53] Lewis' presentation of the issue is arguably far too Manichean. On her account, there are only two options: either the Memorial symbolizes an ethical remorse that brings pain *to* the Germans or it facilitates a psychic catharsis that relieves the pain *of* the Germans. As my analysis of 'The Finger of Blame' shows, repentance can relieve (and justifiably so) if it is linked to the creation of a form of life (namely, cosmopolitanism) that does not maintain itself by usurping and destroying the lives of others. That is not to say, however, that Lewis is wrong to raise the possibility of an emotional catharsis divorced from any kind of political reconstitution. Clearly it is not possible to fully control the way in which memorials are used by the public and that to the murdered Jews has generated its fair share of what might be regarded as inappropriate activity (jumping across the *stelae*, games of hide and seek, selfies that jar with the solemnity of the site, and so on). Trivialization, it seems, has come despite the protection afforded against it by the medium of abstract art.[54] And yet, through their spatial organization, their aesthetic properties, and their minimalist inscriptions, abstract memorials like that to the murdered Jews clearly do favour—if they do not, in fact, seek to elicit—certain kinds of experience and emotions. Inclined, as Quentin Stevens has noted, to be 'sunken rather than raised, void rather than solid, dark rather than light, dispersed rather than spatially concentrated', they have a tendency to evoke sadness, grief, and an abiding sense of death.[55] The issue that remains to be explored, then, is how this symbolization of death actually plays out in political and emotional terms. Exactly what impact does the Memorial to the Murdered Jews have upon the civic trauma it returns to the public sphere through its representation in stone?[56]

II Symbols of Death and Sites of Mourning

In her pathbreaking book *Trauma and the Memory of Politics*, Jenny Edkins argues that memorials to the war dead tend to have a depoliticizing, redemptive effect, hiding the ugly truths about sovereign power and the nation-state that war makes briefly apparent. On her reading, war more or less is trauma—and this not just because it leaves so many slaughtered and mutilated bodies in its wake but because it undoes the mythology of the state as an agent of protection. The shock of the soldiers who are lucky enough to survive does not simply arise from what they were exposed to on the field of battle; it arises also from what that experience of exposure reveals to them about the ideals and institutions for which they were ostensibly fighting. A sense that one has been betrayed by the caretaker is, claims Edkins, scarcely an uncommon experience among veterans, making regulation of the war experience a vital political concern. In her account, memorials to the war dead manage this traumatic experience (and the danger it poses to the reproduction of systems of power) by assigning a sense of order and purpose to what might otherwise appear as a senseless waste of human life. Through memorialization, death is ennobled as heroic sacrifice and the soldier destroyed on foreign soils is turned into the model of the ideal citizen: courageous, loyal, and, above all, selfless. In short, then, in death as in life, the soldiers of war serve the state by deflecting critical attention from the violence that underpins and sustains the political order.[57]

But there are exceptions. These are cases which, in Edkins' words, 'mark the trauma without compromise' by exposing the reality of war as death.[58] One of the public memorials Edkins deems to have broken with convention in this way is the Vietnam Veterans Memorial in Washington, DC designed by Maya Lin—an arresting, and initially highly controversial, piece of public architecture which, on her reading, sets itself apart through its (feminine) conformation in space and its (traumatic) encoding of time. As Edkins points out, critics of the memorial were inclined to associate the 'V' formed by its two black granite walls as they descend into and below the ground with a series of negative feminine tropes. The 'gash in the earth' created by the intersecting walls gave rise to an interpretation in which female genitalia, castration, and the 'open wound' of an unsuccessful war were linked together in a semiotic chain. Was it not all symbolic of an emasculated United States? But there were, of course, other, more positive, ways to read this exposure to (and of) the feminine. Pointedly anti-phallic in the way it sits in, rather than upon, the earth, claimed Edkins, the Memorial did not rise triumphant and indomitable in order to reinstate the social fantasy of completion and sovereignty. Instead, it led visitors down into the underworld and forced them to confront the melancholy fact that many of the soldiers never came back. As she would have it, the black wall of names offers no consolation, no tale of redemption, only an uncanny glimpse of the reality of disappearance and death. The testament that it provides of war is a true testament because it is the testament of the bereaved—the testament, that is, of those who have been deprived of their love objects and forced to live in a state of incompletion.[59]

In addition to the (feminine) way it which it orders space, according to Edkins, Lin's Memorial recommends itself an encounter with the grim reality of death through the way it 'evokes and represents a different temporality'.[60] In contrast to conventional war memorials, she claims—memorials which work to restore the linear view of the state as a progressive institution through heroic narratives of redemption and overcoming—the Vietnam Veterans Memorial evokes the circularity, the untimely repetition and return, characteristic of trauma. On the black wall, as is often pointed out, the names of the dead and disappeared—with the first in 1959 and the last in 1975— begin and end in the centre of the work. In order to read them in the order in which they fell, one must make a circuit around the site and come back to the

The Monumentalization of Shame 143

place where one began. To experience the Memorial in its totality is thus to turn a circle in which one bears witness to thousands of deaths without actually advancing anywhere at all. Nothing is gained and nothing is resolved. For Edkins, the effect of this circular movement, this 'encircling of the trauma', as she puts it, is to strip away the fantasy of healing and recovery. Brought to the end, but no further advanced than at the beginning, the visitor is left with nothing but the unbearable, inconsolable reality of loss.[61] What was it all for? Not unlike a Greek tragedy in this sense, the Memorial opens up an abyssal, traumatic truth (at least for Americans): the war was for nothing and all that life was needlessly wasted.

Edkins' reading of the Vietnam Memorial lends support to the possibility (sketched in section I through a reading Habermas' 'The Finger of Blame') of state symbolization that does some remedial work in relation to civic trauma while maintaining (and demanding) a certain critical distance from the conservative project of political redemption.[62] If she is right about the way the Memorial encourages reflection by symbolizing and encircling the trauma, there are ways of doing public memory that encourage political reconstitution by exposing, rather than masking, the violence that sits at the centre of the political order.[63] Edkins, as we have already noted, is critical of gendered readings of the site which construe its burial in the 'feminized earth' as connotating shame, defeat, and a lack of power.[64] But it is hard not to hear echoes of Loraux's 'female model of memory' in her reading of the 'anti-phallic' site. For here, too, subjects are faced with the loss of something that is without substitution—the absolutely irreplaceable brother or father or son—and here too one encounters a mourning that cannot (and which perhaps does not want to?) accomplish itself. By encouraging visitors to go round and round in an endless circuit, Lin's black wall of names seems to make a mockery of healing and, in that way, draw attention to the limits and fallibility of sovereign power. Did not all those soldiers marked on the wall, all those bodies who now survive only in name, not disappear from the earth because the sovereign made an erroneous judgement about an existential threat to the state? More than simply arresting as art, in other words, the Vietnam Veterans Memorial is dangerous as politics because it draws mourning back into the public sphere and articulates it with a critique of power. How could it not encourage grief-stricken visitors to eventually turn their eyes in the direction of the sovereign and start to question the security that serves as its *raison d'être*? How could it not lead them to see the nation-state, and the friend–enemy distinction it encodes, as a problematic form of political community?

Now, in principle, everything Edkins says about the Vietnam Veterans Memorial should apply to the Memorial to the Murdered Jews of

Europe—*only* more so. Like its counterpart in Washington, DC, the Berlin Memorial is a 'moving composition' in more ways than one. Spread across a large site, it is not an object that can be contemplated (or comprehended) from afar. On the contrary, it draws the visitor in, encloses them within itself, and exposes them to an ambivalent, multi-sensory experience.[65] At the edges, where the *stelae* are at their lowest, it is easy to overlook the transition from public space to ritual space. Yet as visitors walk into the centre of the large, undulating site, they are slowly drawn into, and isolated by, the looming pillars; trapped, as the Jews were, within an unnerving and menacing landscape.[66] As is often observed, the uneven surface and tilting pillars conspire in creating a sense of instability, and the deeper one descends, the more disorientated one tends to become—there is no ground beneath the feet, nothing true to hold on to.[67] To create feelings of discomfort and unease is one of the explicit intentions of the design.[68] Inspired, as Johan Ahr notes, by Primo Levi's reflections in *The Drowned and the Saved*, 'Eisenman wanted his monument to be a proxy for the trauma of living in the concentration camp: to induce disorientation and claustrophobia.'[69] Visitors to the site—especially, one imagines, non-Jewish, German citizens—are expected to feel something of the constriction, the loss of breathing space, that the victims of the Shoah felt. Ideally they should lose their bearings, lose their composure, and, in that way, become awakened (or re-awakened) to the destruction of the human personality that served as the evil core of the crime of their forebears. 'As visitors', writes Karen Baptist, 'we fear that we, too, could lose our individuality amongst the endless standing stelae.'[70] 'I imagine', she adds, 'it feels like death.'

Clearly there is much about the Memorial to the Murdered Jews of Europe to suggest that it, even more than the Vietnam Veterans Memorial, marks the trauma without compromise and refuses redemptive narration.[71] Suggestive of a graveyard and sensed like a tomb, the *stelae* field is an architectural stage where death is not simply evoked as symbol but conjured as experience. One scarcely needs to take the *stelae* to be symbolic of coffins, and the ensemble to be symbolic of a cemetery (both readings being, in a sense, far too literal), in order to understand that the site belongs demonstrably to the underworld and its female deities.[72] Here too one descends, falls into the earth, and becomes engulfed within the trauma of an exposed life. Moreover, as is often suggested, the Memorial offers no coherent narrative to the visitor, no story which, in coming to a natural conclusion, would allow a line to be drawn under the past (*Schlusstricht*). Below ground, in the information centre that was later added to the site, there is, to be sure, lots to read: letters, photographs, names, details of the camps. A timeline can be established and a documentary record compiled. But above ground, in the *stelae* field itself, one reaches the limits of symbolization and encounters a different temporality. Here there is no real beginning or end, no movement forwards towards healing or closure. On the contrary, as Andrew Benjamin points out, the site is a study in incompletion. Neither resolved structure nor complete void, it alludes, through its very form, to what is still missing and still being mourned: the murdered Jews. By leaving visitors no place to occupy except the 'in-between' space of the *stelae*, the no-man's land where presence is marked by absence, appearance by disappearance, the Memorial serves as a reminder that there is no time when the trauma of the Shoah will be over—it belongs always to the 'now'.[73]

By hinting (in the paragraphs above) that the Memorial to the Murdered Jews of Europe is even less compromising in its representation of the open wound, I am not trying to downgrade the significance either of the Vietnam War as a 'civic trauma' for the United States or of the Veterans Memorial as a site where the soldiers who felt doubly betrayed (once by the state for sending them on an inglorious mission and once by the public who disowned them on their return) were rescued from official oblivion by the sovereign body.[74] Charles Griswold is undoubtedly right to claim that 'the internal discord, moral hatred, and institutional damage caused by the enterprise was incalculable'.[75] The point is rather that the Memorial to the Murdered Jews takes on an additional symbolic load because the deaths that it tries to hold in public memory were the result of domestic persecution, not foreign conflict. 'Non-triumphalist' though it may be, the Veterans Memorial still allows the sovereign body to maintain a certain innocence in relation to the lives that were 'lost' (note, not murdered) because it marks them as having been killed somewhere else, by someone else.[76] As even Edkins concedes, the Veterans Memorial remains susceptible to colonization by the narrative of heroic sacrifice (and the cathartic possibilities that attend identification), for it is, after all, still the names of American soldiers, not Native Americans or Black slaves (let alone Vietnamese victims), which are inscribed on the wall.[77] With the Memorial to the Murdered Jews, by contrast, the narrative of heroic sacrifice becomes utterly untenable. In this case, the violence at the heart of the political order is all the more clearly exposed because it is innocent civilians, not citizen-soldiers, who are being honoured in memory and it is the sovereign body which is shown to be directly, not indirectly, responsible for their deaths.

Such distinctions are clearly not without significance for the way 'the people' is able to see (and experience) itself. To the extent that it serves as a mirror, a device for reflecting the people back to itself, the Memorial to the Murdered

Jews inevitably testifies to more than one absence. As well as the absence of the Jews (or rather because of the absence of the Jews), there is the absence of a complete or unified sovereign body: in the place where 'the people', one and indivisible, should reside, there is only disjointedness and irresolution. Located in the centre of Berlin, in the place where the once divided Germany is now supposed to 'come together', the Memorial (and herein, one could argue, lies its great architectural virtue) does not actually seek to make whole what has been smashed. Through its own incompletion, it concedes the impossibility of repair and, with that, the unfulfillable ideal of a sovereign that truly is 'the real unity of them all'. As much a site of absence as presence, it breaks apart the myth of the unified state and calls forth other ways of imagining community, other non-national forms of life, which loosen the ties that bind and give difference breathing space. The message it sends is not so much that the social contract has been dissolved but that the sovereign person can no longer be the pinnacle of judgement, the point at which the power and strength of the multitude is consolidated and given complete licence to decide on the exception. The structure might fairly be described as kenotic (after the Greek *kenosis*: emptying) because it gives up the hope, seemingly once and for all, of gathering the *demos* together as an undifferentiated collection of friends.[78] In short, in this mirror for the people there is ultimately nothing to see. The people are not there because the people were killed.

Between Berlin and Washington, DC, one might reasonably conclude, there really is no comparison. If any memorial is going to induce the critical-emotional experience Edkins and Habermas extol, the experience that culminates in a cosmopolitan re-imagining of political community, it is the Memorial to the Murdered Jews. Somewhat surprisingly, however, critics are not always averse to drawing parallels between the two sites, nor are they persuaded that the Memorial in Berlin is more successful than the one in Washington, DC at encouraging citizens to reflect on the problem of sovereign violence and the friend–enemy distinction. Although by no means unaware of the difference between military sacrifices and civilian murders, for instance, Henry Pickford justifies comparison between the two sites on the grounds that they share an elective affinity in their turn towards abstraction and tilt towards the sublime. On his reading, both are 'performance landscapes', expressive of a late modern preference for the abstract or minimalist over the figurative or representational. Each, in its own way, nods its head towards the so-called unrepresentability thesis pioneered by Jean-François Lyotard, according to which there are phenomena that exceed or defy representation. In the case of such 'limit events' (or so the thesis runs), there is no possibility of fully re-membering or re-cognizing. All one can do is gesture

The Monumentalization of Shame   147

towards them through work that centres absence and which points, in self-referential fashion, to its own inadequacy as historical reflection. The abstract memorial is always, as it were, a counter-memorial: a marking of space that is at the same time an erasure of space.

The paradox of trying to represent the unrepresentable finds a parallel at the level of evaluation. What criteria other than likeness to the object can one appeal to? How, in other words, is one meant to pass judgement upon an impossibility? Like Habermas, Pickford seems persuaded by the idea that abstraction provides the only viable response to the limit event. Anything else leads to embarrassing trivialization. However, this is not to say he thinks minimalist memorials are free of problems, particularly when they are staged as a response to civic trauma. Inherently evocative and gestural, he notes, such memorials are forever in danger of losing their connection to the historical events that inspire them and which they are meant to secure within public memory. If the risk with representational memorials is that they will lack a sufficient 'aesthetic relation' to the event (one that creates the appropriate mood and elicits the right emotions), that with abstract memorials is that they will lack a sufficient 'historical relation' to the event (one that connects it to what happened and builds an understanding of causation and agency). As Pickford would have it, the aesthetic relation and the historical relation are the 'two minimal normative conditions' which a memorial must satisfy in order to be successful. If the former is lost, one ends up with mere documentation and if the latter is lost, one ends up with pure affect.[79]

The reason, on his reading of things, that the Memorial in Washington, DC succeeds while the Berlin Memorial fails, their aesthetic similarities notwithstanding, is that the former maintains an adequate historical relation while the latter does not. Even without the honorary inscriptions later added to the black wall at the request of its sponsors, claims Pickford, Lin's Memorial does enough to establish its relationship to the events that inspired it. In part by providing a record of names and dates and in part by preserving sight lines towards the Washington Monument at one end and the Lincoln Memorial at the other, it maintains an historical relation to the war and the responsibility the nation must shoulder for the lives it destroyed. In short, content and form are integrated in a way that encourages the visitor to reflect on where *they* stand in relationship to the dead. Deprived, by contrast, of contextual markers, according to Pickford, Eisenman's Memorial 'lacks such means by which to anchor its powerful affective response to a determinate historical relation'.[80] With its naming plaque hidden at the edge of the site, its 'aesthetic geography' disconnected from its surrounds, and its information centre buried underground, the Memorial to the Murdered Jews all but loses touch with its genocidal referent. For Pickford, this separation of the historical and the aesthetic is fatal. Without any historical markers to guide reception, the *stelae* are left to stand alone, foreboding but indeterminate. Unable to differentiate memorial from maze, visitors remember only a 'dark experience' and the 'necessary historical consciousness'—the consciousness upon which Habermas' entire defence of the Memorial is based—fails to develop. Death, to be sure, is present, but more as a generic symbol than a historical event.

Pickford's reading of the site suggests it is more likely to facilitate cathartic release than critical reflection. The *stelae* field, he implies, will not focus the visitor's attention on their relationship to the crime and their responsibility to its victims (whether primary or secondary) because it does not name the Jewish victims or declare who murdered them. Agency and causation are assumed rather than declared, obfuscating the meaning of the site. In this, it seems to me, Pickford is by no means misguided. Since the content of public discussion tends to slide quickly out of view, one cannot rely, as Habermas seems to, on citizens coming to the Memorial equipped with a knowledge of the public debates and the 'reservoir of reasons' that informed its inception, design, and placement. The Memorial itself must guide the visitor as to what it is bringing to their attention, why it is necessary to do so, and why it is important that it be sited where it is. At the same time, however, it seems naïve to assume that better historical indexing would, in and of itself, be enough to ensure that the Memorial functions in the way that Pickford wants it to; namely, as a place of self-interrogation where spectators are led to reflect on the relation in which *they* stand—particularly, I would add, if they are citizen-spectators—to the dead.[81] The national significance of the memorial more or less guarantees that it will be subject to a host of pressures—biopolitical as well as political—that cannot but have a bearing on how it is experienced and how it is adjudged a failure or a success.

Long before he enters his verdict about the relative merits of the Washington, DC and Berlin tributes to the dead, Pickford raises, and then immediately dismisses, a 'third desideratum' for a successful memorial: that it establish an appropriate 'moral-political' relation to the event. On his account, one cannot require, as a condition of its success, that a memorial either deliver a didactic/admonitory message or that it provide consolation/catharsis. Since the first is likely to short-circuit the experience of the memorial by subsuming it under a 'proffered lesson' and the second is likely to be contingent on the identity of the visitor (their age, nationality, gender, connection to the event, etc.), the creation of a moral-political relation is not something that can be expected of, or held against, the designer. Pickford is not wrong to suggest some aspects of aesthetic appreciation will always remain in the eye of the beholder or that good art enables a plurality of interpretations and experiences. However, it is hard to see how the Memorial to the Murdered Jews can do the political work Habermas wants (and expects) it to if it does not serve as a warning to Germans about the friend–enemy distinction. As James E. Young has insisted, the purpose of any Holocaust memorial must be 'not to console but to provoke ... not to accept graciously the burden of memory but to throw it back at the town's feet'.[82] If the Memorial to the Murdered Jews provides consolation when it is supposed to admonish, if it brings closure when it is supposed to deny it, one would seem justified in regarding it as having failed in some important respect, regardless of what is introduced by way of signage. The issue that needs to be considered very seriously here, then, is how the power of a memorial to admonish or console might be both encoded in the performance landscape and determinate of the choice of that particular performance landscape in the first place (remembering that both the Washington, DC and Berlin Memorials were the result of design competitions).

It is with this issue in mind that I want to return briefly to the putatively 'normatively successful' Vietnam Veterans Memorial and to readings of it that suggest its ability to console and to heal is in no way unrelated to its design or irrelevant to its selection within the design competition. In *Political Emotions*, Martha Nussbaum argues, effectively with Herman and against Edkins (albeit without mentioning either), that the Veterans Memorial does in fact play a therapeutic role for both the individual and the collective. On her account, the Memorial is a site of healing and reconciliation, working, at one and the same time, to integrate the broken fragments of self and reweave the torn threads of civil association. Although clearly at odds with Edkins' claim that the Memorial denies closure by encircling the trauma, Nussbaum's sense of the cathartic power of the site cannot simply be dismissed as wrongheaded. A great deal of anecdotal evidence points to the fact that the Vietnam Veterans Memorial does make people cry and that visitors to it do experience a certain kind of healing catharsis. 'Be prepared to weep', claimed Arthur Danto in an essay on the Memorial that Nussbaum cites approvingly. 'Tears are the universal experience even if you don't know any of the dead.'[83] Writing in a similar vein, and of a similar personal experience, Stanford Levinson notes that 'many of us' find the Vietnam Veterans Memorial in Washington, DC 'immensely moving' (and Edkins, her critique of healing notwithstanding, does not actually demur).[84] Is it credible to think the 'universality' of this experience bears no relation to the political intent of the memorial?

Nussbaum, for one, clearly thinks not. As she points out, the emotional power of the site is closely tied to the sense of seclusion and intimacy, the home-like milieu, it creates. The Vietnam Veterans Memorial, she notes, is at once cut off from everything else—'[y]ou cannot interact with it without being in its space'—and intensely personal in the way that it addresses its audience—'[t]here is no impersonal symbol, no flag, no message, only the names of individuals'.[85] Akin, in other words, to a private gathering of the bereaved, the site all but closes off peripheral vision in order to grant visitors a complete immersion in the experience of death and to bring them to an 'emotional awareness of shared human possibilities, rooted in bodily vulnerability'.[86] To peruse the endless list of names is, according to Nussbaum, to understand the indiscriminate nature of war and come to the recognition that one's own could easily have been among them. The precarity of life strikes home, conjuring tears for those who lost theirs too early through no fault of their own. Through the 'simple dignity of its design', she writes, the Veterans Memorial simultaneously is and enables a 'straightforward and unpretentious mourning' for all the individuals who never returned.[87] Studiously and, for her, it would seem, *productively* non-partisan in the way it focuses on the human toll of conflict (as opposed to the political causes of conflict), it 'includes all visitors in the experience of grief, bringing them together no matter what they think of the war'.[88] In short, then, by serving as a site of bodily vulnerability—of what is, at one and the same time, the most intimate and most universal, and hence the least political, thing of all—the Memorial achieves exactly what its designer intended it to achieve: 'to bring out in people the realization of loss and a cathartic healing process'.[89]

One would, to be sure, need to be deeply insensitive to the tragedy of the Vietnam War or deeply committed to the merits of institutionalized forgetting to be dismissive of this 'cathartic healing process'. Whatever else might be said about it, the Vietnam Veterans Memorial has succeeded (and succeeded quite spectacularly) in overturning the ban, albeit more implicit than explicit in this context, on recalling the misfortunes and mourning in public. In contrast to the ancient Greeks, who, as we saw in Chapter 2, considered grief a dangerously feminine emotion/failing and displaced it to the anti- (or ante-)political sphere (that is, to the private realm), the modern Americans have secured a place for it in the sacred space of the state capital. As Edkins notes, the Veterans Memorial is a place where 'private grief' is granted 'public support' or, more precisely, where the 'private/public distinction can be overcome in an act of communal mourning'.[90] The problem, however, is that there does not seem to be an intrinsic connection between communal mourning and mourning for community. One can give public support to private grief without at the same time bringing citizens to the recognition that what is invariably 'lost' when the sovereign wages war against a real or perceived enemy is community itself. To the extent that it makes the object of grief the individual body, the name on the wall beneath which visitors leave flowers and letters, the Veterans Memorial does little to focus attention on the violence inherent to the nation-state and its friend–enemy calculus. Instead of the explosive reckoning with sovereign power that the Vietnam adventure should occasion, attention is directed to those personal losses and losses of persons to which every member of the public, as a mortal human, is able to relate. On this point Maya Lin's design statement is particularly instructive:

> We the living are brought to a concrete realization of these deaths. Brought to a sharp awareness of such a loss, it is up to each individual to resolve or come to terms with this loss. For death is in the end a personal and private matter, and the area contained within this memorial is a quiet place, meant for personal reflection and private reckoning.[91]

In the face of this declaration about the way the public architecture of death services the private needs of the living, it is not surprising that the author of a book called *Political Emotions* should raise the question of a collective (not individual) coming to terms and of a public (not private) reckoning. Mindful of the political significance of the Vietnam War, Nussbaum defends the Veterans Memorial on the grounds that it has the same kind of 'deliberative quality' as Greek tragedy.[92] As well as provoking strong feelings of grief, she suggests, it invites critical reflection on the phenomenon of war and the role of the state in waging it—for her, in short, the Memorial is a site of 'mourning and questioning'.[93] Like Pickford, Nussbaum makes a great deal of the fact that the glossy surface of the Veterans Memorial reflects your own image back to you: '[a]s you study the names, you see your own face behind them'.[94] This, she suggests, makes the memorial interrogative as well as contemplative—visitors inevitably feel like the black wall is posing a question to them. One might legitimately wonder, however, whether confronting death 'face to face' in this way really does encourage individuals to question the war and, perhaps more importantly, their own responsibility as citizens for perpetuating the political structure that wages war. Is it capable of bringing them, as Habermas and Edkins hope, to a critical understanding of the conventional nation-state as a political form enmeshed in organized violence or does it merely remind them of their vulnerability as mortal human beings? Can anything be seen at this distance except one name and one face?

By symbolizing death in the way that it does, the Veterans Memorial seems to do much to catalyse grief for the mortal human but much less to incite critique of the sovereign state. In this sacred space, at once secluded and intimate, one does not seem to be addressed as a public person with a political stake in clarifying what happened, why it happened, and how it might be prevented from happening again. One is rather addressed as a private person, a vulnerable human being, who understands loss and can be moved (like a visitor at a funeral?) to a vicarious kind of mourning. To be in this 'sacred space' ultimately appears to be akin to being in the artifice of Gauss' 'Onion Cellar', able, finally, 'to cry like mad'. Only here it is the dead and the disappeared who do the work of the onion. Visitors to the Memorial see the names and peel back the lives in their imagination. Their own image, reflected quietly back to them, helps them to put flesh on the bones of 'all those individuals lost in the war', inducing the emotional outpouring about which everyone, even some of its strongest critics, remarks. 'The designer of the Memorial', notes Griswold, 'wanted it to serve as an occasion for therapeutic catharsis, and in this she succeeded.'[95] But how much of this 'success' is attributable to the fact that the Memorial strips death or, more precisely, *these deaths* of their political significance and displaces them onto a terrain where loss is a strictly private affair, a matter about which each individual must come to terms?

Arguably the most important question to ask in the context of this therapeutic catharsis is that posed by Griswold: 'What truth is grasped, and what not? What is said, and what unsaid?'[96] Inevitably, I would suggest, this recourse to shared human possibilities and the universal truth of bodily vulnerability comes at the expense of the specific lessons of history and the general lessons of politics. Exactly *why* people suffered, and whether that suffering could have been avoided through more astute political judgement or a different understanding of community, becomes less important than the fact *that* they suffered. People were 'lost' and the visitor feels that loss. Hence the 'oceans of emotions' and variety of personal offerings (flowers, mementos, letters) left at the site as if it was a gravestone.[97] The problem, in this instance, is that the strength of emotion seems to be inversely proportional to the clarity of insight. As Griswold notes, contrary to what might be expected from such an exceptional symbolic gesture, the Vietnam Veterans Memorial has a strangely de-politicizing effect, occluding precisely the issues of justice and responsibility that it ought to bring to the fore:

> One is offered therapeutic reconciliation without apology, reconciliation without a stand on the question of justice or responsibility (all without a recognition of the horrendous cost imposed on the other side). This is therapeutic reconciliation

built on a blend of truth, minimal assertion (in the form of the two inscriptions), an invitation to reflection, and deliberate silence—one might even say, evasion.[98]

While Edkins may be right, then, to conclude that the Veterans Memorial is not *simply* a tool of state power, it still seems better suited to the biopolitical objective of catalysing the mourning process than the critical objective of bringing the state into question. Focused on humans and their mortality, rather than sovereigns and their violence, it seems to solicit a (cathartic) grief without inciting a (political) wrath.

It is worth adding, before finally finishing with this example, that there is some evidence to suggest the Memorial has not always proved as therapeutic for the veterans as it has for others. Although Nussbaum dismisses the suggestion all too quickly, I consider it far from irrelevant that some veteran groups saw the memorial as a 'degrading ditch' or a 'wall of shame' and insisted that a more heroic, figurative monument to their national sacrifice be erected at the site. Dismissed by Nussbaum and Danto as banal, the bronze statue of four soldiers that was added to the site in 1982 may well be an artistic failure. Although clearly not without technical merit, it does little to extend, let alone challenge or reshape, the aesthetic convention of the war memorial. On the contrary, in what amounts to a clear tilt towards conservatism, it depicts the servicemen in action in such a way as to make courage, devotion, and sacrifice the central themes. Arguably, however, it is not the conservatism but the resistance to exposure that is most instructive about this supplement to the black wall of names.[99] Reclaimed within the old discourse of heroic sacrifice, the soldiers are no longer exposed to the public as bare life. Unlike the abstract memorial that marks them as a body that did not come back, a life extinguished and laid in the earth, the figurative one 're-covers' them as soldiers by dressing them up in a protective layer of myth. Could it be that the hero-victim would prefer to be recognized as a brave soldier rather than exposed as a mortal human? Might they want something else to be remembered about them other than that they died?

My intention in dedicating so much space to the Vietnam Veterans Memorial is not to muddy the political waters, or not more, at any rate, than they already are. I am not trying to assert that the Vietnam War and the Jewish Shoah are analogous events or even that they play a similarly diremptive role in the public life of America and Germany, respectively. Although both clearly are 'civic traumas' for their respective nations, a war waged overseas against foreign combatants (even one as morally bankrupt as the Vietnam War) is inevitably more easily redeemable than the war waged at home against innocent civilians. Since the crimes of the American sovereign body took place largely offshore, it could engage in a process of mourning without having to fulfil an obligation of repentance. No such option is available to the Germans. My intention has rather been to show how memorials (even the supposedly 'normatively successful' ones) can function as therapeutic instruments in ways that compromise their ability to generate critical reflection. If Nussbaum is right, the success of the Veterans Memorial as a tool of cathartic healing is related quite precisely to the way it circumvents the problem of the nation-state and cultivates an emotional awareness of shared *human* possibilities. Encoded as something that is, at once, intensely personal and completely universal, specific to each individual and common to all humans, death loses its connection to sovereign violence and grief is severed from anger. Might the same be said of the Memorial to the Murdered Jews? Is this another instance in which the negative sublime conspires to produce a therapeutic catharsis rather than a political critique?

Henry Pickford is by no means alone in judging the Memorial to the Murdered Jews of Europe a failure. In a short essay for *The New Yorker*, published in the same year, Richard Brody put forward a remarkably similar thesis. For him, too, the 'inadequacy' of the Berlin Memorial had less to do with the integrity of the design (what Pickford places under the heading of the 'aesthetic relation') than the absence of any clear historical direction in matters of causation and agency. In his account, there is a disturbing vagueness to the Memorial that begins with the title—which Jews, murdered when, where, and by whom?—and which is carried through in the installation as a whole. 'Nothing about the stelae themselves', he notes, 'indicate[s] that the murderers were German (or worked for Germany) and that the murdered victims were Jews.' Like Pickford, Brody is critical of the way the information centre is detached from the Memorial proper, allowing the *stelae* field to operate as a floating signifier. Lacking in historical guides, he suggests, the metaphorical possibilities of the site become all too plentiful. 'The play of imagination that the memorial provokes', he writes, 'is piously generic: something to do with death.' Although by no means emotionally unaffected by the experience of traversing the *stelae* field, therefore, Brody is led to conclude that the Memorial 'hardly serves the function for which it was intended'. Having failed to establish the connection between the Jewish victims and their German murderers, the site is leached of any admonitory element. Ultimately, he suggests, one is left with little more than a feeling of 'general grief in the face of haphazard fortune'. Tears, to be sure, flow here too, but once again it is tears stripped of the 'enduring historical anger' that the crime being memorialized should provoke.[100]

Pickford and Brody might be right. But, as Griswold alerts us, the critical issue is not so much whether their judgement of inadequacy is sound as what it presumes about the Memorial in relation to function: 'inadequate' for what purpose? To say that the Memorial to the Murdered Jews doesn't fulfil its *intended* function is not to say that it doesn't fulfil *a* function (or even that Pickford and Brody are right about what was actually intended). A memorial that succeeds in soliciting grief or sadness, especially one that does so without provoking anger, is clearly doing something in relation to the emotional life of its visitors, even if it is not 'the something' that Pickford and Brody hoped for. As Mark Callaghan has noted, if the purpose of the Berlin Memorial was to 'do penance', other entries to the design competition, specifically one titled *Blowing Up the Brandenburg Gate*, might have sent the message more clearly. 'It would, more than most submissions', he wrote, 'be a commitment to the "self-effacing" nation, a country so determined to present itself to the world as being penitent that it demolished its national icon.'[101] The immediate sense one has (or, at least, which *this one* has) that *Blowing Up the Brandenburg Gate* goes too far is a reminder not only that sovereign repentance has its limits (even when the crime it responds to did not) but also that the designs that win out in national competitions do so because they fulfil certain interests and meet certain needs, not all of which relate to the obligations of anamnestic solidarity. 'For the past sixty years', noted Chin, Franke, and Halpern,

> Germany dealt with the Holocaust primarily through guilt. The Memorial to the Murdered Jews of Europe now presents the opportunity for catharsis, both through debate and by virtue of its presence; the memorial offers a path towards a more positive sense of national identity and provides a template that other countries may follow.[102]

The Jews, it seems important to note, did not ask for the Memorial to be erected. It was rather the Germans who felt the need for it. According to Callaghan, who treats the memorial competition process as a window onto the German unconscious, everything from the initiation of the proposal to the selection of the winning design was reflective of, if not completely overdetermined by, the unique situation of 'the later-born' or *Nachgeborenen*: the Germans of the third generation who played no active role in the Shoah but whose lives have been shadowed (and in some ways diminished) by it through relentless exposure. As he would have it, 'post-unification Germany was drawn to proposals that expressed their own trauma, a vicarious one'.[103] Drawing on the psychoanalytic work of Cathy Caruth, Callaghan takes it as given that exposure to an event through its repeated representation can produce similar, though clearly not identical, psychological effects to exposure to the event itself. Trauma, on this reading, becomes vicarious when one begins to identify, at a very profound level, with the fate of the victims. Callaghan engages in a wide-ranging discussion of the problem of traumatic witnessing and the desire it created within Germany for 'experiential designs' whose primary function is visceral and emotional (as opposed to critical or intellectual). But the crux of the argument is that the *Nachgeborenen* have suffered as a result of their identification with the Jews they were given no chance to save and were drawn, 'perhaps unconsciously', to select a memorial design (Eisenman's *stelae* field) which, rather than commemorate the murder of 6 million Jews, speaks to, and offers consolation for, their own trauma.[104]

Callaghan's thesis is somewhat tendentious but by no means completely implausible. As Judith Lewis Herman, and many other psychoanalysts, have suggested, those who 'bear witness' can, as it were, become infected by the trauma and begin to display similar kinds of symptoms. As Herman succinctly put it: 'trauma is contagious'. However, it might with equal plausibility be argued that the roots of the trauma in question lie in the direct (not vicarious) experience of the later-born themselves and the suffocating presence of the Shoah as an everlasting, inexpiable crime from which they are, at one and the same time, in no way responsible *as individuals* and in no way able to free themselves *as Germans*. Martin Walser may be unique in his willingness to publicly express his irritation at the way the Germans were reminded daily of their 'everlasting shame' or in admitting that he 'wouldn't be able to get through the day, to say nothing of the night, without looking away and thinking about something else'.[105] But his antipathy to the way the memory of the Shoah undoes any claim to innocence or goodness is scarcely unique and speaks of the political unconscious of the nation.[106] As Alexander Mathäs notes, the desperate need for the post-war generation to atone for their father's crimes, has, in the eyes of many, given rise to a culture of remembrance that borders on the obsessive-compulsive. Atonement rituals are meticulously carried out, public opinion is closely monitored, and any deviation from the accepted penitential script is quickly denounced. This is the culture the *Nachgeborenen* have inherited—a culture which effectively pre-determines their relationship to the nation (with the only acceptable stance being self-effacement); which imposes upon them a duty of remembrance they did nothing to earn other than by being German; and which perpetually frustrates their desire for normality.[107] Might the 'trauma' of which Callaghan speaks have arisen less from their identification with the inhuman treatment of the Jews than from the claustrophobia they feel at being trapped by a history not of their choosing?[108]

Arguably, vicarious trauma and the perpetrator trauma are so thoroughly intertwined in this situation there is little chance of working out which is the primary driver behind the Memorial. Seen from a biopolitical perspective, however, it hardly seems to matter since, either way, it is the trauma of the Germans, not that of the Jews, that is critically at stake. If Callaghan is right, they are the ones the Memorial is designed to heal. The risk that German visitors to the site will assume the identity of the victim rather than the perpetrator has certainly not gone unnoticed.[109] And although such 'self-orientated' misinterpretations have tended to be dismissed as the price that must be paid for maintaining the openness of the work of art, it is by no means clear that this experience is exclusive to those who 'misinterpret'. As Callaghan notes, Eisenman's *stelae* field is, in essence, an experiential site that was chosen over many other compelling entries (over 500 were received in all) because of the way it engaged people emotionally. The powerful affective response it generates hinges upon the visitor being interpellated as a victim, overwhelmed and disorientated by the looming pillars. The reason, one could speculate, why the Memorial tends, in practice, to produce the cathartic effect it was meant, in theory, to deny is because every visitor, on entry, becomes a victim, suffocated by the claustrophobic *stelae* field, and on exit, a survivor, able to breathe freely again. Whether it deserves to be regarded as an admonitory, warning monument (*Manmahl*) is thus a moot issue. Baptiste sums up the problem with this symbol of death quite precisely: 'If the Memorial to the Murdered Jews of Europe succeeds as a monument because of its capacity to induce a sublime experience, and if the after effect of that experience is purifying, does it succeed as a memorial?'[110]

Like its aesthetic counterpart in Washington, DC, the Berlin Memorial appears to rely upon a sense of what Nussbaum calls 'similar possibilities' to generate its emotional effects. Were it not for a sense of their own vulnerability and mortality, and the intensification of that sense as a result of their own exposure to the Shoah through various media, citizens would be left unmoved by the experience of walking among the *stelae*—it simply wouldn't, to use Baptiste's phrase, 'feel like death'. The obvious problem with all this is that the possibility to which the Memorial gestures, the possibility of suffocation that began with the withdrawal of legal immunities for the Jews and reached its ghastly conclusion with their exposure to Zyklon B in the gas chambers, was not shared. Only the Jews and other 'internal enemies' such as the Roma and Sinti were abandoned by the law and reduced to a purely biological existence; only they were turned into 'specimens of the species', as Arendt put it, able to be exterminated without loss because each had been turned into an exact replica of the other.[111] All the rest, those who designed, operated, or were complicit in the system that was precisely calculated to create this zone of indistinction between human and animal, retained their individuality (which is not, of course, to say they didn't also suffer). Empathetic identification with the victim is, to be sure, an appropriate, perhaps even an ethically imperative, response to the Final Solution. But only, perhaps, in situations where a certain critical awareness is retained of the difference between identification with the victims and being a victim oneself. Arguably, it is only when one recognizes oneself, or is capable of imagining oneself, as a perpetrator, as someone, that is, who *intentionally* sets out to rob others of their breathing space, that one becomes fully conscious of the friend-enemy distinction as a problem and is led to embrace universalistic constitutional principles.

The victims, for their part, seem to have sensed that the Memorial isn't really about them. Like Habermas, they have been inclined to see it as one more attempt by the Germans to come to terms with themselves. Disregarding it entirely would not, however, appear to be an option, for if it doesn't speak to them, it clearly does speak of them. In *The Drowned and the Saved*, Primo Levi made the paradoxical observation that the 'true witnesses' to the camps, the ones that had plumbed its useless violence to the very bottom, were the ones who were unable to bear witness because they had disappeared into oblivion. Although 'the saved' felt compelled to talk, it was 'the drowned' who knew the truth.[112] Inserted into this frame—a frame unique to the survivor—the Memorial to the Murdered Jews seems to reveal itself as an ambiguous artefact. On the one hand, it testifies, and not without a certain pathos, to a truth that cannot in fact be told, the truth that died when all those inmates of the camps went under and were silenced forever. Not unlike *The Drowned and the Saved*, it attempts to bear witness to what can never bear witness: the ones who drowned, the murdered Jews. On the other hand, it revives the trauma of the survivor. In what is, perhaps, one of the most heartrending chapters in an utterly heartrending book, Levi talks of the sense of shame, irrational but still 'concrete, heavy, perennial', that came belatedly over him upon liberation: the shame, firstly, of having lived for years 'at an animal level', secondly of not having done enough to resist the system and maintain solidarity among the prisoners, and thirdly of having survived, if not at the expense of another, then at least 'in the place of another'.[113] It is these others that now stand in the centre of Berlin. Is it possible (one recoils at the thought) that the Jews as much as the Germans will feel accused by them, the Jews as much as the Germans who will be overcome by shame in the face of bare life?

III Error in Mourning

Memorials, unlike apologies and truth commissions, are mute artefacts. And yet, as Stanley Levison has rightly noted, they are hardly silent. Every time the state allows something to be placed within the symbolically loaded spaces of the capital, the 'consciousness of the polity is being regulated'.[114] 'Government', he writes, 'does indeed speak when it offers sacred space.'[115] Exactly what it says (or perhaps does) when it offers that sacred space is not, however, always self-evident. At first blush, the Memorial to the Murdered Jews of Europe appears to be an attempt to heal the biopolitical fracture between the Germans and the Jews—the fracture which opened up when the Jews were designated as 'life unworthy of life' who could be herded as animals and dispatched as waste—by locating the crime of the Shoah in the very place where the 'we' of 'we, the people' is represented in stone. Viewed, in the way that Habermas suggests, as a form of political communication, it provides an explicit rejection of the 'form of life' that sustained itself by usurping and destroying the lives of others. A world away from the ethos of 'forgive and forget' that Adorno castigated in 1959,[116] the Memorial brings the crime into the symbolic heart of the united Germany, setting it before the public as an enduring reminder of what it can never again be. Here, one might say, is a clear call, addressed to the future, for the adoption of a post-conventional, cosmopolitan identity: a new, shared form of existence in which there is no question that Jewish life is 'grievable life'; that it is life, in other words, 'that qualifies for recognition'.[117]

That the giant, concrete *stelae* field provides an emphatic statement of 'never forget' seems indisputable. But, as James E. Young rightly noted in his pioneering work on monuments and memory, it is incumbent upon the 'critical visitor' to 'ask what precisely it is that is not forgotten'.[118] Since, as he underlined, *what* is remembered depends upon *how* it is remembered, it is not possible to separate message and media, content and form. Making sense of what has been written in stone requires us to pay careful attention to the way in which memorials like that for the Murdered Jews of Europe come to 'stand for', and thus necessarily displace and revise, 'past realities'.[119] Inevitably, according to Young, even the so-called authentic sites like Auschwitz efface as much of the past as they preserve because they feed the illusion of an unmediated history and make the part stand for the whole.[120] But dangers of a different, and by no means less worrying, kind emerge when the traumatic legacy of a crime against humanity drives a political community to seek consolation in the negative pathos of the aesthetic sublime. As we have seen throughout this chapter, the risk in this case is not simply that of historical revisionism undertaken in the name of national pride but of emotional regulation undertaken in the name of national healing. The key question we have posed here relates to the mirroring of the civic trauma: has it been represented in such a way as to spark critical reflection on the nation-state form or is it rather geared towards providing a kind of cathartic relief for the heavy presence of the Shoah in German life? Is it, in other words, a case of victims recovering because the sovereign exposed itself as bare life or of the sovereign recovering because it exposed its victims as bare life?

The analysis presented in this chapter suggests the issue raised by the Memorial to the Murdered Jews may not ultimately be whether it 'marks the trauma' in a compromised or uncompromised way but *whose trauma* it marks and what kind of relief it provides in relation to it. If Habermas is right, hostility to the Memorial among conservatives arises less from the trauma it represents *to* them than from the trauma it represents *for* them. They resist exposure to the Shoah precisely because they understand the demand it makes upon them as members of the German *Kulturnation*—the demand that they stop drawing from the well of tradition that has been poisoned by inexpressible crimes. The 'gasses of an undigested past' to which Habermas refers can be regarded as simply so many testaments to their inability (or their refusal?) to mourn the loss of continuity in their national identity. But, as Callaghan reveals, it is by no means clear that the Germans who actually wanted the Memorial did so purely out of an impulse of anamnestic solidarity or enlightened cosmopolitanism; that is, out of a wish to mourn their lost community with the Jews. Even if we take it to be vicarious, a product of their identification with the Jewish victims, the trauma of the later-born seems to play an overdetermining role in how the Memorial functions and why it was chosen in the first place. Rather than encourage critical reflection on the conventional nation-state, it provides the *Nachgeborenen* with a means of working through the impossible position of being, at once, guiltless and responsible. Too far removed from events even to find solace in holding their parents to account, they have found relief in a memorial that allows them to experience history from precisely the position that has been historically denied to them: the position of the victim. In short, though it is addressed to the Jews, the Memorial actually seems to be *for* the Germans. By positioning them as 'spectators of their own feelings', the *stelae* field fulfils its biopolitical function as a 'moving composition', allowing its visitors to grasp (and thus gain some relief from) their vicarious trauma.[121]

There is, of course, a certain perversity in the suggestion that the Memorial to the Murdered Jews fails because it does not encourage German citizens to reflect on the old *Kulturnation* and the friend–enemy distinction that sits at

The Monumentalization of Shame   161

the heart of the political. Its primary function, ethically speaking, must still be anamnestic solidarity: a demonstration of the fact that the Germans are willing to share in the mourning of the victims of their aggression or, more precisely, to take on that work of mourning as their own. To the extent that the flowers and pebbles ('heavy with sorrow') placed atop the *stelae* reflect a belated awareness that these too were 'grievable lives', as Butler puts it, they are far from insignificant.[122] In the same way that graves dignify the body, marking each life as worthy of remembrance, such offerings rescue the victims of the Shoah from the industrial murder and mass graves that obliterated individuality and denied loss. With them a sense of personhood (and thus of a life that ought not to have been exposed to violence) returns. On this matter, one can but repeat the dictum of Primo Levi: 'every victim is to be mourned'.[123] And yet, a mourning that mourns only the lost life, a mourning that does not see the lost life in relation to the political institution that took it, threatens to descend into sterile sentimentalism. Focused on the half-life of the alienated survivor, it forgets the over-life of the guilty sovereign and the commitment to universalistic constitutional principles that is needed to finally bury it. What, one might ask, comes of such acts of mourning, other, perhaps, than the cathartic experience of release as one leaves the site behind and escapes the claustrophobia of the looming *stelae*?

The risk in all this, I would hazard, is that the healing of the civic trauma (itself hardly a bad thing) becomes an end in itself, divorced from any kind of political transformation. Although the Memorial to the Murdered Jews makes no attempt to hide the crime, it is not clear that the Shoah is represented in such a way as to facilitate critical reflection on the nation-state as a political form historically implicated in state racism. For Habermas, as we have seen, success in coming to terms must ultimately be measured in terms of a break from a poisoned tradition. To properly realize such a break, the 'old trinity of state-people-territory', as Arendt put it, would have to be put to the sword and Germany reborn as a post-national state (a state, if not exactly *without* a national self, at least one without any inherited traditions that would prevent others from being joined into 'the people').[121] But if Pickford, Brody, and Callaghan (among others) are right, this is not how the Memorial functions. On the contrary, by allowing everyone to assume the identity of the victim, it shields spectators from the very 'truths' about the nation-state they ought to be confronting: truths about the constitutive nature of its racial exclusions; about its xenophobic relation to the outside; and about its glorification of military adventurism. Despite its central location and its sombre presence, the Memorial ultimately seems to favour cheap sentimentality over attentive reflection and emotional catharsis over political self-understanding.

Shielded from the problem of the nation-state, the citizen-spectators are able to revel in the sadness without feeling themselves implicated or challenged as members of a political community founded on the distinction between friends and enemies.

Notes

1. As Mark Amstutz puts it: 'Although forgetting is seldom defended as an official government policy, nations, like individuals, can only stand so much truth. Indeed, states, like people, are not eager to acknowledge their errors, sins and shortcomings.' M. Amstutz, *The Healing of Nations: The Promise and Limits of Political Forgiveness*, Lanham, MD: Rowman and Littlefield, 2005, p. 19.
2. As Sanford Levinson has noted, 'All monuments are efforts, in their own way, to stop time … History, of course, moves relentlessly to mock any such beliefs.' S. Levinson, *Written in Stone: Public Monuments in Changing Societies*, Durham, NC: Duke University Press, 1998, p. 7.
3. For a general discussion of the current moment as one of crisis in memory, see J.K. Olick and H. Teichler, 'Memory and Crisis: An Introduction', *Memory Studies*, 14(6), 2021, pp. 1135–1142.
4. In my hometown of Melbourne a lobby group called 'A Monument of One's Own' is currently seeking to address the huge gender imbalance in statues around the city. Of the 580 existing statues, only 9 are of real women (as opposed to mythological figures). One of the leaders of the campaign, Professor Claire Wright, has suggested, by no means improbably, that the lack of statues of women added to the 'respect gap' in Australian civic and political life. See C. Waters, 'Some Day Their Plinth Will (Finally) Come', *The Age*, 3 December 2021, pp. 2–3. For a discussion of similar issues in the United States, see K.M. Murphy, 'Fear and Loathing in Monuments: Rethinking the Politics and Practices of Monumentality and Monumentalization', *Memory Studies*, 145(6), 2021, pp. 1143–1158.
5. I am alluding here to Charles Taylor's well-known suggestion that non- or misrecognition, beyond simply indicating a lack of respect, can 'inflict a grievous wound, saddling victims with crippling self-hatred'. C. Taylor, 'The Politics of Recognition', in A. Gutmann (ed.), *Multiculturalism: Examining the Politics of Recognition*, Princeton: Princeton University Press, 1994, pp. 25–26.
6. Thus Levinson has questioned whether the Memorial to the Confederate Dead in Austin, Texas 'is equivalent to memorializing those who fought to maintain chattel slavery and the abuse of African Americans'. Levinson, *Written in Stone*, p. 81.
7. This is, of course, the title of Levinson's book cited in note 6.
8. See A. Chaudhuri, 'The Real Meaning of the Rhodes Must Fall', *The Guardian*, 16 March 2016 and S. Maddison, 'Why the Statues Must Fall', *The Sydney Morning Herald*, 12 June 2020.
9. H.W. Pickford, 'Dialectical Reflections on Peter Eisenman's Memorial for the Murdered Jews of Europe', *Architectural Theory Review*, 17(2–3), 2012, p. 435.
10. In a recent special edition of the journal *German Politics and Society*, Bach and Nienass insist that the quest for innocence has been a central driver of German memory politics in

The Monumentalization of Shame 163

the post-war period, giving rise to a variety of mechanisms by which to evade the Shoah. J. Bach and B. Nienass, 'Introduction: Innocence and the Politics of Memory', *German Politics and Society*, 39(1), 2021, pp. 1–12.
11. M. Marzynski, 'Good Guilt in Germany', *The Washington Post*, 28 May 2005, p. 25.
12. See J. Ahr, 'Memory and Mourning in Berlin: On Peter Eisenman's *Holocaust Mahnmal*', *Modern Judaism*, 28(3), 2008, p. 285; and Marzynski, 'Good Guilt in Germany', p. 25.
13. D. La Capra, *Writing History, Writing Trauma*, Baltimore, MD: The Johns Hopkins University Press, 2001, p. 23.
14. Seen from this perspective, the memorialization of the victims of the Shoah at the *Yad v'shem* in Jerusalem makes perfect sense. According to Bruno Bettelheim, Israel is, in fact, 'the most appropriate, the best, place to memorialise the victims'. B. Bettelheim, *Surviving and Other Essays*, London: Thames and Hudson, 1979, p. 97.
15. T.A. Kovach and M. Walser, *The Burden of the Past: Martin Walser on Modern German Identity—Texts, Contexts, Commentary*, Camden: Boydell & Brewer, 2008, p. 91.
16. J. Amery, *At the Mind's Limit: Contemplations by a Survivor on Auschwitz and Its Realities*, trans. by S. Rosenfeld and S.P. Rosenfeld, London: Granta, 1999, p. 95.
17. On this point, see T. Brudholm, 'Revisitng Resentments: Jean Amery and the Dark Side of Forgiveness and Reconciliation', *Journal of Human Rights*, 5, 2006, pp. 7–26.
18. 'Just because we cannot atone for it', writes Bettelheim, 'it is wrong to deny or obfuscate it.' Bettelheim, *Surviving and Other Essays*, p. 103.
19. Bettelheim, *Surviving and Other Essays*, p. 103. Bettelheim's reflections on the Nazi attempt to strip the Jews of their autonomy, offered in the page before the text I have quoted, are also highly instructive in this context: 'what happened to them impressed on them that nobody cared whether they lived or died and the rest of the world, including foreign countries, had no concern for their fate'. Although belatedly (and pathetically), memorials provide evidence of that concern.
20. Cited in J. Habermas, *Time of Transitions*, ed. and trans. by Ciaran Cronin and Max Pensky, Cambridge: Polity, 2006, p. 56.
21. See L. Mahlum, 'The Similarities of Difference: A Comparative Analysis of the New England Holocaust Memorial in Boston and the Memorial to the Murdered Jews of Europe in Berlin', *Intersections*, 10(1), 2009, p. 292; and A. Mathäs, 'The Presence of the Past: Martin Walser on Memoirs and Memorials', *German Studies Review*, 25(1), 2002, pp. 8–9.
22. C. Maier, *The Unmasterable Past: History, Holocaust, and German National Identity*, Cambridge, MA: Harvard University Press, 1988, p. 12.
23. Cited in Mahlum, 'The Similarities of Difference', p. 306.
24. It is important to note that 'The Finger of Blame' was written at a time when the 'Holocaust Memorial' was still in the proposal stage but Eisenman's 'stelae field' had emerged as the preferred design.
25. Habermas, *Time of Transitions*, p. 41.
26. Habermas, *Time of Transitions*, p. 38.
27. Habermas, *Time of Transitions*, p. 43.
28. Habermas, *Time of Transitions*, p. 43.
29. 'The goal of the memorial', he writes, 'is to challenge future generations to take a stand.' Habermas, *Time of Transitions*, p. 44.
30. Andrew Benjamin, similarly, assumes that the community being addressed (or, once again, elicited) by the Memorial to the Murdered Jews is a cosmopolitan one. Like

Habermas, he suggests the Memorial responds to the 'categorical imperative' arising from the Shoah itself. 'Part of that imperative', he writes, 'means acting in ways that refuse the return of nationhood defined in terms of that conception of ethnicity and the nation necessitating the violent exclusion of the other. What is demanded, therefore, is the affirmation of the cosmopolitan'. A. Benjamin, 'Now Still Absent: Eisenman's Memorial to the Murdered Jews of Europe', *Architectural Theory Review*, 8(1), 2003, p. 60.

31. This position had already been staked out during the *Historikerstreit*. In his 1988 essay 'A Settlement of Damages', Habermas declared 'The only patriotism which does not alienate us from the West is a constitutional patriotism. A commitment to universalistic constitutional principles which is anchored by conviction has unfortunately only been able to develop in the German *Kulturnation* since—and because of—Auschwitz'. J. Habermas, 'A Kind of Settlement of Damages (Apologetic Tendencies)', *New German Critique*, 44, spring/summer 1988, p. 39.

32. J. Habermas, *A Berlin Republic: Writings on Germany*, trans. by Steven Rendall, Cambridge: Polity Press, 1998, p. 19. Arguably, Walser's critique of the Memorial stems from his failure to acknowledge this political dimension of 'coming to terms' (something he had done earlier in his career). For him, dealing with the past is now exclusively a matter of conscience and thus incapable of public representation. 'Everyone', he writes, 'is alone with his or her conscience. For this reason, public acts of conscience are in danger of becoming symbolic'. Kovach and Walser, *The Burden of the Past*, p. 92. On this point, see also A. Lewis, 'Germany's Metamorphosis: Memory and the Holocaust in the Berlin Republic', *Cultural Studies Review*, 9(2), 2003, p. 108.

33. In one of his earlier interventions into the *Historikerstreit*, Habermas rejects the idea that responsibility does not carry from one generation to the next on the grounds that there is no easy way to separate the 'form of existence' of this generation from the previous one. See J. Habermas, 'Concerning the Public Use of History', *New German Critique*, 44, 1988, p. 44.

34. See Habermas, *A Berlin Republic*, p. 19; and Habermas, *Time of Transitions*, p. 42.

35. Habermas, *Time of Transitions*, p. 44. On the importance of the Memorial as an expression of intentionality and decision, see also Benjamin, 'Now Still Absent', p. 59.

36. Habermas, *Time of Transitions*, p. 45. In *The Texture of Memory*, J.E. Young claims that representational forms of memorialization are hopelessly inadequate in relation to the Holocaust. In his view, only non-representational, self-reflexive memorials or 'counter-monuments' were adequate as vehicles of remembrance for the countless victims of industrial murder. In like fashion, Eisenman claimed he was forced to resort to minimalist technique 'because the Holocaust is unfathomable and representations only trivialize it'. See J.E. Young, *The Texture of Memory: Holocaust Memorials and Meaning*, New Haven, CT: Yale University Press, 1993; and Q. Stevens, 'Nothing More Than Feelings: Abstract Memorials', *Architectural Theory Review*, 14(2), 2009, p. 166.

37. Habermas, *Time of Transitions*, p. 38.

38. Habermas, 'Concerning the Public Use of History', p. 47.

39. Habermas, *Time of Transitions*, p. 42.

40. Habermas, 'Concerning the Public Use of History', p. 44.

41. As far back as 1988, Habermas was referring to the 'traumatic refusal of an ethical imperfection, which has been branded into our national history, to disappear'. Habermas, 'Concerning the Public Use of History', p. 41.

42. See, for instance, J. Habermas, 'Defusing the Past: A Politico-Cultural Tract' in G. Hartmann (Ed.), *Bitburg in Moral and Political Perspective*, Bloomington, IN: Indiana University Press, 1986, pp. 43–49.
43. Habermas, *Time of Transitions*, p. 40.
44. Habermas, *Time of Transitions*, p. 40.
45. Habermas, *Time of Transitions*, p. 46.
46. Habermas, *Time of Transitions*, p. 47.
47. Habermas, *Time of Transitions*, p. 42.
48. Bettelheim, *Surviving*, p. 87. As Bettelheim morbidly observes, the cutting off of Jewish breathing space reached its horrific conclusion in the gas chambers.
49. See Habermas, 'Concerning the Public Use of History', pp. 44–45.
50. Habermas, *Time of Transitions*, p. 45.
51. Habermas, *Time of Transitions*, p. 54.
52. Habermas, *Time of Transitions*, p. 46. On the affective power of abstract memorials, see Stevens, 'Nothing More Than Feelings', pp. 156–172.
53. Lewis, 'Germany's Metamorphosis', p. 115.
54. See Q. Stevens, 'Visitor Responses at Berlin's Holocaust Memorial: Contrary to Conventions, Expectations and Rules', *Public Art Dialogue*, 2(1), 2012, pp. 34-59; and M. Callaghan, 'A Holocaust Memorial or a Memorial to Germany's Vicarious Trauma', *Inter-Disciplinary Press*, 2013, p. 9.
55. Stevens, 'Visitor Responses at Berlin's Holocaust Memorial', p. 36.
56. This approach is consistent with recent research in which attention is redirected away from what memorials *mean* and towards what they *do*. See S. Buckley-Zistel, "Tracing the Politics of Aesthetics: From Imposing, via Counter to Affirmative Memorials to Violence', *Memory Studies*, 14(4), 2021, p. 782.
57. J. Edkins, *Trauma and the Memory of Politics*, Cambridge: Cambridge University Press, 2003, pp. 58–59; 91–98.
58. Edkins, *Trauma and the Memory of Politics*, p. 94. This view of the memorial as a symbol of death is strongly supported by James Tatum: 'The memorial concentrates starkly on mortality and nothing else.' J. Tatum, *The Mourner's Song: War and Remembrance from the Iliad to Vietnam*, Chicago, IL: The University of Chicago Press, 2003, p. 4.
59. Edkins, *Trauma and the Memory of Politics*, pp. 80–81.
60. Edkins, *Trauma and the Memory of Politics*, p. 81.
61. Edkins, *Trauma and the Memory of Politics*, p. 83.
62. According to Edkins, 'the aim of Lin's memorial is not to heal (or rather, conceal) the wound or the lack by a reimposition of masculinity and triumphalism, but to enable a recognition of loss and an acceptance of the scarring'. Edkins, *Trauma and the Memory of Politics*, p. 81.
63. It is, perhaps, in relation to the goal of psychic integration that Edkins' opposition to the biopolitical project of healing is most clearly marked. Incorporation, she insists, is not always something to be desired. See Edkins, *Trauma and the Memory of Politics*, p. 73.
64. Edkins, *Trauma and the Memory of Politics*, p. 77.
65. See Stevens, 'Visitor Responses at Berlin's Holocaust Memorial', p. 42; and Pickford, 'Dialectical Reflections on Peter Eisenman's Memorial for the Murdered Jews of Europe', pp. 428–429.
66. Habermas, *Time of Transitions*, p. 46.

166 The Penitent State

67. As Stevens notes, 'the physical qualities of the MMJE, combined with its lack of representational detail, also create physiological feelings of discomfort, confinement, disorientation, isolation, deprivation and instability, which are intended to produce a sense of apprehension'. Stevens, 'Nothing More Than Feelings', p. 160.
68. As Eisenman insisted, 'You will feel what it is like to be lost in space'. Quoted in Pickford, 'Dialectical Reflections', p. 428.
69. Ahr, 'Memory and Mourning in Berlin', p. 285. See also Stevens, 'Nothing More Than Feelings', p. 166.
70. K. Baptist, 'Shades of Grey: The Role of the Sublime in the Memorial to the Murdered Jews of Europe', *Landscape Review*, 14(2), 2012, p. 83. See also Stevens, 'Visitor Responses to Berlin's Holocaust Memorial', pp. 39–40.
71. See Mathäs, 'The Presence of the Past', p. 15.
72. Both the coffin and the cemetery symbols are advanced by Richard Brody. See R. Brody, 'The Inadequacy of Berlin's "Memorial to the Murdered Jews of Europe"', *The New Yorker*, 12 July 2012.
73. Benjamin, 'Now Still Absent', p. 61. On the point of the Memorial being resistant to normalization and closure, see also Ahr, 'Memory and Mourning in Berlin', pp. 298–299; and E. Grenzer, 'The Topographies of Memory in Berlin: The *Neue Wache* and the Memorial for the Murdered Jews of Europe', *Canadian Journal of Urban Research*, 11(1), 2002, p. 107.
74. As Griswold put it: 'It is as though the nation first sought to purify itself of its loss by shifting the stain to those it had sent to fight, sending them away again ... this time into official oblivion.' C. Griswold, *Forgiveness: A Philosophical Exploration*, Cambridge: Cambridge University Press, 2007, p. 196. As he later points out, the Vietnam Veterans Memorial is neither a top-down nor a bottom-up exercise of power—it was neither imposed upon the people by the government against their will nor forced upon the government by the pressure of civil action. Yet it is nevertheless 'the official expression, so to speak, of the nation's sovereign body'. Griswold, *Forgiveness*, p. 200.
75. Griswold, *Forgiveness*, p. 196.
76. Habermas notes the analogy/disanalogy between the two memorials in his essay 'The Finger of Blame', proving, inadvertently, a certain elective affinity between the two as permanent provocations to complacent understandings of the national identity. Habermas, 'The Finger of Blame', p. 47.
77. As Edkins wryly observes, 'A wall carved with the names of all the Vietnamese victims of the war would be sixty-nine times the size and would stretch the whole distance between the Washington and Lincoln monuments.' Edkins, *Trauma and the Memory of Politics*, p. 75.
78. Whereas Lindstrom links the kenotic element of the memorial to openness in interpretation, I see it as being tied to its designation of the people as not there, as the emptiness at the heart of the state. See R. Lindstrom, 'Berlin's Kenotic Triad of Architecture', *Academia Letters*, August 2021, Article 3407.
79. Pickford, 'Dialectical Reflections', pp. 420–423.
80. Pickford, 'Dialectical Reflections', p. 434.
81. Pickford, 'Dialectical Reflections', p. 433.
82. J.E. Young, *At Memory's Edge: After-Images of the Holocaust in Contemporary Art and Architecture*, New Haven, CT: Yale University Press, 2000, pp. 7–8. In a similar vein,

Habermas has suggested the Memorial to the Murdered Jews should function as an irritant, adding that '[a]nyone who wants something more comfortable or more discursive has not grasped the meaning and the point of the project'. Habermas, *Time of Transitions*, p. 44.
83. A.C. Danto, 'The Vietnam Veterans Memorial', *The Nation*, 31 August 1985, p. 155.
84. Levinson, *Written in Stone*, p. 122; Edkins, *Trauma and the Memory of Politics*, p. 79.
85. M. Nussbaum, *Political Emotions: Why Love Matters for Justice*, Cambridge, MA: The Belknap Press, 2013, p. 287.
86. Nussbaum, *Political Emotions*, p. 258. As Nussbaum notes, one of the conditions of the competition for the design of the Vietnam Veterans Memorial was that it make no political statement about the war. In order to heal divisions, the Memorial had to remain studiously neutral in relation to one of the most contentious episodes in American foreign (and domestic) policy. Hence the shift from the political register to the human register. In this 'memorial to humanity', as James Tatum has put it, it is that which is personal and that which is human, not that which is civic, that takes pride of place. See Nussbaum, *Political Emotions*, p. 286; and Tatum, *The Mourner's Song*, p. 17.
87. Nussbaum, *Political Emotions*, p. 286.
88. Nussbaum, *Political Emotions*, p.287.
89. Nussbaum, *Political Emotions*, p. 286.
90. Edkins, *Trauma and the Memory of Politics*, p. 80.
91. Maya Lin, Design Statement, cited in Edkins, *Trauma and the Memory of Politics*, p. 79.
92. Nussbaum, *Political Emotions*, p. 288.
93. Nussbaum, *Political Emotions*, pp. 284–285.
94. Nussbaum, *Political Emotions*, p. 287.
95. Griswold, *Forgiveness*, p. 205.
96. Griswold, *Forgiveness*, p. 198.
97. Griswold, *Forgiveness*, p. 202.
98. Griswold, *Forgiveness*, pp. 207–208.
99. See Nussbaum, *Political Emotions*, p. 286; A.C. Danto, 'The Vietnam Veterans Memorial', pp. 153–154; and Levinson, *Written in Stone*, pp. 122–123.
100. Brody, 'The Inadequacy of Berlin's "Memorial to the Murdered Jews of Europe"', passim.
101. M. Callaghan, *Empathetic Memorials: The Other Designs for the Berlin Holocaust Memorial*, London: Palgrave Macmillan, 2020, p. 220.
102. S.M. Chin, F. Franke, and S. Halpern, 'A Self-Serving Admission of Guilt: An Examination of the Intentions and Effects of Germany's Memorial to the Murdered Jews of Europe' in J. Zarankin. *Reflections on the Holocaust*, New York: Humanity in Action Inc., 2011.
103. M. Callaghan, 'A Holocaust Memorial or a Memorial to Germany's Vicarious Trauma?', *Inter-Disciplinary Press*, 2013, p. 1.
104. Callaghan, 'A Holocaust Memorial', p. 3.
105. Kovach and Walser, *The Burden of the Past*, p. 86.
106. Lewis, 'Germany's Metamorphosis', p. 109.
107. As Mathäs has noted, the later-born are at once 'more reluctant to bear the responsibility for their ancestor's crimes' and yet 'accountable for the preservation of the memory of those crimes'. A. Mathäs, 'The Presence of the Past: Martin Walser on Memoirs and Memorials', *German Studies Review*, 25(1), 2002, p. 1.

108. As Callaghan notes, 'Though Germany was the perpetrator of the Holocaust, one might argue that the victims include the post-war generation of Germans—the *Nachgeborenen*—who continue to deal with the resonating effects of a legacy that must always haunt them'. Callaghan, 'A Holocaust Memorial', p. 4.
109. See Callaghan, *Empathetic Memorials*, p. 248.
110. Baptist, 'Shades of Grey', p. 83.
111. H. Arendt, 'Mankind and Terror' in *Essays in Understanding*, New York: Schocken Books, 2005, p. 304.
112. P. Levi, *The Drowned and the Saved*, London: Penguin Books, 1988, pp. 63–64. In the preface to *Survival in Auschwitz*, Levi wrote of his need to bear witness as follows: 'The need to tell our story to "the rest", to make "the rest" participate in it, had taken on for us, before our liberation and after, the character of an immediate and violent impulse, to the point of competing with our other elementary needs.' See P. Levi, *Survival in Auschwitz*, New York: Touchstone, 1996, p. 9.
113. Levi, *The Drowned and the Saved*, pp. 56–62.
114. Levinson, *Written in Stone*, p. 139.
115. Levinson, *Written in Stone*, p. 127.
116. T. Adorno, 'What Does Coming to Terms with the Past Mean?' in G. Hartmann (ed.), *Bitburg in Moral and Political Perspective*, Bloomington, IN: Indiana University Press, 1986, pp. 114–130.
117. J. Butler, *Precarious Life: The Powers of Mourning and Violence*, London: Verso, 2004, p. 34.
118. J.E. Young, 'Memory and Monument' in G. Hartmann (ed.), *Bitburg in Moral and Political Perspective*, Bloomington, IN: Indiana University Press, 1986, p. 105.
119. Young, 'Memory and Monument', p. 105.
120. Young, 'Memory and Monument', p. 106.
121. The phrase is taken from Callaghan, 'A Holocaust Memorial', p. 9.
122. Ahr, 'Memory and Mourning in Berlin', p. 295.
123. Levi, *The Drowned and the Saved*, p. 9.
124. H. Arendt, *The Origins of Totalitarianism*, New York: Harcourt, 1976, p. 282.

4
An Exercise of Sovereignty in the Mode of Contrition

If the first rule of politics is to never admit you're wrong, never say you're sorry, political apologies make for a truly strange spectacle.[1] Even for those inclined to scepticism, there is something uniquely absorbing about the moment when the sovereign surrenders its inviolability, falls to its knees before the wronged other, and begs for their forgiveness. One cannot quite believe what one is seeing because it is fundamentally at odds with everything one has learnt about sovereign power in theory and practice. Does not its defining feature lie precisely in the fact that it is untouchable? And yet, in what is, perhaps, one of the great curiosities of the late twentieth and early twenty-first centuries, political or state apologies (by which I mean those offered by a duly authorized representative of a sovereign people) have emerged as an instance of the exception become norm.[2] 'Twenty years ago', claimed Danielle Celermajer back in 2008, 'the idea that a political leader might apologize on behalf of the nation to a section of its (current and former) population for past wrongs would have seemed anomalous, if not absurd.' Today, she added, the list of collective, representative apologies runs on almost endlessly.[3] More than a decade later, neither demand nor supply shows much sign of waning. As Mark Gibney, editor of the book that announced the 'age of apology', ironically noted in 2021, it is now the absence (not the presence) of political apology that raises questions.[4] 'Anomalous', then? Not at all. 'Absurd'? This is what we need to discover.

The question of whether there is any sense in political apologies has been on the agenda for some time now. For the most part, however, political philosophers have been more interested in working out *what* makes for a good political apology (what might be called its ethico-normative conditions of sincerity) than *how* a political apology is made (what might be called its juridico-political conditions of possibility).[5] Attention has thus been predominantly focused on ascertaining what a sovereign would need to do in order to demonstrate that it really was sorry for the injustices of the past. Since a political apology, unlike a personal apology, is invariably offered by a representative (by someone, that is, who speaks on behalf of a sovereign body and in relation to things done 'in its name'), some criteria, other than an expression of remorse, seem to be needed to prove that the sovereign means what it says when it says sorry. What, ask the moral philosophers, might take the place of emotion, the so-called engine of apology, as an index of sincerity in cases where the apologizer did not do anything wrong *personally* and would therefore only be capable of a confected remorse?[6] Although by no means idle, this preoccupation with sincerity and, more precisely, with whether a political apology can ever be truly sincere has meant that the question of *how* political apologies relate to the legal order of the state has been left largely unaddressed. For the political philosophers, it seems, it is enough that the agent offering the apology has the authority to do so. Exactly where that authority is derived from, what it entitles the representative of the sovereign polity to do (or say), and how that entitlement impacts upon the act of apology itself scarcely rate a mention.[7] Would it matter if we approached political apology less as an ethical gesture than as an act of sovereignty?

Just how much it might matter becomes apparent when one asks why a sovereign should feel the need to apologize for its actions at all. For even if we accept, as I think we must, that the sovereign is a continuous agent, an 'artificial person', as Hobbes put it, that extends through time, at once outliving and connecting the various 'natural persons' (whether monarchs or assemblies) who have represented it and acted in its name, the justification for political apology remains elusive.[8] Since the authority to determine what is lawful and unlawful ultimately rests with the sovereign, there is no standard beyond its own against which it is *required* to measure its actions and no entity beyond itself to whom it is *obliged* to submit to judgement.[9] The only agent, other, of course, than God, that 'Sovereign of Sovereigns', as Hobbes put it, which could convict it of injustice and force it to atone for its actions is itself.[10] But what sovereign would take cause against itself for things done by itself? And what possible impact could this have upon its authority even if it did? The more closely one looks at it, therefore, the more perplexing the phenomenon of political apology seems to become. What is it exactly—what reason, what purpose, what pressure—has it to fall to its knees and do penance for past acts? And what kind of penance does a political apology ultimately amount to if the sovereign retains the same rights, including the right to go beyond the law, which it enjoyed before? Could it be that the idea of a political apology is really just a nonsense, an inherently 'abortive ritual', as Michel-Rolph Trouillot so vividly put it?[11]

The paradox implicit in a sovereign saying sorry for acts that it was authorized to perform and which, failing some radical overhaul of the social contract, it would appear to have the authority to perform again escapes even some of the best observers. In an otherwise insightful article, for instance, Stephen Winter depicts political apologies as institutional responses to 'politically *authorised* wrongdoings'; that is, to 'acts of state—done by the law either directly or through negligence'. On his account, the act of wrongdoing 'burdens the political authority'; the act of apology unburdens it.[12] Exactly how authorized acts, 'done by the law', become wrongs that burden the sovereign is, however, left unclear. Must we assume that the sovereign now has no choice but to bow down before a universal morality beyond its own law; that the reputational costs of not accepting human rights norms (and retrospectively applying them) are now so high as to have effectively taken the decision to apologize out of its hands? A similar problem arises in a paper on official apologies by Ernesto Verdeja. 'State violations', notes Verdeja, 'are normally framed as "necessary" responses to some perceived threat.' In situations of emergency, acts of 'harassment, abuse, massacre and terror' become 'officially sanctioned methods of dealing with some minorities or political enemies'. Verdeja takes it as given that the state should apologize for these violations of 'basic social norms'.[13] Yet it is once again not entirely clear why the sovereign should apologize for breaching social norms in situations of emergency. Is that not what it is authorized and, in fact, expected to do? Should we assume that apologies are only appropriate where it can be shown the appeal to necessity was self-evidently fallacious or can the sovereign be expected to apologize regardless of how well founded the threat appeared at the time because basic social norms are inviolate no matter what the circumstances?[14]

In section I of this chapter, I pay close attention to the work of two of the rare critics—Alex Reilly and Michael Fagenblat—to have pondered these questions in a profound and serious way. Each remains local to the extent that he addresses himself specifically to the apology to the 'Stolen Generations' (the victims of a racial policy of forced child removal) offered by Prime Minister Kevin Rudd on behalf of the sovereign people of Australia. Yet, by analysing that apology with reference to the political theology of Carl Schmitt, both Reilly and Fagenblat lend the particular instance a more general significance. Since it is explicitly based in the theory of sovereignty, their work sheds considerable light not just on the case of Australia but on the nature and limits of political apologies more generally. Indeed, although each arrives at a rather different conclusion, both wrestle with the problem of sovereign transcendence and, more specifically, with the fact that the gesture of political apology seems to sit in tension with the authority the sovereign person has conventionally enjoyed to declare a state of exception and go beyond the law. On what basis, they ask, can sovereigns be called to apologize for past actions that, legally speaking, they had a right (and potentially even a duty) to perform? And what can a political apology, whose transformative potential pivots around the promise of 'never again', actually mean if the sovereign retains its discretionary right to suspend or override the law in the future? Is there any ethical or political merit in saying 'never again, unless ...'?

This chapter is indebted to Reilly for refusing to take for granted that a sovereign can make a meaningful apology. As he quite sensibly asks: doesn't its right to decide on the exception both secure it against accusations of wrongdoing and vitiate its commitment to non-repetition? However, as the choice of title makes clear, the chapter centres on Fagenblat's highly evocative, yet also somewhat elusive, characterization of political apology as an 'exercise of sovereignty in the mode of contrition'.[15] Although scarcely alone in conceiving political apology as an 'act of contrition' or a symbolic form of 'public penance', Fagenblat can be credited with recognizing it as a most unusual manifestation of the transcendent power of the sovereign in relation to the law.[16] In apologizing, he claims, the sovereign uses its prerogative to go beyond the law not, as is conventional, to license violence but to practise atonement. Awake, finally, to the damage its untrammelled will does to others, it subjects itself to a painful reckoning with its own moral ground beyond the law, finding in the Christian code of ethics a reason to change not just one or two policies but its entire character. As Fagenblat would have it, a political apology does more (much, much more) than provide a belated form of recognition to the victims of injustice. It re-constitutes the sovereign as an essentially other-orientated, essentially non-violent, being; a being that fulfils the promise of 'never again' by renouncing the absolute, divine-like power of decision that allowed it to cause harm in the past.

Fagenblat's account of political apology makes two strong claims to our attention. In the first place, it serves as a something of corrective to the dominant 'membership theory' of political apology pioneered by Melissa Nobles in which the 'act of contrition' is considered primarily in terms of its implications for the victim, not the perpetrator.[17] Political apologies, on this membership theory, revise, and in an inherently progressive way, the rules of inclusion and exclusion that determine who enjoys full citizenship rights in the polity. By providing belated recognition to the victims of an unjust policy of racial discrimination, apologies demonstrate that they will henceforth be fully included in (and ought never have been excluded from) the political community. But what of the political agent who says sorry? On what authority do *they* issue such an apology and what happens to *their* status as a result of the gesture of contrition? Rather than dodge these questions, Fagenblat confronts them head on, seeking to both account for, and explain the implications of, political apology with reference to the theory of sovereignty. Extending Schmitt's *Political Theology* in a novel way, he reads apology as a historically unprecedented and politically radical manifestation of the decision on the exception—a decision which, in enacting a Christian ethic of respect for others, radically changes our sense not only of what the sovereign can do but of what the sovereign can be.

Secondly, Fagenblat gives an account of the symbolism of political apology that is not only unusually rich but which also helps to reveal its precise implications as the act of a *sovereign* entity. Thus far, most of the literature that engages the figurative or performative nature of political apology does so in the context of debates about whether symbolic gestures ought to be backed up by concrete actions. The key question here has been whether political apologies can stand alone as illocutionary speech acts (speech acts which, in J.L. Austin's famous formula, 'do things by saying things') or are nothing but empty symbols if they are not 'backed up' by concrete forms of amends.[18] Concerned more with the question of *what* is being signified than *whether* signification is meaningful in and of itself, Fagenblat traces the peculiar symbolism of *sovereign* contrition back to the Christian conceptualization of kenosis. Used in Christian theology to refer to the renunciation of divine power and, more precisely, to the assumption by God of the form of man in Christ, kenosis figures in Fagenblat's analysis as the symbolic model (and symbolic ideal) of radical humility implicit in political apology. As he compellingly argues, the true ethical significance of this kind of *political* act of contrition lies in the way the sovereign re-enacts the incarnation by 'foregoing the very power that constitutes its sovereignty'.[19] No sovereign, he suggests, can make an apology without consciously giving up the power that connects it to the divine: immunity from judgement and invulnerability to suffering.

Fagenblat, it seems to me, takes the logic of political apology as an ethical gesture about as far as it can go, revealing, along the way, precisely what it would need to be in order to be genuinely transformative. As striking and illuminating as it may be, though, his account makes the mistake of reading sovereignty in terms of apology rather than apology in terms of sovereignty. In line with the concept of kenosis, Fagenblat treats political apology as a radical act of abasement in which the sovereign relinquishes its immunity and makes a sacrifice of itself. And yet, if there is one thing we learn from Schmitt, it is that the sovereign always acts in defence of the life *of* the state and the life *in* the state. While it is happy to leave well enough alone in normal times, the threat of death—not least of all its own death—stirs it into action. In *Political Theology*, the text upon which Fagenblat's whole analysis hinges, Schmitt repeatedly underlines that the state only ever 'suspends the law in the exception on the basis of its right to self-preservation'.[20] In this respect, I will suggest, political apology is, in fact, no exception. While the gesture does indeed involve a sacrifice, it is not, as Fagenblat would have it, the sacrifice of self for other but rather of one self for another self. In the act of political apology, I will suggest, the sovereign divides its earlier, tainted self from its current, innocent self to cleanse the body politic of the stain of sin. Rather than empty itself of the power to abuse, it relieves itself of the weight of shame, regenerating the body politic in a renewed innocence. A resurrection to be sure.

As I go on to discuss in the following sections, this places political apology squarely within the frame of 'shame management', albeit not in the way such a therapy is commonly understood. In many cases the restorative power of apology as an act of recognition is linked to its capacity to alleviate the misplaced shame of the victims who are inclined to blame themselves for what happened.[21] The analysis presented here suggests that it is not simply (or even primarily) the trauma of the victims and its shameful excess that is 'managed' or 'assuaged' by apology. As Robert Manne (one of the most prominent public advocates of an apology for the forced removal of Indigenous children) noted, revelations of Stolen Generations did considerable damage to the national self-image of non-Indigenous Australians. In part because the violation in question was easy to identify with and in part because it had occurred so recently, stories of child removal provided a culturally disorientating, traumatic blow to collective pride.[22] Manne was hardly overstating the matter when he said 'Australians have found this dimension of their history exceptionally difficult to face'.[23] With revelations about forced removals, a shadow fell across the nation, or perhaps it would be better to say that an ever-present, but largely ignored, disquiet about dispossession re-emerged in a particularly forceful, shame-inducing way. By exercising its right of exception 'in the mode of contrition', I argue, the sovereign did not just make it clear that Indigenous people were not to blame, it also made a double for itself, a representation of what it once was (but claimed no longer to be), which could be sacrificed on the cross to provide Australians with a cathartic release from the burden of shame. The problem confronting Indigenous people was thus not so much whether the apology was sincere or insincere but whether it had produced the structural change that would be genuinely transformative of Indigenous life.

I A Rape of the Soul So Profound

Scholars are now in the habit of attributing the devastating effects of settler colonialism to the fact that it is 'a structure not an event'.[24] Since, in the settler variant of colonialism, the invaders come to stay, Indigenous peoples are necessarily deprived of the resources (particularly that critical resource called land) they need to sustain their way of life. It is thus not by chance or accident, by some unhappy confluence of events, that settler colonialism has proved destructive of their societies and their lives. Although the events of colonial history may turn this way and that, generally doing damage to but sometimes also giving succour to Indigenous peoples, their prior occupation of the land makes them an obstacle to colonialization and hence a target for elimination. As Patrick Wolfe famously put it, since territoriality is non-negotiable in this form of colonialism, 'elimination is an organizing principal of settler society rather than a one-off (and superseded occurrence)'—the overriding objective is always 'biocultural assimilation', with the line between biological absorption and cultural assimilation invariably being blurred.[25] One need not, however, reject the idea that settler colonialism is a structure, not an event, to countenance the possibility that certain exceptional events can alter that structure in ways that foster survival rather than accelerate elimination. One such 'event', frequently celebrated by advocates of restorative justice for overcoming the amnesia of the settler-colonial state and providing healing for Indigenous life, is political apology.[26] It is with this possibility of a transformative event in mind that I turn to our example.

On 13 February 2008, the then prime minister, Kevin Rudd, offered a nationally unprecedented apology to Indigenous people on behalf of the sovereign body of Australia. The apology was addressed specifically to the members of the so-called Stolen Generations: the children of Aboriginal and Torres Strait Islander descent who were forcibly, yet lawfully, removed from their parents and placed in non-Indigenous families and institutions during the course of the twentieth century. The practice of forced removal operated in a range of jurisdictions and under a range of policy settings—racial absorption, cultural integration, social assimilation—blurring the line between a eugenic programme aimed at 'breeding out the colour' and a welfare measure aimed at 'uplifting the native'. However, even in its supposedly more benign phases, the policy was sufficiently stepped in racial assumptions and sufficiently destructive of Aboriginal life to warrant accusations of genocide.[27] In contrast to regular forms of child removal, which are only undertaken where there is substantiated evidence of abuse and neglect, Aboriginal and

Torres Strait Islander children were taken from their families and communities (and thereby exposed to various kinds of institutional abuse) on the entirely arbitrary basis of their racial identity.[28] The assumption was always that Aboriginality was a barrier (if not a threat) to the colonial project and thus something that needed to be eliminated, as much for the benefit of the children as for the unity of the sovereign body. In effect, therefore, the exceptional measure of a forced removal was both an expression of, and the solution to, the biopolitical fracture state racism opened up between 'the People', whose form of life had to be protected, and 'the people', whose form of life had to be eliminated. Had it succeeded, it would have ensured that Aboriginality (and thus people who identified as Aboriginal) disappeared.

The question of whether the crime of genocide had been committed in Australia proved to be one of the most controversial aspects of the debate that followed the publication of the *Bringing Them Home* report in 1997. Although the forcible transference of children from one group to another group 'with the intention of destroying that group' is one of the means of genocide listed in the 1948 United Nations Convention on the Prevention and Prosecution of the Crime of Genocide, establishing an 'intention to destroy' with the certitude required by the law proved difficult in the Australian context. While undeniably underpinned by racist assumptions, forced removals were defensible as misguided humanitarianism, particularly during the post-war assimilationist era, and were generally understood as such, even by Australians who came to the belated recognition that the thing most lacking about the policy was humanity.[29] Indigenous people, quite understandably, have been inclined to pay less attention to the niceties of legal definition and what the colonizer intended than the practical effects of racial practices upon their way of life. As Larissa Behrendt wrote,

> [f]or Indigenous plaintiffs, it doesn't matter whether the crime of genocide was committed as it was defined by international law and it doesn't matter whether there was intention or not. What seems to be more important from the Indigenous perspective are the effects of the actions of the government—these actions have amounted to damage to Indigenous people, families and communities and they choose to use the word 'genocide' to describe it.[30]

By evoking the concept of genocide in this way, Indigenous people have effectively spanned 'the gap between law and life', as Behrendt puts it, underscoring just how profound a trauma the Stolen Generations (and dispossession more generally) was, and still is, for Indigenous people. They 'choose' the word genocide deliberately because forced removal did not simply do damage to particular Indigenous lives, it did damage to the whole Indigenous way of life.

The devastating nature of that damage was revealed only too clearly by the *Bringing Them Home* report. Composed largely of first-person testimony, the report released stories into the public sphere that had not been widely circulated before and which spoke with distressing candidness of the disruption to the Indigenous way of life cause by forced removal and the profound 'loss' (of liberty, language, kinship, culture, continuity, trust) that accompanied it. The president of the commission for the inquiry, Sir Ronald Wilson, was by no means wrong when he noted '[g]rief and loss are the predominant themes of this report'—to read it as a whole was to listen to a seemingly endless song of mourning.[31] As a *de facto* national exercise in truth telling, *Bringing Them Home* shone an unflattering light on Australia. More than simply drawing attention to the racial distinctions that had been used to determine who was included in (and, of course, who was excluded from) the community of rights-bearing citizens, it exposed a history of racial engineering. Accused of genocide, Australia suddenly found itself in the company of the very countries—Nazi Germany for one, South Africa for another—it prided itself on being different from, engendering a sense of shame that was largely unprecedented.[32] This truth-telling exercise was, however, also exposing of the 'inner life' of the Stolen Generations themselves, with Wilson describing its subject matter as 'so personal and intimate' that it would not ordinarily be discussed in the public domain.[33] In *Bringing Them Home*, a 'rape of the soul so profound' (this being the phrase Peter Read adopted to explain the impact of forced removal) was put on public display and its victims laid bare in their unimaginable, unresolved grief.[34]

After the history of forced removals was brought to the attention of the wider Australian public, forcing it to confront a deeply unpalatable truth about itself, a long, and frequently highly acrimonious, debate ensued about the appropriate measures of redress. However, it was the recommendation of the Human Rights and Equal Opportunity Commission for an official apology that galvanized supporters of the Stolen Generations. Resisted for ten years by the conservative government of Prime Minister John Howard on the grounds that members of the current generation should not be held responsible for the mistakes of their predecessors, the demand for an apology became divisive of public life, making its eventual delivery by the newly elected Rudd government in 2008 an even more momentous occasion than it would already have been. Symbolically chosen as the first item of business in the first full sitting of the new parliament, the Rudd apology became, at one and the same time, an attempt to recognize the extraordinary damage that had been done to Indigenous life and to mark a temporal rupture in the life of the Australian state. 'There comes a time in the history of nations', declared Rudd,

> when their peoples must become fully reconciled to their past if they are to go forward with confidence to embrace their future. Our nation, Australia, has reached such a time. That is why the parliament is today here assembled: to deal with this unfinished business of the nation, to remove a great stain from the nation's soul and, in a true spirit of reconciliation, to open a new chapter in the history of this great land, Australia.[35]

Only by addressing this 'dark chapter', Rudd went on, could 'we' bring 'the first two centuries of our settled history to a close'.[36] For him, and the nation, the apology was thus both a moment of reckoning and the beginning of something new. But what exactly had been reckoned with and what exactly was new?

II Reckoning with Exceptionalism: Political Apology as an Act of Sovereignty

Advocates of restorative justice have tended to champion political apologies as symbolic acts of contrition which, in reckoning with historical forms of misrecognition, perform a number of valuable functions. In the first place, it is said, they affirm or acknowledge the human and civil dignity of the victims of discrimination, reversing or, as Govier and Verwoerd have put it, 'unsaying' the message of moral worthlessness implied by the original violation.[37] Secondly, they work to affirm or reaffirm normative principles of universal justice and respect, signalling to the victim group that the discriminatory treatment they received in the past is no longer considered acceptable and will not be repeated in the future. Thirdly, and relatedly, political apologies help to re-establish trust in the institutions of the state, providing victims with *prima facie* evidence of a renewed commitment to principles of neutrality, reliability, and fairness. Fourthly, they reshape the historical record of the nation, overturning monumental histories that remember the achievements and the triumphs while forgetting the abuses and the violations. Finally, and in part because of all the other functions listed above, political apologies are believed to promote healing and reconciliation. Since the recognition of wrongdoing serves, at the same time, as a recognition of undeserved suffering, it provides what Barkan calls a form of 'psychic amends'. Victims are able overcome their feelings of grief and alienation—are able, that is, to complete the process of mourning because the polity has come to accept *their* truth.[38] One sticking point to unequivocal assent has, however, always remained: how does one guarantee the sincerity of a political apology?

For all their evident merits, political apologies, like the one offered by Prime Minister Rudd, have tended to invite suspicion, particularly as the practice has spread globally. The more that the gesture of apology has cemented itself as a political norm, deployed by sovereign states around the world as an alternative way of doing justice to wrongdoing, the more moral critics have worried about its potential manipulation, in Machiavellian fashion, as a tool of 'reputation management' or 'image repair'. The critical issue in this regard is not so much that apologies are, *by their very nature*, empty symbolism or even that they are a poor substitute for material reparations (as Jana Thompson has duly noted, just as an apology can seem hollow in the absence of reparations, reparations can appear utilitarian in the absence of an apology).[39] It is rather that the use of apology in a political, as opposed to a personal, context immediately puts its sincerity in doubt. Since, or so the critics assume, strategic calculation is not simply endemic to political life, but one of the defining conditions of the political game, no official or state apology can ever be morally uncontaminated. Behind every act of state, even an act of contrition like an apology, must sit a strategic concern with the national interest. As Charles Griswold put it: 'some level of hypocrisy is no doubt intrinsic to the expression of political apology (for narrowly self-interested motivations are ineliminable when the agent is a political entity)'.[40] Looked at from an ethico-normative perspective, then, the issue is not really whether self-interest contaminates the moral purity of the gesture (for that much can be safely assumed); it is rather whether the gesture can retain some ethical value even in the face of those narrowly self-interested motivations.

It is completely understandable, given this set of assumptions, that political philosophers have tended to see their critical task in terms of reducing the risk of a purely self-interested (and therefore *utterly* insincere) atonement ritual. Working from the entirely plausible assumption that a completely inauthentic apology would be worse than no apology at all, they have sought to establish the (ethico-normative) conditions that would need to be satisfied to demonstrate that the sovereign, if not devoid of instrumental motivations, had at least engaged in a painful acknowledgement of its violent deeds. Inevitably, differences of opinion have emerged as to the precise nature of this 'sincerity test'[41]—the issue, firstly, of whether a political apology ought to include a request for forgiveness or, secondly, be supported by material amends being among the most contentious.[42] Notwithstanding the ongoing nature of these disputes, a broad consensus has emerged around a number of essential felicity conditions. Firstly, that a political apology must be framed as an exceptional event—that it must meet the ceremonial conditions (right location, right time, right tone) by which watershed moments in the life of the polity are distinguished from the day-to-day business of the state. Secondly, that it must be offered by the right person—by someone who not only has the requisite moral standing but who is also duly authorized to act as a representative of the people. Thirdly, that it must publicly name and explain the injustice to which it is responding—that it must be quite specific in describing the injustice in question and in accounting for its occurrence. Finally, that it must include a solemn commitment not to commit similar acts in the future—that it promises 'never again'.[43]

Implicitly or explicitly, most critical analyses of empirical cases rely upon this 'sincerity test' to differentiate between authentic and faux contrition or, as Matt James puts it, the apology from the quasi-apology and the non-apology.[44] Thus, when Tony Barta and Damien Short questioned the value of Prime Minister Rudd's (seemingly meritorious) apology to the Stolen Generations, it was on the grounds, firstly, that it did not properly name the injustice and secondly that it was not accompanied by any offer of financial restitution.[45] Both accused the prime minister of having failed to accurately describe the harm, his apology speech having studiously avoided any reference to the term 'genocide' despite the fact it had been used in the *Bringing Them Home* report and was preferred by many of the victims.[46] In their judgement, this omission made the apology an ambiguous act of recognition/non-recognition, remembering and forgetting, doing more than a little damage to its 'felicity'. As Barta sharply put it, at the same moment that the apology exposed a history of injustice, it 'buried a history of genocide'.[47] In a similar fashion, both took aim at the attempt to 'compensate' the victims of forced removal through welfare measures rather than financial restitution. Working on the basis that 'practical amends' are needed not so much to complement as to *underwrite* the 'symbolic amends' of apologies, Short claimed that the lack of reparations had 'significantly diminish[ed] the quality and sincerity of the apology'—a point which many Indigenous critics reiterated.[48]

At first blush, this ethico-normative approach to the issue of political apologies seems eminently sensible. Since the demand for state apologies shows no sign of abating and the political stakes of the gesture are high (healing or hurt), one ought to have some criteria for differentiating the sincere from the cynical. However, in their resolve to establish the felicity conditions of official apologies, political philosophers have been surprisingly inattentive to the nature of the agent that offers or, as I will go on to underline, *performs* them. Political apologies, they have repeatedly stressed, need to be offered by someone duly authorized to speak on behalf of the people; by someone, that is, who is entitled to 'bear the sovereign person'.[49] And yet, beyond worrying about the possible 'non-identity' of this sovereign person in cases of historical injustice (beyond worrying, that is, about the possibility that the 'sovereign person' who committed the offence might not, because of the passage of time, be the same 'sovereign person' being called on to apologize for it),[50] they have given little thought to the kind of qualities and powers that it possesses. Once the necessary corrections are made for the fact that the sovereign person (in our case a prime minister) may have no personal relationship to the wrong and thus be incapable of feeling genuine remorse, the usual conventions and expectations are assumed to apply: an apology is an apology is an apology. Arguably, however, we stand little chance of truly understanding the phenomenon of *political* apology unless we can come to grips with the kind of authority the sovereign person possesses and the way in which that authority works not simply to enable but also to disable gestures of contrition. The critical issue here, as will we see, is less whether the sincerity conditions of apology have been met in the particular case than whether the nature of sovereign authority makes them unattainable in any case.

The first and most important issue that needs to be reckoned with in this context is that of sovereign prerogative. In the liberal tradition that begins with Locke, the authority of the sovereign (by which I mean the things that it enjoys a *right* to do) is strictly delimited by the social contract. In contrast to Hobbes, who gave the sovereign 'the whole power of prescribing the rules' (thereby rendering it completely immune to accusations of injustice),[51] Locke restricts its authority to the protection of natural rights. Since, in his account, the state of nature is not a condition of war but a condition of civility, the 'Supreme Power' has no other end than the protection of the 'property' individuals *already* hold in their bodies, their movements, and their things; that is, in their life, liberty, and estate. Power is entrusted to it for this purpose and this purpose alone. In this revival of natural law theory, it is thus entirely possible for the sovereign to be found guilty of abusing the trust that is placed in it or of acting beyond the authority it acquires through the mechanism of the social contract. Since positive laws (the '*Municipal Laws* of Countries') are 'only so far right', according to Locke, 'as they are founded on the Law of Nature', the sovereign is not free, as it is in Hobbes, to do as it will.[52] If the 'Supreme Power' acts in ways that are at odds with the law of nature, infringing on those 'natural rights' to life, liberty, and property which exist prior to its creation, it will have exceeded the limits of its contractual authority and exposed itself to the penalty, if that is the right word for it, of civil rebellion.

Although Locke never mentions official apologies, and would doubtless have been perplexed by the very idea, it is his or some similar account of political authority that underpins and justifies the demand for sovereign acts of contrition. Since, in his view, the authority of the sovereign is bound by natural law, it can be held to account—or, in accord with the current fashion, made to atone—for 'any exercise of power beyond moral right'.[53] Should it exceed what nature is willing to sanction by enacting laws (or issuing decrees) that jeopardize rights to life, liberty, and estate, it can be rightly expected to apologize. That, at any rate, seems to be the logic at work in Winter's reference to wrongdoings 'done by the law', Verdeja's reference to violations that are 'officially sanctioned', and many similar formulations. The assertion in each case is that 'the lawful' and 'the official' cannot be equated with 'the just' or 'the moral'. The mere fact that something is done in accordance with the law or is sanctioned by officialdom does not mean that it is not in breach of the laws of nature (or, as Verdeja puts it, 'basic social norms'). In insisting that the sovereign answer for the damage it has done to the lives of others through the exercise of its supreme power, demands for apology implicitly, and sometimes explicitly, invoke this gap between municipal law and natural right. No sovereign, they presuppose, is immune from moral scrutiny or permitted to act with impunity. Norms and standards—derived from natural law and now referred to as human rights—exist outside the municipal law, the violation of which gives rise to claims for various forms of redress.

As always, however, things are not quite as straightforward as they first appear. While Locke makes every effort to hold the 'Supreme Power' in check, he concedes that the law cannot provide for all exigencies. On some occasions, the sovereign will find it necessary to act in ways that are either outside or in violation of the law, so as to better fulfil the purpose for which it was instituted in the first place: the protection of the public good.[54] In the *Two Treatises*, Locke refers to such exercises of sovereign prerogative as 'the power of doing public good without a rule'.[55] Precisely when a sovereign might be justified in acting without a rule is, of course, a matter of contention. Necessity, as Locke knew only too well, is always 'the tyrant's plea'. However, that did not mean that the exercise of sovereign prerogative (its freedom to use its supreme power, as it were, 'without right') could be eliminated or even strictly delimited. Even in the most well-ordered state, a sovereign might still find cause, potentially very good cause, to act beyond the scope or in violation of the law. In such cases, according to Locke, there was 'no judge on earth' who could determine whether it had misused its prerogative because necessity, by its very nature, has no law, natural or municipal. Should the people feel aggrieved, their only recourse was to 'appeal to heaven' and wait (but for how long?) for that inscrutable sovereign of sovereigns to deliver its verdict on the justness of their cause.[56]

In more recent times credit is usually given to Carl Schmitt ('the Hobbes of the twentieth century')[57] for placing this issue of sovereign prerogative squarely before our eyes. In *Political Theology*, Schmitt locates the specificity of the sovereign as a political 'agent' or 'person' in the authority that it, and it alone, enjoys to act without a rule or, in what amounts to the same thing, to make a decision. As he empathically declares in the first line of the text: 'sovereign is he who decides on the exception'.[58] *Political Theology* followed closely in the wake of debates (tackled directly by Schmitt in *Die Diktator*) over the kind of powers the German president might exercise under Article 48 of the Weimar Constitution in times of emergency. However, for Schmitt, it was ultimately of little consequence whether the Constitution explicitly provided for such a 'right of exception' or made no mention of it. With Hobbes and Locke, he took the view that the sovereign person was ultimately *free to decide* when the circumstances necessitated special measures and what those special measures might be because that was the role it had been authorized to play in the political order.[59] And like them too, Schmitt insisted that acts performed in the state of exception would, by definition, be without a rule and without a judge on earth. 'The exception in jurisprudence', he noted, 'is analogous to the miracle in theology.'[60] Since neither emanates from within the order they effect (the first being outside law, the second outside nature), neither is amenable to evaluation or judgement. Such emergency measures are, as it were, 'measures beyond measure'.

One of the few scholars to have taken stock of this issue of prerogative and its relation to apology is Alex Reilly. In a short paper, instructively entitled 'Sovereign Apologies', Reilly draws on the work of Carl Schmitt to expose the paradox that perpetually threatens to unravel political apology as an act of contrition. If, on the one hand, according to Reilly, we accept that the sovereign has the right to decide on the exception and adopt special measures (like the forced removal of children) in situations of real or perceived emergency, then it cannot be accused of having done anything wrong when it discriminates through, or against, the law. 'The work of Schmitt', he writes, 'requires us to take seriously the possibility that the state has nothing to apologise for when passing extreme laws, as its lawful power extends to the exceptional.'[61] If, on the other hand, we accept that the sovereign can do wrong and does have cause to apologize, it can only be because we believe that it cannot (or ought not) exempt itself from legal constraint as and when *it* deems necessary. Set out in this way, the conjunction 'sovereign apology' emerges as a logical contradiction—either the concept of sovereignty works to strip apology of the thing that makes it meaningful (namely, an admission of wrongdoing) or the concept of apology works to strip sovereignty of the thing that makes it meaningful (namely, a right of exception). 'To be genuine', suggests Reilly, a political apology would have to recognize 'that the capacity of the sovereign is, or at least ought to be, limited.'[62] Yet that would require the sovereign to renounce precisely the right of exception in which the essence of its authority resides.

As Reilly would have it, then, the Australian Government's apology to the Stolen Generations (and by implication all such 'sovereign apologies') was really a sleight of hand. Notwithstanding the fact that it appeared to meet many, though not all, of the 'sincerity conditions' stipulated by normative theorists, it was rendered meaningless by the fact that it contained 'no reflection on the nature of governmental power or on the extent of the State's sovereignty.'[63] If 'the apology' was an admission of 'wrong', it was not of the fact that the sovereign has no right to the prerogative power that enabled such abuse but of the fact that the assumptions that drove it to make use of that prerogative power were, *on that occasion* and *with the benefit of hindsight*, mistaken.[64] In effect, the apology conceded that Aboriginal people, in their difference, had posed no threat to the political unity of the state and consequently ought not to have been the target of measures like forced removals aimed at their biological/cultural elimination. Put simply, there was no emergency.[65] The apology did not, however, concede that this should have been obvious at the time or that circumstances could never arise in which the exercise of that prerogative power against (or, as is commonly said, 'for the benefit of') Aboriginal people might not, once again, be necessary. As Reilly himself concludes: 'it would seem then that the same laws could be passed again and that future apologies may be necessary.'[66] Hardly what one would call a transformation.

The problem Reilly identifies with sovereign apologies is not simply of academic interest. For, at the very moment that Kevin Rudd was delivering his apology to the Stolen Generations, the Australian Government was once again interfering (with the assistance of the armed forces) in the domestic affairs of Indigenous peoples in the Northern Territory of Australia. The Northern Territory Emergency Response or 'Intervention', as it came to be known, was launched on the pretext of yet another crisis in the welfare of Indigenous children and led to the introduction (enabled by the Northern Territory National Emergency Response Act 2007) of a number of emergency measures that only applied to citizens of Aboriginal or Torres Strait

Islander descent: restrictions on the purchase of alcohol, quarantining of welfare payments, acquisition of parcels of land, special initiatives in employment, education, and health, and restrictions on pornography, among many others. In order to enact such emergency measures, it had been necessary for the Australian Government to temporarily suspend a range of other legislative instruments, not least of all the Racial Discrimination Act 1975. Asked about the legitimacy of the intervention, the prime minister who initiated it, John Howard, employed exactly the same Schmittian logic that enabled the policy of forced removals: 'What matters more: the constitutional niceties or the care and protection of young children?'[67] In an irony that was not lost on commentators, then, the sovereign was, at one and the same time, repenting the use of and making use of its prerogative powers in relation to a racially defined minority, revealing all too clearly that it retained the right to decide who might be included in (and, of course, who might be excluded from) the category of full citizen. As Indigenous scholar Nicole Watson observed,

> Australian Parliaments have a long tradition of enacting legislation for the purpose of coercing behavioural change in Aboriginal people. It is often preceded by moral panic buttressed by racial mythology. Until Australian Parliaments abandon this tradition, gestures such as the Apology will achieve little towards reconciling the nation.[68]

Reilly, to be sure, is by no means alone in questioning whether states can fulfil the promissory aspect of apology. Yet his critique of sovereign apologies is by no means as easily refuted as those which discredit the promise of 'never again' on the basis that, in politics, the parties, people, and policies are forever changing. Jana Thompson has, for instance, answered those sceptical about the capacity of states to act consistently over time by demonstrating that they are transgenerational entities. The mistake made by those who claim that politicians are only able to make commitments 'for the term of their office' or that policies are 'subject to reversal as soon as other people take power', she writes, is to conflate office-bearers with the office and the government of the day with the institution of the state. While leaders and governments can (and do) overturn the policies of their predecessors, many obligations, like many entitlements, are still passed from one generation to another. 'Skeptics', claims Thompson, 'exaggerate the problem': '[i]f states can make treaties and accept obligations of reparation, then they should be able to make genuine apologies'.[69] Reilly's point, however, is not that states are incapable of making long-term commitments. It is rather that the sovereign reserves the right to break all such commitments whenever (it deems) the circumstances necessitate. Sovereign prerogative comes, as it were, 'with the office' and is thus something of a transgenerational entitlement in its own right. Indeed, since citizens rely upon the sovereign to ensure the polity survives from one generation to the next, overcoming whatever crises may arise, its right to decide upon the exception does not just override but *legitimately* overrides all other obligations and entitlements.

By encouraging us to think about political apologies in relation to sovereign authority, then, Reilly throws considerable doubt not so much on the sincerity as on the very possibility of the gesture. For him, the infelicity of the apology to the Stolen Generations, rent as it was by the 'need to apologize' on the one hand and the 'impossibility of doing so' on the other, was not an isolated failure but entirely symptomatic of the aporetic nature of sovereign apologies more generally.[70] Since, on his account, the one thing that could demonstrate the felicity of an apology is the one thing that is incompatible with the idea of sovereignty—namely, the renunciation of the right to decide upon the exception—there is really no such thing as a *political* apology. That is not to say that victims will not welcome the admission of errors in previous exercises of sovereign prerogative or find them reassuring for the future, but simply that such admissions do not do anything to transform the authority of the sovereign person or alter settler colonialism as a structure. Indeed, since the promise made by a political apology can be legitimately broken in situations of crisis or emergency, it is doubtful whether it can really be considered a promise at all. 'The paradox at the heart of sovereignty', notes Reilly, 'is that the absolute sovereign cannot bind itself for the future.'[71] Say, or unsay, what it will, in other words, it simply cannot commit to 'never again'.

If Reilly is right, a political apology, however sincerely offered, really is an 'abortive ritual', albeit for reasons different than those offered by Trouillot, and ought not be relied upon.[72] However, there is another layer to the paradox of sovereign apologies that escapes his attention and which, theoretically at least, opens up new possibilities: this is the paradox entailed in making use of the right of exception to pass negative judgements on prior uses of the right of exception. Since it is only by standing above the law that the sovereign is able to pass judgement upon it or, to be more precise, it is only by transcending the legal order that it is able to declare that which was previously done *in the name of the people* and *by way of the law* unjust, a political apology would appear to rest upon the very same authority to decide on the exception that makes it possible for states to violate rights. Just as it is the sovereign decision on the exception that enables discrimination, it is the sovereign decision on the exception that enables redress. In both cases, it is 'the power to do public good without a rule' that enables 'special treatment' for a particular group or 'special measures' for a particular situation. If sovereign apologies have an ambiguous quality, then, it does not just arise from the fact that the sovereign cannot be accused of wrongdoing or that it is incapable of renouncing its right to decide upon the exception; it arises from the fact that it must make use of precisely that right to decide on the exception in order to make an apology at all. Paradoxically, in other words, every political apology would seem to be at once a critique and an expression of sovereign prerogative.

Two judgements are possible about the meaning of political apology as a 'speech act' here. The first is that every sovereign apology represents a kind of performative contra-diction: an unsaying that, in simultaneously critiquing and affirming the right of the exception, cancels itself out. The second is that a sovereign apology represents a kind of performative pre-diction: an unsaying that, in making ethical use of the right of the exception, reveals a new sovereign in the making. This second view hinges on the idea that a political apology is not just another expression of the power of exception but a wholly exceptional use of that power of the exception that leaves nothing unchanged, including, it would seem, the power to decide on the exception itself. In a seminal yet largely ignored essay, Michael Fagenblat characterizes this novel use of the power of exception, this exception *within* an exception, as an 'exercise of sovereignty in the mode of contrition'.[73] On his reading of things, a political apology differs significantly from conventional exercises of the right of exception because it constitutes an act of self-abasement rather than self-assertion. In saying sorry for past mistakes, he claims, the sovereign undergoes a radical transformation from a self-orientated to an other-orientated being, recreating itself in a relational mould in which the violence of pure will gives way to the vulnerability of ethical relation, independence to interdependence. However, in order to make sense of this, it is necessary to return to, and delve yet more deeply into, the issue of authority and the symbolism of political apology.

Like Reilly, Fagenblat begins his essay on the apology to the Stolen Generations from the premise that the defining characteristic of the sovereign as a political actor is that it answers to no one else. Unlike political agents constituted *under* the law, he notes, here in full agreement with Schmitt, the sovereign sits at the pinnacle of the legal order and is thus 'in need of no justification beyond itself'.[74] Like Reilly too, Fagenblat is drawn, logically and necessarily, by this Schmittian starting point to the conclusion that 'sovereign apologies' have a paradoxical quality:

in whose name and on the basis of what authority could a sovereign power apologise? Only in the name of itself and on the basis of its own authority. But then there would be no need to apologise for the very notions of what is right and wrong would simply be derived from sovereignty.[75]

Unlike Reilly, however, Fagenblat treats the absence of legal cause (the fact that, technically speaking, no sovereign *needs to* or can be *forced to* say sorry) as the making rather than the unmaking of political apology as an act of contrition. For him, it is precisely because a sovereign apology is entirely gratuitous from a strictly legal point of view, an assumption of responsibility *in excess of the law*, that it has transformative potential. As he points out in his discussion of the Australian case, a political apology is probably best seen as 'a reckoning of the sovereign with its own moral ground beyond the law'.[76] But what exactly is meant by reckoning here and what exactly is its impact upon the settler-colonial dynamic?

One way to explicate Fagenblat's conception of political apology as a reckoning of the sovereign with its own moral ground *beyond the law* is by comparing it to an ethical gesture with which we are historically more familiar; namely, that of mercy or pardon. In legal theory, the sovereign act of mercy is commonly conceived as an entirely arbitrary exemption from a law. In granting it, the sovereign decides not to punish someone who deserves to be punished; someone, that is, whose guilt is not in doubt.[77] Yet mercy can also be conceived as the imposition, by the sovereign and upon itself, of a 'higher law'. In granting it, one might plausibly argue, the sovereign does not simply decide to release another from the law, it decides to subject itself to a law beyond the law or, to be more precise, to an ethical code that exceeds the law and which provides a justification for setting it aside; in this instance, an honour code of Greco-Roman origins in which mercifulness is understood as a virtue. In an analogous, if somewhat inverted, way, the sovereign act of apology could be seen as a voluntary act of subjection to an ethical code (albeit, in this case, a Christian one centred upon respect rather than honour). Since, in showing contrition, the sovereign does something that is beyond its responsibilities within the law, an apology too is expressive of what Fagenblat calls a 'surplus ethical spirit'.[78] Clearly in the first instance, that of mercy, the beneficiary of this surplus is a perpetrator, while in the second instance, that of apology, the beneficiary is a victim. Yet, in both cases the sovereign could be regarded as having freely chosen to inflict a loss upon itself. In the first case it decides to forgo payment of a debt that it is owed under the law and in the second case it decides to make payment for a debt that it does not owe under the law.

The comparison with mercy makes it easier to see why Fagenblat is inclined to see political apology not as the subjection of the sovereign to an external power (whether the international community, the United Nations, or even God) but as a 'deployment of sovereignty against itself in the name of a good that goes beyond its own political legitimacy'.[79] Just as the sovereign act of mercy entails a voluntary sacrifice of payment in the name of honour, the sovereign act of apology entails a voluntary sacrifice of immunity in the name of respect. The only difference, though it is clearly a significant one, is that the 'good' in question is now of Christian, not Greek, origin.[80] Unlike the heroes of Homer's world who take account of others only to the extent that it affects their own standing, the heroes of Christ's world take account of others because they consider them intrinsically worthy—each one the child of God. Followers of Christ (which, on Fagenblat's account, most Westerners, even atheists, still implicitly are) cannot be indifferent to the suffering of others and especially not to others that suffer *because* of them. Respect entails a concern for the other as an independent centre of value and a responsibility to repair whatever damage one might have intentionally or unintentionally done to that centre of value. However seemingly secularized the setting in which they take place, he concludes, political apologies are inherently Christian in nature. In apologizing, the sovereign makes its own 'appeal to heaven', as it were, acceding to the demands of its victims, not because it is legally required to or because necessity commands, but because it makes a decision to voluntarily subject itself to a 'Christian code of ethics'.

For Fagenblat, the implications of this voluntary submission to the Christian code of ethics are far more significant than they first appear. In line with Schmitt, he takes the view that the sovereign person remains largely invisible during normal times when reliance upon procedure obviates the need for decision. Only in those moments when it exercises its right to decide on the exception does the sovereign person reveal itself as something more than the sum total of its laws. In these inherently exceptional situations, analogous, in Schmitt's account, to the miracle in nature, the sovereign at once shows that it is not fully contained by the constitutional order *and* that it wants to be known or identified in a particular way (e.g. as brutal, merciful, magnanimous, criminal, contrite, etc.). For Fagenblat, in other words, the true character of the sovereign person or the true identity of the sovereign people is only ever fully manifest in those exceptional situations when it voluntarily chooses to seek an ethical ground for its otherwise ungrounded power:

> As in a miracle, it is in the exceptional act beyond the law that the truth of the sovereign is revealed. A miracle is the revelation of the transcendence of God over the laws of nature. It is precisely the power of the exception to the law that provides proof, for those who need it, of true sovereignty. Now, the political act of the

> Apology was exceptional in just this sense. Here too it was a matter of the sovereign revealing itself by transcending the very laws that it had created. It proved, for those who need it, and I think we generally do, that there is something to 'Australia' that goes beyond the laws of the state.[81]

The significance of political apology in this account is thus not confined to the fact that it requires a representative of the sovereign people to '[touch] a moral point of view beyond the sovereign power of the state'.[82] It extends also to the fact that, in touching on that moral point of view, that representative reveals the sovereign people as wrongdoers who have cause to repent, and who are thereby exposed to humiliation and rejection.[83] As Fagenblat noted of the Rudd apology, while the sovereign person was free to take a stand (or perhaps we should rather say a fall) in relation to its own past policies and actions, it was 'utterly dependent on the freedom of Indigenous people to receive, reject, ignore or defer [its apology]'.[84]

To think about political apology as an exercise of sovereignty in the mode of contrition is, then, to undergo a kind of gestalt shift in which we begin to understand that the true significance of the gesture might reside less in what it recognizes than in what it risks.[85] Since an apology is, by its very nature, an admission of wrongdoing, it cannot be performed without tearing down the walls states commonly erect against unpalatable truths: denial, displacement, excuse, and so on.[86] Responsibility must be assumed in a way that leaves the sovereign standing naked in its violence. Moreover, since political apologies, like all apologies, can be rejected or refused by their addressee, they leave the sovereign at the mercy of those it previously exposed to death in the state of exception. Should the victims decide that the apology ought not be accepted, whether because they judge it to be insincere or the wrong in question to be beyond atonement, the sovereign body will be left to suffer in a state of shame. Arguably, an apology without this element of risk would be no apology at all. If the gesture is not to be purely perfunctory, the possibility of the perpetrator remaining unforgiven, the parties unreconciled, has to be left open. But this means political apologies are far from inconsequential for the 'Supreme Power'. When a sovereign apologizes, it effectively sacrifices its immunity and 'comes out of hiding', exposing itself, firstly, to a sense of shame before the ugly truth, and secondly to the possibility of rejection (of political exile and death) by the wronged other.[87]

By drawing attention to this element of risk, Fagenblat gives us as good a set of reasons as might be mustered for treating political apology as transformative of sovereign authority. Historically speaking, he claims (and by no means unreasonably), the decision on the exception has revealed the sovereign as

An Exercise of Sovereignty in the Mode of Contrition   191

a 'congenitally violent' being. Since any measure that exceeds or breaks the law is, technically speaking, a violation of right, the decision on the exception carries logical connotations of violence and illegality, of the sovereign as 'outlaw'. Hence Derrida's suggestion (against the specifically American usage) that all sovereigns, insofar as they operate outside the law, are 'rogues'. 'Abuse of power', he notes, 'is constitutive of sovereignty itself.'[88] Yet it is not just as a matter of formal logic that the sovereign has appeared as a congenitally violent being in the state of exception. Since the decision to suspend or exceed the law is classically prompted by existential crises, by the appearance of threats or the identification of enemies (including internal enemies), it regularly manifests in measures that entail real physical and emotional violence; that is, in precisely those acts of harassment, discrimination, abuse, and massacre that Verdeja takes to be indicative of acts of state in situations of emergency. As the example of the Stolen Generations testifies all too well, the sovereign that suspends or overrides the law in the state of exception invariably emerges as an imperious actor for whom others are little more than instruments of its untrammelled will. It is nothing if not terror unbound.[89]

All of this is, however, a far cry from the penitent sovereign which issues an apology to the victims of its own excess. Is not this exercise of sovereignty in the mode of contrition, this sovereignty of self-sacrifice that justifies itself through an appeal to ethics rather than an appeal to necessity, something quite new? On first appearances, as we have noted, acts of apology bear a similarity to acts of mercy, creating the impression we have in fact seen something of this self-sacrificing, ethical sovereign before. And yet, as Nietzsche persuasively argues in *On the Genealogy of Morality*, in acts of mercy the sovereign actually reveals (or seeks to impose) its nobility of spirit and will to power. In refusing to collect payment, it underscores the fact that it is wealthier, unimaginably wealthier, than all its debtors. Indeed, since only the richest of all can 'incur loss without suffering', says Nietzsche, acts of mercy are one of the principal means by which the sovereign distinguishes itself as sovereign, revealing precisely through its generosity that it is 'above the law' (and proudly so).[90] In acts of apology, by contrast, the sovereign expresses a certain humility of spirit and will to powerlessness. In saying sorry, it lowers or humbles itself before the victims of its own excess, in 'recognition and critique', says Fagenblat, 'of its own founding authority'.[91] Moreover, since the sovereign is 'precisely not free', as he puts it, 'to determine whether or not [its apology] will be accepted', the gesture places it in a relation of dependence. Say (or unsay) what it likes, the issue of sincerity is not for it to judge. Put simply, then, if the act of mercy is a means by which the sovereign asserts its own being, the act of apology is a means by which it 'atones for its own being'.[92]

In Fagenblat's analysis, this 'essentially other-orientated', 'essentially non-violent' sovereign of the apology finds its symbolic model in a little-known Christian concept associated with the incarnation of God as man. 'I think it is hard to understand the Apology as *an act of sovereignty*', he writes, 'whether this refers to the power of the state or that of the people, without reference to the notion of kenosis.'[93] As intimated earlier, kenosis figures in Fagenblat's analysis of the apology to the Stolen Generations as a way of conceptualizing the kind of sovereignty entailed by (or implicit in) acts of apology more generally:

> Kenosis is a radical reconception of the idea of the sovereignty as a mode of radical humility and even abasement, of Christ as 'the form of God' who 'emptied himself ... humbled himself and became obedient unto death'. Usually it refers to the free act of assuming the position of the sacrificed on the cross. It is an exercise of sovereignty that *foregoes its own absolute power* by becoming sacrificed. In a sense, the Apology went further, for here the abasement of the sovereign went beyond the point of assuming the position of the victim in order to assume the more debased position of the perpetrator. The point, however, is that the humbling of sovereignty defines Christianity from the very outset. Indeed what makes the Apology of a sovereign nation, whether in Australia or elsewhere, so strikingly new in political history and political theology is that here, finally, sovereignty has deployed its transcendence with respect to the law in order to practice humility rather than violence.[94]

In the kenotic process, then, which is at once an *emptying out* and a *submitting to*, sovereignty is radically refigured as absence rather than presence, unworthiness rather than worthiness. By apologizing, the sovereign man does not just admit to mistakes, he voluntarily divests himself of that God-like supremacy—beyond judgement, beyond suffering—which has served as his distinguishing feature and gives himself over to those he has promised not to harm ever again: obedient unto death. A sovereign who apologizes is thus a sovereign who is radically transformed; a sovereign, as Fagenblat puts it, who has succeeded in 'overcoming its own essential violence'.[95]

III A New Sovereign?

Although it is, at first, tempting to dismiss this idea of a new, essentially non-violent, essentially other-orientated sovereign as a metaphysical conceit, it gains in plausibility when one starts to think about sovereignty in historical terms. As Fagenblat rightly points out, the disenchantment of the Mortal Sovereign (king) brought about by the democratic revolution bears a very strong resemblance to the disenchantment of the Immortal Sovereign (God) brought about by the Christian revolution. In effect, democratization introduced into the secular realm what incarnation introduced into the sacred: a sovereign stripped of its divinity and brought down to earth; a sovereign, that is, whose 'humbling' defined it from the very outset. As the symbolic locus of sovereignty in democracy, 'the people' make for a frail, and thus potentially contrite, power. Unlike the kings of the *ancien régime*, who could do no wrong, the people of the nation-state were inherently fallible. Enjoying no greater claim to authority than their own covenants, the possibility, if not the likelihood, that they would slip up was there from the beginning. In their ignorance, their vanity, their greed, and their many other mortal failings, they were destined to commit sins against the *Grundnorm* of equality that would have to be made good at a later date. As incredible as it first appears, therefore, Fagenblat's sense that a new kind of sovereign appears, if only momentarily, in the act of apology is by no means inconsistent with conventional accounts of democratic authority. Its Christian overtones notwithstanding, the exercise of sovereignty in the mode of contrition would appear to find its ultimate juridico-political condition of possibility in that great revolution of the early modern period which saw sovereign authority became grounded in human covenant rather than divine right.

Many commentators, unfamiliar with the concept of kenosis, have clearly been inclined to read things in this way. Kora Andrieu has, for instance, connected the 'growing practice' of political apologies to the fact that the sovereign person is no longer 'untouchable'. As a result of the democratic revolution that made 'the people' rather than 'the divine' the source of political authority, sovereigns have become 'questionable entities' who must answer for their violations of right.[96] According to this reading, political apologies are just one expression, albeit a very dramatic one, of the fact that sovereigns have lost the immunity they once enjoyed as God's representatives on earth and are now accountable to the ever-evolving democratic principle of equality (and the domestic and global public that polices it). For Andrieu, this humbling of the sovereign is most apparent in the *content* of political apologies. By saying sorry to those exposed to violence as a result of their exclusion from the category of 'the people', sovereigns at once '[redefine] the community's rules of membership' and demonstrate their obedience to the democratic taboo against discrimination.[97] However, in Andrieu's account it is the *form* political apology takes that provides the most telling sign of this new, humble sovereign. Less divine command than 'open conversation', according to her, political apologies fill the gap left by the 'missing transcendent' with an 'immanent process of deliberation'.[98] Political apologies, she writes, echoing Martha Minow, are 'no soliloquy'. They are rather an 'intersubjective process' in which the sovereign not only enjoys no privilege but assumes a position of vulnerability with respect to the victims, knowing all the while that its attempt to unsay could just as easily be refused as accepted.[99]

The idea that political apologies are revelatory of the new sovereign of the democratic age, a sovereign who cares rather than abuses and who talks rather than commands, is clearly not without appeal. If, following Fagenblat, a sovereign apology really does represent a voluntary submission to a (Christian/democratic) code of ethics in which all life is valued equally, it would seem tantamount to a renunciation of precisely that power to abuse which Derrida takes to be constitutive of sovereignty itself. Although the right of the exception will (as Reilly noted) remain the signature feature of the supreme power, it should not result in the 'same laws' as before because the sovereign has declared it will never again go rogue. Henceforth the power to go beyond the law will be tied to the need to care for life *in an indiscriminate way*—it will be the power of a fallible sovereign who, aping that looped video of Willy Brandt, will be required to fall and fall again to heal the wounds it inflicted. And yet, if sovereign apologies really are an expression of a new sovereign who cares for life, they may not be politically transformative in quite the way that Fagenblat, Andrieu, and many others imagine. For when remembrance becomes painful, when it casts shame upon the sovereign body, the need for healing ceases to be a matter for the victims alone. As our reading of *The Inability to Mourn* revealed in Chapter 1, when 'the People' (upper-case P) are forced to confront the violence used against 'the people' (lower-case p) *in their name*, they can be narcissistically wounded in a way that places them at risk of mass melancholia. Should we then see apology as a sacrificial gesture, the humiliating 'about-face' of a sovereign that has long since lost faith in its deeds and itself, or as a biopolitical operation, a performative 'unsaying' of the trauma undertaken with the intent of restoring life and motion to the *whole* social body?

On this point, Fagenblat, in many ways against his own intentions, is in fact highly instructive. Following the work of Danielle Celermajer, he takes the view that revelations about forced removals, particularly those conducted under the eugenic idea of 'breeding out the colour', induced a crisis of identity among Australians. Genocidal in implication, if not perhaps in intent, forced removals were not easily dismissed as isolated acts of injustice for which one or two people might be held to account. By adopting policies that sought the elimination of Aboriginal people, whether culturally or biologically, the

Australian state had treated friends as enemies—treated them far worse, in some ways, than any of the real enemies they had engaged in their foreign wars. The fact that they had done so in good conscience and with the support of the law pointed, in Celermajer's apposite phrase, to something deeply amiss with 'the moral grammar of the political community'.[100] Only a completely skewed view of right and wrong could have made the elimination of another culture or people appear acceptable and necessary. As she rightly went on to note, '[t]he wrong that the apology was addressing expanded beyond the specific events to encompass the cultural and political constitution of the Australian nation itself'.[101] The fact that Australians of the current generation did not feel guilty for what they had done did not, therefore, prevent them from feeling ashamed of who they were. As Fagenblat glosses the point, revelations about forced removals triggered a certain 'moral excess' among the public, making guiltless Australians feel ashamed of 'whatever it was that made one Australian'.[102]

Fagenblat likens this experience of living in a 'state of shame' to that endured by Christians after the fall. Just as Christians, regardless of what they had done or not done, could still feel ashamed of their beginnings, Australians, though now at a temporal distance from the injustice of dispossession, could still 'feel ashamed of how [they] were created'.[103] Fagenblat does not have a great deal to say about the pain associated with this experience other than to allude to the 'terrible psychological affects' that go along with being 'constituted in a shameful state'.[104] However, his sense of the shock produced by revelations of Stolen Generations chimes perfectly with Piotr Sztompka's idea of a 'cultural trauma' induced by the return of 'memories of collective sins committed by the community to which we belong'.[105] Once admitted or, at least, no longer denied, historical injustices do more than simply compromise institutional legitimacy. They pop the narcissistic bubble of national self-congratulation, saddling citizens with an abiding sense of shame that is difficult to shake off. And the more profound this feeling of loss—this loss of love *for oneself*—the more likely it is that it will call forth extraordinary measures.[106] When the experience of collective shame 'takes hold', notes Fagenblat, an imperative is created for the sovereign to do what only it can: use its right to go beyond the law to 'change the very identity of the state'.[107] 'The sovereign alone', he writes, 'can assuage the moral or spiritual excess [of the experience of shame]' by atoning for itself.[108] In the extraordinary act of apology, it responds to, and averts, the crisis of self-loathing to which the law has no answer by representing itself in the form of a penitent.

Although Fagenblat sees political apology as being all about 'the other', therefore, his analysis indicates that it also offers something very valuable to 'the self'. Indeed, for all the emphasis he places upon kenosis, the sovereign sacrifice of absolute power, he remains acutely conscious of how the story of God's incarnation in the form of Christ ends; namely, in the miracle of resurrection and the regeneration of life. In the act of incarnation, God effectively splits something off from himself, something that can be burdened by sin and offered as a sacrifice, so that all sinners, united in the body of Christ, can be reborn, purified of sin, innocent again: 'the old has passed away, behold, the new has come'.[109] In apology, similarly, the sovereign seems to split something off from itself that can be burdened with shame and offered as a sacrifice so that 'the people', united in the body of the sovereign, can be freed of their excess moral burden. In this secular adaptation of the kenotic process, performed on the political stage, the sovereign effectively divides itself into two through the assertion of a temporal rupture between past and present. Wrongdoing is displaced onto a prior self, the sovereign people pre-apology, in order that the current self, the sovereign people post-apology, can be reborn in renewed innocence. Is this not what the prime minister of Australia was alluding to when he claimed the apology to the Stolen Generations would 'remove a great stain from the nation's soul' and allow it to 'begin anew'?[110]

Although, once again, inclined to look like a metaphysical conceit, the splitting that functions as the condition of possibility of the Christian kenosis ceases to appear quite so foreign to the political realm once we remind ourselves that the capacity to double itself has been one of the most redoubtable attributes of sovereign power.[111] As Ernst Kantorowicz famously noted in *The King's Two Bodies*, the medieval period found a solution to the problem of discontinuity in rule by supplementing the king's 'body natural', which inevitably succumbs to death, with the king's 'body politic', which lives on eternally.[112] As Kantorowicz would have it, this doubling of bodies rescued (*inter alia*) the institution of monarchy from the recurrent problem of succession. Old kings could pass away and new kings could be sworn in without creating any rupture in the continuity of the state because the 'body politic' was understood as an immortal entity that lived in each king while they were alive and lived outside of them after they died. As Kantorowicz shows, the coronation rite performs the symbolically essential function of passing the 'body politic' from one 'body natural' to another. In the ritual of coronation, the king's two bodies, having become temporarily separated as a result of the passing of the sovereign, were once again rejoined as the heir to the throne incorporated the body politic into himself. With the anointment of the new king, the sovereign power once again acquired a vehicle for its expression and the vehicle for its expression acquired the sovereign power.

An Exercise of Sovereignty in the Mode of Contrition   197

Fagenblat helps us to see that a similar form of doubling comes into play in the gesture of political apology, only in this instance it is not the death of the living sovereign but the living of the dead sovereign that throws the state into disarray. Since, in the medieval context of divine right, the king can do no wrong, the only challenge was to ensure that the continuity of sovereign rule was *not* broken. The concept of the 'body politic' answered this problem by allowing sovereignty to live outside the 'body natural' who happened to exercise it at any one time. However, in modern cases like the one under discussion here, where it is a matter of a sovereign having done wrong, the challenge is to symbolically mark discontinuity rather than continuity. So long as the body politic fails to disassociate itself from the body natural that used sovereign power to commit crimes, it continues to carry the taint of the crime within itself and feel the burden of shame. This, I would suggest, is why the gesture of apology acquires such significance as a performative. If the ritual of coronation is all about getting the body politic *in* to the king, the ritual of apology is all about the getting the body politic *out* of him. In political apology, a public stage is found for announcing the split between the two. When the sovereign falls to its knees, it symbolically announces the separation of the body politic from the body natural who abused the prerogative power that was placed in its hands. A sovereign doubled opens up the possibility of a sovereign sacrifice, allowing shame to be sloughed off and the body politic to be born anew.[113]

That this kind of doubling is intrinsic to the act of apology at both the personal and the political level is widely recognized. Thus, while Ernesto Verdeja never invokes the concept of the king's two bodies, he is by no means unaware of the 'expressive ambiguities' that surround official apologies in 'transitional scenarios'. An official apology, he suggests, must simultaneously establish a continuity with, and a break from, the sovereign body. In order to issue an apology for 'earlier state actions', the apologizer must identify as an authorized representative of the same sovereign body that committed the offences (since in the absence of such continuity the fault ceases to be his or hers, as duly authorized representative, to apologize for). At the same time, the apologizer must dis-identify with *that* sovereign body, repudiating what it did and was, in order to invest the sovereign body on whose behalf he or she *now* says sorry with legitimacy:

> The official apology seeks to establish a continuity of state authority and responsibility, while simultaneously stating in no uncertain terms its rejection of the previous leadership. This double movement is part of a broader effort at founding a new political order (rejection of the past) while claiming the right to do so

legitimately (demanding to be recognised as the legitimate successor authority); as such, successor elites are forcefully making a claim of separation from and continuity with the past, with all of the symbolic ambivalence that this entails.[114]

Although Verdeja's language in this passage contains no theological overtones, none of the ritual elements are missing. The act of 'official apology' is at once a scene of doubling (the sovereign that was/the sovereign that is), a sacrificial rite (rejection of the sovereign that was), and a sacrament of rebirth (a new political order).

The line between political apology as an ethical practice and political apology as an instrumental practice begins to become very blurred here. Is it, as one hopes, an act of sovereignty that imposes an ethical limit on power, an act that creates (or finally manifests) a new, essentially other-orientated, essentially non-violent sovereign? Or is it, as one fears, an act of sovereignty that exposes the biopolitical investment of power, an act that symbolically asserts a new identity in order to slough off the shame of the past? Put differently, does it reveal a 'new sovereign' in the sense of having developed an unprecedented concern for the other or a 'new sovereign' in the sense of having regained a lost innocence? Fagenblat clearly wants apology to be an expression of a radically new, other-orientated sovereignty. Yet much of his analysis on the state of shame points to a different conclusion: it is not apology that brings about a change in the nature of sovereignty, but sovereignty that brings about a change in the nature of apology. Understood as a performative, the exercise of sovereignty in the mode of contrition ultimately betrays itself as a biopolitical technique of healing and revitalization. Against the creeping death of shame, it creates a new political order—an order worthy of love and devotion, an order for which citizens need feel no shame. Exactly what makes apology ethical is thus unclear. If the primary aim of this exercise of sovereignty in the mode of contrition is to assuage the moral excess of the experience of shame, it would seem to be addressing the other not as an independent 'moral subject' to whom one must 'face up', as Fagenblat puts it, but as a means to an end.[115] Symbolically speaking, such a political apology repeats the violence that it is meant to amend by once again using the other to invigorate the body politic.

IV 'A True Renaissance': Apology, Reason of State, and Indigenous Resurgence

If the 'state of shame' is indeed the crisis that (at least in this instance) necessitates the exercise of sovereignty in the mode of contrition, a political apology is not quite the ritual that normative theorists have imagined it to be. Once the shame of the perpetrator enters into the equation, its status as an essentially 'other-orientated', essentially 'non-violent' gesture is thrown into doubt. Exactly whose hurt is being managed here? The victim's? The perpetrator's? Both at the same time? Strangely enough, given the emphasis the restorative model of justice places upon moral repair, the idea that the victim and the perpetrator might both suffer, the first from the trauma of violation, the second from the trauma of exposure, is widely recognized, as is the idea that the symbolic gesture of apology might bring relief to both. As Darío Páez has written, 'the offender group is ashamed and symbolically punished, the victim group is revalorized and symbolically rewarded, and both groups can feel pride and a positive emotional climate'.[116] Páez, like McAlinden, represents the 'shame management' function of apology as beneficial to victim and perpetrator alike, but one might legitimately wonder who profits most from that 'positive emotional climate'. As Juno Gemes notes, one of the most remarkable features of the apology to the Stolen Generations was how euphoric it made (non-Indigenous) Australians feel:

> One sensed immediately that the mood of the nation had changed. On television screens across the nation, in public squares, schools, viewed at home, we had all participated in a seminal catharsis in our personal and national narrative. Sharing the emotional truths of our personal histories had the power to awaken in 'us' a sense of 'we' in all our cultural diversity. It is the meta narrative of what we all are—what it means to be an Australian.[117]

Well, might one ask, then, as Sara Ahmed astutely did, 'who is doing the healing and who is being healed'?[118]

The public record provides ample proof that the apology to the Stolen Generations was greeted by Indigenous people as a significant moment of healing and reconciliation.[119] By exposing itself in its violence, the sovereign validated their sense of injustice and created a much-needed outlet for a grief which, for want of recognition and restitution, had morphed into an intergenerational trauma. 'For members of the Stolen Generations, their descendants and families', noted the co-chair of the Stolen Generations Alliance, Christine Fejo-King,

> it was a day filled with high emotions. We shed tears of sadness and joy. We hugged with happiness and for comfort. And for many of us, it was the relief and peace we had been searching for, for so long ... Saying 'Sorry' was the right thing to do. Past government policies and practices or removing Indigenous children have damaged

so many peoples' lives. Saying 'Sorry' acknowledged the past, the trauma it caused at the time, and the hurt and suffering it continues to cause today.[120]

By no means unrepresentative, such comments would seem to bear out Weyneth's claim about the remedial power of sorry: 'when issues are especially intractable or a society fundamentally divided an apology can offer a starting point for healing.'[121] As well as being the right thing to do ethically speaking, saying sorry appeared to be the right thing to do therapeutically speaking because it allowed a long-suspended process of mourning to resume its natural course. In the absence of recognition, the ability of Indigenous people to come to terms with their irreparable losses (and, of course, renew their trust in the Australian Government) had been severely compromised. The past remained an open wound. By openly admitting to the nation, and to the world, that they had been wronged, the apology provided that recognition by which trauma is turned into mourning.

The belated recognition of Indigenous life as grievable life spoke, once again, of a kind of affirmative biopolitics in which those once deprived of protection and targeted for elimination were to be granted an equal chance to live and flourish. In the speech that followed the apology proper, Prime Minister Rudd made a point of asking non-Indigenous Australians to imagine for a moment if this had happened to them, underlining the point that suffering was suffering and every life deserved to be as free of it as possible. It was by no means insignificant in this regard either that the apology was accompanied by a promise of a renewed commitment to 'close the gap' between Indigenous life and non-Indigenous life across a range of socio-economic indicators, notably those of infant mortality (which, at the time, were four times higher among Indigenous people) and life expectancy (which was an appalling seventeen years lower among Indigenous people). Keen to avoid the accusation of 'political posturing', not to mention the charge that apologies were 'merely symbolic', Rudd went so far as to make a concrete proposal for a joint policy commission to tackle the problem of Indigenous housing. Given the violence to which Indigenous life had been exposed, this commitment to provide 'shelter' could hardly have been more symbolically loaded.

And yet, for all the assurance the apology provided that Indigenous life now mattered, a sense of ambivalence remained. In a speech given at the National Press Club, the former chairman of the Council for Aboriginal Reconciliation, Patrick Dodson, simultaneously celebrated the apology as an epic gesture and questioned whether it would create the foundation of a better relationship. On the one hand, he noted, credit had to be given to the Australian people for recognizing past wrongdoing and disavowing the 'misguided attempt to destroy our people'. In a metaphorical appeal to the drought that had, at that point, already been plaguing Australia for a number of years, Dodson alluded to the apology as a 'climatic shift', finding in it grounds to hope that the 'crippling long dry spell [in the political cycle] may have just ended'.[122] On the other hand, he wondered whether it would mark the beginning of a relationship where the settler state was truly responsive to 'the imperatives of Indigenous life' and genuinely invested in their 'survival as peoples'. Although the apology had, he suggested, made it possible to imagine Australia as a different place, it had not yet made it a different place. The challenge that remained was to give constitutional and institutional expression to the kind of relationship that the apology intimated. 'Let us not pretend', he noted, 'that the journey from this point will not be challenging. It must involve the capacity of our leaders and opinion makers to imagine a renewed nation and to be prepared to take and support the steps towards a true renaissance.'[123]

Dodson's 'true renaissance' spoke of another kind of rebirth and thus, at least implicitly, of another kind of biopolitics: not the rebirth of the Australian nation but the rebirth of Aboriginal nations; and not the biopolitics of national healing but the biopolitics of Indigenous resurgence. Although clearly supportive of the apology and the commitment it made to improve Indigenous lives, Dodson left the audience in little doubt that it was a necessary but not sufficient condition of that true renaissance. As a therapy for the trauma of child removal (and, via that, for the trauma of national shame), the apology could be credited with creating a shift in the emotional climate. 'For the first time in many years', noted Dodson, 'the resolution of the unfinished business between us seems possible.' However, when it came to the rebirth of Aboriginal nations, something altogether different was required. If Indigenous peoples were going to survive and thrive 'as peoples', changes to the political architecture of the nation were needed that demonstrated 'the imperatives of Indigenous life' were understood and respected. Without those changes, relating specifically to the exercise of sovereignty and rights to land, a suspicion would be inevitably aroused that the primary work being done by the apology was restorative work for the settler culture. It might simply be a case, as Povinelli had argued all along, of the settlers wanting Aboriginal people to feel better so that they could too:

> in this liberal imaginary, the now recognized subaltern subjects would slough off their traumatic histories, ambivalences, incoherencies, and angst like so much outgrown skin rather than remain for themselves the wounded testament to the nation's past bad faith. The nation would then be able to come out from under

the pall of its failed history, betrayed best intentions, and discursive impasses. And normative citizens would be freed to pursue their profits and enjoy their families without guilty glances over the shoulders into history or at the slum across the block.[124]

This reading of apology—as a means of recovering from the shameful exposure of crimes—brings us back to the problem with which we began: the instrumental value of political apologies for the state. However, it does so within a framework which, because it is biopolitical rather than normative in nature, casts the instrumentality of the state in a different, rather more ambiguous light. Normative theorists have long insisted that it is naïve to imagine victims of injustice are the only ones who have an interest in apology. The state also has its 'reasons'. For the most part, however, those 'reasons of state' have been understood in terms of reputation and legitimation. In the democratic age, it is suggested, where respect for human rights serves as the criterion of the 'good state', sovereigns apologize in order to enhance their reputation and supply a deficit in legitimacy. This is not to say, of course, that they rush to apologize in every instance. Since legitimation hinges not simply on the justness of the act but on its reception by the public (some of whom might be opposed to confessions of injustice on the grounds that they generate, rather than allay, the state of shame), a delicate balance needs to be struck between what is admitted and what is denied: hence the kind of recognition/non-recognition characteristic of the apology to the Stolen Generations[125] The point, nevertheless, is that states recognize moral authority as a valuable commodity and seek to accumulate it in the same way as they accumulate capital. The challenge from a normative perspective is thus to ensure that they don't acquire it too cheaply—don't acquire it, that is, at the expense of the victims by substituting 'genuine apologies' for 'gestural politics'.[126]

Things take on a rather different and rather more confusing complexion if we assume that the 'reasons' states apologize relate less to legitimacy than to vitality or perhaps to legitimacy only insofar as it contributes to vitality. As the analysis provided in this chapter indicates, there are grounds for thinking that the sovereign decision on the exceptional gesture of apology responds to a perceived threat to the life of the body politic—a threat of an essentially psychological nature that arises from an unfinished process of mourning and manifests in emotional excess: impacted grief on the one side, debilitating shame on the other. The risk of 'gestural politics' in this context is not simply that it compromises the ethical status of the gesture, but that it threatens

An Exercise of Sovereignty in the Mode of Contrition   203

to accentuate the crisis to which it responds. Apologies that fail not just in the eyes of those who are addressed by them but in the eyes of those who witness them add insult to injury, increasing the sense of anger on the one side and deepening the sense of shame on the other. It is thus in the interests of the sovereign, for reasons that have nothing to do with ethics, to make its act of contrition as felicitous as possible. Only by apologizing sincerely can it ensure that the life it governs is restored to emotional normality. What kind of critique, then, could one make of this kind of apology? Should one applaud it because it meets the 'sincerity test' stipulated by normative theorists? Condemn it because it treats apology as a means to another end? Or applaud it again because the end it seeks—the healing of victims and perpetrators alike—is ultimately a good end?

The normative fog that surrounds political apologies as tools of healing in settler societies is understandable. On what grounds could one be critical of healing? But the fog is inclined to evaporate quite quickly once attention is focused on the subject of the 'healing'. As the work of Watson and Dodson in Australia, and Coulthard and Million in Canada, makes clear, in this instance it is not just Indigenous life which is in need of healing but the Indigenous 'form of life'.[127] This is not to say that there is no Indigenous trauma or that there is no healing value in symbolic acts of recognition. Judging from the reflections of Christine Fejo-King, the catharsis precipitated by the apology was no illusion. But there is a reason disappointment among Indigenous people often follows the cathartic moment of apology. Ultimately, what they seek is not healing for their *individual* wounds, but the restoration of their *collective* way of life, and the tendency to assume the former is a precondition for the latter is simply another ruse of colonial power.[128] Restoration of the Indigenous 'form of life' is what Coulthard has in mind when he speaks of a 'biopolitics of resurgence'—this is a biopolitics which, as he puts it, 'refuses to be coopted by scraps of recognition, opportunistic apologies, and the cheap gift of political and economic inclusion'.[129] It is also what Dodson has in mind when he invokes the idea of a true renaissance, implicitly criticizing the apology for bolstering 'life' rather than the Indigenous 'form of life'. Here, as in Canada, the bold promise of 'never again', impossible to truly enact without treaty agreements recognizing Indigenous sovereignty, was reduced to a commitment to improve the health of Indigenous people and close the gap in life span. Australia would say sorry not by supporting the renaissance of Indigenous life but by giving Indigenous people a little more life.[130]

Notes

1. D. Páez, 'Official or Political Apologies and Improvement of Intergroup Relations: A Neo-Durkheimian Approach to Official Apologies as Rituals', *Revista de Psicologia Social*, 25(1), 2010, p. 2.
2. I use the term 'political apology' synonymously with official apologies, state apologies, and sovereign apologies to refer to apologies offered by a duly authorized representative of the state for injustices perpetrated against its own citizens. The chapter is thus not concerned with apologies offered by politicians for personal transgressions or with apologies offered by one state to the citizens of another state. For discussions of intrapersonal and interstate apologies, respectively, see A. Lazare, *On Apology*, Oxford: Oxford University Press, 2004; and J. Lind, *Sorry States: Apologies in International Politics*, Ithaca, NY: Cornell University Press, 2008.
3. D. Celermajer, 'Apology and the Possibility of Ethical Politics', *JCRT*, 9(1), winter 2008, p. 14.
4. M. Gibney, 'Introduction to a Symposium on Political Apology', *Journal of Human Rights*, 20(5), 2021, p. 580.
5. This distinction between the ethico-normative and the juridico-political maps quite neatly onto Stephen Winter's distinction between 'qualitative conditions', which relate to the better and worse of political apology, and 'existence conditions', which relate to the possibility or impossibility of political apology. This chapter agrees with Winter (and coincidently Trouillot) that apologies can only be offered by agents not subjects. Political apologies, it assumes, only make sense where the apologizer is the sovereign (the agent that *represents* the people) not the nation (the ethno-national hodgepodge that *is* the people). However, it goes further than Winter's institutional account by delving more deeply into the kind of authority exercised by the sovereign person and the way in which that authority both enables and disables the offer of apology. See S. Winter, 'Theorising the Political Apology', *The Journal of Political Philosophy*, 23(3), 2015, p. 263; and M. Trouillot, 'Abortive Rituals: Historical Apologies in the Global Era', *Interventions: International Journal of Postcolonial Studies*, 2(2), 2000, pp. 171–186.
6. The expression comes from Nicholas Tavuchis and the issue is discussed at length by Govier and Verwoerd. See N. Tavuchis, *Mea Culpa: A Sociology of Apology and Reconciliation*, Stanford, CA: Stanford University Press, 1991; and T. Govier and W. Verwoerd, 'The Promise and Pitfalls of Apology', *Journal of Social Philosophy*, 33(1), 2002, pp. 74–75.
7. Thus, in an extended discussion of the issue of authority and the right of a leader to speak in the name of the state, Ernesto Verdeja makes no mention of sovereignty. The key issue for him is whether the representative of the state is a 'legitimate voice'. See E. Verdeja, 'Official Apologies in the Aftermath of Political Violence', *Metaphilosophy*, 41(4), 2010, pp. 575–576.
8. For a discussion of Hobbes' conception of the state as an agent to whom actions can be attributed, see Q. Skinner, 'Hobbes and the Purely Artificial Person of the State', *The Journal of Political Philosophy*, 7(1), 1999, pp. 1–29.
9. Hobbes insisted that the sovereign could not be subject to the civil laws without undermining his standing as the highest authority. To set the laws above the sovereign would be to set a power to judge and to punish above 'him', which would in effect 'make a new sovereign'. As Charles Tarlton neatly put it, the sovereign 'is accountable, if at all, only

to God'. See T. Hobbes, *Leviathan*, Oxford: Oxford University Press, 1998, 29: 9; and C. Tarlton, 'The Despotical Doctrine of Hobbes, Part II', *History of Political Thought*, 23(12), 2002, p. 63.
10. Examples of mortal sovereigns apologizing (or at least attempting to apologize) to the immortal one are not, of course, unknown in literature, with one prime example being King Claudius in *Hamlet*. See A. Escobedo, 'On Sincere Apologies: Saying "Sorry" in Hamlet', *Philosophy and Literature*, 41(1A), 2017, pp. A169–A171.
11. Although I borrow the concept of the 'abortive ritual' from Michel-Rolph Trouillot's seminal article on state apologies, the grounds upon which I make the claim are slightly different. Trouillot takes aim at the wrongful assumptions that apologies for *historically distant* wrongs make about collective *subjects*. As he would have it, collective apologies are required to attribute the characteristics of the (liberal) individual to the collective subject to cover up for the fact that the continuity needed between the wrongdoer past and present and the victim past and present to make the gesture meaningful is absent. Apologies offered by Christians for the Crusades or Americans for plantation slavery are cases in point. As Trouillot notes, the difference between an agent and a subject is crucial here because we do tend to assume that agents, like sovereigns, extend through time, while collectives like 'Christians' or 'Americans' change over time. While it is well taken, therefore, his critique of apology would not seem to apply to the case we are examining and, depending on the time frame, may not even rule out an apology for slavery. Recent work from Tom Bentley comes closer to the kinds of problems with sovereign apologies that I raise in this chapter in the sense that they too focus upon the absence of any higher power before which the sovereign might prostrate itself and from which it might receive forgiveness. However, while I am interested in the way this forces the sovereign to double itself and become, in a sense, its own confessor, Bentley is interested in the way it obviates the possibility of forgiveness. Since, as he puts it, there is no higher authority in the domestic or international arena to offer absolution, political apologies inevitably fail as rituals of purification. The argument of this chapter is that a kind of purification—a purification that is at once spiritual and emotional—*is* achieved by political apologies because the sovereign doubled—the sovereign split, like the Father and the Son in Christianity, into two entities—effectively absolves itself of its sins. See M. Trouillot, 'Abortive Rituals: Historical Apologies in the Global Era', *Interventions: International Journal of Postcolonial Studies*, 2(2), 2000, pp. 174–178; and T. Bentley, 'Settler State Apologies and the Elusiveness of Forgiveness: The Purification Ritual That Does Not Purify', *Contemporary Political Theory*, 19(3), 2020, pp. 381–403.
12. S. Winter, 'Theorising the Political Apology', pp. 274, 277.
13. E. Verdeja, 'Official Apologies in the Aftermath of Political Violence', *Metaphilosophy*, 41(4), 2010, p. 569.
14. The paradox here was acknowledged by Bronwyn Leebaw in 2008 when she described transitional justice as 'a process that condemns as shameful actions that may previously have been championed as a matter of duty to a particular political community'. B. Leebaw, 'The Irreconcilable Goals of Transitional Justice', *Human Rights Quarterly*, 30, 2008, p. 101.
15. M. Fagenblat, 'The Apology, the Secular and the Theologico-Political', *Dialogue*, 27(2), 2008, p. 16.

16. See, for instance, Z. Kampf and N. Löwenheim, 'Rituals of Apology in the Global Arena', *Security Dialogue*, 43(1), 2012, pp. 43–60; and Bentley, 'Settler-State Apologies and the Elusiveness of Forgiveness', pp. 381–403.
17. See M. Nobles, *The Politics of Official Apologies*, Cambridge: Cambridge University Press, 2008.
18. See D. Celermajer, 'Apology and the Possibility of Ethical Politics', *Journal of Cultural and Religious Theory*, 9(1), 2008, pp. 14–34; and Nobles, *The Politics of Official Apologies*, pp. 139–144.
19. Fagenblat, 'The Apology', p. 28.
20. C. Schmitt, *Political Theology: Four Chapters on the Concept of Sovereignty*, Chicago, IL: University of Chicago Press, p. 12.
21. See, for instance, A.-M. McAlinden, 'Apologies as "Shame Management": The Politics of Remorse in the Aftermath of Historical Institutional Abuse', *Legal Studies*, 1, 2021, pp. 4–6.
22. See R. Manne, 'In Denial: The Stolen Generations and the Right'. *The Australian Quarterly Essay*, April 2001.
23. R. Manne, 'Sorry Business', *The Monthly*, March 2008, no. 32, p. 9.
24. The phrase is taken from the influential article by Patrick Wolfe. See P. Wolfe, 'Settler Colonialism and the Elimination of the Native', *Journal of Genocide Research*, 8(4), 2006.
25. As Wolfe goes on to note, 'the logic of elimination can include officially encouraged miscegenation, the breaking-down of native title into alienable freeholds, native citizenship, child abduction, religious conversion, resocialization in total institutions such as missions or boarding schools, and a whole range of cognate biocultural assimilations'. Wolfe, 'Settler Colonialism and the Elimination of the Native', p. 388.
26. Leela Ghandi has used the phrase 'postcolonial amnesia' in reference to the wish among the formerly colonized to erase the painful memories of colonial subordination. While it is possible the same occurs in settler-colonial states, the amnesia I am speaking of concerns the wish, characteristic of such states, for the colonisers to forget how they acquired the land and what they did to keep it. In her seminal work on the cultural politics of emotion, Sara Ahmed associates the refusal to apologize with forgetting and sees it as a means by which to cut the present off from the past. The position taken in this chapter is precisely the opposite. As I go on to suggest, it is actually the act of apology that succeeds in cutting off the present from the past by carving out a temporal rupture between the colonial and the post-colonial. See L. Ghandi, *Postcolonial Theory*, St Leonards: Allen and Unwin, 1998, p. 4; S. Ahmed, *The Cultural Politics of Emotion*, Edinburgh: Edinburgh University Press, 2014, p. 118.
27. For a discussion of this question, see A. Dirk Moses, *Genocide and Settler Society: Frontier Violence and Stolen Indigenous Children in Australian History*, New York: Berghahn Books, 2005.
28. See R. Manne, 'Aboriginal Child Removal and the Question of Genocide, 1900–1940' in Dirk Moses (ed.), *Genocide and Settler Society*, 223.
29. See R. McGregor, 'Governance, Not Genocide: Aboriginal Assimilation in the Postwar Era' in Dirk Moses (ed.), *Genocide and Settler Society*, pp. 290–312.
30. L. Behrendt, 'Genocide: The Distance Between Law and Life', *Aboriginal History*, 25, 2001, pp. 132, 142.

An Exercise of Sovereignty in the Mode of Contrition 207

31. Sir Ronald Wilson in B. Olubas and L. Greenwell, 'Re-membering and Taking Up an Ethics of Listening: A Response to Loss and the Maternal in "the Stolen Children"', *Australian Humanities Review*, 15 October 1999, p. 1.
32. I follow Bernard Williams and Sara Ahmed here in assuming an intrinsic connection between shame and exposure. Shame arises less from the disgraceful act itself than from the fact of having been 'caught' in the act by others. In effect, it is the gaze of the other that brings about the disgrace. See B. Williams, *Shame and Necessity*, Berkeley, CA: University of California Press, 1993, pp. 75–103; Ahmed, *The Cultural Politics of Emotion*, p. 104.
33. Sir Ronald Wilson in Olubas and Greenwell, 'Re-membering and Taking Up an Ethics of Listening', p. 1.
34. P. Read, *A Rape of the Soul So Profound: The Return of the Stolen Generation*, London: Routledge, 1999.
35. Commonwealth, Parliamentary Debates, House of Representatives, 13 February 2008, p. 170 (Kevin Rudd, Prime Minister).
36. Commonwealth, Parliamentary Debates, House of Representatives, 13 February 2008, p. 172 (Kevin Rudd, Prime Minister).
37. Govier and Verwoerd, 'The Promise and Pitfalls of Apology', p. 70.
38. On the benefits of (felicitous) political apologies, see E. Barkan, *The Guilt of Nations: Restitution and Negotiating Historical Injustice*, Baltimore, MD: Johns Hopkins University Press, 2000, pp. 323–324; J. Thompson, 'Apology, Justice and Respect: A Critical Defence of Political Apology' in M. Gibney (ed.), *The Age of Apology*, Philadelphia, PA: University of Pennsylvania Press, 2008; K. Andrieu, '"Sorry for the Genocide": How Public Apologies Can Help Promote National Reconciliation', *Millennium: Journal of International Studies*, 38(3), 2009, pp. 3–23.
39. J. Thompson, *Taking Responsibility for the Past*, Cambridge: Polity, 2002, pp. 38-54.
40. C. Griswold, *Forgiveness: A Philosophical Exploration*, Cambridge: Cambridge University Press, 2007, p. 151. For similar views about the insincerity of political apologies, see M. Cunningham, '"Saying Sorry": The Politics of Apology', *The Political Quarterly*, 70(3), 1999, pp. 287–288; R. Joyce, 'Apologising', *Public Affairs Quarterly*, 13(2), 1999, pp. 159–160; Govier and Verwoerd, 'The Promise and Pitfalls of Apology', pp. 144–147; J. Thompson, 'Apology, Justice and Respect: A Critical Defense of Political Apology' in M. Gibney, R.E. Howard-Hassman, J.-M. Coicaud, and N. Steiner (eds.), *The Age of Apology*, Philadelphia, PA: University of Pennsylvania Press, 2008, pp. 34–38; M. Gibney and E. Roxstrom, 'The Status of State Apologies', *Human Rights Quarterly*, 23, 2001, pp. 912–914; Verdeja, 'Official Apologies', p. 568; Kampf and Löwenheim, 'Rituals of Apology in the Global Arena', pp. 43–60; and M. Thaler, 'Just Pretending: Political Apologies for Historical Injustice and Vice's Tribute to Virtue', *Critical Review of International Social and Political Philosophy*, 15(3), 2012, p. 260.
41. Thaler, 'Just Pretending', p. 261.
42. According to Kora Andrieu, for instance, 'The primary object of an apology is forgiveness and, ultimately, reconciliation between the offender and the offended.' According to Charles Griswold, by contrast, 'When we move to the political level, the appropriate vocabulary is not that of forgiveness but of apology and the acceptance thereof.' See Andrieu, '"Sorry for the Genocide"', p. 5; and Griswold, *Forgiveness*, p. 172.
43. See Gibney and Roxstrom, 'The Status of State Apologies', pp. 926–937; Thompson, 'Apology, Justice and Respect', pp. 40–44; Verdeja, 'Official Apologies', pp. 570–572; D.

Celermajer, *The Sins of the Nation and the Ritual of Apologies*, Cambridge: Cambridge University Press, 2009, pp. 250–258; M. James, 'Wrestling with the Past: Apologies, Quasi-Apologies and Non-Apologies in Canada' in Gibney et al. (eds.), *The Age of Apology*, pp. 137–153.

44. James, 'Wrestling with the Past', pp. 137–153. See also M.-S. Lotta, 'The Art of Apology: On the True and the Phony in Political Apology' in M. Buschmeier and K. von Kellenback (eds.), *Guilt: A Force of Cultural Transformation*, Oxford: Oxford University Press, 2021.
45. See T. Barta, 'Sorry and Not Sorry, in Australia: How the Apology to the Stolen Generations Buried a History of Genocide', *Journal of Genocide Research*, 10(2), 2008, pp. 201–214; D. Short, 'When Sorry Isn't Good Enough: Official Remembrance and Reconciliation in Australia', *Memory Studies*, 5(3), 2012, pp. 293–304.
46. Short, 'When Sorry Isn't Good Enough', p. 299.
47. Barta, 'Sorry and Not Sorry', p. 201. Glen Coulthard has made a similar critique of Prime Minister Harper's apology for the residential schools system in Canada, arguing that 'there is no recognition of a colonial past or present, nor is there any mention of the much broader system of land dispossession, political domination, and cultural genocide of which the residential school system formed only a part'. One could also note here, as Emma Dolan has recently done in other contexts, that apologizing to women as victims can sometimes be an 'easy recognition'. See G. Coulthard, *Red Skin, White Masks: Rejecting the Colonial Politics of Recognition*, Minneapolis, MN: University of Minnesota Press, p. 125; and E. Dolan, 'The Gendered Politics of Recognition and Recognizability through Political Apology', *Journal of Human Rights*, 20(5), 2021, p. 619.
48. Short, 'When Sorry Isn't Good Enough', p. 299. See also A.D. Moses, 'Official Apologies, Reconciliation, and Settler Colonialism: Australian Indigenous Alterity and Political Agency', *Citizenship Studies*, 15(2), 2011, p. 152.
49. Although the distinction is rarely drawn, Short, following Austin, rightly refers to this as a 'preparatory condition' rather than a 'sincerity condition'. See Short, 'When Sorry Isn't Good Enough', p. 296.
50. For a discussion of the problem of non-identity, see S. Winter, 'Theorising the Political Apology', pp. 276–278.
51. Hobbes, *Leviathan*, 18: 10.
52. J. Locke, *The Two Treatises of Government*, Cambridge: Cambridge University Press, 2: 12.
53. I. Hampsher-Monk, *A History of Modern Political Thought: Major Political Thinkers from Hobbes to Marx*, Oxford: Blackwell, 1992, p. 111.
54. Locke, *The Two Treatises*, 2: 159. As Klosko notes, 'In order to preserve the Country, the King must take emergency measures, some of which could violate the law and the rights of citizens.' G. Klosko, *History of Political Theory*, vol. 2, Belmont, CA: Thompson Wadsworth, 1995, p. 123.
55. Locke, *The Two Treatises*, 2: 166.
56. Locke, *The Two Treatises*, 2: 168.
57. G. Schwab, 'Introduction' in Schmitt, *Political Theology*, p. lii.
58. Schmitt, *Political Theology*, p. 5.
59. Schwab, 'Introduction' in Schmitt, *Political Theology*, pp. xiv–xlix.
60. Schmitt, *Political Theology*, p. 36.

An Exercise of Sovereignty in the Mode of Contrition   209

61. A. Reilly, 'Sovereign Apologies' in J. Evans, A. Reilly, and P. Wolfe (eds.), *Sovereignty: Frontiers of Possibility*, Honolulu, HI: University of Hawaii Press, 2013, p. 196.
62. Reilly, 'Sovereign Apologies', p. 209.
63. Reilly, 'Sovereign Apologies', pp. 205, 210.
64. Bentley makes a similar point when he writes that '[t]he state can admit to specific wrongs and express remorse for particular, even grave, misdemeanours. But it cannot bitterly recant the violent truth of its origins. This would be to invalidate the legitimacy of the state itself ... it is unthinkable that the state would denounce its existence or voluntarily relinquish its sovereignty'. Bentley, 'Settler State Apologies and the Elusiveness of Forgiveness', p. 396.
65. Reilly, 'Sovereign Apologies', p. 197.
66. Reilly, 'Sovereign Apologies', p. 213.
67. John Howard cited in N. Watson, 'The Northern Territory Emergency Response: The More Things Change the More They Stay the Same', *Alberta Law Review*, 48(4), 2011, p. 912.
68. Watson, 'The Northern Territory Emergency Response', p. 906. See also D. Million, *Therapeutic Nations: Healing in an Age of Indigenous Human Rights*, Tucson, AZ: University of Arizona Press, 2013, p. 22.
69. J. Thompson, 'Apology, Justice, and Respect', p. 38.
70. Reilly, 'Sovereign Apologies', pp. 209–210.
71. Reilly, 'Sovereign Apologies', p. 213.
72. Once again, unlike Trouillot, whose critique of political apologies rests on the way they misunderstand (or make false claims about) collective *subjects*, Reilly's is based upon the authority of the sovereign as an *agent*. See Trouillot, 'Abortive Rituals', pp. 174–177.
73. Fagenblat, 'The Apology', p. 16.
74. Fagenblat, 'The Apology', p. 21. This point, and the negative implications it carries for the possibility of state apologies, has been recently reiterated by Tom Bentley. See Bentley, 'Settler State Apologies and the Elusiveness of Forgiveness', p. 395.
75. Fagenblat, 'The Apology', p. 21.
76. Fagenblat, 'The Apology', p. 24.
77. Thus Derrida will describe 'the right of grace' by which a monarch pardons a criminal, 'a law which inscribes in the laws a power above the laws', as at once the most 'elevated' and 'noble' and the most 'dangerous' and 'arbitrary' right of all. See J. Derrida, *On Cosmopolitanism and Forgiveness*, London: Routledge, 2001, p. 46.
78. Fagenblat, 'The Apology', p. 23.
79. Fagenblat, 'The Apology', p. 21.
80. As he writes at the beginning of his essay: 'How are we to understand this symbolic reshaping of the national character that reconciliation and apology sought to accomplish? And how are we to explain the euphoria that accompanied it? Only by way of Christianity'. Fagenblat, 'The Apology', p. 16.
81. Fagenblat, 'The Apology', p. 24.
82. Fagenblat, 'The Apology', p. 21.
83. While careful not to overstate the 'empirical effects' of the apology to the Stolen Generations, therefore, Fagenblat is nevertheless at pains to note that 'it is only on rare occasions that a nation-state, in this case the Parliament of Australia, exercises its sovereign power in order to re-imagine the basic character of the nation'. Fagenblat, 'The Apology', p. 16.

210   The Penitent State

84. Fagenblat, 'The Apology', p. 26.
85. I have discussed this idea of risk in apology in P. Muldoon, 'After Apology: The Remains of the Past', *Australian Humanities Review*, 61, 2017, pp. 138–139.
86. As Tavuchis noted, 'to apologise is to declare voluntarily that one has no excuse, defence, justification, or explanation for an action (or inaction)'. N. Tavuchis, *Mea Culpa: A Sociology of Apology and Reconciliation*, Stanford, CA: Stanford University Press, 1991, p. 17.
87. As Sara Ahmed notes, 'It may be anxiety about the unfinished nature of the apology as a social action that makes it such a troublesome topic for official representatives of nation states'. Ahmed, *The Cultural Politics of Emotions*, p. 116.
88. J. Derrida, *Rogues: Two Essays on Reason*, Stanford, CA: Stanford University Press, 2005, p. 102.
89. One is reminded here of Machiavelli's claim that the Prince only has two instruments at his disposal to maintain a state: law and force. N. Machiavelli, *The Prince*, London: Penguin, 2003, p. 56.
90. F. Nietzsche, *On the Genealogy of Morals*, trans. by W. Kaufmann and R.J. Hollingdale, New York: Vintage, 1997, 2: 10.
91. Fagenblat, 'The Apology', p. 26.
92. Fagenblat, 'The Apology', p. 27.
93. Fagenblat, 'The Apology', p. 27.
94. Fagenblat, 'The Apology', pp. 27–28.
95. Fagenblat, 'The Apology', p. 28.
96. Andrieu, '"Sorry for the Genocide"', p. 4.
97. The delegitimation of discrimination (and hence the need to apologize for it) clearly has a great deal to do with the revelations of the Shoah. John Borneman has, in addition, suggested that the proliferation of apologies has much to do with the way the end of the Cold War diminished 'pressures for internal unity'. See J. Borneman, 'Public Apologies as Performative Redress', *SAIS Review*, 25(2), 2005, pp. 54, 59.
98. Andrieu, '"Sorry for the Genocide"', p. 14.
99. See Andrieu, '"Sorry for the Genocide"', pp. 13–14; Minow, *Between Vengeance and Forgiveness*, Boston, MA: Beacon Press, 1998, p. 114. In a similar vein, John Borneman has suggested that apologies 'affirm that both the victim and wrongdoer are equal, in the sense that both are intersubjective political agents exercising free will, the minimal condition of humanity in democratic states'. Borneman, 'Public Apologies as Performative Redress', p. 54.
100. D. Celermajer, 'The Apology in Australia: Re-covenanting the National Imaginary', in E. Barkan and A. Karn (eds.), *Taking Wrongs Seriously: Apologies and Reconciliation*, Stanford, CA: Stanford University Press, p. 162.
101. Celermajer, 'The Apology in Australia', p. 162.
102. Fagenblat, 'The Apology', p. 22. Much the same point was made by Elizabeth Povinelli in 1998 when she noted that 'Australian state officials represent themselves and the nation as subjects shamed by past imperial, colonial, and racist attitudes that are now understood as having, in their words, constituted "the darkest chapter" of the nation's history and impaired its social and economic future'. Povinelli also anticipates, at least in broad outline, the argument of this chapter by suggesting the state 'makes shame and reconciliation—a public, collective purging of the past—an index and requirement of a

An Exercise of Sovereignty in the Mode of Contrition 211

new abstracted national membership'. See E. Povinelli, 'The State of Shame: Australian Multiculturalism and the Crisis of Indigenous Citizenship', *Critical Inquiry*, 24(2), 1998, pp. 581, 580.
103. Fagenblat, 'The Apology', pp. 23-24.
104. Fagenblat, 'The Apology', p. 23.
105. P. Sztompka, 'Cultural Trauma: The Other Face of Social Change', *European Journal of Social Theory*, 3(4), 2000, p. 454.
106. Although I think Ahmed is right to suggest the feeling of shame already does some restorative work—since it 'shows we are now good and caring subjects'—I think the emotion is inclined to become so unbearable as to elicit grand gestures of destruction and reconstruction. Almost invariably the shamed seek, as it were, to 'abandon their identity' either by terminating it through suicide (as did Ajax) or, in a symmetrically identical move, transforming it through atonement. See Ahmed, *The Cultural Politics of Emotion*, pp. 109-110. I have discussed this loss of love for country and its relationship to the apology at length in P. Muldoon, 'A Reconciliation Most Desirable: Shame, Narcissism, Apology and Justice', *International Political Science Review*, 38(2), 2017, pp. 213-227.
107. Fagenblat, 'The Apology', p. 23.
108. Fagenblat, 'The Apology', p. 25.
109. Fagenblat, here quoting from Corinthians, pp. 25-26.
110. Fagenblat, 'The Apology', p. 26.
111. Of course, as Kantorowicz suggests, the inspiration for the concept of the king's two bodies is none other than the incarnation of Christ. See E.H. Kantorowicz, *The King's Two Bodies: A Study in Medieval Political Theology*, Princeton, NJ: Princeton University Press, 1957, p. 16.
112. Kantorowicz, *The King's Two Bodies*, pp. 7-23.
113. Here, again, I think Ahmed is instructive: 'In shame, I feel myself to be bad, and hence to expel the badness, I have to expel myself from myself.' On my reading, apology is precisely this action of expelling the self from the self. Ahmed, *The Cultural Politics of Emotion*, p. 104.
114. Verdeja, 'Official Apologies in the Aftermath of Political Violence', p. 576.
115. Fagenblat, 'The Apology', p. 26.
116. Páez, 'Official or Political Apologies and Improvement of Intergroup Relations', p. 12.
117. J. Gemes, 'Witnessing the Apology', *Australian Aboriginal Studies*, 1, 2008, p. 118.
118. Ahmed, *The Cultural Politics of Emotion*, p. 35.
119. See A. Dirk Moses, 'Official Apologies', pp. 152-155.
120. C. Fejo-King cited in Dirk Moses, 'Official Apologies', p. 153.
121. R. Weyneth, 'The Power of Apology and the Process of Historical Reconciliation', *The Public Historian*, 23(3), 2001, p. 24.
122. See P. Dodson, 'After the Apology', *Arena Magazine* 94, p. 23.
123. Dodson, 'After the Apology', *Arena Magazine* 94, pp. 20-22.
124. Povinelli, 'The State of Shame', p. 582; Mihaela Mihai may well have been more right than she knew when she suggested that apologies are more likely to succeed if they 'encourage citizens to feel good'. M. Mihai, 'When the State Says "Sorry": State Apologies as Exemplary Political Judgements', *The Journal of Political Philosophy*, 21(2), 2013, p. 203.
125. See Mihai, 'When the State Says "Sorry"', p. 201.
126. Cunningham, 'Saying Sorry: The Politics of Apology', p. 288.

127. Dodson, 'After the Apology'; Watson, 'The Northern Territory Emergency Response'; Coulthard, *Red Skin, White Masks*; Million, *Therapeutic Nations*.
128. As Million points out, making healing from trauma a prerequisite for the exercise of self-determination is one of the ways in which the neoliberal state blocks and undermines the Indigenous struggle for autonomy. Million, *Therapeutic Nations*, p. 105. On this point, see also K. Maxwell, 'Settler Humanitarianism: Healing the Indigenous Child Victim', *Comparative Studies in Society and History*, 59(4), 2017, pp. 974–1007.
129. Coulthard, *Red Skin, White Masks*, p. 173.
130. This conclusion is also in accord with Lisa Stevenson's sense of biopolitics as being completely indifferent to the kind of life it cares for. Since biopolitics is, in essence, concerned with human beings as members of the species, it can mobilize forms of 'care' that actually endanger 'ways of life' like, in her case, the Inuit in Canada. See L. Stevenson, *Life Beside Itself: Imagining Care in the Canadian Arctic*, Oakland, CA: University of California Press, 2014.

5
The Therapy of Reconciliation

Unlike public memorials and political apologies, truth commissions do not at first glance appear to be institutions in which the sovereign body offers itself up to its victims in a grand gesture of repentance. Instead, they look very much like a standard vehicle of democratic accountability, albeit one operating on a much larger scale, in which the objective is the far more mundane (though still completely indispensable) one of documenting rights violations and correcting the historical record. To the extent, however, that they also require the sovereign body to bear witness to the suffering of victims and lay the evidence of wrongdoing before itself, truth commissions share a certain elective affinity with public memorials and political apologies as collective acts of reckoning and repentance. Unlike criminal trials which, by their very nature, individualize guilt, truth commissions work to unearth *systemic* injustices that implicate (and cast dishonour upon) the body politic as a whole.[1] Through them, as Ignatieff puts it, 'former regimes are shamed into unalterable moral disgrace [and] their inner moral essence is named and defined for all times by an objective process of fact-finding'.[2] And yet, to assume the only truths with which truth commissions deal are the objective facts and the only emotions they conjure are shame may be to neglect the greater part of the operation they (or, at least, some of them) perform. As I seek to show in this chapter, truth commissions, like the other exceptional institutions of the penitent state, are as much about the recovery from memory as they are the recovery of memory.

In genealogies of the truth commission as a public exercise in the recovery of/recovery from memory, precedence should, by rights, be given to Chile. While national inquiries into gross violations of human rights had already been conducted elsewhere, the Chilean Commission, held between 1990 and 1991, was the first to pair truth and reconciliation and thus, implicitly at least, to make the former serve the latter. In Chile, and for the first time, the discovery of the truth about past wrongs was linked not to criminal prosecution (which amnesty laws prohibited), or simply to historical correction, but to psychological repair.[3] In seeking to uncover the fate of the dead and disappeared, it had attempted not simply to ascertain the facts but to console the grief-stricken and, as Mark Sanders put it, 'join in the work of mourning'.[4] As fortune would have it, however, this pre-eminence in truth and reconciliation turned out to be relatively short-lived. In part because of the novelty of putting amnesty into the service of truth and reconciliation (into the service, that is, of memory rather than forgetting),[5] in part because of the international prominence of Apartheid as a crime against humanity, and in part because of the message of forgiveness championed by its famous chairperson, Desmond Tutu, the South African Truth and Reconciliation Commission (TRC), whose hearings extended between 1995 and 1998, quickly eclipsed its Latin American predecessor. As if overnight, the South African experiment in national healing became a world-historical event, establishing truth and reconciliation as a genuine rival to the Nuremberg model.[6]

In large measure because the South African TRC did rival Nuremberg as an institutional vehicle for coming to terms with the past, the most influential debates about the merits of truth and reconciliation have hitherto been fought on the terrain of justice. As far as its critics are concerned, truth and reconciliation is inherently inferior to prosecution and punishment both as a means of restoring the rule of law and of demonstrating to victims that their rights (and thus *they*) matter. However justifiable it might be on prudential or pragmatic grounds, they argue, it sacrifices accountability for civility, justice for peace, in ways that moral reason finds difficult to sanction. Where rights have been violated (and particularly where they have been egregiously violated), there is a 'duty to prosecute' that circumstances might render unfeasible, but which remains, for all that, the gold standard. In the eyes of its supporters, by contrast, truth and reconciliation is less a political expedient, a measure that one is forced to adopt when prosecution becomes dangerous and/or impractical, than a form of justice in its own right. In truth and reconciliation, they suggest, restoration *for* the victim (as well as the community to which the perpetrator and the victim belong) is prioritized over retribution *against* the perpetrator in a way that reframes, but does not diminish, justice. Rather than a sacrifice imposed upon the victims, in other words, truth and reconciliation puts them (and their 'experience of injustice') at the centre, giving rise to what one commentator called a 'more ambitious and expansive vision of justice'.[7]

Truth and reconciliation found a powerful advocate in Desmond Tutu and *No Future without Forgiveness*, his personal memoir of the South African TRC, can be read as one long defence of the proposition that 'retributive justice ... is not the only form of justice'.[8] Whether Tutu and his allies ever succeeding in convincing themselves, let alone others, that the concept of restorative justice was sufficiently coherent or robust to challenge the presumption that retributive justice simply '*is* justice', as Judith Shklar once sharply put it, is nevertheless doubtful.[9] For all their insistence that truth and reconciliation was 'victim-orientated'—that it offered the violated an opportunity to tell their story, receive recognition for their suffering, and regain their human and civil dignity—they were never so assured of its moral claim as to completely cease appeals to political necessity. If they championed truth and reconciliation, in other words, it was often on the understanding not that it was the best but that it was the best that could be hoped for under the circumstances.[10] In this, as in most matters concerning the South African TRC, *No Future without Forgiveness* is illuminating as much for its passionate defence of restorative justice as for its lapses and inconsistencies. As tireless as Tutu was in championing truth and reconciliation as a model, his favoured means of rebutting those who argued the amnesty provisions of the Commission allowed perpetrators to get away with murder was to remind them of the carnage that surely would have unfolded had South Africa taken the path of prosecution and punishment.[11]

This prudential justification of truth and reconciliation as a tool for averting carnage did little to discourage the impression that the TRC, for all its novelty as an institution, was simply another manifestation of the very old political tendency to prioritize peace over justice—an impression that Tutu himself often encouraged. 'If there was no amnesty', he claimed in an interview (here falling back on the conventional conception of justice as retributive justice), 'then we would have had justice and ashes.'[12] His point, rendered with admirable economy, was that there are circumstances where it is not only, as it is in Kant's happy rendering of *fiat iustitia, pereat mundus*, 'the rogues' of the world who perish when justice is done.[13] Everyone perishes. The whole world is reduced to ashes. In circumstances such as this, suggests Tutu, one faces a very simple decision: does one want life at the expense of justice or justice at the expense of life? In short, amnesty or ashes? Thus pragmatism will out.[14] Unless doubts exist about the validity of the counterfactual—was it really amnesty or ashes?—the choice between 'justice' and 'peace' is hardly a choice at all. When legal prosecution comes at the expense of life, it turns into a self-defeating value, destroying the very thing to which it might render justice or restore dignity: living beings. That, at any rate, was the 'moral defence' of amnesty that Tutu (and many others) found convincing and which they regularly used to bring discussions of amnesty to a full stop.[15]

To give pragmatism the final word in this matter is, however, to overlook what was, in fact, truly novel about the TRC. For if the question of life was always at the centre of this experiment in truth and reconciliation, it was never simply within the terms of a pragmatic calculus, according to which life only acquires value in relation to death. For the pragmatist in Tutu, amnesty is preferable to 'justice and ashes' because it, at least, allows life to go on. The wager, persuasive in its simplicity (if not, perhaps, in its counterfactual), is that a morally compromised life is still better than no life at all. However, the more closely one examines the workings of the TRC, the more apparent it becomes that 'life' had been granted another, much more subtle, significance. Within that context, life was not simply something that was 'there' or 'not there', something that could be preserved or destroyed in its simple facticity. It was rather something variable in strength, something that could be depleted or invigorated, damaged or repaired, as a result of the political forces being brought to bear upon it. As Tutu, now switching into the role of the non-pragmatist, revealed through his commitment to a *restorative* justice, the value of truth and reconciliation did not simply lie in preventing death but in enhancing life—in mending wounds, healing divisions, and restoring what had been lost. In short, rather than content itself with avoiding the destruction *of* life, the TRC addressed itself *to* life as a governable object in the hope (and seemingly in the knowledge) that it could be regulated and modified, healed and revived, through judicious use of the restorative powers of truth telling.

Whatever their philosophical merits, therefore, the principled (deontological) attack upon, and the prudential (utilitarian) defence of, the South African TRC only served to obscure what its critics and supporters alike were always at least dimly aware; namely, that the model of truth and reconciliation could not be fully comprehended or understood within the terms of the so-called peace for justice trade.[16] Perhaps Derrida didn't mean everything he implied when, in reflecting upon the global proliferation of 'scenes of repentance', he referred to the South African experiment with public truth telling as a 'therapy of reconciliation'.[17] Whether by accident or design, however, the phrase is strikingly apt. When Minister for Justice Dullah Omar introduced the Promotion of National Unity and Reconciliation Act into the South African Parliament in 1995, he described the TRC as an instrument by which 'to heal our country'.[18] Similarly, in his introduction to its Final Report, Desmond Tutu presented the TRC as a vehicle for 'the crucial process of attempting to heal a traumatised and deeply divided people'.[19] Rather than peace or justice, then, it was 'healing' that loomed large from beginning to end. As statement after statement testified, healing was the core mission of the TRC, served as a key justification for each of its committees (Amnesty, Human Rights Violation, Reparation and Rehabilitation), and constituted the principal criteria against which it would be judged. So entwined did therapy and the TRC become, in fact, that the only question anyone really wanted to ask of it in the end was whether it had succeeded in 'healing the nation'.[20]

Precisely what healing meant and how it was to be achieved was, however, never all that clear. In some cases, the concept was specifically invoked within the psychoanalytic frame of the 'talking cure'. In one of those vague gestures to Freud that have become so familiar, truth telling was presented as a therapeutic experience for victims that allowed them to achieve closure.[21] Pamphlets and posters distributed by the TRC to encourage victims to come forward and tell their story explicitly played on the popular notion that 'revealing is healing' by carrying the slogan: 'The Truth Hurts, But Silence Kills'.[22] At other times healing was deployed as an all-purpose metaphor for the 'mending' of broken people and broken relationships, shrouding the work of the TRC in a vague but permissive mysticism. Some of the early commentary on the TRC sought to bring greater conceptual rigour to discussions of healing by questioning the salience of applying the therapeutic analogy to whole nations and exploring precisely what, if indeed anything, truth telling could do to heal traumatized subjects.[23] Later analyses deepened these critiques by interrogating the 'rhetorics', the 'ethos', and the 'practices' of healing at work in the TRC.[24] By and large, however, critical assessments of the TRC (including many of those just mentioned) have continued to circle around the twin concerns of treating nations as subjects of trauma and bringing therapy into politics.[25] Endlessly referred back to the problems of scale (does it make sense to treat a collective as if it was an individual?) and autonomy (isn't it justice and peace rather trauma and therapy that belongs to the political?), 'healing' has paradoxically emerged as one of the most ubiquitous, yet most elusive, concepts of the TRC.

Arguably, one of the main reasons why analyses of the TRC as a therapeutic exercise rarely get past these problems of scale and autonomy is because the concept of healing always comes pre-packaged. Since healing, generally speaking, means nothing outside of the physical, psychological, and spiritual frameworks that furnish it with both an 'object' upon which to work (the body, the psyche, the soul) and a 'theory' to guide that work (medicine, psychoanalysis, theology), it is hard to 'think it' or think about it outside those forms of analysis that are, at once, situated at the unit level and foreign to the political domain. In the majority of cases, whatever sense is made of the 'therapy of reconciliation' comes down to whether it is read as a spiritual exercise that seeks healing for the soul in acts of repentance and forgiveness (in the manner of Amstutz and Philpott) or a psycho-therapeutic exercise that seeks healing for the psyche in acts of catharsis and cathexis (in the manner of Minow and Hutchinson).[26] The question that naturally arises in this context is whether these spiritual and therapeutic exercises can be made to work for collectives or ought to be part of politics at all. Is it meaningful to speak of the 'national soul' or the 'national psyche'? Can nations show remorse or experience catharsis in the same way as individuals? Presented in this way, it is hard not to conclude, as does Lund, that 'the use of such medical analogies in statecraft is actually misleading'.[27] Applied at the collective level, she asserts, healing can be little more than rhetoric and, given the interventions it has licensed historically in Africa, a dangerous rhetoric at that.

In an attempt to get past, or at least think differently about, these recurring problems of scale and autonomy, this chapter shifts the focus from models of healing to models of governing. Rather than approach the TRC as an application (or misapplication) of a particular therapeutic discourse, it tries to construct an understanding of the kind of institution it was by asking a set of simple questions about its operation: what is being governed, through what techniques, and with what effects? More specifically, the chapter seeks to gain some critical purchase on the 'healing mission' of the TRC by analytically disentangling the two biopolitical rationalities it could plausibly be regarded as having mobilized: pastoralism and governmentalism, or what Foucault calls the *ratio pastoralis* and the *ratio gubernatorial*.[28] So long as one adheres to the view of its functionaries, I will suggest, the Commission bears a striking resemblance to the Christian model of pastoral power in its beneficent concern for the welfare of 'all and each' (*omnes et singulatim*).[29] Tasked with healing a wounded and divided people, the commissioners were inclined to see themselves as pastors whose task was to bear attentive witness to the story of each individual as a means of restoring the entire flock to health. And yet, as I go on to show by taking an outside perspective, this beneficent concern for 'all and each' was ultimately overridden by—or, more accurately, subsumed within—a more fully modern governmental rationality that tapped into (and arguably exploited) individual trauma to generate a national catharsis. Fearing the return of violence, the emergency yet to come, the TRC staged an emotional spectacle of such intensity and power it provided a transition point in the collective grieving process. Precisely where that healing operation—focused more on the population than the individual—left the victims is something the analysis seeks to discover.

This chapter focuses upon South Africa, in part because it is hailed as a landmark in truth and reconciliation and in part because its 'exalted status'[30] means there is a wealth of primary and secondary material to draw upon. However, it should not be assumed that the South African experiment in truth and reconciliation was a completely novel therapeutic intervention into the life of the population. On the contrary, what we see in South Africa is a consolidation and extension of therapeutic technologies that had already been deployed elsewhere and which have since been further developed and refined.[31] Truth telling, as the establishment of commissions in countries as distinct as Peru and Canada testifies, is a mobile and flexible technology, whose critical value to (even causal connection with) healing and reconciliation is increasingly taken for granted. The mere fact that a new institution has been created around it, and for it, confirms its status as an imperative: truth commissions have become necessary because truth itself has become necessary—it simply *must* be told. Significantly, however, the truth that must now be told is not just the 'factual truth' that acts as the handmaiden of justice or the 'moral truth' derived from the exercise of critical reason, but the 'narrative truth' (or, even more revealingly, the 'healing truth') that resolves trauma. As Pierre Hazan has noted, the 'new doxa' which both underpins and justifies the truth commission as an institution of exception comes courtesy of Judith Lewis Herman's *Trauma and Recovery*: '[r]emembering and telling the truth about terrible events are prerequisites both for the restoration of the social order and for the healing of individual victims'.[32]

One of the benefits of examining the South African TRC in this context lies in the power it has to puncture these assumptions. If the 'exalted case' does not fully succeed, maybe none of the others do either. The analysis begins with an account of the pastoral model as a way of making sense of the 'soul craft' of remorse and forgiveness that dominated the discourse of the TRC and became central to its conception of healing. I then go on to complicate this view by exposing the biopolitical significance of the choice of transitional vehicle (truth commission over criminal tribunal), the parameters of its operation (the period, the cases, the duration), and the techniques it deployed (testimony and witnessing). Through such means, I suggest, the TRC generated a cathartic effect which, regardless of its implications for the individuals giving testimony, made it possible for the nation as a whole to put the past behind it and 'get on with life'. I conclude by suggesting that truth and reconciliation was not simply, as many critics have claimed, a tool of depoliticization—a means by which a moral and political crisis was converted into an emotional and psychological one.[33] It was also, and just as importantly, a tool of politicization—a means by which the emotions and the psyche were brought across the threshold from the private to the public and made available to political manipulation. In the TRC, I will suggest, the 'inner life' of subjects was exposed to power in a hitherto unprecedented way, precipitating a whole new moral and political crisis from which we are yet to extricate ourselves.

I All and Each: The Return of the Pastorate?

The religious tenor of the TRC—evident in its personnel, its liturgies, and its ethics—has been widely noted and widely criticized.[34] Staffed by men of the cloth, introduced with prayers and hymns, and conceived as exercises in reconciliation, the hearings of the Commission were so at odds with normal juridical processes they provided critics with an easy target. For predictable, though not unpersuasive, reasons, Tutu's promotion of forgiveness as a 'civic sacrament' proved to be something of a lightning rod, with many critics questioning its place in this (or indeed any) transition from authoritarianism to democracy. To champion forgiveness in a public institution, especially one charged with painting as complete a picture as possible of gross violations of human rights, was, they argued, to undermine accountability, confuse the private with the public, and place undue pressure upon the victims who had every right to feel angry and indignant.[35] Lurking beneath the problem of forgiveness was, however, a more deeply rooted set of concerns about the appropriate relation between the theological and the political. For some, the overtly Christian character of the TRC spoke of a failure to break from the colonial deference to Western values; for others, it demonstrated a clear violation of the separation of church and state; and for others still, it amounted to an attempt to build a democratic nation on a non-pluralist, and thus inherently unstable, moral foundation.[36]

Although by no means wrongheaded, such critiques never quite got to the heart of the matter because they placed more emphasis on Christian symbols of faith and piety than on Christian systems of power and governance.[37] If it was Tutu's robes and prayers (and, of course, his praise of forgiveness) that captured the public gaze and disturbed the critics, the pseudo-religious character of the TRC was always more powerfully manifest in its resemblance to the 'shepherd–flock relation' characteristic of the Christian model of pastoral power. Explicitly adopted as an alternative to the Nuremberg model, the Commission more or less defined itself as a public institution by the fact that it did not punish. Instead, like the Christian pastorate with its 'care for the flock' ethos, it operated as a completely beneficent power whose 'only *raison d'être*', as Foucault put it in his seminal discussion of the pastoral form of governance, was 'doing good'.[38] Frameworks have, of course, a way of shaping the reality they are elicited to explain so it is, perhaps, not entirely surprising that the resemblance between commissioner and public on the one hand and pastor and flock on the other should become more and more uncanny once one approaches the TRC with the pastoral model in mind. My objective in this section is not, however, to show that the TRC was a precise copy of this pastoral model of governmentality. It is rather to use that model to try and shed light on, and reveal some of the attraction of, its attempt to give succour to life and 'heal through truth'.

Arguably, the two structural features that best revealed the affinity between the TRC and the Christian pastorate were its benevolent and individualizing approach. Tasked with providing healing or, to the extent that the two ideas were differentiated, delivering salvation, the Commission consciously took on the character of a 'benevolent power'; a power whose purpose was to listen rather than command, and whose forum and offices were structured accordingly.[39] In order to avoid what Tutu and others referred to as the intimidation of judicial proceedings, the Commission constituted its 'hearings' as a non-adversarial, 'safe space' in which the disclosure of emotion took precedence over the adjudication of facts.[40] Even the hearings of the Amnesty Committee—in effect the committee for the sheep who had strayed off course—were intended, as far as possible, to be a non-judgemental domain in which perpetrators could speak openly of the emotional toll that having to uphold the system of Apartheid had taken on them.[41] In a similar way, the priority given to healing made it incumbent on the officers of the Commission, from the highest to the lowest, to resist all the seductions of power and selflessly devote themselves to the well-being of others. Tutu would, of course, embody this ethos to perfection by conceiving his position as chief commissioner, not in terms of a right to rule but in terms of a duty to save. All would, however, symbolically mark their position of service by inverting the order of the courtroom and rising to their feet when witnesses entered to give evidence.[42]

Consistent with the model of the pastorate too, the TRC was an 'individualizing power' whose mission proceeded on the basis that 'to care for all is to care for one and to care for one is to care for all'. As Minister for Justice Dullah Omar made clear from the very outset, the Commission had not been established in the interests of any particular group within the South African flock. It was not exclusively for the benefit of the liberation movement, still less for the benefit of any one arm of that liberation movement. The only entities with which it was truly concerned were the wounded nation and the wounded individual in what Foucault calls their 'paradoxical equivalence'.[43] In the annals of the TRC, the double nature of this operation—to heal the nation by healing the individual and to heal the individual by healing the nation—would appear just as frequently as its paradoxical quality would go unremarked. On the one hand, as Tutu (and many others) suggested, the mission of the TRC was to heal a 'wounded people'.[44] Since Apartheid was, in essence, a 'sick system', affecting and infecting everybody like a plague, it had to be treated globally, at the level of the whole South African nation. On the other hand, as Tutu (and many others) also suggested, the mission of the TRC was to heal the 'wounded individual'. As the flesh upon which the wounds of Apartheid had been inflicted, they assumed an absolute, and not a relative, importance: each story mattered, each one deserved to be heard, because each one carried the scars of the nation within itself.[45] Hence the strange 'paradoxical equivalence' that would return over and over: to heal the nation was to heal the individual and to heal the individual was to heal the nation.[46]

Identifying these structural features gives us our first intimation of the exceptional character of the TRC and why it captured the imagination of so many. As Foucault notes, one of the most striking features of the pastoral model of governance is that 'all the dimensions of terror and of force or fearful violence, all these disturbing powers that make men tremble before the power of kings and gods, disappear'.[47] Instead, one encounters an institution that wants only to do good; which attends with as much care to those who have stuck to the path as those who have strayed from it; and whose only objective is the welfare of all and each. At the risk of essentialism, the ideal it imitates is less that of the all-powerful, sovereign father than that of the all-forgiving, sacrificing mother. Serving as a sympathetic witness to stories of pain and loss, enjoined in the mourning process, the Commission found its essence as a power in the kenotic surrender of power. Rather than inspire fear, pass judgement, or dispense punishment, it wanted nothing more than to look after the damaged life that had been temporarily placed into its care and heal it through compassionate identification. In this, as in almost every other respect, it was an exception to the cold, dispassionate force of the law and clearly understood itself as such. 'Tutu cried', wrote Albie Sachs. 'Judges do not cry'.[48] And it was ultimately in the expression of those tears that the TRC differentiated itself from the institution of the court and revealed itself as something wholly other to sovereign power.

To go no further than these structural features would, however, be to overlook the micro-mechanisms by which the TRC exercised its pastoral power. In Foucault's account (which is the one I will rely upon here), the real essence of the pastorate as a structure of governance lies in the complex relations of responsibility that run forwards and backwards between pastor and flock. For the pastor, it is a matter of 'total responsibility': he must ensure the welfare of 'all and each'; take on the deeds and misdeeds of the flock as his own; be prepared to risk his physical and spiritual life for them; and serve as much through his flaws as his merits as their principal example. For the flock, it is a matter of 'total obedience': they must renounce their will; confess the inner truths of the hidden soul; consent to be guided in the conduct of their everyday life; and take direction, above all, in matters of conscience. Ultimately, as we shall see, it is through the enactment of these relationships of responsibility that the TRC would reveal its deeper affiliation with the pastorate and show itself not just as a vehicle for bearing witness but as an instrument for the governance of life. Appointed, as it were, to guide their multi-racial flock to the chosen land of the 'new South Africa', the commissioners took on the role of soul shepherds, encouraging personal acts of apology and forgiveness as a way of healing all and each. The officers who were, in principle, expected to care and obey were thus, in practice, inclined to insist upon a certain kind of care and obedience themselves: firstly, to the authority of the Commission as an instrument of healing and secondly, to a model of restorative justice that demanded resentment be set aside for the sake of life.

As with every therapeutic operation, all of this began with a diagnosis. As Deputy Chair Alex Boraine noted, the Commission could scarcely be expected to deliver healing to South African society if it did not start with 'an honest assessment ... of the sickness within that society'.[49] And for him, as for Tutu, the issue was quite straightforward, at least as a general proposition: ultimately the cause of that sickness was to be found in what South Africa had hidden from itself, in what it had disappeared from the public world; in short, in secrecy. Conversely, the healing that it sought was to be found in putting the truth before itself, in the exhumation of those missing bodies; in short, in exposure.[50] Consistent, again, with the idea of a paradoxical equivalence between 'all and each', the assumption guiding the entire healing operation was that it would be just as beneficial for society to hear the truth as it would be for individuals to tell it. If the victims and the perpetrators were ever to put the past to rest, it was essential that they return to their memories and speak publicly of what they had suffered and what they had done. Giving testimony was a critical part of *their* healing process.[51] At the same time, having each individual publicly confront the truth was considered fundamentally important to the health of the nation. The only way, according to Boraine, that South Africa could heal the tear in *its* national soul was to 'come out of a period in which its society was based on lies and deceit'.[52] In short, then, in Minow's pithy summary: 'expose the terrible secrets of a sick society and heal that society'.[53]

The more the hearings of the Commission proceeded, however, the more this assumed relation between exposure and healing was tested. The key problem in this regard, as one of the slogans of the TRC inadvertently highlighted, was that of pain: however much one might agree with the proposition that silence kills, the fact remained that the truth *still* hurt.[54] On the one hand, as was widely admitted, it was painful for the victims and the perpetrators to tell their stories and expose their grief and/or guilt in public. Frequent requests by victims for the return of body parts and human remains showed just how intimately memory and mourning were related and provided an all too visceral expression of the agonizing pathos behind the unrealizable wish to 'make whole again'.[55] While Tutu was keen to cite cases of people who found talking to the Commission therapeutic, even he had to admit that there were victims who, instead of finding relief, 'went away more traumatised than before' and perpetrators who, instead of enjoying release, suffered 'the penalty of public exposure and humiliation'.[56] On the other hand, as was also widely admitted, it was painful for the survivors, the secondary victims, and the public to hear their stories.[57] If revelations about the fate (or final resting place) of the dead and the disappeared brought some comfort to the relatives whose mourning had remained in state of suspension, there was no guarantee that even 'a very good dose of the truth', as one observer put it in suggestively medicinal terms, would lead to healing.[58] Similarly, for many members of the general public, the disclosures of the TRC often proved far from restorative.[59] As Antjie Krog noted in her autobiographical commentary, *Country of My Skull*:

> Flesh and blood can in the end only endure so much... Every week we are stretched thinner and thinner over different pitches of grief... how many people can one see crying, how much sorrow wrenched loose can one accommodate... and how does one get rid of the specific intonation of the words? It stays and stays.[60]

Even if no one at the Commission doubted that the wounded needed to speak and South Africa needed to listen, therefore, they were hardly insensitive to the toll that truth telling had taken (and might yet still take) both upon the truth-tellers, who had been asked to bear their souls, and the nation, which had been asked to give up its innocence. In opening up a space for storytelling, the TRC had simultaneously opened up a space for grief and anger that it was, at one and the same time, eager to engage and desperate to contain. Through the voices of damaged life (sometimes as much those who worked for the Apartheid state as those who rebelled against it), trauma entered the public sphere with a force that did not seem to have been anticipated and which constantly threatened to disrupt the efforts the Commission was making to heal a divided people. Ever proximate, ever entwined, grief flowed into anger and anger into grief in ways that undid the truth-tellers, broke the commissioners, and tested the limits of the witnesses. 'How many people can one see crying, how much sorrow wrenched loose can one accommodate'?—these were, to be sure, the salient questions and Antjie Krog was by no means the only one to ponder the problem of vicarious trauma and the risks of incorporation in the face of those harrowing tales of loss. Was it possible, as Dumisa Ntsebeza suggested, that South African society was 'in danger of its own success in exposing the truth'?[61]

The apparent success of the TRC in exposing the truth opened up two different problems for the commissioners. The first of these related to their own role as doctors of the soul.[62] Notwithstanding the fact they had been tasked with healing the nation, claimed Tutu, the commissioners were themselves wounded people, whose pain compounded every day they presided over the hearings.[63] Exposed, as it were, to the toxic truth over and over and over again, they had effectively borne the brunt of the healing operation.[64] Had anyone been more completely enjoined in the work of mourning than them? In the postscript to *No Future without Forgiveness*, Tutu went so far as to say the role assigned to the commissioner was more taxing even than that assigned to Jesus. While the latter had acted like a 'dishwasher', able to manage all the pain and anguish that came to him in his ministry because he could, in turn, 'pass it on to the Father', the former had been given no choice but to absorb it all themselves. 'It may be', he wrote (vividly capturing the character of vicarious trauma), 'that we have been a great deal more like vacuum cleaners than dishwashers, and have taken into ourselves far more than we can say of the pain and devastation of those whose stories we have heard.'[65] For the commissioners, in short, the threat of psychic overload loomed large, raising the issue of their responsibility as 'wounded healers': were they to forget themselves to save the flock (thereby putting the healer at risk) or forget the flock to save themselves (thereby putting the healing at risk)?[66]

The second problem related to how the needs of the individual might be balanced against the needs of the nation. Again, in striking agreement with the Christian model of the pastorate, the Commission had proceeded on the presumption that narrative truth (a bit like good pasturage) would nourish and restore provided it was shared around equitably. If those who had too much (the insiders burdened by the truth) shared with those who had too little (the outsiders yearning for the truth), both would in the end be healed. Hence the only questions it really needed to address were the technical ones of how it might 'bring forth' truths not widely known and 'distribute them' to the nation.[67] The more it proceeded, however, the more the needs of the individual and the nation seemed to diverge, raising the possibility that what was good for the one might not be good for the other. Thus a second paradox emerged. Might encouraging individuals to tell their story, without which the process of national healing would inevitably grind to a halt, work to re-traumatize them? Or might encouraging the nation to bear witness to that testimony, without which the recovery of each individual would be jeopardized, turn into a vicarious trauma for them?[68] The 'haunting question', yet to be answered, wrote Boraine, was whether 'the needs and objectives of the state' are 'synonymous with those of the violated individual'.[69]

The consensus surrounding the restorative power of truth telling notwithstanding, then, the Commission found itself wrestling with the same ethical dilemmas that had troubled the pastorate from the beginning.[70] As Foucault goes to some lengths to explain, pastoral power is characteristically implicated in two seemingly irresolvable paradoxes from which an entire suite of ethical conundrums arises. In the first place, the requirement that the shepherd should take care of (or keep his eye on) all and each creates significant problems, not only of a technical but also of an ethical nature. What happens in situations where the needs of one place the needs of all in jeopardy? Should the shepherd abandon the whole flock in order to save a single sheep that has gone astray or abandon that sheep to avoid compromising the well-being of the whole flock? Similarly, and secondly, what happens in situations where the needs of the flock put the well-being of the shepherd in jeopardy? Should the shepherd be prepared to risk his own (physical or spiritual) life in order to save his flock? Or should he protect his own body and soul first and foremost so that the flock does not lose its carer? In short, then, the problem that appears at the very centre of the pastorate is the problem of sacrifice— the problem, to restate the dilemmas in reverse order, of 'the sacrifice of the shepherd for his flock' (one for all) and 'the sacrifice of the whole of his flock for each of the sheep' (all for one).[71]

To the extent that they embraced their pastoral role, therefore, the commissioners found their responsibilities as carers for life rather more complicated than the 'healing through revealing' mantra suggested. Instead of simply facilitating the discovery and distribution of truth, they were required to actively shape the sacrificial ethics that would allow that truth to be safely revealed and received. In his attempts to both articulate and legitimate this 'ethics', Tutu drew inspiration from a range of different, and arguably incompatible, cultural inheritances: the Greco-Roman, with the concept of magnanimity, the African, with the concept of *ubuntu*, and the Christian, with the concept of reconciliation. However, in a feat of alchemical skill, all were fused together into that radiant compound known as 'restorative justice'.[72] In general terms, this restorative justice found its point of differentiation from retributive justice in the rejection of punitive measures that take something away from the perpetrator and the endorsement of recognition measures that give something back to the victim. And yet, in the ministrations of the TRC the concept took on a much broader range of connotations and gave rise to a far more exacting set of demands. Concerned, in essence, with 'healing', 'harmony', and 'humanization', restorative justice was not just something dispensed by authorities in the form of recognition but something expected of subjects in the form of generosity. Ultimately, as Pumla Gobodo-Madikizela acknowledged, restorative justice was equivalent to the emotional discipline every individual needed to show (or the emotional sacrifice they needed to make) to ensure that *they themselves* made the transition from 'vengeful citizens' to 'caring citizens'.[73]

A crucial link was in this way established between national objectives and individual conduct. If they wanted to reach the Promised Land of that 'new', undivided South Africa, every citizen had to act not just as a *beneficiary* but also as an *agent* of a 'restorative justice' by making the necessary sacrifices. This, in essence, meant that the general principle guiding the TRC—'that there is a need for understanding not vengeance'—became the specific duty of every individual. In the face of the painful truths that threatened to drag the nation back into discord, each member of the flock had to assist the goal of healing/harmony by 'rehumanizing'; that is, by trying to understand the situation, and affirm the dignity, of 'the other'. Listening to the victims, acknowledging the injustices they suffered, and responding to their pain with apologetic remorse was, of course, a crucial part of this ethics of rehumanization.[74] But it was by no means the whole of it. 'This kind of justice', wrote Tutu, 'seeks to rehabilitate both the victim and the perpetrator.'[75] If South Africa was to be truly healed and harmonized, it was vital that the victims *also* be 'a little more generous, a little more understanding, in judging the perpetrators of human rights violations'.[76] In dehumanizing others, he claimed, those perpetrators had dehumanized themselves, and it was only by understanding them and, if possible, forgiving them that they too could be brought back to the fold of humanity and 'rehumanized'.[77]

Seen from the pastoral perspective of the Commission, the greatest challenge lay in the fact that this ethic of rehumanization—the ethic that demanded sacrifices *from all parties*—could not be enforced. Since the integrity of the restorative form of justice (as well as the pastoral power of the Commission) would have been irretrievably damaged by coercive tactics, 'generosity of spirit' could not be inculcated through any means other than the promotion of examples. Hence the critical significance that began to be attached to the attitude of the chief commissioner. Although effectively the symbol of the entire healing operation, Tutu did not, as we have seen, make any attempt to deny the gruelling nature of the task he had been asked to perform. In *No Future without Forgiveness*, he alludes more than once to the physical and emotional toll of the work, half-attributing his own brush with cancer to the demands of bearing witness: 'my own illness seemed to dramatise the fact that it is a costly business to try to heal a wounded and traumatised people and that those engaging in that crucial task will perhaps bear the brunt themselves'.[78] And yet, as if in perfect alignment with the pastoral ideal of 'sacrificial reversal'—the idea that 'the pastor must be prepared to die to save his sheep'[79]—Tutu declared himself happy to absorb these 'costs' so that the nation might recover from its trauma. Called, he supposed, as much by God as by the president to serve as the shepherd of the entire South African flock, he took on the expenditure of himself as both a vocation and a privilege.[80] Attentive to all, forgiving of all, Tutu would become the symbol of reconciliation par excellence, an example to citizens everywhere of the sacrifices required to heal a nation ('one for all').

Inevitably, however, one example could not suffice. If the people were to be brought to the view that everyone (and not just one exceptional one) was capable of rehumanizing, other examples had to be evoked as a way of showing what was necessary and celebrating what was possible. Hence, whenever Tutu praised Mandela for his 'breathtaking magnanimity' and 'willingness to forgive', it was always, paradoxically enough, as a way of showing that there were no exceptions, that even those who suffered most egregiously could put their resentment aside for the sake of life.[81] Indeed, as if to drive home the message that anyone can do (and everyone *must* do) what Mandela had done, Tutu would cite case after case of expressions of magnanimity, *ubuntu*, and reconciliation on the part of ordinary citizens—white and Black alike.[82] It is in this spirit that we would hear of Johan Smit of Pretoria who lost his young son in an African National Congress (ANC) bomb blast, but who has 'no anger' (except perhaps for the Apartheid government), and of Babalwa Mhlauli (daughter of one of the Craddock Four) who declared herself 'ready to forgive' the security men who brutally murdered her father.[83] And, of course, since all of this was but the compassion of God working in the hearts of the creature he had made in his own image, this generosity towards each was within the reach of all:

> mercifully and wonderfully, as I listened to the stories of victims I marvelled at their magnanimity, that after so much suffering instead of lusting for revenge they had this extraordinary willingness to forgive. Then I thanked God that *all* of us, even I, have this remarkable capacity for good, for generosity, for magnanimity.[84]

While Alex Boraine insisted there could be no reconciliation without truth, therefore, it might be more accurate to suggest there could be no truth without reconciliation (or *ubuntu* or magnanimity).[85] As a result of its intimate connection with grief and anger, truth telling turned out to be a remedy and a poison all in one whose famed 'restorative powers' actually hinged upon the ability of the commissioners to inculcate a sacrificial ethics of rehumanization through the celebration and promotion of exemplars. Subtly, but surely, extraordinary generosity of spirit was instantiated as the norm, putting pressure on the truth-tellers to bring their emotions into alignment with the ethos of restorative justice and become 'caring citizens'. The inevitable consequence of this was that little public credit was granted to those whose emotional life resisted the insistent demand for forgiveness, magnanimity, or *ubuntu*. Instead of being regarded as a proof of self-worth or a demonstration of agency, the anger, resentment, and indignation of victims was treated as an expression of emotional recalcitrance or emotional pathology—at best, the unforgiving were seen as cases of pathological resentment; at worst, as a threat to peace (and, most likely, to themselves). They were the ones keeping the wounds open. As well as exposing the crimes of Apartheid, then, the victims were also required to expose themselves not simply *in* the agony of their loss but *to* the power of the Commission and its sacrificial ethics.

That the Commission was actually seeking to exert a pastoral *power* was most clearly in evidence when its attempts to bring individual conduct into line with this ethic of rehumanization met resistance. Of this there were many instances, both at the Human Rights Violation Committee (where forgiveness was promoted) and at the Amnesty Committee hearings (where remorse was promoted).[86] However, the spectacular case of Winnie Madikizela-Mandela, in which victim and perpetrator effectively appeared together in the one person, did as much as any to reveal the pressures and counter-pressures brought into play when generosity of spirit turned into a more or less explicit demand. Brought before the TRC to answer questions in relation to the murder of Stompie Seipei, allegedly at the hands of her famous 'Football Club', Madikizela-Mandela dismissed the testimony against her as ludicrous and refused to show the remorse required for rehumanization. Tutu, unable to simply impose his will, but cognizant of what was at stake with such a high-profile public figure, implored Madikizela-Mandela to live up to her greatness by apologizing:

> I beg you, I beg you, I beg you please—I have not made any particular finding from what has happened here. I speak as someone who has lived in this community. You are a great person and you don't know how your greatness would be enhanced if you were to say, 'sorry, things went wrong, forgive me'. I beg you.[87]

In his own memoire, Tutu recalls this episode as the moment when Madikizela-Mandela put her pride to one side and made her first, if tentative, public apology.[88] Others, however, will describe it as an embarrassing plea for a sign of remorse that was only reluctantly and half-heartedly complied with.[89] Frederik Van Zyl Slabbert gives an especially damning account of her resistance to the demand of moral transformation, recalling a 'Winnie Mandela who glared at Desmond Tutu with fixed, bitter eyes while he begged her to say that she felt just a little bit sorry. Her entire attitude said "Stompie was a traitor, he betrayed the struggle" … Can't the meddlesome priest understand this?'[90]

For many critics, the Commission's attempt to meddle in the emotional interior through its sacrificial ethics of rehumanization was deeply problematic *as politics*, in part because it was completely beyond the scope of the law and in part because the demand tended to fall harder upon the victims than the perpetrators. By connecting the transformation of the nation to the transformation of the individual, the TRC built the impression that it was not enough for subjects to simply respect human rights; they also had to undergo a moral reformation through acts of remorse and forgiveness. Under the aegis of restorative justice, in other words, generosity of spirit was turned into a matter of political necessity, drawing power into what Tutu called the 'secret places of the soul'.[91] More worrying still, since expressions of remorse proved to be the exception rather than the norm, the burden of this restorative justice fell disproportionately upon those who had already made the most extraordinary sacrifices for the greater good. In the TRC, as Nagy ironically underlined, 'national reconciliation was indeed premised upon moral transformation, but of *victims*: as forgiving rather than angry, and generous rather than demanding'.[92] They, above all, were expected to show grace. A risk was thus created of a perverse double sacrifice in which those who had given all for freedom were asked to give it all again for the sake of those poor 'lost souls' who had denied it to them.[93]

Unsurprisingly, it was the ever-more blurred line between promoting an ethics to the victims and imposing an ethics upon them that became one of the mainstays of critiques of the pastoral operation of the TRC.[94] While it was at least defensible, to use Derrida's formulation, as a 'freely given gift', forgiveness threatened to turn into an inherently unethical, coercive demand whenever it emerged as a social expectation.[95] Represented as a requisite sacrifice, critical to healing and humanization, forgiveness militated against a more reflexive engagement with the violence of Apartheid, delegitimated the righteous anger of the victims, and brought a halt (far too prematurely) to the mourning process. Those who continued, quite justifiably, to feel resentful about the indignities of state racism or found themselves incapable of forgiving those responsible for the death or disappearance of their love objects suddenly found themselves cast as obstacles to the realization of the new South Africa. If, as Tutu maintained, there was indeed no future without forgiveness, the resentful and unforgiving were responsible for holding the whole country back and putting it at risk of an endless cycle of violence. As Sisonke Msimany, in agreement with earlier work by Thomas Brudholm and Sonali Chakravarti, has recently underlined, the sacrifice of one for all and all for one appeared, for all intents and purposes, to be non-negotiable: 'forgiveness became a national mantra, and reconciliation an official ideology. Progress towards nation building was measured by the march of forgiveness. To be a good new South African, you had to leave anger in the past'.[96]

All of this was, of course, made worse by the fact the remorse was not deemed critical to the future in the same way (why not *No Future without Apology*?) and rarely offered up as a freely given gift. And yet, as Nagy more or less concedes, one can hardly blame the TRC for the moral turpitude of the perpetrators.[97] One can only judge it on the basis of the moral vision at work in its pastoral enterprise and, as the enthusiasm of so many critics, Martha Nussbaum not least among them, testifies, that vision was by no means wholly unattractive.[98] If we can take Tutu as our authority, the idea that underpins the entire framework of this restorative justice is that we belong in a 'bundle of life'.[99] Rather than autonomous rights-holders who exercise claims over and against one another, our lives are entwined in ways that enjoin and in fact necessitate the exercise of ethical generosity. Since we dehumanize ourselves when we dehumanize others and, conversely, humanize ourselves when we humanize others, we can only live our lives fully when every other life is fully lived. Abandoning those who strayed from the path only serves to diminish us as individuals and damage the bundle of life that binds and nourishes us all. Restorative justice, at least on Tutu's account of it, embraces this relational, communitarian conception of existence and sets out the ethical stance or emotional discipline needed to repair the damage violence does to life; namely, generosity of spirit. As Trudy Govier glosses it, relations with others are so fundamental to this particular conception of existence as to make forgiveness essential to survival: 'if a person does not forgive, her existence—and that of the others on whom she depends—will be at risk'.[100] In short, resentful life is a danger to life.

It is by no means irrelevant to post-facto judgements of the TRC that one of the most robust justifications for this 'inward dimension of the commission's work' should have come from psychologist and aide to the Human Rights Violation Committee Pumla Gobodo-Madikizela.[101] Although hardly inclined to underestimate the difficulty of remorse and forgiveness as ethical gestures, Gobodo-Madikizela underlined their utility for the 'bundle of life' pastoralism knows as 'the flock' by claiming they facilitated the rehumanization (a term she equates with a kind of moral/psychic healing) of self and other simultaneously. 'When perpetrators apologise', she noted, 'they are *acting as human beings*.'[102] Indicative of their wish, however unrealizable, to restore the loss suffered by the victim, the pain of remorse did not simply affirm the humanity of the victim (rescuing them, as it were, from the position of 'dehumanized other'); it demonstrated that the perpetrator still belonged to the ranks of moral human beings. Similarly, the act of forgiveness, in graciously responding to the pain of that remorse, worked to simultaneously readmit the perpetrator to moral humanity and affirm the victim as a moral agent. 'The act of forgiveness', wrote Gobodo-Madikizela, 'resists separating perpetrators from [the] network of human others.'[103] At the same time, it reveals the humanity of the victim by showing them capable of bringing negative emotions like anger and resentment to heel. Not only, in other words, was 'generosity of spirit' morally necessary, it was also psychologically beneficial—resistance to it simply harmed everyone.

Against those like Nagy, then, who suggested the Commission had lowered ethical standards by privileging reconciliation over responsibility (or, more precisely, over legal accountability) Tutu (and the other commissioners) could reasonably claim to have elevated ethical standards by making reconciliation everyone's responsibility.[104] Instead of encouraging citizens to exact satisfaction from each other in accordance with their legal entitlements (that is, to 'get their due'), he had asked them to reinvigorate the bundle of life from which *all* drew nourishment by becoming masters of their resentments. The fact that this was an ambitious goal did not, *ipso facto*, make it an undesirable one. On the contrary, as Nigel Biggar, among many others, argued, Tutu (and the TRC) deserved credit for reminding us of a dimension of our justice tradition that had been neglected since Kant. Long accustomed to the right of retribution, he suggested, we had forgotten a whole other tradition according to which 'justice is that which defends, restores and promotes healthy community'.[105] Variously described as expansive, generous, holistic, visionary, and restorative, this other justice was not to be disparaged for giving up on accountability but celebrated for recognizing the inseparability of individual and community and calling human beings to be the best, least vindictive, version of themselves they could be. In the battle against residual anger and resentment the TRC was, to be sure, unlikely to be completely victorious, but as Nussbaum pointed out, 'our institutions should model our best selves, not our worst'.[106]

Seen in this light—the light cast by the model of the pastorate—the attraction of the TRC is by no means incomprehensible. While critics found it difficult to get past the fact that (retributive) justice was not done and that the meddlesome priest asked wounded subjects to apologize and forgive, there was still something commendable about the way it had attempted to care for life and heal the biopolitical fracture in the population. Was not this stubborn refusal to divide life from itself the perfect response to the crime against humanity known as Apartheid? Was not the ethic of rehumanization, premised as it was on every individual exercising their moral agency and taking responsibility for the well-being of others, the perfect antidote to the denial of equality? As Charles Villa-Vincencio, director of the research department at the TRC, pointed out, if 'the ultimate goal of justice' is not retribution but 'healing and a better world in which to live', the Commission could be said to have fulfilled the requirements of justice better than any criminal tribunal could have done.[107] As the name itself implied, 'restorative justice' was a life-enhancing rather than life-destroying justice. Unlike its retributive counterpart, which, as Villa-Vincencio (aping Nietzsche) noted, had never quite freed itself of the 'reek of cruelty', it was a justice dedicated to the mending of wounds and the recovery of what was lost—a model of affirmative biopolitics if ever there was one. Did not such a healing justice, a justice that staunchly resisted the so-called death-dealing spirits of hatred, resentment, bitterness, and revenge, deserve to be commended?[108]

The more, then, we are drawn into the self-understanding of the Commission, the more difficult it becomes to find fault with its healing operation.[109] Although the moral/emotional demands it placed on citizens were exceptionally high, they seemed more than justified by the threat the death-dealing spirits posed to individual and collective well-being. For all the sacrifice it entailed, especially for the victims, the ethic of rehumanization at least held out the promise of restoring that 'bundle of life' in which all were enmeshed and upon which all relied. All that could be expected of resentment was the unravelling of that bundle all over again. However, there is reason to doubt whether the sacrificial ethics of the pastorate—'one for all', 'all for one'— captures the true character of the therapeutic operation the TRC performed. As a vehicle for national healing or, as Pupavac put it, 'mass psychotherapy',[110] the TRC could not afford to be quite so dedicated to singularity, to the welfare of all and each, as Tutu and his fellow commissioners frequently made out.[111] For the sake of the future, the population as a whole needed to be 'moved' towards healing and reconciliation and for that to happen the 'inner dimension' had to be 'worked' in other ways. In section II, I adopt an outside perspective to flesh out a quite different operation upon memory in which healing became associated not with forgiving but with purging. If the logic of the *ratio pastoralis* was to offer sacrifice without limit, to inculcate an 'unconditional generosity' so as to restore the bundle of life, that of the *ratio gubernatorial* was to build pressure without relent, so as to create a cathartic upheaval in the population as a whole.

II For the Sake of the Future: Flushing the Wound and Clearing the Air

Critical accounts of the TRC have been magnetically drawn to the battles waged over remorse and forgiveness as instruments of healing in the pastorate of souls. All the while, however, another understanding of the healing process was in evidence that had little to do with the ethic of rehumanization and the demand for generosity of spirit: catharsis.[112] As in the model of the pastorate, this other healing process was extolled as something that would be to the benefit of all and each: catharsis was what wounded individuals would undergo as they told their stories, and catharsis was what the wounded nation would undergo as it bore witness to those stories and shared in the mourning process. Unlike the 'healing as reconciliation' achieved through conscious acts of remorse and forgiveness, however, the 'healing as catharsis' achieved (for the individual) through a purging of emotions and (for the nation) through an identification with suffering avoided any entanglement in questions of ethical responsibility and sacrifice. As an organic process, induced by the application of powerful external stimuli, catharsis did not rely upon anyone disciplining their resentments in the name of some higher ethical ideal—be it magnanimity, *ubuntu*, or reconciliation—to achieve its 'healing effect'. Instead, it worked in a largely involuntary way as the buildup of emotional pressure forced the release of suppressed affect. Coming to grips with this other healing process requires a shift in perspective, away from the pastoral reason of those who held office in the Commission and towards the governmental reason embedded in the institutional form as a 'stage' for suffering.

Before beginning with this alternative reading of the TRC, it is worth pausing briefly to note the surprisingly central place this other healing process assumes in the thought of its famous chief commissioner. Compared to the concept of forgiveness, which Tutu invokes over and over again, the concept of catharsis is only explicitly referenced a few times in *No Future without Forgiveness*.[113] However, the more one reads his post-hoc reflections on the Commission with an eye to the so-called hydraulic model of the emotions, the more central catharsis begins to appear to his therapy for damaged life. Time and time again, sickness is coded as stagnation, health as movement, in a way that makes emotional 'flow' the key to healing. If there is one thing upon which Tutu insists, it is that 'the wounds of the past must not be allowed to fester'—'for the sake of the future' it was essential that they be 'opened up' and 'flushed out'; that feelings be moved.[114] Beneath the world of generous spirits that he celebrates and champions, then, lies a more primary, more organic, world of swirling emotions in which there are 'damns' and 'floodgates', containers (like the soul) where feelings are 'held' and sluices (like the mouth) through which they can 'flow'. So insistent is this hydraulic theme, in fact, that one might well wonder what Tutu really imagines healing requires: is it remorse and forgiveness that is restorative of life or the 'gushing forth' of feelings that have been 'bottled up'?[115] Whatever the case (and ultimately, from a governmental perspective, it doesn't really matter what Tutu thinks), there is little doubt that the institutional form of the TRC—under whose heading I will include the ends for which it was instituted, the parameters under which it operated, and the techniques that it deployed—conspired, as it were, of its own accord, to produce a cathartic effect.

Instructively, the idea that truth commissions actually work better than criminal tribunals as instruments of emotional catharsis appears to have been part of the justification for this choice of 'transitional vehicle' in South Africa all along.[116] It is hardly an accident, for instance, that one of the arguments most frequently adduced in defence of the amnesty provisions of the TRC (according to which perpetrators were granted immunity from criminal and civil prosecution in exchange for the 'full disclosure' of their politically motivated deeds) was that criminal trials prevent truths from coming out and feelings from being transformed.[117] Given, it was suggested, the first concern of the defendant in trials is not to disclose information but to create reasonable doubt, the likelihood that victims would find relief from the 'anxiety of not knowing' or, for that matter, the perpetrators from the 'weight of their guilt' was considered relatively slim. As Chief Justice Ismail Mahomed noted when relatives of Steve Biko issued an action contesting the constitutional validity of the amnesty provision, to refuse immunity to the perpetrators was to effectively erect a dam not just against the truth but against the emotions:

> The alternative to the grant of immunity from criminal prosecution of offenders is to keep intact the abstract right to such a prosecution for particular persons without the evidence to sustain the prosecution successfully, to continue to keep the dependents of such victims in many cases substantially ignorant about what precisely happened to their loved ones, to leave their yearning for the truth effectively

unassuaged, to perpetuate their legitimate sense of resentment and grief and correspondingly to allow the culprits of such deeds to remain perhaps physically free but inhibited in their capacity to become active, full and creative members of the new order by a menacing combination of confused fear, guilt, uncertainty and sometimes even trepidation.[118]

At the centre of this bleak picture (which is, at the same time, a justification of truth and reconciliation as therapy) lurks a barely concealed worry about 'festering wounds'; that is, about impacted grief and repressed guilt. While the duty to prosecute remains the gold standard as far as justice is concerned, an 'abstract right', as Chief Justice Mahomed puts it, that cannot be morally forsworn, insisting upon it runs the risk of leaving the victims and perpetrators stuck just where they are; ignorant about the fate of their loved ones on the one hand and burdened by the guilt of their wrongdoings on the other. Since criminal trials are procedurally designed to safeguard the defendant (not least of all against self-incrimination), focused upon establishing the facts of the case, and geared towards the dispensation of punishment, they do not simply hamper but actively work against the disclosure of information that might allow emotional resolution. Indeed, as the judgment of the Court underlined, since the victims have no real opportunity, and the perpetrators no real incentive, to tell the full story, trials are inclined to leave them at once imprisoned by their emotions and alienated from each other. Victims will be saddled with their resentment and grief, perpetrators with their guilt and fear, with the result that neither their wounds nor the rift between them is healed. Whatever the verdict—guilty or innocent—citizens are prevented from becoming fully active and creative (fully, as it were, alive) and the menace to the future remains.

What made the model of truth and reconciliation so attractive by comparison was that it flushed things out. As was widely noted (and as I will go on to discuss in more detail when I examine the specific practices of the Commission), the TRC differentiated itself from criminal trials through two key innovations—truth telling (as against forensic evidence) and sympathetic witnessing (as against impartial judgement)—each of which had the express purpose of encouraging victims and perpetrators to 'open up'.[119] Since, in this context, 'truth' was largely equated with personal disclosure for the purposes of healing (what was called 'narrative truth' or 'emotional truth'), rather than factual evidence for the purposes of adjudication (what was called 'juridical truth' or 'forensic truth'), everybody was free to tell *their* story, in *their* way. No one was required to stick strictly to the facts or keep their feelings to themselves.[120] Similarly, by insisting that the hearings (even, to the extent that it was possible, those of the Amnesty Committee) be a non-adversarial, safe space in which compassion took precedence over judgement, the TRC removed the barriers to disclosure that trials, if only for procedural reasons, tend to erect. In short, in the hearings of both the Human Rights Violation Committee and the Amnesty Committee, conventional juridical procedures were set aside (or, at the very least, substantially qualified) so that participants were free not just to testify but to vent. Better, it would appear, to forgo (retributive) justice if it meant getting things out.

As well as heeding the structural advantages that truth commissions almost always enjoy over criminal tribunals as vehicles of catharsis, it is necessary to attend to the specific terms under which the TRC operated. As was commonly, and sometimes critically, observed, the Promotion of National Unity and Reconciliation Act (1995) that established the TRC actively delimited, through a series of temporal and typological parameters, both the cohort of wounded subjects that could appear and the period during which the nation would be exposed to their traumatic stories.[121] Firstly, the Act determined that the opportunity to testify before the Commission would be limited to those who had been wounded during the period 1960 to 1994 (with the offer of reparations being further restricted to those who actually gave testimony—this was commonly referred to as the 'closed list' approach). Secondly, the Act restricted the category of 'victim' to those who had suffered gross violations of human rights (murder, abduction, torture, and severe ill-treatment). Finally, the Act declared that the Commission should take no more than two years (later extended to three) in which to complete its work. Timely completion was, in fact, a key theme among officials, with Thabo Mbecki, the ANC leader who succeeded Nelson Mandela as president, insisting that the TRC 'should conclude its work as quickly as possible' so as not to leave a legacy of unfinished business.[122]

Tutu, for one, made no attempt to hide from the fact that these parameters were entirely arbitrary from a moral point of view. While he did not deny that the dates which bookended the TRC made a certain kind of sense—with the first, 21 March 1960, corresponding to the Sharpeville Massacre (after which a number of Black political organizations were outlawed and the liberation struggle abandoned its commitment to non-violence) and the second, 10 May 1994, corresponding to Nelson Mandela's inauguration as president—'we could quite legitimately', he claimed, 'have gone right back to the days of Jan van Riebeeck' (the Dutch explorer who founded Cape Town in 1652).[123] Similarly, while limiting the category of victim to those who suffered gross violations of human rights was not without justification, it would, once again, he suggested, have been quite legitimate to have determined 'that all who were not white qualified automatically as victims since they had run the gauntlet of apartheid's viciousness'.[124] The only thing, on his account, that really spoke in favour of the restricted mandate was the feasibility of the healing mission. Had the Commission broadened the historical period under investigation or included all those who ran the gauntlet of Apartheid, the possibility of closure would have disappeared over the horizon. Similarly, had the Commission been granted a longer time frame in which to complete its work, the country would have been at risk of becoming permanently 'bogged down' in its painful past.[125]

Such justifications were nothing if not revealing. Doubtless no society can take on the painful past in its entirety or allocate endless time to working it through. But that does not mean the decisions it makes in relation to what it 'stages' and 'plays back' to itself have no bearing upon the justice it delivers or the biopolitical effects it produces. As well as protecting the nation against an interminable grieving process, the parameters under which the TRC operated compressed and intensified the suffering it put on display, more or less ensuring that Apartheid would not re-appear before the public in any form other than traumatic drama. As many critics noted, albeit without drawing out the biopolitical implications, the Commission more or less disregarded the 'daily pain', as Walaza put it, or the 'daily pinpricks', as Tutu put it, caused by 'ordinary' cultural denigration and 'overt' racial legislation (particularly the Pass Laws, the Land Act, and the Group Areas Act).[126] Instead, it focused almost exclusively on the most secret, the most violent, assaults upon individual dignity perpetrated by both sides in the struggle, with psychological suffering (or mental anguish) being a key measure of ill-treatment.[127] Critics have not failed to note that this focus on personal trauma erased the moral distinction between violence perpetrated by a criminal state and violence perpetrated by the liberation movement. Without the systemic injustice of the racialized legal structure to provide context, every individual who violated the rights of another, regardless of whether they served the criminal state or opposed it, was classified as a perpetrator in a way that grossly misrepresented the ethics of the struggle.[128] What generally went unremarked, however, was the dramatic impact created by this concentration upon 'exceptional pain'. If it was far more widespread and ultimately more damaging, 'daily pain' (or what Kim Wale has recently termed 'continuous identity wounding')[129] did not make for such a great spectacle. But who could not be moved to tears when horror was piled upon horror in an endless series of gruesome torture stories?[130]

We turn now to a more detailed analysis of the two practices that most clearly differentiate truth commissions from criminal tribunals and which

The Therapy of Reconciliation   239

are generally deemed intrinsic to their healing power: truth telling (testimony) and sympathetic listening (witnessing). In principle, the dialectic of testimony and witnessing set up by the TRC acted as a public analogue of the therapeutic contract between patient and therapist in which the former assumes responsibility for speaking the truth of their experience and the latter for validating that experience as the truth.[131] Naturally, as Minow, among others, pointed out, the public setting altered the dynamics of this relation in a fundamental way: 'a commission', she duly noted, 'cannot create the bond of commitment that exists between therapist and client'.[132] Yet this did mean that the relation between testifier and witness mediated, firstly through the Commission, and secondly through the mass media, was wholly without therapeutic value. In her view, the act of giving testimony before the Commission and the public could still be psychologically beneficial because it transformed a 'seemingly private experience into a public one'.[133] When survivors recount their stories in the presence of sympathetic witnesses, she suggested (here drawing explicitly upon the work of Judith Lewis Herman), their experience of terror ceases to be a matter of private humiliation and becomes a matter of public responsibility. Personal traumas are located in the larger political context, allowing them to be re-lived and re-experienced in a less alienating, and thus ultimately restorative, way:

> Coming to know that one's suffering is not solely a private experience, best forgotten, but instead an indictment of a social cataclysm, can permit individuals to move beyond trauma, hopelessness, numbness, and preoccupation with loss and injury. Even those who are too afraid or too much in pain to testify can gain some benefit from hearing the testimony of others that may parallel their own experiences. Integrating personal devastation within the larger context of political oppression can be crucial to the therapeutic result.[134]

Just how restorative truth telling turned out to be for the alienated survivor is, however, a matter of contention (an issue I will return to in the final section of this chapter.[135] However, the point that is often overlooked in these discussions of healing is that it is not just the victims but the social body more generally for whom truth commissions provide therapeutic benefits. Irrespective, I would suggest, of whether it brought closure or repeated trauma for those giving testimony, the TRC still made two crucial contributions to the production of a national catharsis through truth telling. Firstly, it helped to convert the incommunicable (and thus untransmissible) experience of pain into a form that was capable of wider circulation.[136] By providing a space in which pain could be narrated and rendered into story, the TRC was able to turn it into common currency: the incomprehensible became comprehensible, the inaccessible accessible, and with that the door was opened to the possibilities of compassion as 'fellow-felling'; that is, to the kind of collective sharing in sorrow that it went to such lengths to promote. As we have already noted, the experience of vicarious trauma was by no means uncommon among those working in and around the Commission and was responsible for rendering more than one commissioner undone.[137] From the very outset, however, a concerted effort was made to broaden the circle of witnesses by broadcasting the proceedings of the Commission as widely as possible through a range of media: print, radio, television, and the internet. Subsequently celebrated as a means of guaranteeing that nobody could thereafter say they didn't know, this publicity enjoyed a more immediate utility as the means by which the nation as a whole could bear witness to the spectacle of suffering and become enjoined in mourning process.[138]

Secondly, storytelling allowed the pain of Apartheid to 'reach' a national audience in the other (emotional) sense of the word by shifting it onto the terrain of intimacy. Viewed simply as a structure of oppression, Apartheid had little power to move people, even when they recognized it as politically and economically unjust—which was not, of course, always the case. By its very nature, however, storytelling at the TRC (especially the stories told in the hearings of the Human Rights Violation Committee) exposed Apartheid as individual trauma, allowing it to touch people in a highly charged way. As Minow noted, none of the stories told before the Commission consisted of a 'plain statement of facts'—by their very nature they were visceral and emotional acts of self-exposure.[139] For Verdoolaege (and others), this emotional exposure was, in fact, one of the great contributions of the TRC. Her misgivings about the way the Commission pressured victims to forgive notwithstanding, she still credited it for having created an 'open forum' at which they could 'pour out their emotions, ventilate their frustrations, and relive their experiences as openly and freely as they desired'.[140] But, of course, 'by exposing personal suffering in a public way', as Minow put it, the Commission also made it possible for others, distant in all senses of the word, to identify with the victims and participate in the cathartic moment of their public testimony.[141]

Although any number of cases could be used to illustrate this double effect of storytelling, that of Yazir Henry, a torture victim who testified before the Human Rights Violation Committee, is instructive precisely because it became such a widely circulated case. In the report on his testimony published in the *Cape Argus* which, as he points out, was only one of the many times in which his story was exchanged, Henry is portrayed as a traumatized subject, marked by a pain that is variously described as 'appalling', 'overwhelming', and 'concentrated'. In this retelling (and what else is retelling other than an instrument of circulation?), Henry's story, 'his harrowing tale', is purposefully dramatized as a catharsis. Attention moves to his voice as it rises and falls 'with his emotions' and to his body as it contorts with the effort needed 'to relieve the appalling pain'. The point being made could scarcely have been more transparent: in order to tell his story, Henry must, quite literally, spill everything and exhaust himself. However, it is the transmission of pain from victim to audience, referenced in the final lines of the report, which most clearly reveals the possibilities inherent within victim testimony for the diffusion of this cathartic effect. Thanks to the TRC, runs the report, this 'nightmare of concentrated pain' has 'etched itself into the consciousness of all who heard it' and now, thanks to the *Cape Argus* (and, of course, all the other news outlets who covered the story), can etch itself into the consciousness of all those who didn't hear it first-hand. By way of publicity, a harrowing tale had been circulated around the nation and, by that means, turned into a cathartic experience for all.[142]

Through a variety of means, then, the TRC exercised a decisive influence over the way in which the crime of Apartheid was represented to (and re-experienced by) the public as witness. By restricting the period under consideration to the most violent period of Apartheid rule; by attending only to the most outrageous violations of individual rights (killing, torture, abductions, and severe ill-treatment); by limiting the time frame in which those violations were brought before the public; and by displacing a systemic injustice onto the terrain of intimacy; the TRC intensified, compressed, and personalized the event of Apartheid to the point where it resembled nothing so much as a 'terrible drama'. If the audience came to 'see' Apartheid, it was not in an abstract or formal way, as a structure of colonial rule or system of radicalized capitalism, but in a concrete or personal way, as a series of devastating assaults upon individual dignity committed by everybody and upon everybody. One of the reasons Antjie Krog's *Country of My Skull* achieved such critical acclaim was that its intimate narration managed to capture (far better, according to Villa-Vincencio, than the report of the Commission itself)[143] the intensity of that terrible drama played out on the national stage. Mirroring the TRC, and functioning, in effect, as the dramatic copy of the real drama that it enacted, it made raw human suffering, suffering removed from all considerations of colour, or party, or language, its entire focus.[144] To witness the horror and agony that the TRC unveiled (all in a highly concentrated form) was, in effect, to suffer a vicarious trauma and be moved to catharsis.

Doubtless a great deal of this terrible drama has now been lost in translation. As Colin Bundy noted, one of the common failings of writers who discuss the TRC 'academically' is their failure to credit 'the potency and intensity of the testimony it elicited'.[145] By its very nature, he suggested, scholarly writing tends to miss the 'dramatic impact' live broadcasts had upon the 'popular psyche' of South Africans during that brief period of time. For the public assembled as audience by way of the mass media, however, the emotional impact was nothing short of profound: 'there is horror in the testimonies, and grief and pain and anguish; there is courage, cowardice, resilience, self-knowledge and denial. The cumulative account provides an explicit and terrible record of violence, vindictiveness and brutalization'.[146] How could one not be moved to tears by it? If it was commonly used in a derisive sense, therefore, the term 'Kleenex Commission' (or, in Afrikaans, the *Snot-en-trane Kommissie*—Snot-and-Tears Commission) did, in fact, capture something of the essence of the TRC—as Tutu himself freely admitted.[147] For him, the Commission was nothing if not 'a place where people could come to cry, to open their hearts, to expose the anguish that had remained locked up for so long, unacknowledged, ignored and denied'.[148] In *No Future without Forgiveness*, he inadvertently underlined the centrality of this anguished exposure to the national healing operation by presenting the 'piercing wail' of Nomonde Calata (whose husband, Fort Calata, was one of the Craddock Four murdered by the security forces) as the 'defining sound' of the TRC. Harrowing, as it were, all the way down, the Commission did not need to solicit remorse or forgiveness or, ultimately, even words to have a cathartic effect. The piercing wail of one grief-stricken widow, carried over the airwaves, was enough to open the emotional floodgates.

If they shared an interest in restoring life, then, the two rationalities of power at work in the Commission—the *ratio pastoralis* and the *ratio gubernatorial*—were actually quite distinct in terms of their targets, their techniques, and their effects. Although both were mobilized for the political purposes and sought, above all, to prevent the past from coming back and poisoning the present, each undertook a different operation upon memory and sought a rather different kind of healing. In the case of pastoral power, everything hinged upon the moral transformation of the subject in the face of the truth. Without the freely given gift of remorse and, even more importantly, forgiveness, the bundle of life would be compromised and the future jeopardized. Pastoral power demanded (personal) sacrifice for the sake of (collective) life. Governmental power (and herein perhaps lies its comparative advantage as an instrument of 'healing') has no need of this moral transformation and hence of that ever-so-precarious generosity of spirit needed to buttress reconciliation. All that was required was the transmission of pain and the purging of affects. This is not to say, of course, that acts of remorse and forgiveness were entirely irrelevant to it. To the extent that they added to the emotional intensity of the terrible drama, scenes of reconciliation (and irreconciliation) between perpetrator and victim contributed their fair share to the power of the TRC to move people. It is simply to say that it was entirely possible to generate a cathartic effect without any citizen making a conscious decision to put the needs of the nation above their own needs as individuals.

The sense in which this emotional discharge, operating independently of the domain of agency, can be said to have 'healed' is clearly difficult to determine with any precision. Less a sustained work of mourning in the way Freud envisaged than a curating of cathartic moments, the TRC might best be understood as a valve that released emotional pressure and allowed feelings (and tears) to flow through and around the social body. 'Although the very trappings of therapy may disturb many who seek justice', noted Minow, 'a truth commission can clear the air with acknowledgment of the casualties of violence.'[149] And, in the end, a clearing of the air—a ventilation—might well be the best way of describing what the TRC achieved through its determination to share the stories (and grief) of victims. Presented with the risk of festering wounds, the TRC succeeded in catalysing a cathartic process by staging a terrible drama. The fact that some victims were not able to tell their story and that others did not find the telling of it restorative; the fact that some stories either did not reach an audience or failed to elicit the requisite sympathy; the fact that some perpetrators were denied amnesty or found the experience of disclosure too shameful to bear; and the fact, finally, that some victims received no reparations and others found the reparation they did receive inadequate was ultimately neither here nor there. Seen from the perspective of a biopolitically inflected *raison d'état*, intent on mobilizing resources around potential risk and hazards to life, all that really mattered was that the wounds had not been allowed to fester and the emotions began to flow again.

III The Gift of Sight

One of the most famous cases from the TRC is that of Lucas Baba Sikwepere, a young Black man who lost his sight after a notorious Cape Town policeman shot him in the face. Standing before the Human Rights Violation Committee, Sikwepere uttered the following, endlessly recited, words: 'I feel what has been making me sick all the time is the fact that I couldn't tell my story. But now ... it feels like I've got my sight back by coming here and telling you the story.'[150] Like a distant echo of the miracles of Christ, the healed eyes of Sikwepere speak symbolically of the power of a restorative justice to give back sight to the blind. Thanks to the space of truth and grief that the TRC made available, Sikwepere himself now 'sees'—sees what has been making him sick and what was needed to restore health. Having lived the half-life of the alienated survivor, he finds a cure for the darkness of his trauma in the public telling (and, of course, the public recognition) of his story. But if Sikwepere now sees, he too is supposed to be the miracle worker of a restored sight. Along with all those other truth-tellers who exposed their personal suffering in a public way, it is Sikwepere who has made it possible for the country to see *itself* properly for the first time. By opening up their wounds to each and every eye, they exposed South Africa for what it truly was and, in that way, gave it an opportunity to get its (moral) sight back.

Whether the TRC represented Apartheid back to the South African public in a way that allowed it to see that systemic failing is nevertheless questionable. One of the most redoubtable critiques of the TRC (one that begins with the work of Mahmood Mamdani and is reiterated by almost every critic thereafter) is that its individualizing, therapeutic focus rendered it (and all who watched the drama it staged) blind to the structural injustice of Apartheid as a system of racial exploitation built through discriminatory legislation.[151] Intent on exposing the gross violations of human rights committed on all sides (murder, torture, and severe ill-treatment), the Commission elided the very crime against humanity within which (and against which) the violence of the armed resistance had emerged. Amidst the many stories, the story of Apartheid (and its institutional legacy) went missing. For the critics, as we have noted, the distortion created by this restricted focus was twofold: firstly, it placed the violence of the Apartheid state and the violence of the liberation movement on the same moral plane and, secondly, it allowed the beneficiaries of an inherently exploitative system to maintain their innocence. While the violation of the individual through violent excess was placed centre-stage, the violation of the race through economic exploitation was hidden behind the curtain. So long as they were not themselves revealed as torturers or murderers, therefore, those who had unjustly enriched themselves through Apartheid could weep with the rest while holding on tightly to their ill-gotten gains.[152]

One of the clearest indications that the TRC blinded the public (and was itself blind) to the structural injustice of Apartheid is the way it took up the question of reparation as a matter of individual healing rather than economic amelioration. Wendy Orr, deputy chairperson of the Reparations and

Rehabilitation Committee, was completely up front in suggesting that 'the concept of psychological healing became deeply entrenched in the work of the TRC and it also became one of our defined objectives in reparation'.[153] In the first instance, this meant nothing more complex than holding out the promise of reparations to entice people to testify. Since victims had initially been reluctant to appear before the Commission, reparation was used to encourage them to come forward, tell their stories, and, by that means, submit themselves to the therapeutic process. Hence the rather curious analogy that was sometimes drawn between reparations and amnesty, with both being treated as 'rewards' for disclosure. However, beyond the role they played as a handmaiden to testimony, reparations were also understood as a therapy for the trauma caused by the violation of individual rights. For Tutu, testimony and reparations were, in fact, but two complementary treatments within a broader process, according to which national healing would be achieved through the treatment of individual wounds:

> The nation said, in effect to victims: 'We acknowledge that you suffered a gross violation of your rights. Nothing can ever replace your loved one. But as a nation we are saying, we are sorry, we have opened the wounds of your suffering and sought to cleanse them; this reparation is as balm, an ointment being poured over the wounds to assist in their healing'.[154]

With everything centred on psychological healing, it was almost inevitable that no problem should impose itself with greater urgency than how to get the 'balm of reparation' onto those wounds as quickly as possible. As Orr's account of the proceedings of the Reparations and Rehabilitation Committee reveals, many concerns were raised along the way about the principal measure that the TRC ultimately recommended to the president: 'the individual reparation grant'. As well as admitting to the difficulty of determining the 'degree of suffering' experienced by different victims (whose pain was greater?) and the absence of any 'ready formula for establishing the monetary value of suffering' (what is pain really worth?), the members of the Committee questioned whether, even if they were able to work out the sums, the victims would want to be 'so crassly "bought off?"'[155] However, if there was one worry that overrode all the others, it was not how to calculate the reparations, or what form they should take, but simply that they be delivered in a timely manner. As the title of Orr's essay on the subject—'Reparation Delayed Is Healing Retarded'—makes abundantly clear, the imperative from a therapeutic perspective was not that there be reparations of this or that type but that there be reparations *of some type* as soon as possible. To delay compensation for those who testified before the Human Rights Violations Committee while perpetrators were granted immediate amnesty was to rub salt, rather than balm, into their wounds. 'Looking at the process in retrospect', she wrote,

> my sense is that one of our failures was our inability to deliver some form of reparation or supportive intervention almost immediately. The fact that perpetrators felt the benefit of a positive amnesty decision at once, while victims have had to wait years for the token amount allowed by the urgent reparation regulations (and will have to wait even longer for whatever final reparation is actually delivered) has not facilitated healing.[156]

Thus, while it is self-evidently true, as Jana Thompson has noted, that the 'unjustly killed' cannot be 'brought back to life' by reparations, the operational premise of the TRC was that the unjustly treated (and the secondary victims of the unjustly killed) could be.[157] What Orr didn't say, but others did, was that the collapse of reparations as a mechanism for inducing victims to alienate their pain was likely to rebound not just upon the TRC but upon the security of South Africa more generally.[158] Although they were more inclined to extol testimony and the cathartic experience it made possible, many at the Commission were, in fact, also acutely conscious of the contribution reparations could make to the healing mission. Just as, at some level, they knew that testimony facilitated catharsis, they knew that reparations facilitated cathexis; that is, a reinvestment of libidinal energy in life and the future. Rather than a way of doing justice by acknowledging suffering, in other words, reparations were understood as a means of shifting the focus of wounded subjects from what they had lost to what they might gain, from a concern with the dead to a concern with the living. The failure to deliver timely reparations was thus readily correlated with the failure to secure the future. It is by no means surprising, therefore, that Tutu threw his weight behind the 'urgent interim measures' or was at pains to remind people that the persistence of such a huge economic disparity between Black and white (beyond being manifestly unjust) placed the whole therapeutic process in jeopardy.[159]

Claire Moon is, then, quite right to conclude that the TRC 'transformed the moral and political crisis about South Africa's past into an emotional or psychological one'.[160] Irrespective of whether the logic driving it was pastoral reason (*ratio pastoralis*), governmental reason (*ratio gubernatorial*), or a mixture of both, it was the emotional and psychological legacy of Apartheid, not the economic or political one, which became the main drama. However, the suggestion, more or less explicit, that the moral and political crisis is primary, the emotional and psychological one secondary, runs the risk of remaining blind to the problems that arise when the emotional and psychological domain is conceived in terms of emergency (or the state of exception) and made a target of therapeutic intervention. As I have tried to show in this chapter (as indeed throughout this book), the problem with exceptional institutions like the TRC does not simply lie in the *displacement* of the crisis *from* the political to the psychological terrain but in the *placement* of the psychological as a site of crisis *within* the political terrain. In the hearings of the TRC, personal suffering was exposed in a public way, allowing power to gain access to (and make strategic use of) the inner self. If Lucas Baba Sikwepere sees, he is also seen, laid bare before a public commission whose role it becomes to prise open the inner world of subjects and expose them in their trauma so that the social body might become enjoined (and rejoined) in the work of mourning or the catharsis of grief.

Like Minow, Hamber and Wilson are inclined to see the survivor's desire for public validation (the desire to have their story and their tears *witnessed*) as a vital part of that work of mourning. 'Speaking at public hearings like those of the South African TRC', they write, 'can break an enforced silence and represent a point of closure and transition in the grieving process.'[161] On their view, the TRC (in both its hearings and its reparation policy) created 'possibilities for the internalization of loss and Freud's work of mourning (*trauerarbeit*) that [did] not exist through legal channels'.[162] And yet, like many before and after, they remain deeply sceptical about the merits of encouraging survivors to relive their trauma under these kinds of institutional constraints. The issue, for them, is not just the fragility of the therapeutic relation when a commission or, even more tenuously, the general public is called upon to play the role of sympathetic witness. It is also about the different temporal frameworks that govern public commissions and personal grieving. As exercises in national reconciliation operating in a limited time frame, truth commissions are structurally ill suited to the slow work of mourning in which, as Freud pointed out, subjects only discover the nature of their loss and what it actually means to them *in stages*. A truth commission instructed to finish its work as quickly as possible and leave no legacy behind it can never truly accommodate (and may in some cases actually endanger) that slow work of mourning.[163]

Concerns about the risks truth commissions pose to survivors have often been offset by the fact that the practice of truth telling allows the alienated and marginalized to return to the public stage as fully enfranchised citizens. Although otherwise quite critical of truth commissions and their sacrificial ethics, for instance, Michael Humphrey insisted public testimony ought still to be celebrated for 'making individuals who were socially abject—homo sacer/invisible people—visible and socially equal'.[164] Similarly, in *Sing the Rage*, Sonali Chakravarti defends victim testimony as a form of political action in the Arendtian sense—an appearing before others in the manner of speech and deed—that marks the return of the excluded to the political realm. Pushing against Arendt's fear that public discourse degrades into cheap sentimentality when it is invaded by emotions, she, like Humphrey, supports the South African TRC on the grounds that it

> allowed previously disenfranchised and second-class citizens, such as black, Asians, and 'coloured' in South Africa, to testify in public and thus represented the first political institution to offer those groups the dignity and equality that Arendt understands to be foundational to political life.[165]

Chakravarti's endorsement is, to be sure, qualified by the fact that the TRC was largely deaf to the anger of these second-class citizens, denying them through various means (especially its emphasis upon forgiveness) the right to 'sing the rage' and have their emotional experience of injustice noted by, and reflected in, the new political order. In a sense, however, the plea for forgiveness that was central to the *ratio pastoralis* only adds weight to her claim because it shows the Commission saw the victims not just as people entitled to speak but as moral agents who were quite capable of bringing their resentment to heal for the sake of higher political objectives. Demanding though the sacrifice might be, there was still nobility in it being freely chosen.

Thinking about the TRC as an instantiation of the *ratio gubernatorial* leads to rather different conclusions. In this case, one can concede the value of public testimony as a way of overcoming exclusion and invisibility without fully disposing of Arendt's critique. For the problem is not (or not simply) that victim testimony draws emotional life into the public arena, blurring the distinction between the intimate and the political spheres and thus, on Arendt's spatial conception of politics, perverting the true character of both. It is rather that the exposure of trauma threatens to turn the victim into the object under discussion rather than one of the discussants of the object, stripping them of the very dignity they were supposed to regain through their testimony. As Chakravarti herself notes, politics assumes an elevated status for Arendt because it is the only field of human activity or the only component of the *vita activa* in which human beings disclose 'who' they are rather than 'what' they can do; that is, their individuality and identity rather than their skills and talents.[166] For Arendt, in other words, the uniqueness of the public realm or 'space of appearances', as she instructively puts it, does not simply lie in being

The Therapy of Reconciliation 249

seen but in *how* one is seen or, more to the point, what is seen *about* one. Only in this realm, she claims, do human beings 'make their appearance explicitly', differentiating themselves as actors from all those other living or inanimate things which merely show up.[167] The worry here is that the truth-tellers who facilitate the national catharsis by exposing personal suffering in a public way are in danger of crossing the line where testament *to* trauma turns into a testament *of* trauma or, as Agamben puts it, the 'speaking being' into the 'living being'.[168] Once that line is crossed, it is no longer their unique character but their psychological disorder that is on display—they have become a 'what' rather than a 'who', entering the public sphere not as a reflecting agent but as an object upon which others reflect.[169]

The risk of objectification for those who render themselves emotionally vulnerable by exposing their inner life in testimony is not just a matter of speculation. Called to reflect on his experience of truth telling after the fact, Yazir Henry is nothing if not ambivalent about his encounter with truth telling. On the one hand, he commends the TRC for providing a space that 'did not and does not exist elsewhere in our society': a space in which people were able to speak freely, bear their souls, and 'tell their stories of abuse and violation'. For him, the hearings provided an opportunity to both 'face himself' and 'face the nation', to appear in public in the nakedness of his truth and 'be judged only for who [he] was'.[170] On the other hand, he criticizes the TRC for failing to honour and protect that space. Having exposed himself to the view (and the judgement) of others, Henry suffered the bitter, if all too common, experience of losing control of his own story. Able, now, to be inserted in other contexts and other histories, he found identities being 'imposed' on him that were not simply misconceived but which inhibited his ability to recognize himself—the 'most hurtful' of these being that of the 'agonized confessor or the betrayer that should be pitied'.[171] The irony here is marked. Driven to testify in the belief that 'there was nothing further to lose', Henry had come to the tragic realization that he did in fact have something else to lose; namely, his ability to story himself:

> The lack of sensitivity with which my story was treated once it left the confines of that space and became part of the public domain was immediately apparent—my face and the story of my life were flashed across the country, on television, in newspapers, magazines and books, and often out of context. It was out of my control and done without my permission.[172]

The possibility that truth telling might lead as much to the loss as to the recovery of agency appears in other signature cases as well. Who or what, one might wonder, was Nomonde Calata for the public assembled as 'sympathetic witnesses' when that 'piercing wail' issued from her? An actor, a victim, a vast wound of grief? Reflecting back twenty years after the event, Pumla Gobodo-Madikizela declared it an act of defiance and a call to arms:

> [t]here was a sense that Mrs Calata was at last reclaiming her agency, with the violent movement of her body thrown back as she let out her wailing cry. She was confronting this violent history told on the stage of the TRC, exposing those responsible for her irreparable loss.[173]

Talk of exposure is, to be sure, not misplaced here. But the phenomenon cuts both ways. The fact that Tutu saw fit to describe this as the 'defining moment' of the TRC speaks volumes about the significance of this 'wailing cry' to the exposure of that violent history. If it made sense to talk of transitional points in the collective and not just the individual 'grieving process', this, it seems, was the outstanding candidate. Who would now deny the irreparable losses brought about by the system of Apartheid or feel no responsibility for sharing in the work of mourning? And yet, Gobodo-Madikizela's sense that 'much of what happens in the afterlife of historical trauma is enigmatic, muddy, elusive, and unpredictable' seems more than a little apposite here. For if Nomonde Calata was confronting a violent history, the violent movement of her body was also 'bearing witness to the shards of her brokenness'.[174] Like Yazir Henry, she had not simply exposed those responsible for her irreparable loss but exposed herself in—exposed herself *as*?—the fragments of her loss.

In *Country of My Skull*, Antjie Krog characterizes that haunting sound as an 'indefinable wail', pointing compassionately, but also suggestively, to its liminal, uncanny character as that which could not be storied; as that which defied the talking cure because it defied language itself. In one sense, that meant it got closer to the 'truth' of Apartheid and its violation of body and soul than anything that could be parcelled up in words.[175] What else could have made irreparable loss so palpable? What else, ironically enough, signalled the impossibility of closure more clearly than that 'defining sound' of the TRC? But, in another sense, it meant something genuinely other had made its way into the space of appearances, something that could not be assimilated in any form other than as spectacle. In that moment, Nomonde Calata 'appeared' as a liminal figure, straddling an uncertain boundary between *zoë* and *bios*, wounded animal and speaking citizen. What was she except a body in pain; a body turned, by way of a public exercise in truth telling, into a spectacle of an all too corporeal, all too bestial mourning that was unable to accomplish itself *in words*? If Calata's 'voice' is definitive, it is also in-definitive, as exceptional as the exceptional institution that amplified it, because it is a cry of agony that fails to reach the threshold of speech and which, as a result, can only be heard as a symptom of trauma. Should we assume that such sounds resound because they expose those responsible or because they expose those damaged? Alongside Nomonde Calata's wail before the TRC it is surely Nomfundo Walaza's warning about the TRC that should, at this point, be ringing loudly in our ears: '[t]he pain of blacks is being dumped into the country more or less like a commodity article—easy to access and even easier to discard'.[176]

The already muddy gets muddier still. As Sara Ahmed observes, 'stories of pain involve complex relations of power', making it difficult to ascertain their true political effects.[177] Those called to bear witness can respond in a variety of ways to the demand pain makes upon them: they can feel disgust in the face of an exposure too intimate, resent being confronted by lives that have been damaged (especially if they feel directly or indirectly responsible for those lives and that damage), find themselves lured by, perhaps even titillated by, the morbid fascination of trauma, or simply remain completely indifferent to those beyond their immediate circle of concern. Moreover, as Ahmed insists (and Yazir Henry warns), compassion itself—despite the reputation it has acquired courtesy of Rousseau as a natural sentiment—does not stand outside those complex relations of power. If the feeling of pity can sponsor attempts to alleviate pain, it can also work to lower the other to the status of passive object (the 'thing' that arouses 'our' emotions) and to elevate the self to the position of saviour. In the therapeutic dynamic set up in truth commissions, where sympathetic witnesses are the means by which storytellers overcome their trauma, the risk of reproducing the asymmetry between victim group and perpetrating community is high. Strange inversions from perpetrator to saviour are hardly inconceivable, for here, as Ahmed puts it, 'the one who gives to the other [in the form of recognition] is the one who is "behind" the possibility of overcoming pain'.[178] Even if it holds no value for the victim, in other words, pity can 'restore' the perpetrator and purge *them* of their guilt and shame.

In matters as complex and intricate as this one, simple conclusions are no doubt best avoided. In part because the experience of public testimony is deeply personal and in part because the quality of sympathetic witnessing is highly variable, it may not, ultimately, be possible to arrive at any definitive statements about the merits of truth commissions as instruments of healing. At the very least, however, it seems prudent to acknowledge the vast distance that separates the exceptional institution from the therapeutic suite and the implications that has for those who expose themselves in truth telling.[179]

Since it is fundamental to this kind of institution that testimony be given in a public setting and for political purposes (healing, closure, reconciliation, cleansing), it will always be subject to the pressure of restoring the social body to 'normal life'. Critical accounts of the South African TRC often assume that the problem was not so much the exceptional institution itself as the way in which the emotional life of vulnerable people was handled within it. Had the Commission been more willing to listen to the anger of victims and acknowledge its political significance, it might have facilitated a more radical kind of political transformation.[180] But the conclusion towards which the analysis provided here seems to inexorably push is that the TRC was precisely structured to drive a wedge between the emotional and the political: to reveal damaged life as objects of pity (and voyeuristic allure) while concealing the political structures that did the damage.

Notes

1. On this point, see B. Leebaw, 'Legitimation or Judgement? South Africa's Restorative Approach to Transitional Justice', *Polity*, 36(1), 2003, p. 27; S. Chakravarti, *Sing the Rage: Listening to Anger after Mass Violence*, Chicago, IL: University of Chicago Press, 2014, p. 57; and M. Mihai, *Negative Emotions and Transitional Justice*, New York: Columbia University Press, 2016, pp. 18–19; 28.
2. Ignatieff cited in Chakravarti, *Sing the Rage*, p. 58.
3. See D. Weissbrodt and P.W. Fraser, 'Report of the Chilean National Commission on Truth and Reconciliation', *Human Rights Quarterly*, 14(4), 1992, p. 602; and K. Klep, 'Tracing Collective Memory: Chilean Truth Commissions and Memorial Sites', *Memory Studies*, 5(3), 2012, p. 261.
4. M. Sanders, 'Ambiguities of Mourning: Law, Custom and Women before South Africa's Truth and Reconciliation Commission', *Law, Text, Culture*, 4(2), 1998, p. 129.
5. As Priscilla Hayner has noted, 'blanket amnesties require no individual identification of crimes or perpetrators, usually preventing any judicial action on all human rights abuses that took place prior to the date the amnesty was granted. The South African process, in contrast, turned the amnesty application process into a tool to uncover details of past crimes, making South Africa the first country in the world to hear detailed testimony about crimes directly from the perpetrators themselves'. In a similar vein, Andrew Schaap has suggested that what was most fascinating about the way transitional justice was pursued in South Africa was that 'amnesty was linked to reckoning with the past rather than simply wiping the slate clean'. See P. Hayner, 'Same Species, Different Animal: How South Africa Compares to Truth Commissions Worldwide' in C. Villa-Vincencio and W. Verwoerd (eds.), *Looking Back, Reaching Forward: Reflections on the Truth and Reconciliation Commission of South Africa*, London: Zed Books, 2000, p. 36; and A. Schaap, *Political Reconciliation*, London: Routledge, p. 113.

6. See P. Hazan, *Judging War, Judging History: Behind Truth and Reconciliation*, Stanford, CA: Stanford University Press, 2010, pp. 33–34; and S. Msimang, 'All Is Not Forgiven: South Africa and the Scars of Apartheid', *Foreign Affairs*, 97(1), 2018, p. 32.
7. The final phrase of this paragraph is taken from E. Kiss, 'Moral Ambition within and beyond Political Constraints: Reflections on Restorative Justice' in R.I. Rotberg and D. Thompson (eds.), *Truth v. Justice: The Morality of Truth Commissions*, Princeton, NJ: Princeton University Press, 2000, p. 69. However, the question of where truth and reconciliation stands in relation to justice was thoroughly, if inconclusively, canvassed by a range of contributors to that volume of essays. See also C. Villa-Vincencio, 'The Reek of Cruelty and the Quest for Healing: Where Retributive and Restorative Justice Meet', *Journal of Law and Religion*, 14(1), 1999–2000, pp. 165–187; D. Little, 'A Different Kind of Justice: Dealing with Human Rights Violations in Transitional Societies', *Ethics and International Affairs*, 13, 1999, pp. 65–80; M. Osiel, 'Why Prosecute? Critics of Punishment for Mass Atrocity', *Human Rights Quarterly*, 22, 2000, pp. 134–135; and R. Aldana, 'A Victim-Centered Reflection on Truth Commissions and Prosecutions as a Response to Mass Atrocities', *Journal of Human Rights*, 5(1), 2006, pp. 107–126.
8. D. Tutu, *No Future without Forgiveness*, London: Rider, 1999, p. 51.
9. J. Shklar, *The Faces of Injustice*, New Haven, CT: Yale University Press, 1990, p. 94. As Gutmann and Thompson noted in their seminal essay on the moral foundations of truth commissions, 'restorative justice remains relatively undeveloped as a conception of justice'. A. Gutmann and D. Thompson, 'The Moral Foundations of Truth Commissions', in Rotberg and Thompson, *Truth v. Justice*, p. 29.
10. Thus Charles Villa-Vincencio will speak of a 'national compromise regarding justice' and Alex Boraine will claim 'full justice is not always possible in a society in transition'. See C. Villa-Vincencio, 'Getting On with Life: A Move towards Reconciliation' in Villa-Vincencio and Verwoerd (eds.), *Looking Back, Reaching Forward*, p. 200; and A. Boraine, 'Truth and Reconciliation in South Africa: The Third Way', in Rotberg and Thompson (eds.), *Truth v. Justice*, p. 147.
11. Tutu, *No Future without Forgiveness*, pp. 25, 52, 54.
12. Interview with Desmond Tutu, *Index on Censorship*, 5, 1996, p. 41. Similarly, in *No Future without Forgiveness*, Tutu notes: 'We could very well have had retributive justice, and had a South Africa lying in ashes—a truly Pyrrhic victory if ever there was one.' Tutu, *No Future without Forgiveness*, p. 27.
13. I. Kant, 'Perpetual Peace: A Philosophical Sketch' in F. Reiss (ed.), *Kant: Political Writings*, Cambridge: Cambridge University Press, 1991, p. 123.
14. As Villa-Vincencio noted, even strong advocates of prosecutorial justice like Diane Orentlicher recognized that states are not required to take action that 'poses a threat to vital national interests'. Villa-Vincencio, 'The Reek of Cruelty', p. 179.
15. As Boraine, among many others, noted, 'It is morally defensible to argue that amnesty was the price South Africa had to pay for peace and stability.' Boraine, 'Truth and Reconciliation in South Africa', p. 156.
16. See, for instance, M. Minow, *Between Vengeance and Forgiveness*, Boston, MA: Beacon, 1998, pp. 52–90; Villa-Vincencio, 'The Reek of Cruelty', p. 175; E.K. Yamamoto and S.K. Serrano, 'Healing Racial Wounds?' in R.L. Brooks (ed.), *When Sorry Isn't Enough: The Controversy over Apologies and Reparations for Human Injustice*, New York: New York

254   The Penitent State

University Press, 1999, pp. 492–500; and M. Minow, 'The Hope for Healing: What Can Truth Commissions Do?' in Rotberg and Thompson, *Truth v. Justice*, pp. 240–255.
17. J. Derrida, *On Cosmopolitanism and Forgiveness*, London: Routledge, 2001, pp. 28, 41. In a similar vein, Daniel Philpott has referred to 'the medicine of reconciliation'; Minow to the displacement of 'justice' by 'health'; and Humphrey to the substitution of 'medication for adjudication'. See D. Philpott, 'Beyond Politics as Usual' in D. Philpott (ed.), *The Politics of Past Evil: Religion, Reconciliation and the Dilemmas of Transitional Justice*, Notre Dame, IN: University of Notre Dame Press, 2006, p. 13; Minow, *Between Vengeance and Forgiveness*, p. 63; and M. Humphrey, *The Politics of Atrocity and Reconciliation: From Terror to Trauma*, London: Routledge, 2002, p. 108.
18. D. Omar, 'Introduction' to Promotion of National Unity and Reconciliation Act. https://www.justice.gov.za/trc/legal/justice.htm
19. *Truth and Reconciliation Commission of South Africa Report*, vol. 1, 74. See also Tutu, *No Future without Forgiveness*, pp. 33, 78.
20. See, for instance, N. Walaza, 'Insufficient Healing and Reparation' in Villa-Vincencio and Verwoerd (eds.), *Looking Back, Reaching Forward*, pp. 250–255. In a telling slip, Pumla Gobodo-Madikizela would refer to the Act as the National Healing and Reconciliation Act of 1995. P. Gobodo-Madikizela, 'Remorse, Forgiveness and Rehumanisation: Stories from South Africa', *Journal of Humanistic Psychology*, 42(1), 2002, p. 9.
21. According to Tutu, for instance, 'many bore witness to the fact that coming to talk to the Commission had had a marked therapeutic effect on them'. Tutu, *No Future without Forgiveness*, p. 33. See also E. Kiss, 'Moral Ambition within and beyond Political Constraints', p. 72; Y. Henry, 'Where Healing Begins' in Villa-Vincencio and Verwoerd (eds.), *Looking Back, Reaching Forward*, pp. 166–173.
22. Tutu, *No Future without Forgiveness*, p. 81.
23. M. Minow, 'The Hope for Healing: What Can Truth Commissions Do?' in Rotberg and Thompson, *Truth v. Justice*, pp. 240–241; M. Ignatieff, 'Articles of Faith', *Index on Censorship*, 5, pp. 110–122; B. Hamber and R. Wilson, 'Symbolic Closure through Memory, Reparation and Revenge in Post-Conflict Societies', *Journal of Human Rights*, 1(1), 2002, pp. 35–53; Leebaw, 'Legitimation of Judgement?', pp. 23–51; R. Wilson, *The Politics of Truth and Reconciliation in South Africa*, Cambridge: Cambridge University Press, 2009. See also D. Mendeloff, 'Truth-Seeking, Truth-Telling, and Postconflict Peacebuilding: Curb the Enthusiasm?', *International Studies Review*, 6(3), 2004, pp. 363–369.
24. G. Lund, '"Healing the Nation": Medicolonial Discourse and the State of Emergency from Apartheid to Truth and Reconciliation', *Cultural Critique*, 54, 2003, pp. 88–119; C. Moon, 'Healing Past Violence: Traumatic Assumptions and Therapeutic Interventions in War and Reconciliation', *Journal of Human Rights*, 8(1), 2009, pp. 71–91; E. Hutchinson, *Affective Communities in World Politics: Collective Emotions after Trauma*, Cambridge: Cambridge University Press, 2016, pp. 247–266; Chakravarti, *Sing the Rage*, passim.
25. Hence one of Claire Moon's strongest objections to the TRC is that it 'projected an anthropomorphic image of the nation, constituting it as an individual person with a single body and psyche'. Similarly Lund, echoing Minow, asks, 'Can a therapeutic process work for collectivities?' See Moon, 'Healing Past Violence', p. 82; and Lund, '"Healing the Nation"', p. 109.
26. See M. Amstutz, *The Healing of Nations: The Promise and Limits of Political Forgiveness*, Lanham, MD: Rowman and Littlefield, 2005, pp. 187–210; D. Philpott, 'Beyond Politics

The Therapy of Reconciliation 255

as Usual' in D. Philpott (Ed.), *The Politics of Past Evil: Religion, Reconciliation and the Dilemmas of Transitional Justice*, Notre Dame, IN: University of Notre Dame Press, 2006, pp. 11-42; Minow, 'The Hope for Healing'; and Hutchinson, *Affective Communities in World Politics*, pp. 247-266.

27. Lund, '"Healing the Nation"', p. 108.
28. Foucault refers to these as the *ratio pastoralis* and the *ratio gubernatorial*. M. Foucault, *Security, Territory, Population: Lectures at the Collège de France 1977-1978*, New York: Picador, 2007, p. 232.
29. Foucault, *Security, Territory, Population*, pp. 115-135.
30. Torpey, '"Making Whole What Has Been Smashed": Reflections on Reparations', *Journal of Modern History*, 73(2), 2001, p. 144.
31. One of the common criticisms levelled against the Chilean Truth and Reconciliation Commission, for instance, was that it had not allowed victims to tell their story—an error the South African Truth and Reconciliation Commission went to great length to correct. As Bronwyn Leebaw has pointed out, South African leaders who attended the IDASA conference where the form of the TRC was determined were persuaded by Jose Zalaquett's suggestion that 'by taking testimony, and acknowledging past abuses, truth commissions might help to address the trauma suffered by victims and survivors of past abuses'. Leebaw, 'Legitimation or Judgment', p. 38. On this point, see also a conversation with the Chilean playwright Ariel Dorfman recorded in P. Meiring, *Chronicle of the Truth Commission*, Vanderbijlpark: Carpe Diem Books, 1999, pp. 172-173; and Boraine, 'Truth and Reconciliation in South Africa' in Rotberg and Thompson, *Truth v. Justice*, pp. 142-143. On the extension of the therapeutic governance pioneered by the TRC to other contexts, see P. Hayner, 'Same Species, Different Animal: How South Africa Compares to Truth Commissions Worldwide' in Villa-Vincencio and Verwoerd (eds.), *Looking Back, Reaching Forward*, pp. 32-42; Moon, 'Healing Past Violence', p. 85.
32. See Hazan, *Judging War, Judging History*, p. 35; and J.L. Herman, *Trauma and Recovery*, New York: Basic Books, 1992, p. 1.
33. See Leebaw, 'Legitimation or Judgement?', p. 26; Moon, 'Healing Past Violence', p. 84; and V. Pupavac, 'War on the Couch: The Emotionology of the New International Security Paradigm', *European Journal of Social Theory*, 7(2), 2004, passim.
34. Concerns about the role played by religion in the TRC have been raised endlessly but see, for instance, L. Graybill, 'South Africa's Truth and Reconciliation Commission: Ethical and Theological Perspectives', *Ethics and International Affairs*, 12, 1998, pp. 43-62; A. Gutmann and D. Thompson, 'The Moral Foundations of Truth Commissions' in Rotberg and Thompson, *Truth v. Justice*, pp. 22-44; P. Hayner, 'Same Species, Different Animal: How South Africa Compares to Truth Commissions Worldwide' in Villa-Vincencio and Verwoerd (eds.), *Looking Back, Reaching Forward*, pp. 32-41; J. VanAntwerpen, 'Reconciliation Reconceived: Religion, Secularism, and the Language of Transition' in W. Kymlicka and B. Bashir, *The Politics of Reconciliation in Multicultural Societies*, Oxford: Oxford University Press, 2010, pp. 25-47.
35. See Hayner, 'Same Species, Different Animal', p. 40; Kiss, 'Moral Ambition within and beyond Political Constraints', pp. 84-87; T. Brudholm, *Resentment's Virtue: Jean Amery and the Refusal to Forgive*, Philadelphia, PA: Temple University Press, 2008, pp. 42-62; Chakravarti, *Sing the Rage*.

36. See C. Griswold, *Forgiveness: A Philosophical Exploration*, Cambridge: Cambridge University Press 2007, pp. 180-183 and Lund, "'Healing the Nation'", pp. 104-107.
37. I follow Foucault here in assuming the essential aspect of the relationship between religion and politics in modern Western societies is not found in the interplay between church and state but between pastorate and government. See Foucault, *Security, Territory, Population*, p. 191.
38. As Foucault goes on to note, 'pastoral power is a power of care. It looks after the flock, it looks after the individuals of the flock, it sees to it that the sheep do not suffer, it goes in search of those that have strayed off course, and it treats those that are injured'. Foucault, *Security, Territory, Population*, pp. 126-127.
39. Thus Deputy Chair Alex Boraine would characterize the TRC as 'a compassionate and a sympathetic state-appointed commission' and Elizabeth Kiss would speak of 'norms of respectful listening, which allow people to tell stories without interruption'. Boraine, 'Truth and Reconciliation in South Africa', p. 154; Kiss, 'Moral Ambition within and beyond Political Constraints', p. 73.
40. Thus Tutu would write, 'We wanted to engender an atmosphere that would be welcoming, friendly and affirming. We did not want the witnesses traumatised and upset by insensitive cross-examination.' Tutu, *No Future without Forgiveness*, p. 88. Contrary to what I am arguing here, Chakravarti suggests the desire to gather material evidence often triumphed over the need to stay attuned to the psychological legacy of violence. Victims, she says, were frequently denied the opportunity to talk about or fully explore the emotional impact of past experience. Chakravarti is, however, focused almost exclusively on anger—precisely the emotion, in other words, that the Commission was most keen to silence in the name of healing. The fact that anger was not given its due is not, therefore, inconsistent with the argument being made here; namely, that the operation of the Commission was fundamentally shaped by the objective of 'healing'. Indeed, while I think Chakravarti is absolutely right to suggest the Commission failed to deal properly with the psychological legacy of Apartheid, she more or less concedes the objective of healing (at least on the Commission's pastoral understanding of that process) when she notes that 'the act of forgiveness was the pivot upon which the transition to a more peaceful future rested, and each individual act of forgiveness was seen as a sacrifice necessary for the success of the nation'. Chakravarti, *Sing the Rage*, pp. 57-78.
41. See Villa-Vincencio, 'Getting on with Life', p. 203; W. Verwoerd, 'Towards the Recognition of our Past Injustices' in Villa-Vincencio and Verwoerd (eds.), *Looking Back, Reaching Forward*, p. 157.
42. Kiss, 'Moral Ambition within and beyond Political Constraints', p. 73.
43. 'I do not distinguish between ANC wounds, PAC wounds and other wounds—many people are in need of healing, and we need to heal our country if we are to build a nation which will guarantee peace and stability.' Omar, 'Introduction'. As I will go on to discuss, Foucault refers to this symmetry between all and each as a 'paradoxical equivalence' because the interests of one are sometimes in tension with the interests of all and the interests of all in tension with the interests of one. Foucault, *Security, Territory, Population*, pp. 129, 169.
44. Tutu, *No Future without Forgiveness*, p. 87.

The Therapy of Reconciliation 257

45. As the deputy chair of the Commission Alex Boraine noted: 'We care about every witness, young and old, Black and White, men and women, it makes no difference.' Boraine, cited in M. Sanders, 'Remembering Apartheid', *Diacritics*, 32(3/4), 2002, p. 67.
46. As Rosemary Nagy has noted, 'This image of the wounded nation had the effect of conflating individual acts of torture with the suffering of the nation as a whole. And consequently, catharsis of individual victim's stories could also stand in for national reconciliation as a whole.' R. Nagy, 'The Ambiguities of Reconciliation and Responsibility in South Africa', *Political Studies*, 52, 2004, p. 718.
47. Foucault, *Security, Territory, Population*, p. 128.
48. A. Sachs, 'His Name Was Henry' in W. James and L. Van De Vijver (Eds.), *After the TRC: Reflections on Truth and Reconciliation in South Africa*, Athens, OH: Ohio University Press, 2001, p. 98.
49. Boraine, 'Truth and Reconciliation in South Africa', p. 142.
50. It is perhaps worth noting here that the idea that lies are harmful and poisonous, truth nourishing and restorative has long roots in the Christian tradition. Like food with regards to the body, it is all a question of what one takes in to the soul and asks it to digest. See S. Gayland, 'Machiavelli's Medical *Mandrogola*: Knowledge, Food, and Feces', *Renaissance Quarterly*, 74, 2021, pp. 63–64.
51. This view was inherent in the 'revealing is healing' mantra of the TRC and underpinned its whole commitment to testimony. As Boraine wrote, 'Explicit in the Act was an affirmation of the healing potential of truth telling.' The orthodox nature of this view of the healing powers of truth telling is evident in the number of times it was uncritically endorsed by commentators. Thus Lyn Graybill would write: 'psychology tells us that suppressing stories leads to stress, depression and anxiety; sharing stories in a supportive setting leads to healing'; and Pumla Gobodo-Madikizela would claim '[f]or the victims, being given a voice for the first time, being able to speak before an official body, gave them the sense of affirmation and validation that is so crucial to victims of trauma'. See Boraine, 'Truth and Reconciliation in South Africa', p. 152; Graybill, 'South Africa's Truth and Reconciliation Commission', p. 49; and Gobodo-Madikizela, 'Remorse, Forgiveness, and Rehumanisation', p. 11.
52. Boraine, 'Truth and Reconciliation in South Africa', p. 151. As Nagy noted, 'It was expected that the moral conscience of passive bystanders would be reawakened during the witnessing of victim and perpetrator testimony.' Nagy, 'The Ambiguities of Reconciliation and Responsibility in South Africa', p. 715.
53. Minow, *Between Vengeance and Forgiveness*, p. 66. In a similar vein, Kiss would write: 'If telling the truth about their wounds can heal the wounded … perhaps listening to such stories can help heal societies'; and Humphrey would note 'speaking out is believed to be a liberating and empowering act and a step towards individual and social healing'. See Kiss, 'Moral Ambition within and beyond Political Constraints', p. 72; and Humphrey, *The Politics of Atrocity and Reconciliation*, p. 107.
54. In her chapter 'Confronting Anger', Chakravarti notes how the pain of those who gave testimony before the TRC was often too great (and too subtle) to be either investigated or contained. Pain, one might say, overflowed the space that had been allocated to it by the Commission. Chakravarti, *Sing the Rage*, pp. 68–70.

258   The Penitent State

55. See C. Rassool, L. Witz, and G. Minkley, 'Burying and Memorialising the Body of Truth: The TRC and National Heritage' in James and Van de Vijver, *After the TRC*, p. 125; and Sanders, 'Remembering Apartheid', p. 70.
56. Tutu, *No Future without Forgiveness*, pp. 48, 186. As Gutmann and Thompson also noted, 'many welcomed the chance to testify, and said they experienced some relief and less hostility towards their former oppressors. But in many other cases, testifying reopened old wounds, produced continuing psychological distress, and generated hostility toward the new government and the TRC itself'. Gutmann and Thompson, 'The Moral Foundations of Truth Commissions', p. 30.
57. N. Walaza, 'Insufficient Healing and Reparation' in Villa-Vincencio and Verwoerd (eds.), *Looking Back, Reaching Forward*, p. 252.
58. Ntsebeza, 'The Uses of Truth Commissions: Lessons for the World', in Rotberg and Thompson (eds.), *Truth v. Justice*, p. 162.
59. Boraine, 'Truth and Reconciliation in South Africa', p. 153.
60. A. Krog, *Country of My Skull*, London: Vintage, 1999, p. 73.
61. Ntsebeza, 'The Uses of Truth Commissions', p. 165.
62. Interestingly, Tutu devotes a whole chapter of his memoire to this question. See *No Future without Forgiveness*, pp. 153–171.
63. Tutu, *No Future without Forgiveness*, p. 155.
64. Minow sums the issue up as follows: 'Sympathetic listeners who work with survivors may be engulfed by anguish, overcome by despair, and awash with mourning. All of these reactions are understandable response to identifying with the survivors, feeling guilty form causing the patient to re-experience pain in the retelling, dwelling with the contagious hopelessness of victims, becoming overwhelmed by the enormity of reported suffering and confronting such human evil'. Minow, *Between Vengeance and Forgiveness*, p. 74.
65. Tutu, *No Future without Forgiveness*, pp. 232–233.
66. Tutu, *No Future without Forgiveness*, p. 233.
67. Boraine, 'Truth and Reconciliation in South Africa', pp. 141–157; Tutu, *No Future without Forgiveness*, pp. 10–37.
68. A. Allan, 'Truth and Reconciliation: A Psycholegal Perspective', *Ethnicity and Health*, 5(3-4), 2000, p. 192.
69. Boraine, 'Truth and Reconciliation in South Africa', p. 150.
70. As Rosemary Nagy later noted, 'the promise of truth fell short of initial aspirations'. Nagy, 'The Ambiguities of Reconciliation and Responsibility in South Africa', p. 715.
71. Foucault, *Security, Territory, Population*, pp. 128–129.
72. In *No Future without Forgiveness*, Tutu explicitly links the concept of restorative justice with both *ubuntu* and reconciliation. And, while not used quite so interchangeably with restorative justice, the concept of magnanimity would also be deployed on many occasions, particularly in relation to Mandela, as a way of denoting the necessary generosity of spirit. *No Future without Forgiveness*, pp. 34–36, 51.
73. Gobodo-Madikizela, 'Remorse, Forgiveness and Rehumanisation', p. 11.
74. Gobodo-Madikizela, 'Remorse, Forgiveness and Rehumanisation', p. 20.
75. Tutu, *No Future without Forgiveness*, p. 51.
76. Tutu, *No Future without Forgiveness*, p. 204. So earnest was the Commission in this endeavour, in fact, it consistently blurred the very distinction between victim and perpetrator: '*Ubuntu* means that in a real sense even the supporters of apartheid were

victims of the vicious system which they implemented and which they supported so enthusiastically.' See Tutu, *No Future without Forgiveness*, p. 35.
77. Tutu, *No Future without Forgiveness*, p. 35. In a similar vein, Charles Villa-Vincencio, the director of research for the TRC, would claim: 'The testimony of amnesty applicants shows the extent to which many of the nation's worst perpetrators were themselves victims of a political system and cultural milieu that promoted violence.' Villa-Vincencio, 'Getting on With Life', p. 204.
78. Tutu, *No Future without Forgiveness*, p. 232.
79. On the notion of sacrificial reversal, see Foucault, *Security, Territory, Population*, p. 170.
80. Tutu, *No Future without Forgiveness*, p. 233.
81. Tutu, *No Future without Forgiveness*, pp. 7, 20, 39.
82. As Nagy notes, 'the TRC praised individual victims who harboured no bitterness as heroes in the New South Africa'. Nagy, 'The Ambiguities of Reconciliation and Responsibility in South Africa', p. 718.
83. Tutu, *No Future without Forgiveness*, pp. 36, 115, 118.
84. Tutu, *No Future without Forgiveness*, p. 76.
85. In South Africa, according to Gobodo-Madikizela, 'the language of "reconciliation" defined the way that society dealt with its traumatic past' (p. 19).
86. See A. Verdoolaege, 'Managing Reconciliation at the Human Rights Violations Hearings of the South African TRC', *Journal of Human Rights*, 5(1), 2006, 61–80; T. Brudholm, *Resentment's Virtue: Jean Amery and the Refusal to Forgive*, Philadelphia, PA: Temple University Press, 2008, pp. 30–34; Chakravarti, *Sing the Rage*, pp. 57–78; and F. Van Zyl Slabbert, 'Truth without Reconciliation, Reconciliation with Truth' in James and Van De Vijver (eds.), *After the TRC*, p. 69.
87. Tutu, *No Future without Forgiveness*, p. 135.
88. Tutu, *No Future without Forgiveness*, p. 136.
89. H. Adam and K. Adam, 'The Politics of Memory in Divided Societies' in James and Van De Vijver (eds.), *After the TRC*, p. 44.
90. Van Zyl Slabbert, 'Truth without Reconciliation, Reconciliation with Truth' in W. James and L. Van De Vijver (eds.), *After the TRC*, p. 66.
91. Tutu, *No Future without Forgiveness*, p. 82.
92. Nagy, 'Reconciliation and Responsibility in South Africa', p. 719. In a similar vein, Humphrey has claimed that '[i]n the process of national reconciliation it is those who have suffered the most, the victims, who are usually asked to make the greatest efforts to reconcile. It is their forgiveness that puts the past to rest'. Humphrey, *The Politics of Atrocity and Reconciliation*, p. 107.
93. Gobodo-Madikizela, 'Remorse, Forgiveness, and Rehumanisation', p. 29.
94. See, for instance, Brudholm, *Resentment's Virtue*, pp. 26–34; P. Muldoon, 'The Moral Legitimacy of Anger', *European Journal of Social Theory*, 11(3), 2008, pp. 299–314; Chakravarti, *Sing the Rage*, pp. 65–68.
95. Derrida, *On Cosmopolitanism and Forgiveness*, pp. 32–33.
96. S. Msimany, 'All Is Not Forgiven', p. 32.
97. Nagy, 'The Ambiguities of Reconciliation and Responsibility in South Africa', p. 716.
98. Although Nussbaum takes issue with Tutu's contrition/forgiveness ethics, seeing in it a subtle variety of retributivism, she endorses the TRC's sponsorship of an 'unconditional

generosity' and 'forward-looking' approach. See M. Nussbaum, *Anger and Forgiveness: Resentment, Generosity, Justice*, Oxford: Oxford University Press, 2016, pp. 237–246.
99. Tutu, *No Future without Forgiveness*, p. 35.
100. T. Govier, *Forgiveness and Revenge*, London: Routledge, 2002, p. 96.
101. Gobodo-Madikizela, 'Remorse, Forgiveness, and Rehumanisation', p. 8.
102. Gobodo-Madikizela, 'Remorse, Forgiveness, and Rehumanisation', p. 20.
103. Gobodo-Madikizela, 'Remorse, Forgiveness, and Rehumanisation', pp. 13, 14.
104. Nagy, 'The Ambiguities of Reconciliation and Responsibility in South Africa', pp. 722–724.
105. Biggar, *Burying the Past*, p. 12.
106. Nussbaum, *Anger and Forgiveness*, p. 249.
107. Villa-Vincencio, 'The Reek of Cruelty', p. 186.
108. See Tutu, *No Future without Forgiveness*, p. 122.
109. As Herbert and Kanya Adam have astutely noted, owing to Tutu's international stature, 'his hopes and predictions have entered the academic literature as empirical facts'. Adam and Adam, 'The Politics of Memory in Divided Societies', p. 43.
110. Pupavac, 'War on the Couch', p. 159.
111. At one point in *No Future without Forgiveness*, Tutu virtually lays claim to a kind of pastoral perfection by suggesting the TRC would have been 'more than justified' had only 'one person' seized 'the opportunity of unburdening themselves of the heavy weight of their anguish'. Tutu, *No Future without Forgiveness*, p. 127.
112. This view of the South African TRC as a cathartic operation is shared by Sonali Chakravarti and I am in full agreement with her suggestion that catharsis should not be the primary goal of truth commissions either for the witness or the audience. As she rightly points out, 'Applying the idea of catharsis to victim testimony attributes too much significance to one moment of emotional expression rather than to the larger process of political transformation'. However, for the reasons outlined in Chapter 6, I think she is wrong to treat the method of the TRC as 'a type of Aristotelian catharsis'. Missing in the TRC was precisely the clarification in relation to political error that the Greek tragedies studied by Aristotle achieved and which Chakravarti believes can and should come from an engagement with anger. If Aristotle is right, tragic catharsis goes beyond any simple discharge of emotion. Chakravarti, *Sing the Rage*, pp. 70–71.
113. See Tutu, *No Future without Forgiveness*, pp. 127–128, 226.
114. TRC Report, vol. 1, p. 7, para. 27.
115. Tutu, *No Future without Forgiveness*, pp. 76, 82, 114.
116. See, for instance, Chakravarti, *Sing the Rage*, pp. 43–44.
117. According to Elizabeth Kiss, for instance, 'prosecutions would have yielded much less truth about what happened and why, and far fewer opportunities for closure, healing and reconciliation'. Kiss, 'Moral Ambition within and beyond Political Constraints', p. 69. For similar claims, see M. Minow, 'The Hope for Healing', pp. 237–240; R.C. Slye, 'Amnesty, Truth, and Reconciliation' in Rotberg and Thompson (Eds.), *Truth v. Justice*, pp. 170–188; Boraine, 'Truth and Reconciliation in South Africa' in Rotberg and Thompson (Eds.), *Truth v. Justice*, p. 150; Ntsebeza, 'The Uses of Truth Commissions' in Rotberg and Thompson (Eds.), *Truth v. Justice*, p. 162; R.L. Brooks, 'Reflections on Reparations' in J. Torpey (ed.), *The Politics of the Past*, Lanham, MD: Rowman and Littlefield, p. 111; and Aldana, 'A Victim-Centered Reflection on Truth Commissions', p. 112.

118. *Azanian Peoples Organization (AZAPO) and others v. President of the Republic of South Africa and others*, Constitutional Court of South Africa, Case No. CCT 117/96 (25 July 1996).
119. M. Minow, 'The Hope for Healing', pp. 243–247.
120. See Aldana, 'A Victim-Centered Reflection on Truth Commissions and Prosecutions as a Response to Mass Atrocities', p. 111.
121. For a critical perspective on the temporal parameters, see C. Bundy, 'The Beast of the Past: History and the TRC' in James and Van de Vijver, *After the TRC: Reflections on Truth and Reconciliation in South Africa*, Athens, OH: Ohio University Press, 2001, p. 17.
122. Tutu, *No Future without Forgiveness*, p. 79.
123. Tutu, *No Future without Forgiveness*, p. 78.
124. Tutu, *No Future without Forgiveness*, p. 79.
125. Tutu, *No Future without Forgiveness*, pp. 78–79. See also pp. 27, 59.
126. As Mahmood Mamdani noted, the TRC 'ignored apartheid as experienced by the broad masses of the people of South Africa'. In a similar vein, Lyn Graybill claimed 'The TRC ignores the massive denial of human rights experienced by millions of ordinary people.' See N. Walaza, 'Insufficient Healing and Reparation' in Villa-Vincencio and Verwoerd (eds.), *Looking Back, Reaching Forward*, p. 252; Tutu, *No Future without Forgiveness*, p. 14; M. Mamdani, 'Amnesty or Impunity? A Preliminary Critique of the Report of the Truth and Reconciliation Commission of South Africa', *Diacritics*, 32(3/4), 2002, p. 38; Graybill, 'South Africa's Truth and Reconciliation Commission', p. 54; and B. Leebaw, 'Mobilizing Emotions: Shame, Victimhood and Agency' in M.N. Barnett (ed.), *Humanitarianism and Human Rights*, Cambridge: Cambridge University Press, 2020, p. 153.
127. Mamdani, 'Amnesty or Impunity?', p. 40. As is often noted, the TRC did hold certain industry hearings for business, the media, the judiciary, etc. However, the public face of the Commission was undoubtedly the hearings of the Human Rights Violation Committee. See Humphrey, *The Politics of Atrocity and Reconciliation*, p. 111.
128. See, for instance, Leebaw, 'Legitimation or Judgement', passim.
129. K. Wale, 'Knotted Memories of a Betrayed Sacrifice: Rethinking Trauma and Hope in South Africa', *Memory Studies*, 2022, p. 4.
130. As Mark Sanders noted, 'What has captured the hearts of observers … is the testimony heard at the human rights violation hearings.' M. Sanders, 'Ambiguities of Mourning: Law, Custom and Women before South Africa's Truth and Reconciliation Commission', *Law, Text, Culture*, 4(2), 1998, p. 107.
131. See Herman, *Trauma and Recovery*, pp. 147–151 and D. Laub, 'Truth and Testimony: The Process and the Struggle', *American Imago*, 48(1), 1991, p. 85.
132. Minow, 'The Hope for Healing', p. 246. See also Chakravarti, *Sing the Rage*, p. 70.
133. Minow, 'The Hope for Healing', p. 244.
134. Minow, 'The Hope for Healing', p. 244.
135. According to Paul Ricoeur, the benefits of this 'public exercise in memory and mourning' were 'undeniable in therapeutic, moral, and political terms'. P. Ricoeur, *Memory, History, Forgetting*, Chicago, IL: University of Chicago Press, 2004, p. 484. Others have, however, been rather less sanguine. For critical perspectives, see, for instance, Sanders, 'Ambiguities of Mourning', p. 107; D. Mendeloff, 'Truth-Seeking, Truth-Telling, and Post-conflict Peacebuilding: Curb the Enthusiasm?', *International Studies Review*, 6(3), 2004, pp. 363–369; B. Leebaw, 'The Irreconcilable Goals of Transitional Justice', p. 115; and K.

Brounéus, 'The Trauma of Truth Telling: Effects of Witnessing in Rwandan Gacaca Courts on Psychological Health', *Journal of Conflict Resolution*, 54(3), 2010, pp. 408-437.

136. Hannah Arendt was, I think, quite right to suggest that bodily pain is the most private and least communicable experience of all. H. Arendt, *The Human Condition*, Chicago, IL: University of Chicago Press, 1958, pp. 30-31.
137. As Rassool, Witz, and Minkley note, 'At the visual core of the TRC hearings were descriptions, representations and conflicts around bodies in various states of mutilation, dismemberment and interment within the terror of the past. Again and again, witnesses made claims in respect of body parts and human remains, making their visibility, recovery and repossession a metaphor for the settlement of the pasts of apartheid.' C. Rassool, L. Witz, and G. Minkley, 'Burying and Memorialising the Body of Truth: The TRC and National Heritage' in James and Van de Vijver (eds.), *After the TRC*, p. 125.
138. As the deputy chair of the Commission Alex Boraine noted with respect to the 'critical decision' to open the TRC to the media: 'this method ensured a strong educative opportunity so that truth-telling, healing, and reconciliation were not confined to a small group but were available to the entire nation'. Boraine, 'Truth and Reconciliation in South Africa', p. 146. See also Minow, *Between Vengeance and Forgiveness*, pp. 74-75.
139. Minow, 'The Hope for Healing', p. 245.
140. Verdoolaege, 'Managing Reconciliation', p. 62.
141. Minow, 'The Hope for Healing', p. 244.
142. Y. Henry, 'Where Healing Begins' in Villa-Vincencio and Verwoerd (eds.), *Looking Back, Reaching Forward*, p. 167. The witnessing, and thus the transmission, of pain is a common theme in discussions of the TRC. See Minow, 'The Hope for Healing', pp. 243-245. For a discussion of Henry's anger at the appropriation of his story, see Chakravarti, *Sing the Rage*, p. 77.
143. C. Villa-Vincencio, 'On the Limitations of Academic History' in James and Van De Vijver (eds.), *After the TRC*, p. 25.
144. Krog, *Country of My Skull*, p. 68.
145. Bundy, 'The Beast of the Past', p. 9.
146. Bundy, 'The Beast of the Past', p. 9.
147. Tutu, *No Future without Forgiveness*, pp. 83, 124.
148. Tutu, *No Future without Forgiveness*, p. 114.
149. Minow, 'The Hope for Healing', p. 251.
150. See Tutu, *No Future without Forgiveness*, pp. 128-129; Krog, *Country of My Skull*, p. 31; Minow, 'The Hope for Healing', p. 235.
151. See, for instance, M. Mamdani, 'Amnesty or Impunity? A Preliminary Critique of the Report of the Truth and Reconciliation Commission of South Africa', *Diacritics*, 32(3/4), 2002, pp. 32-59; Mamdani, 'A Diminished Truth' in James and Van De Vijver (eds.), *After the TRC*, pp. 58-61; Graybill, 'South Africa's Truth and Reconciliation Commissions', p. 54; Moon, 'Healing Past Violence', p. 85; Leebaw, 'Legitimation or Judgement?', p. 39; Chakravarti, *Sing the Rage*, p. 67; Torpey, '"Making Whole What Has Been Smashed"', pp. 144-146.
152. As John Torpey has written, 'The TRC failed to have a bigger impact on post-Apartheid South African life in part because it did not—and perhaps, given the terms of its mandate, could not—address the sharp economic inequalities between black and white that the Apartheid state left behind.' Torpey, '"Making Whole What Has Been Smashed"', p. 145.

The Therapy of Reconciliation   263

153. W. Orr, 'Reparation Delayed Is Healing Retarded' in Villa-Vincencio and Verwoerd (eds.), *Looking Back, Reaching Forward*, p. 240.
154. Tutu, *No Future without Forgiveness*, p. 57.
155. Orr, 'Reparation Delayed Is Healing Retarded' in Villa-Vincencio and Verwoerd (eds.), *Looking Back, Reaching Forward*, p. 244.
156. Orr, 'Reparation Delayed Is Healing Retarded' in Villa-Vincencio and Verwoerd (eds.), *Looking Back, Reaching Forward*, p. 247.
157. J. Thompson, *Taking Responsibility for the Past*, Cambridge: Polity, 2002, p. 48.
158. See N. Walaza, 'Insufficient Healing and Reparation' in Villa-Vincencio and Verwoerd (eds.), *Looking Back, Reaching Forward*, p. 255.
159. Tutu, *No Future without Forgiveness*, p. 221. The same concern about the threat to healing posed by the 'ever-widening gap between wealth and poverty' was raised by the deputy chair, Alex Boraine. See Boraine, 'Truth and Reconciliation in South Africa', p. 154.
160. Moon, 'Healing Past Violence', p. 84.
161. Hamber and Wilson, 'Symbolic Closure through Memory Reparation and Revenge', p. 41.
162. Hamber and Wilson, 'Symbolic Closure through Memory Reparation and Revenge', p. 41.
163. As Hamber and Wilson note, 'For survivors, the state's desire to build a new post-conflict society often means sloughing off the past too easily, and asking survivors to engage in a premature closure before all the psychological processes around truth and recompense are fully internalized.' Hamber and Wilson, 'Symbolic Closure through Memory Reparation and Revenge', p. 45.
164. Humphrey, *The Politics of Atrocity and Reconciliation*, p. 119.
165. Chakravarti, *Sing the Rage*, p. 83. Mihai defends storytelling on similar grounds, See Mihai, *Negative Emotions*, p. 34.
166. Arendt, *The Human Condition*, p. 179.
167. Arendt, *The Human Condition*, pp. 198–199.
168. On this point, see J. Edkins, *Trauma and the Memory of Politics*, Cambridge: Cambridge University Press, 2003, p. 214. As Chakravarti notes elsewhere in her book, the possibility of being seen as a citizen, rather than just a victim, was often lost. 'By allowing anger to be interpreted as an individual mental health concern rather than a politically significant criticism', she writes, 'the commission denied its systemic causes.' See Chakravarti, *Sing the Rage*, p. 72.
169. My comments here are informed by Arendt's 'spatial conception' of the different spheres of life—intimate, political, international—in which politics acquires its distinction as the domain in which citizens appear before each other in the mode of speaking and acting. Arendt, *The Human Condition*, pp. 179–180. See Chakravarti, *Sing the Rage*, pp. 79–105.
170. Henry, 'Where Healing Begins', p. 168.
171. Henry, 'Where Healing Begins', p. 167.
172. Henry, 'Where Healing Begins', p. 169.
173. P. Gobodo-Madikizela, 'Why Memories of the Truth and Reconciliation Commissions Still Ache', *The Conversation*, 29 November 2018.
174. Gobodo-Madikizela, 'Why Memories of the Truth and Reconciliation Commission Still Ache'.
175. As Jenny Edkins notes of trauma: 'It is outside the realm of language and to bring it back within that realm by speaking of it, by setting it within a linear narrative form, is to destroy it'. Edkins, *Trauma and the Memory of Politics*, p. 214.

176. Cited in Krog, *Country of My Skull*, p. 244.
177. S. Ahmed, *The Cultural Politics of Emotion*, Edinburgh: Edinburgh University Press, 2015, p. 22.
178. Ahmed, *The Cultural Politics of Emotion*, p. 22. See also B. Leebaw, 'Mobilising Emotions' in M.N. Barnett (ed.), *Humanitarianism and Human Rights*, p. 146.
179. As Chakravarti notes, 'When individuals are made vulnerable by having to disclose traumatic experiences in the context of victim testimony, there is an even greater need to be vigilant about how their testimonies will be used by the state.' Chakravarti, *Sing the Rage*, p. 47.
180. Chakravarti, *Sing the Rage*, p. 75.

6
A Different Catharsis?

Penance and Purification in the Society of the Spectacle

Although the institutions of exception examined in this book are novel in many respects, they are not entirely without precedent. As I intimated in Chapter 2 (and as a number of other commentators have implicitly or explicitly recognized), tragedy played a somewhat similar role—part interrogative, part cathartic—in the political life of the ancient Greeks. Not unlike the public memorial, the political apology, and the truth commission in this sense, the tragic festival of the Great Dionysia (at which the works of Aeschylus, Sophocles, and Euripides were originally performed) was something of an anomaly in the city-state, a space of mourning and reflection that remained institutionally separated from the rest of its life.[1] In contrast to those other political spaces, more or less continuously available, where citizens exercised their sovereign authority and affirmed their identity as a city—I am referring here, in particular, to the Assembly (*ekklesia*), the Council (*boule*), and the Courts (*dikasteria*)—tragedy only gathered the Athenian public once a year and seemingly only for the purpose of putting it (and its civic ideology) into question. Here, as is often noted, civic trauma made its covert return to the space of appearances as the tragedians exposed the city in its deepest conflicts, ripped apart by reckless transgression and unreconcilable antagonisms. Loraux, astute as ever, locates the exceptionality of tragedy in its representation of 'off-limits' topics; for it is as if, in tragedy, the democratic city had purposely set up a stage 'for the tangling and untangling of actions that anywhere else it would be dangerous or intolerable even to think about'.[2]

One of the things that should emerge quite quickly from the discussion that follows is that tragic plays represent a (still largely untapped) resource for thinking about the problem of 'coming to terms' because they too engage with alienated survivors and guilty sovereigns in their mutually constitutive pathology. In Euripides' *The Trojan Women*, a play set in Troy but performed less than a year after the Athenians had laid waste to the island of Melos, centre stage is given over to the survivors of a war of extermination and the irreparable losses—of family, friends, city, and hope—that they have suffered.

Described by one commentator as an 'unambiguously female drama', the play gives voice to the mothers, wives, and daughters of the slaughtered heroes (in much the same way as the Truth and Reconciliation Commission (TRC) did in South Africa), forcing its Greek audience to view things from the perspective of the victims and become enjoined in their mourning.[3] Elsewhere, notably in the great Theban plays of Sophocles, one meets guilty sovereigns of the likes of Oedipus and Creon whose inhumanity, more than simply causing the downfall of their families and cities, poses the problem of the irreversible and irreparable. Left standing after others have fallen, each enjoys a shameful over-life that the city must find a way to manage lest the entire community succumb to a destructive pollution (*miasma*).

Arguably, however, it is less the tragic plays than the civic institution of tragedy that assumes the greatest relevance in the current context. For, beyond engaging with the exceptional, with actions that go too far and mourning that lasts too long, Greek tragedy was itself an institution of exception that played a critical role in the life of democratic Athens. As David Carter, building upon the pioneering work of Simon Goldhill and Olga Taxidou, notes in *The Politics of Greek Tragedy*, the plays of Aeschylus, Sophocles, and Euripides do not just 'tell political stories', they 'also have a function in the political life of the state'.[4] Like many before him, struck by the absence of any clear lessons in Greek drama, Carter is inclined to limit that function to its capacity to provoke reflection: 'the didactic function of tragedy', he writes, 'goes no further than to make the audience think'.[5] However, the insistence with which the problem of loss and the associated themes of memory, mourning, and revenge return in Greek tragedy suggests there may be warrant for going at least a little bit further.[6] In tragedy, as we have just noted, the grieving woman and the shameful man (who is also a figure of grief in the sense of having to come to terms with lost honour) are granted the public exposure vigorously denied them in the day-to-day activity of the *polis*, suggesting the Athenians needed a public vehicle for coming to terms with the wounded remainders of their glorious action.[7] Could it be that the institution of the Great Dionysia was, among other things, a means by which to wrestle with the past and mourn lost love objects?

Just how far we are justified in reading the civic institution of tragedy in this way is, of course, a matter of contention and any attempt at its demonstration would exceed the scope of this book by a long way. But it can hardly be an accident that the problem of 'the unburied' (symbol, par excellence, of the unfinished work of mourning) returns so frequently in the Greek plays.[8] Although readers of *Antigone*, bound by Hegel's spell, have been inclined to treat the exposed corpse of Polynices as a means by which Sophocles explores competing principles of justice—the rights of the city versus the rights of the family—it also serves as a most fitting metaphor for the subject matter of tragedy itself: the past that has not yet been properly buried. 'Tragedy', as Adrian Poole points out, 'always deals with toxic matter bequeathed by the past to the present.'[9] Here, figuratively speaking, the dead live on, sometimes as walking ghosts, sometimes as treasured memories, but always as unfinished business that shows up the limits of any attempt at institutionalized forgetting. In tragedy, those notoriously long-forgotten crimes never stay forgotten long. Instead, they impose themselves on the present: firstly, upon the kin to whom the 'duty of memory', the duty of mourning *and* vengeance, falls directly, and secondly, upon the city where the undisclosed, unexpiated crime manifests as a life-sapping pollution. To cite Poole once more: 'the living dead' of tragedy are not just a problem for their 'nearest and dearest', 'they also bear down heavily on a whole city, people, community, or culture'. Who needs tragedy, he asks? Anyone, it seems, in need of coming to terms with the past or, as he puts it, 'allaying ghosts collective as well as personal'. Tragedy finds its utility here, not just as something that encourages reflection but as an institution that is 'socially no less than psychologically progressive, a means of freeing the future from the past'.[10]

If Poole is even half right about tragedy being a socially and psychologically progressive institution that frees the future from the past, it would seem to hold out considerable promise for our own attempts at coming to terms— but perhaps (or so I will suggest) as much because of the dissimilarity as the similarity between it and our modern institutions of truth telling and societal catharsis. Tragedy, to be sure, is difficult to ignore as a precedent and a guide because it is nothing if not a genre of reckoning: if cities, heroes, and frontiers (notably those separating beast and human, friend and enemy, public and private) fall within the plays, it is generally because the past insists on being accounted for. In tragedy, trouble is, quite literally, passed down the line, as Antigone bitterly laments: 'how many griefs our father Oedipus handed down!'[11] In the same way, it is hard not to think about the festival of the Great Dionysia and the critical mirror it creates for the city of Athens without being reminded of our own more recent efforts at 'reflecting back' in sovereign acts of repentance and redress. As we have discovered, memorials, apologies, and commissions are also a kind of stage upon which the nation-state makes a (less than edifying) representation of itself. And yet, one glaring difference remains between tragedy and our more recent institutions of exception where memory, mourning, and revenge have, once again, become deeply intertwined: the 'distinctive property' of tragedy, as Nicole Loraux put it, was 'to keep at a distance the crucial problems and "inner ills" of the city'.[12] If, and it remains a very big 'if', the Greeks did in fact use tragedy as a means of coming to terms with civic trauma, it was a trauma made safe by examining it at a spatial and temporal remove. Modern states, by contrast, have tended to set the civil wound before the public in all its immediacy and horror, insisting that it needs to be confronted 'face to face'.

The distance tragedy put between the Athenians and their own civic failures can easily incline us to the view that we moderns are much better at facing up to our crimes than them. We, at least, as they now say, 'take ownership'—and perhaps there is something in that.[13] However, I want to use this chapter to explore the possibility that the displacement utilized by the Greeks in the civic institution of the Great Dionysia was a strength rather than a weakness because it facilitated a more radical kind of self-examination than our own institutions of exception allow. Driven by the biopolitical imperative of healing, we have been inclined to stage our own civic traumas in ways that facilitate catharsis but which potentially inhibit ongoing reflection on the structural problem of action as the source of irreversible consequences and the nation-state as a political form based upon exclusion or 'othering'. Could it be, I ask (duly conscious of the speculative nature of the enquiry), that in prioritizing healing and reconciliation, our modern institutions of exception fail where tragedy succeeded, bringing the public together in a tearful festival that is freighted with emotional power but lacking in ethical substance? Although, in what follows, I set up tragedy as a counterpoint, my aim is not to romanticize the institution of the Great Dionysia or present it as the model to follow—even though, in agreement with Simon Critchley, I think the attention it brings to the unhealed/unhealable wound does have 'the virtue of a certain realism'.[14] It is rather to read tragedy selectively (as a pre- or non-biopolitical institution of exception) in order to sketch a form of civic catharsis in which emotional discharge remains tied to critical reflection and political insight is privileged over therapeutic reconciliation.

I The Presentation of the Wound and the Cathartic Event

One of the many insights that can be gleaned from Loraux's work on the divided city of ancient Greece (discussed at length in Chapter 2) is that there are essentially two sources of mourning for the 'civic self': defeat at the hands of a foreign enemy and self-laceration through internal war. Both entail the loss of the city. Just as Miletus is 'lost' to the Persians, Athens is 'lost' to the factions. Of the two, however, it is clearly the second loss that is the more difficult with which to come to terms. Sophocles effectively sums up the Greek (and perhaps the modern) view when he has the messenger in *Oedipus Rex* say: 'The pains we inflict upon ourselves hurt most of all.'[15] In the face of such self-inflicted trauma, the Greeks, as we have seen, believed nothing could be done by way of amelioration. Since the loss of the brother, and, by extension, the brotherhood that is the civic body, was irreplaceable/unmournable, the only 'solution' was to forget the entire affair. Let Lethe do its work. The one place where the public could be exposed to such loss, and a kind of catharsis achieved, was in the theatre of Dionysius, and even there only on the condition that it remain at a safe distance. In tragedy, as Simon Goldhill puts it, misfortune was always 'enacted at the scene of the other—other places, other times, other people'.[16] If Athens and its civic ideology was always implicitly 'on the stage', it was only so reflexively, as a site to which the troubles that befell other cities in other times could be imaginatively returned; in effect, as the introjection of what was already a projection.[17]

The possibility, opened up by the advent of the multi-racial polity (a phenomenon closely tied to the history of colonialism), of figuring internal war as a war against 'foreigners' has clearly made it that much more difficult for us moderns to keep these two sources of mourning for the civic self apart. To the extent that the destruction of the racial 'other', the cause of so much sovereign repentance in the post-World War Two period, was premised on the idea that there was no brotherhood to begin with, it does not fit very comfortably into the category of a 'self-inflicted wound'. Only when these assaults on the racial other within are recast as 'crimes against humanity' does the idea of self-wounding return without ambiguity. In the figure of humanity one once again finds that all-encompassing 'brotherhood' (and, of course, since we have left this particular Greek myopia behind, sisterhood too) whose every crime is that of self upon self, human against human. However, if one considers the extent to which individual nation-states have taken ownership of these crimes, treating them precisely as a source of mourning for their civic self, the gap between the ancients and moderns on this issue may not ultimately be so great. Coming to terms with the past is almost invariably regarded as a national responsibility and the task of bearing witness as a penance for failing to show not just human but civic solidarity. As with the Greeks, in other words, the loss that is felt most keenly is still the loss of self that occurs when brothers and sisters are not treated as brothers and sisters (generally, in the modern instance, because of their race) and violence turns inwards rather than outwards.[18]

Where we do appear to differ markedly from the ancient Greeks is in relation to the presentation of these kinds of self-inflicted wounds. At least since the 1990s, the trauma that Greek tragedy was forced to keep at a distance—that is, to dislocate *from* Athens what it staged *for* Athens—has been brought back home and displayed in all its immediacy and horror.[19] In the case of the Memorial to the Murdered Jews of Europe (and other efforts at displaying national tragedy through memorialization), the crimes of the past are quite literally, to return to Stanley Levison's phrase, 'written in stone'.[20] One has no hope of moving them somewhere else or, perhaps more to the point, onto *someone* else. The site of the memorial is the concrete location of responsibility. But if political apologies and truth commissions appear like ephemeral pieces of public theatre by comparison, they are hardly any easier to evade as 'writings'. To the extent that they too create an official record of past offences, rewriting the national story in such a way as to put discrimination at its centre, they are just as unmoveable as the *stelae*. For the citizen-spectators called to bear witness at these events there is no escape from the (ugly) truth about their nation and thus, of course, about themselves. Whenever they look to the centre, either to the capital of the nation or the book of the nation, the violence done to the body of the other stares back at them.

The modern insistence on locating the injustice in *this* place goes hand in hand with the insistence on assigning it to *this* time. Where the Greek tragedians pushed the divisions of the present back into the past (into the mythical age of Homer), we draw the divisions of the past into the present as if the passing of time had no bearing upon their power or significance. This is not to say, as we have seen, that acts of public penance that return the body politic to the scene of the crime are either uncontroversial or uncontested. Martin Walser's infamous description of the Memorial to the Murdered Jews as a 'nightmare the size of a football field' dedicated to the 'perpetual presentation of our shame' is but one expression of resistance to the current insistence on exhuming the past and making it present.[21] And yet, if there is one thing that marks the age of apology, it is the belief that civil wounds, no matter how long ago they were inflicted, are alive in the present (as a kind of intergenerational, traumatic overrun) and are fully our responsibility to address.[22] A key premise of the restorative justice paradigm is that wrongdoing, like everything else passed down from our ancestors, is a part of our civic inheritance that cannot simply be cast aside as if it had nothing to do with the present generation and its 'well-being'.[23] If we are not directly responsible for having inflicted the wounds, we are responsible for ensuring that their effects are not reproduced in the present or transmitted as a burden to future generations. In short, so long as the guilty sovereign lives on in (or as) trauma, there is no 'unfinished business' that is not *our* business to finish.[24]

A Different Catharsis? 271

The immediacy with which our modern institutions of exception recall the wounds of the past to the present and make them 'our' responsibility makes it easy to forget that they are still a matter of mediation; still, for all intents and purposes, a theatrical spectacle. Between the wound that is exposed and the public that is exposed to it (and by it) stands a whole series of things—techniques, conventions, devices, and calculations—whose mediating effects are difficult to discern and whose political implications are certainly yet to be properly clarified.[25] Indeed, as much as one might grant, with Guy Debord, that '[t]he spectacle is not a collection of images, but a social relation among people mediated by images', determining the nature of that social relation in this case is hardly straightforward.[26] In principle, every expression of sovereign repentance is geared towards restoring an ethical relation between perpetrator and victim. In the gesture of repentance, the political community atones for its crimes precisely in order to make relations 'social' again. Assuming, however, that things can only appear *as they are mediated*, any judgement about the merits of such exceptional institutions is likely to be premature until the devices of representation they mobilize have been more closely analysed in their aesthetic, political, and psychological interrelations (in the way I have attempted in previous chapters). One question that certainly needs to be asked in this context is this: if it is the displacement of the wound that allows tragedy to open up a space for questioning, might the emplacement of the wound not work to close such questioning down? Is it possible, in other words, that the proximity of the misfortune to the here and now, the insistent way in which we are brought 'face to face' with it, actually narrows the space of reception and judgement, facilitating an emotional but not fully critical appropriation of its meaning and significance?

Doubtless a more thoroughgoing study than can be mustered here would be needed to confirm this hypothesis. However, by returning to the counter-example of tragic drama, we can at least provide some grounds for believing that proximity encourages the emotional to overrun the critical, leading to a rather different kind of catharsis than that achieved by tragedy. As Aristotle famously pointed out (and here I draw primarily upon Dennis Schmidt's brilliant commentary on his *Poetics*), tragic drama is an imitation (*mimesis*) of an action (*praxis*) in which calamity and suffering—'death, torture, woundings and the like'—are represented in such a way that they induce an emotional *and* moral purge (*katharsis*).[27] The task that falls to an interested spectator like Aristotle (as well, of course, to all those who have tried to make sense of his *Poetics*) is thus to explain, firstly, how it is that tragedies produce this cathartic effect, and secondly, what kind of effect the catharsis actually is. How is it that an audience can be moved to tears by the fate of a fictional character remote from them in time and space? And what, if any, bearing do these tears have upon the character of the citizen-body? Does the tragic festival (as Plato imagined) appeal to the basest feelings in the individual and spread an epidemic of uncontrolled grief or does it rather (as Aristotle *appeared* to claim) carry ethical significance as a reflection on why things go wrong in political life?

For Aristotle, one key to the puzzle of tragedy as cathartic event is found in those plot devices that make the shift from high to low—overman to outcast, sovereign to suppliant—at once completely unexpected and entirely plausible. As well as being itself the imitation (*mimesis*) of an action, tragedy encourages a certain kind of mimetic identification between audience and protagonist by utilizing the devices of 'reversals' (*peripeteiai*) and 'discoveries' (*anagnorisis*). In the paradigmatic case of Oedipus, it is the discovery of his true identity that brings about a dramatic, and unexpected, reversal in fortune. As he (and we) learn—but too late, of course—who he really is, Oedipus the saviour turns into Oedipus the pariah. In the blink of an eye we see the man and his kingdom collapse, both undone by actions prosecuted under mistaken premises. Oedipus, notoriously, takes out his eyes in horror at the spectacle he has made of himself, but as he and the audience now realize, he has actually been blind all along. Unaware of who he really was and thus of *what he was actually doing* when he murdered Laius and married Jocasta, he remains oblivious to his irreversible breaches of the most sacred of taboos until the effects (like Oedipus himself) have multiplied and run beyond his control. When the great fall comes—and few fall harder than Oedipus—it is thus as surprising as it is plausible.

As Aristotle notes, the catharsis of tragedy depends upon the audience realizing that what happens to Oedipus could just as easily happen to them. Once they grasp that they too act blindly, never fully aware of who they are or what they are doing, they are moved to feelings of 'pity and fear'—pity for the undeserved suffering of the hero and fear that a similar fate might just as well befall them. But, as Schmidt is careful to point out, the catharsis that tragedy solicits has a bearing upon political life (or goes beyond a simple emotional purge) because it relates to the revelation we have about action rather than the identification we have with character. Following Aristotle, who instructively insisted one could have tragedy without character-study but not without plot-action (*praxis*), Schmidt links the catharsis of tragedy to the glimpse it offers, through the temporal concentration it produces, 'into the possibilities of action as such'.[28] Unlike epic, he notes, which makes use of narrative in order to unfold a story that takes place over a long period of time, tragedy makes use of dialogue, 'the supreme form of language in action', to heighten the tension. Used in conjunction with the plot devices of reversals and discoveries that change everything in a flash, the dialogic form works to compress the drama and, as it were, heat it up. For Schmidt, the 'alchemy of pity and fear' is the product of this compression and heat. Exposed, over a short period of time, to a dramatic upheaval in the life of the hero, the audience of citizen-spectators is able to 'enjoy' a diluted but still powerfully affecting sense of what happens to those 'who suffer a *praxis*'.[29]

As Schmidt would have it, the benefit of suffering a praxis by proxy is that it brings insight into the nature of action, into its opacity and contingency, without having to experience a trauma: 'one learns to see, without, like Oedipus, needing to go blind'.[30] For him, it is only because it preserves this relationship with sight (with seeing 'things'—life, action, and the life of action that is politics—more clearly) that the catharsis of tragedy exceeds an emotional purge and becomes beneficial to the soul. 'Just as sometimes the air is uncommonly clear after a storm', he writes, 'so too does the soul achieve a sort of clarification after fear and pity have moved through it.'[31] Aristotle, instructively, was of the view that the ethical nature of this clarification would be placed in jeopardy by tragic spectacles that were too visually dazzling. If the playwright resorted to gimmicks to startle the audience, exploiting, for instance, the horror of bloody eye sockets, the soul would be 'kidnapped' by the staging and the catharsis bungled. Only when this imitation of an action brings us to an understanding of error (*hamartia*), of how we go wrong and why we go wrong, does it produce a catharsis that contributes to ethico-political life.[32] Oedipus, we see, fails through no fault (or perhaps little fault) of his own. Blind to his own identity, he is unable to grasp how his actions pollute his family and his city until it is too late. His suffering, like that of many of the tragic heroes, arises from the untimeliness of his knowledge—if only he had been recognized or, perhaps more to the point, recognized himself sooner. But the knowledge Oedipus 'wins' the hard way is 'won' by the audience the easy way. As pity and fear move through them, they learn about what can happen, even to the best, when one is required to exercise a form of reflective judgement; that is, to make decisions (and to act upon them) under conditions of imperfect knowledge.

The central claim of Schmidt's highly illuminating account, then, is that the 'kathartic effect is indexed not to the characters and our feelings about them, but to the action and the reflection of the possibilities of human life that such action offers us.'[33] As spectators to the pain of others in tragedy, we learn about the opacity and contingency that belongs not to this or that action but to human *praxis* as such. No-one who finds themselves, like Oedipus, at the crossroads where decisions have to be made can be completely confident they are doing the right thing because no-one ever enjoys full knowledge of their identity or situation. As Schmidt notes, the spheres of knowing and acting are incommensurate and it is by illuminating that gap between knowledge and action that tragedy sheds light on our errors of judgement, including, perhaps, the error we make in judging other actors too harshly for their poor decisions. Sophocles' *Oedipus Rex* shows the audience that good people can go wrong, badly wrong, because judgement is an imperfect science. For Aristotle (and here he differs sharply from Plato) there is simply no way around this. Errors of judgement cannot be eradicated from human *praxis* because the knowledge (of self and situation) upon which they are based can never be total—can never, in other words, be divine. For Schmidt, catharsis is the healthy response the audience has in the face of this revelation about the non-sovereign nature of action (about our inability, that is, to control it from beginning to end). Being in the theatre gives them an insight into the truth of *praxis*—an abyssal truth which, being difficult to confront directly, might otherwise elude them.[34]

The significance of this focus upon *praxis* for our enquiry is worth underlining (especially since Aristotle's *Poetics* is not always read in this action-centred way). Of particular note here is the way tragedy, *as a mimesis of an action*, shapes the cathartic experience, preserving within it a certain critical or interrogative power. As Olga Taxidou (in agreement with Schmidt) has pointed out, the performative element of tragedy to which Aristotle draws our attention—the fact that it does not just expose the audience to a collection of characters but re-enacts a drama upon a civic stage in a distant time and place—undoes the illusion of intimacy and helps to ensure that the pity and fear experienced by the audience retains an intellectual as well as an emotional dimension. 'In emphasizing the crucial role of action over character', she writes, 'Aristotle is proposing a reading of tragedy that allows for a rather dispassionate experience on the part of the audience.'[35] In saying this, Taxidou is not suggesting the audience is insensitive to what is happening on stage, simply that their sensitivities are not so bound up with the fate of the hero as to preclude reflection upon the nature of error. Since feelings of pity and fear are triggered by an insight into the frailties of *praxis* rather than a simple identification with the suffering of heroes, tragedy does not have the corrupting influence that Plato feared. Quite the contrary. In tragedy, emotional purgation is not so much the enemy of critical understanding as the means of it—to watch a tragic play is to undergo a paradoxical 'cleaning by mud', an experience that is as intellectual as it is emotional and as spiritual as it is physical.[36]

A Different Catharsis? 275

Perhaps because it is something of a blind spot in Aristotle too, Schmidt does not pay much attention to the so-called 'civic dimension' of tragedy.[37] The cathartic insight the genre yields into the nature of *praxis* is understood largely at the level of the individual and what might happen in life. Yet, it does not take much to recognize that the question of *hamartia* (of how we go wrong and why we go wrong) is of the greatest significance to the city as well. As tragedy shows again and again, bad decisions—by which I mean decisions that turn out to be bad or which become cognizable as bad *in hindsight*—do not just cause the downfall of the hero, they bring ruin to the city.[38] In the theatre (and here we see one expression of its transgressive, boundary-dissolving character) the personal and the political are so inextricably intertwined that the destruction of one becomes the destruction of the other. A powerful case could in fact be made that the 'true protagonist' of tragedy, as Simon Critchley puts it, 'is not the tragic hero, but the city itself'.[39] In many, though perhaps not all, the plays, the fractures in the civic self that Lethe helps bury are exhumed with devastating force, drawing our attention to way the city is never entirely at one with itself and never fully capable of holding the past where it belongs.[40] Again and again we see the *polis* ripped apart by unquiet graves, as if tragedy had no other purpose than to bring civic trauma to consciousness or, to cite Critchley once more, to reveal the city in its 'attempt to confront and cleanse monstrous pollution'.[41]

For evidence of this we scarcely need to look further afield than Aristotle's favoured example of the *Oedipus Rex*. As the symbolic head of Thebes, Oedipus is more or less interchangeable with the civic self.[42] Hence the error he makes when he falls into that unbridgeable gap between knowledge and action does not just cast a shadow over his sovereignty, it pollutes the city and robs it of vitality—here, as ever in tragedy, legitimacy and life are thoroughly interwoven. With the (as yet undisclosed) murder of father by son and marriage of son to mother—the first an inverted version of Thucydides' symbolic reduction of civil war, the second a perversion of the ancient symbol of reconciliation—a plague takes hold that makes babies shrivel in the womb, drying up all life at its source. Nothing can flourish, nothing can grow. As in the divided states of today, the renewal of the city of Thebes hinges upon the discovery of a buried truth and, as in those states too, exhumation exposes something that few can bear to see: what Oedipus, in a clear-eyed estimation of the monstrosity of his deeds, calls 'crimes too huge for hanging'.[43] Ironically enough, in his investigative digging into the murder of Laius, Oedipus succeeds only in digging up himself. Up on stage, the sovereign unmasks the sovereign and in doing so reveals himself in a new light: 'I've stripped myself', he says, 'exposed my guilt'.[44] Having lived all of his life hidden from himself,

Oedipus now seems to have no higher desire than to bring the crime—which is, of course, nothing but himself—out into the open. Exposure, the calamity he suffered at the beginning of his life when he was abandoned to the elements by the caretakers of the child, assumes, near the end of it, a rather different significance as the voluntary self-punishment of the caretaker of the city. Appalled, as it were, by what he now sees about himself, the guilty sovereign makes a decision to stand naked in his shame.

It is precisely at this point of the drama, however, that we, the audience begin to realise just how hard it can be to hold the ugly truth of sovereign violation (and all its category disturbing effects) in our sight. In one sense, of course, Oedipus can now lay claim to being the good sovereign who does the right thing. By uncovering himself as the murderer of Laius and standing naked before his subjects, he placates the gods and brings an end to the curse that has destroyed life in the city. The miasma lifts and vitality returns. However, when crimes too huge for hanging are brought out into the open, they do not have an entirely salutary effect on the political community. At the same time as it ends the plague, the act of exposure severs the relation of mutual regard between people and sovereign: henceforth Oedipus can no longer look upon the city or the city look upon him. 'Now I've exposed my guilt', he says, 'could I train a level glance on you, my countrymen? Impossible.'[45] Creon, reciprocally, will upbraid the guards for allowing Oedipus to leave the palace and present himself in public: 'Never expose a thing of guilt and holy dread so great it appalls the earth, the rain from heaven, the light of day!' 'Kindred alone', he goes on, 'should see a kinsman's shame. This is obscene.'[46] Although his crimes are committed unknowingly, Oedipus breaks every taboo and erases every distinction to the point where he is, in a very real sense, *constitutionally* wrong. The question is thus not simply whether he can bear the light but whether the light can bear him. In striking out his eyes, Oedipus secures himself against a public gaze incapable of disguising its horror. But how is that public to be protected from him? Must they strike out their eyes before the ugly truth of this ill-constituted sovereign body too? Ultimately it is left to Creon to end the obscenity of this exposure by leading Oedipus inside the palace and then into exile. Only with his departure can the city open its eyes again.

As well as delivering insight into the non-sovereign, boundless nature of *praxis*, then, *Oedipus Rex* delivers insight into the dreadful legacy of 'going wrong' and the difficulty of not looking away in the face of the truth. As Terry Eagleton has suggested, tragedy 'rubs our noses in the irreparable'. Through its performance we receive a striking testament of the fact that '[t]ruth is unaesthetic'—'it reminds us of beauty only by negation'.[47] In mythical Thebes, patricide and incest (both instances of something—hate and love—that turns inward when it should turn outward) emerge as the hidden truth of the symbolic order, with the jumbled pairs 'mother-wife', 'son-husband', 'father-brother' serving not simply to undermine the legitimacy of the sovereign but to throw doubt on the very existence of the boundaries and demarcations that sustain political life.[48] Always doubled, always divided, always two where there should be one (father and brother) and one where there should be two (son and husband), Oedipus emerges as the unassimilable truth of the hidden double: the barbarism *in* civilization, the wildness *in* the city, the beast *in* the sovereign. To see Oedipus stripped in his guilt is, in other words, to see more than one can bear: a pollution so deeply mixed into the body of the sovereign that it is beyond purification. The messenger who says barely anything effectively still says it all when he remarks: 'I tell you neither the waters of the Danube nor the Nile can wash this palace clean.'[49] Best, then, if the king must wander that he wander outside the city, away from Thebes and back into the wilds where the categories of civilization are not expected to apply and no-one is forced to look on.

Oedipus would never be seen in, or by, Thebes again. But he would, of course, be seen in and by Athens. Sophocles' masterpiece, hailed by Aristotle as the high-point of tragic drama, would be staged over and over for the civic festivals of the Dionysia, allowing the city of Athens to watch the spectacle of the city of Thebes reeling from the spectacle of Oedipus. In the city of democracy, the guilty sovereign, whose crimes offend against nature and exceed the law, will be granted the over-life that his own city denied him—an eternal return which, even now, still returns. However, unlike the over-life of that other guilty sovereign we encountered in Chapter 1 whose crimes, being fully intentional, truly were too huge for hanging, Oedipus does not survive in the imagination by virtue of an unconscious defence mechanism triggered in the psychological emergency. Instead he lives on as an aesthetic object, which, having been consciously produced, is fully available to human comprehension and reflection. By putting Oedipus on the stage, Sophocles makes it possible for the city to see what, in the affairs of the city itself, is difficult, if not impossible, to see: a thing of guilt so great it appals the earth. In drama, the horror of the leader gone wrong and the city polluted—a horror by no means unknown to Athens—is staged in such a way as to make it assimilable. In short, Oedipus (and his crimes) can be buried in Athens (as they literally are in *Oedipus at Colonus*), but only because Athens (and its crimes) had first been transported to Thebes.

Would we be justified in seeing this as a kind of 'working through'? Is it possible, in other words, that tragedy does not just stage mourning as a site of contest but is itself an instrument of it; a civic tool in which distancing (or doubling) provides a means for reflecting upon and dealing with loss? The idea is by no means implausible. 'If tragedy is all about doubling', notes Critchley, 'then the subject who is doubled over in tragedy is the *polis* itself, divided and in some cases destroyed by the opposed forces that constitute what Hegel would see as the substance of ethical life.'[50] In tragedy, the original trauma of politics—the primacy of division—is replayed over and over as wives kill husbands (and vice versa), parents kill children (and vice versa), and brothers take their bloody revenge upon each other.[51] And yet, if tragedy is the endlessly repeated story of the divided city—of the city that loses itself— it is a story held sufficiently far away from its witnesses as to make it amenable to critical reflection and cathartic incorporation. As well as being doubled on stage, the city is doubled *through* staging, creating a critical mirror for the audience to reflect upon itself. Assembled as a city, but away from the factional divides and historical grievances of *their* politics, the citizens of Athens found themselves exposed to a diluted form of the original trauma of politics and suffered a *praxis* by proxy. For this collective subject, the catharsis of tragedy cannot just be about, and may not even be primarily about, the pity and fear one has as a private individual about what can happen in life.[52] It must also be about the horror they feel (and the clarity they achieve) *as citizens* in the face of those unassimilable political truths from which they were perpetually in flight: that the city is divided, not united; that the boundaries which constitute it—particularly the boundary between friend and enemy, public and private—are unstable; and that the wounds of the past can neither be forgotten nor healed.[53]

Doubtless it would be going too far to suggest that tragedy was less the show than the substance of Athenian democracy. If the Assembly, the Council, and the Courts were given over to the more mundane business of governing and the containment of a thoroughly agonistic culture, they were hardly insubstantial supplements to the annual tragic festival of the Great Dionysia. And yet, as a site where the problem of the city—the problem of the city as an ununified unity—was reflected and engaged at the most profound level, tragedy played a far more significant role in Athenian political life than has often been credited. In tragedy, and in tragedy alone, the actions that bring the city into conflict with itself and others, the actions that expose it in its divisions and embroil it in the problem of life, are put on display and, in that way, made available for critical reflection and affective engagement.[54] Only here, in this exceptional institution, was the body of citizen-spectators given an opportunity to look in the mirror and take stock of the damage that the city had done to itself and others through the creation (and imperial expansion) of a democratic form of life. As Paul Cartledge observes in a piece bearing the instructive subtitle 'Theatre as Process in Greek Civic Life', tragedy provided Athens with a much-needed time and space to *process* a turbulent history and bring its own civic ideology into question.[55]

But—and this, it seems to me, is the critical point—not through a direct confrontation with that turbulent history. Following Froma Zeitlin, it does not seem unreasonable to conclude that the displacement to other places and other times that was characteristic of Greek tragedy played an indispensable role for Athenians, not simply as a guardian of reputation but as a vehicle of mourning. Of course, by locating all the troubles somewhere else, tragedy allows Athens to 'escape the tragic' and sustain an image of itself as the city of order and justice. On the rare occasions when it makes an appearance within the plays (*Oedipus in Colonus* being one), it is as the beautiful city of sanctuary and reconciliation: the other place where refuge is offered and wounds are healed. But displacement is also (and more importantly) what makes it possible for the Athenian audience to plumb the depths of civic discord. Thebes, on Zeitlin's reading, is like a 'shadow self' of Athens, a city within the city, that allows it to 'play with and discharge' both its attraction to and its terror of 'the irreconcilable, the inexpiable, and the unredeemable'.[56] If Thebes has a political function, in other words, it is not simply to make Athens look good (though it clearly does that too), it is to open the door to reflection and catharsis through the repetitive re-enactment of civic trauma. As Zeitlin notes, it is essential not for Thebes but *for Athens* that the city of Oedipus continually survive its self-inflicted wounds. However catastrophic the disasters that befall it, she writes, Thebes must 'remain intact as a theatrical enclosure so that within its closed confines yet another play may be staged that reenacts in some way these same intricate and inextricable conflicts that can never be resolved'.[57] Put simply, to return to a phrase from Jenny Edkins, Thebes is the place where Athens 'confronts its trauma without compromise'.

In keeping with the desire not to romanticize, it should be noted here that the 'theatrical enclosure' provided by tragedy was by no means fully secured against 'leakage'. In *Antigone Interrupted*, Bonnie Honig rightly ponders whether the Greek 'institutions of exception' that returned mourning to the public stage—with the first being the funeral oration and the second being tragedy—were able to spark, without at the same time inflaming, the inner fires of disruption and loss. For her, the performance of grief within Sophocles' *Antigone*—particularly that of Creon whose cry of '*aiee!*' upon the death of his wife Eurydice undoes the very distinctions between man and woman, public and private, democracy and aristocracy, economic and uneconomic mourning, which the play sets up—'highlights the concern that exception-institutions like these cannot turn to totally constructive purposes the very forces and emotions those institutions seek to contain, manage, elicit'.[58] On her reading, the problem depicted by the play—the problem not just of *who* one should mourn but of *how* one should mourn—is ultimately uncontained by it. When Creon succumbs to the very practice he has forbidden and 'mourns like a woman' in public, it is no longer clear what separates the *polis* from the *oikos* or democracy from aristocracy—grief has gotten off the leash and out of the house.[59] The performance of *Antigone* thus puts at risk the political function of tragedy as an exception-institution that arouses prohibited forces and emotions so as to sublimate and derive insight from them.[60] To acknowledge the risk is not, however, to deny the effort taken to minimize it. As arresting, even devastating, as its portrayal of interwoven familial/civic trauma often is, tragedy never renounces its aesthetic (and might we also say psychological?) commitment to displacement. The limit on proximity, inadvertently set by Phrynicus when he brought the Athenians face to face with the siege of Miletus, was never transgressed.[61]

The point we must come back to here, then, is the point with which we began: the catharsis of tragedy can be critical as well as emotional because the praxis suffered by the hero and by the city is 'mediated by the distance of the theatre'.[62] As Schmidt and many other commentators on the Great Dionysia confirm, it is the tragic form, with its aesthetic conventions, its spatial and temporal displacements, and its concern with action, that enables the audience to engage both critically and emotionally with what happens on stage. If the truths revealed by tragedy are confronting in their ugliness, the medium itself is not confrontational in the literal sense of the word because the audience is not being brought 'face to face' with disasters of their own making.[63] 'Tragedies', notes Martha Nussbaum, 'deal with matters that are difficult to confront, but they do so in a way that is made palatable to a squeamish audience.'[64] As well as the seductions of poetry, which soften 'death, torture, woundings and the like' by cloaking them in aesthetic dress, there is the sense of otherworldliness created by the adaptation of the Homeric stories from long ago. As the debacle of the *Capture of Miletus* revealed, in the absence of that sense of distance secured through myth, the emotional overruns the critical and the possibility of ethical insight is severely curtailed. Miletus was simply too close to the present and the heart to give rise to universal truths about the nature of *praxis* or the irreparable effects of going wrong. All the audience could see was itself.[65]

II Proximity and Intimacy

At the end of his discussion of the Great Dionysia in *Love, Sex and Tragedy*, Simon Goldhill asks: '[w]here in the public life of Western society could we look for any such equivalent critical and emotional civic engagement?'[66] To which critics (including this one) have been tempted to answer: in those new institutions of exception in which the state returns attention to *its* civil wounds—the public memorial, the political apology, and the truth commission.[67] Timothy Garton Ash was, perhaps, overstating the resemblance between the ancients and the moderns when he declared that the objective of the South African TRC was simply to 'establish the truth, insofar as it can ever be established; if possible to achieve a collective catharsis, very much as Aristotle envisaged catharsis in Greek tragedy; and move on.'[68] The reason, however, he is able to make such allusions (and the reason he is not alone in making them) is because the similarity between these ancient and modern institutions of exception is, in fact, quite striking.[69] Just as the institution of tragedy functioned as a 'ritual of the city as a city',[70] the institutions of repentance function as a ritual of the state as a state. In both cases, an audience composed of the citizen-body is given an opportunity to go back over (or represent) a cataclysmic action in which suffering takes centre stage; in both cases, that audience is invited to reflect upon the problem of error or going wrong (*hamartia*) in politics; and in both cases it is forced to suffer, or led to undergo, a catharsis of pity and fear.[71]

Taking a lead from Charles Segal, one could, in fact, push the analogy further still and suggest that these ancient and modern 'institutions of exception' are functionally similar in the way they help citizens negotiate crises in the state, and not just by purging them of troubling emotions but by granting them a kind of 'double vision'.[72] For not only are these exceptional institutions sites where the audience of citizen-spectators gets to see and hear its 'others' (the ones, that is, which they have either excluded from their politics or attempted to exterminate through their wars), they are also sites where those citizen-spectators are encouraged to look otherwise at the political world and rethink the nature of community. In both the modern and the ancient case, it is the voices of the excluded and attacked that provide the means by which the state holds a critical mirror up to itself, exposing the ways in which (to invoke Habermas' phrase) it has sustained itself by usurping and destroying the lives of others. If one can look past the fictional setting, the agonized laments of the wives and mothers that issue from the stage in *The Trojan Women* are not so different from those that ring out from the report into the Stolen Generations or the hearings of the South African TRC, and nor are they absent at the Memorial to the Murdered Jews where the mute *stelae*, with fitting pathos, are left to do all the talking. In all these instances, polyphony becomes the order of the day as the audience gets access to voices that bring into question the distinctions upon which the democratic political order is founded: friend and enemy, public and private, the sacred and the everyday.[73] Evocatively, if temporarily, another kind of politics appears in the space of appearances; one in which human vulnerability, exposure to violence, and mourning in the face of loss emerge as an alternative basis for community.

And yet, bearing in mind Loraux's caution against the 'demon of analogy', one might fairly question how deep these resemblances truly run. As we have already noted, there is one obvious difference between our modern institutions of exception and that of the Great Dionysia: with state repentance there is no mythical world of Homeric invention standing between audience and wound (and thus no displacement in space and time) to create the sense of distance which almost all commentators on Greek tragedy deem indispensable to its ability to engage citizens both critically and emotionally in the action. While the civil wounds of the modern nation-state are still mediated through an institutional form and still subject to the conventions of a genre, they turn out to be a far more distressing sight to behold because the 'discoveries' and 'reversals' that they bring into play bear directly upon the audience itself. When the exhumation finally takes place and the stories of damaged life are returned to the light, the political community inevitably discovers something unpleasant about *its* identity, something many within it would prefer remained buried. Like Oedipus, it suffers a moment of belated or tragic recognition (*anagnorisis*) that changes the whole way it sees itself and, of course, is seen by others.[74] The reversal this discovery brings about can take a variety of different forms—it is the liberal shown up as illiberal, the peaceable shown up as violent, the civilized shown up as barbarian. But in every case, it is a difficult thing to confront because it points to the fact that the citizen-body, once again like Oedipus, is 'constitutionally wrong'. Tiresias, as usual, hits the nail on the head: 'How terrible—to see the truth when the truth is only pain to him who sees!'[75]

If the exceptional institutions associated with the healing of nations are no less a theatre than the theatre of Dionysius, then, it would seem to be a theatre in which the audience is the actor most brutally exposed.[76] Addressed in their shameful complicity, if not their direct guilt, the citizen-spectators at these events are effectively offered no place to hide. Like the Spanish public forced to bear witness to the bodies exhumed from mass graves, they are brought face to face with what they, or at least those who exercised sovereign power, went to great lengths to disappear. In such cases, to be exposed *to* the wound is to be exposed *by* the wound (and suffer the sense of shame that falls upon those shown up as constitutionally wrong). Naturally one worries—more out of respect for the disappeared than the language—about straining this metaphor any further. But in a sense, of course, every attempt at recovering historical memory, every public recognition of a past injustice, is a bit like an exhumation. Through truth telling, the body bearing the marks of foul play is exposed to the light again and in the quietness of its destruction it delivers its silent accusation. The fact that such accusations can, in the majority of cases, no longer be heard by the law does nothing to diminish their power as a 'voice' of admonition.[77] For in these moments of exposure a question inevitably imposes itself: what kind of a society does this or, since the second question logically follows the first, what kind of a society *is* this?[78]

The tortured and destroyed body that reappears after it is disappeared may well be the ultimate expression of the unaesthetic nature of truth, for it is truly a disgusting sight, as ugly to behold as the ugliness to which it bears witness. Testifying to an infringement of the burial rite as well as the civic right, it 'speaks' (as does the exposed body of Polynices in *Antigone*) of a crime doubled over, of an offence to earth and heaven that puts not just the civility but the humanity of the perpetrator into question. Is any truth more clearly revealed by such exhumations than that of Hobbes' *homo homini lupus est*? But, of course, when it comes to the so-called 'ugly truth', it may be just a matter of degrees. In the age of apology, almost every re-presentation of the civil wound has the potential to give rise to a sense of shame among 'the people' because they are the ones who variously committed, observed, disregarded, or benefited from the mistreatment of those exposed to death in the state of exception. To the extent that such representations reflect the violence of the citizen-body back to itself like a critical mirror, they too give it every reason to feel disgusted in itself. For this citizen-body, there is none of the safety, and none of the comfort, the Greeks derived from gazing at their misfortunes obliquely. Instead, the civil wound is pressed hard upon the public as witness, forcing it to face itself not analogically and indirectly but bluntly and truthfully in its constitutional wrongness. Or so it would seem.

Since the constitutionally wrong are obscene to behold, and never more so than when one recognizes them as a reflection of oneself, it does not seem unreasonable to ask whether that 'constitutional wrongness' really is what the spectacle of repentance makes visible to the audience. Is it possible that such events actually evade the ugly truth; that the illusion of a shared humanity they create through their proximity and intimacy allows us to look away from the structural problems of the state? As we have already observed on a number of occasions, one index (perhaps the true index) of the power exercised by public memorials, political apologies, and truth commissions as biopolitical interventions is the way they 'move' the audience through empathetic identification. As the citizen-spectators listen to the stories of those who suffered *for no good reason*, they are brought to the realization that it might just as well have been them. For, if there really was 'no good reason'—no deviance, misdemeanour, or crime—to merit suffering, the only thing separating the exposed from the protected was blind luck. Pity for the other, who *was* damaged, is thus tied up with fear for the self, who *might* have been damaged, in a way that bears a certain resemblance to the experience of the citizen-spectators at the performance of Greek tragedy. Arguably, however, the catharsis generated in our modern institutions of exception loses the political significance it carried in Great Dionysia because the sense of similar possibilities it relies on takes its bearings from character rather than action. By pivoting around the intimacies of undeserved individual suffering, the truth telling performed in the modern institution of exception tends only to cultivate a sense of the tragedy of human existence; a sense, in other words, that bad things can happen to anyone as a result of our universal exposure, *as human beings*, to the vicissitudes of life. The role of state racism in allocating life chances, in variously exposing and protecting different lives (and different forms of life), is obscured, inhibiting critical interrogation of the friend–enemy distinction at the heart of the nation-state form.

The great irony here is that the assumption of similar possibilities that arouses compassion for the wounded other is the assumption that vitiates the need to interrogate the nation-state as a structure of organized violence. Seen from a critical perspective, the most important question to pose in the face of those stories of damaged life is not 'what if this had happened to us?' but rather 'why did this not happen to us?' Only in the presence of that question is emotional identification with character likely to turn into critical interrogation of action. Only then might the citizen-spectators assembled as witness come to the realization that the pain and suffering the modern institution of exception puts on display has nothing to do with the 'tragedy of life' and everything to do with the sovereign state and the biopolitical logic that serves it with its 'reasons' for protecting who it protects and exposing who it exposes. The value of tragedy as a counterpoint in this context is that it helps the audience come to terms with loss, not so much by trying to heal it away as by clarifying its causes. Tragedy, at least on the sympathetic reading I have provided here, is spectacle as clarification, not spectacle as voyeurism. It stages suffering not to enable sympathetic identification but to provide insight into the frailty of action, the contingency of political boundaries, and the truth of the irreparable. All the audience is inclined to see in the modern institution of exception is themselves or, more accurately perhaps, an unlucky version of themselves.[79]

It is, to be sure, extremely hazardous, methodologically and politically, to generalize across the three different institutions of exception examined in detail in this book: the Memorial to the Murdered Jews of Europe, the Apology to the Stolen Generations, and the South African sTRC. Not only are they embedded in different historical contexts and staged through different institutional structures, they also respond to quite specific national 'crises'. At the same time, we are not lacking in evidence that the interest in healing common to them all overdetermines the way they operate as public spectacles, tipping the balance in favour of emotional discharge rather than critical reflection. Quentin Stevens may, perhaps, have exaggerated the situation when he chose 'nothing more than feelings' for the title of one of his essays on the Memorial to the Murdered Jews.[80] But his sense of things being 'felt' rather than 'seen' is by no means at odds with the argument developed in this book, nor is it restricted to the one institution of exception (the Memorial) that he examines in detail.[81] In all of the cases examined, one can detect a certain disconnect between the emotional and the critical. Although the suffering of 'the other' is earnestly staged and keenly felt, the link between that suffering and the political structures of the nation-state seems to be obfuscated rather than clarified. Indeed, by encouraging us to re-cognize loss and grief as part of the human condition, as something, in other words, that we share with those we have othered, we allow psychological identification to displace political insight. In the modern institution of exception, it is all about character rather than action.

III Catharsis without Clarification?

According to Honig, 'our debt to Sophocles is his invitation, still fresh and unfortunately, still much needed, to look hard at the myriad ways in which we silence the grief that in our politics we yet do so much to generate'.[82] The point is compelling, but not in its entirety. For while it is obvious that 'our politics' has been a source of grief, it is less obvious that allowing that grief to speak will have beneficial outcomes (not least for those for whom 'our politics' has brought so much grief). Although our modern institutions of exception resemble the ancient in their willingness to engage with mourning, they seem to lack that aspect of double vision that Segal perceives and champions in tragedy. Overdetermined by an interest in healing, the memorial, the apology, and the commission incline towards a purely therapeutic catharsis or what, to underline the contrast with tragedy, might be described as a catharsis without clarification. In all of the cases we examined, the interest in healing works, at one and the same time, to open and close our eyes.

On the one hand, it encourages us to see the victims of sovereign violence as people like us, vulnerable human beings who are exposed to harm and who suffer loss. On the other hand, it allows us to continue largely as before by inhibiting reflection on the nature of action and the limits of the state form. Arguably, this seeing and unseeing are but two sides of the same coin. The basis upon which we are able to feel the pain of the other and share in their mourning is the forgetting of the fact that the nation-state is founded on the friend–enemy, public–private distinction. Sharing in the suffering of others becomes easy (or, at least, easier) because it does not carry with it the responsibility of critically interrogating the political form in which 'the people' is constituted through the exclusion of others—others whose lives are thereby placed at risk. Emotional identification in shared mourning, one might hazard, is the precise form of seeing/unseeing sponsored by our modern institutions of exception. Consoled by the grand myth of similar possibilities (the idea that this could just as easily have happened to us), we forget that the modern, biopolitical state is inherently selective in its valuation of life, invariably exposing some as it shields others.

Two important qualifications must, however, be introduced in relation to this 'thesis'. In the first place, Schmidt's (ethical) reading of the *katharsis* of tragedy is by no means uncontested. While Goldhill too is of the view that 'the "pity" and "fear" aroused by tragedy leads to a cleansed *moral awareness* of what it means to be a citizen' (emphasis added), others treat it as little more than an emotional purge.[83] According to Simon Critchley, for instance, '[i]t is highly dubious that Aristotle wishes to attribute any ethical significance to tragedy'. 'A more minimalist view of catharsis', he adds, 'would simply see it as the outcome of the emotions of pity and fear aroused by the drama.'[84] Terry Eagleton, even more damningly, suggests Aristotle valued tragedy precisely because 'it performs the politically vital service of draining off from the polis a perilous surplus of pity and fear'—both of which he regarded as socially enfeebling emotions. On this reading of things, tragedy invigorates more than it enlightens because it functions (in proto-biopolitical fashion) as 'a kind of public therapy for a citizenry in danger of emotional flabbiness'.[85] Although I'm inclined to think that Schmidt's reading is better or, at least, more faithful to Aristotle than Critchley's or Eagleton's because it leaves room for the reflexivity that both of them attribute to (and continue to celebrate in) tragedy, there is ultimately no way of really knowing what the plays did to, or for, their audience.[86] One must admit the possibility, however reluctantly, that the Great Dionysia really was just a great release valve.

Secondly, although I have purposely exaggerated the contrast between the ancient and the modern for the purposes of this argument, our own institutions of exception may not be quite as radically other to tragedy as I have thus far made out. While the biopolitical investment in healing clearly does impact upon the way these institutions of exception function in the political life of the state, they are not entirely without reflexive power. The more one reviews them (or views them again) through the lens of tragedy, the more one can recognize the way in which they too function as 'other places', a kind of shadow state within the state, where the political community is reflected back to itself and citizens are granted a glimpse, however fleeting, of the problematic character of the friend–enemy, public–private distinctions upon which the state is founded. As noted earlier, in recreating the sense of disorientation and claustrophobia of the concentration camp, the Memorial to the Murdered Jews allows citizens to suffer a trauma by proxy and similar effects are induced by other institutions of truth telling that force citizens to revisit scenes of 'death, torture, woundings and the like' in a temporally concentrated way. Indeed, if Adrian Poole is right and 'tragedy represents the critical moments when words fail', then there is clearly more than a little bit of tragedy lurking in political apologies and truth commissions.[87] Nomonde Calata's 'indefinable wail' (to take just one example) would scarcely be out of place among *The Trojan Women* and points, in its own way, to the danger of the friend–enemy calculus and the limits of psychological repair. Amidst all the talk of a therapeutic catharsis and collective mourning, that indefinable wail emerges as the abyssal truth that sparks critical reflection precisely because it is defies identification. Like tragedy, it issues a sharp reproof to the discourse of healing and reconciliation, forcing the political community to confront the irreconcilable, the inexpiable, and the unredeemable.[88]

Although it has come to appear self-evidently necessary, then, an interest in healing may well be a barrier to critical reflection—particularly on our own *constitutional* wrongness. Shame is an uncomfortable emotion, especially when it lingers, because it goes to the core of our being. The value of apologies (and other gestures of repentance) for the constitutionally wrong lies precisely in the fact that they allow them to shake off that sense of shame and get on with life. Not even the sincerest of apologies is, however, an adequate response to injustice unless it is accompanied by critical interrogation of the nature of political community and the underlying causes of the biopolitical fracture that sees some people within 'the people' exposed to exclusion and extermination. Critchley, it seems to me, glibly underestimates the significance of repentance to the revaluation of damaged life when he writes, 'the political world is stuffed overfull with sham shame, ham humility, and carefully staged tearful apologies: I'm so sorry; I'm so, so sorry. But true shame is something else'.[89] But he may well be on to something with the idea of 'true shame'. If the shame of Oedipus is politically productive, it is because its inexpiable character reveals something—something truly terrible—about the nature and frailty of action (*praxis*). The truth we grasp through the staging of *Oedipus Rex* is abyssal (for there is clearly a horror attached to the gap between knowledge and action), but it is a truth nonetheless. What insight into the political do we gain from the presentation of the wound in the theatres of the modern nation-state? If the analysis presented here has any merit, the answer may well be very little or, at least, not enough. Although the institutions of exception we have examined clearly do have cathartic effects, those effects seem to arise from a precise inversion of the movement of Greek tragedy: where the latter politicizes suffering by linking it to the blindness of action, the former de-politicizes action by reducing it to the universality of suffering. Presented as the essence of community, the loss and grief suffered by *all* vulnerable humans becomes, in fact, the mask of the political, shielding the citizen-spectators from precisely the question of *hamartia* (error) that tragedy brings so powerfully to the fore.

Notes

1. N. Loraux, *Tragic Ways of Killing a Woman*, Cambridge, MA: Harvard University Press, 1991, p. 64.
2. Loraux, *Tragic Ways of Killing a Woman*, p. 33.
3. See D.M. Carter, *The Politics of Greek Tragedy*, Exeter: Bristol Phoenix Press, 2007, pp. 131–139 and M. Nussbaum, 'Compassion and Terror', *Daedalus*, 132(1), Winter 2003, pp. 10–11. Jenny Edkins and Mark Sanders are among those to have noted that truth commissions tend to show 'women in mourning'. See J. Edkins, *Trauma and the Memory of Politics*, Cambridge: Cambridge University Press, 2003, p. 213; M. Sanders, *Complicities: The Intellectual and Apartheid*, Durham, NC: Duke University Press, 2002, pp. 198–199.
4. Carter, *The Politics of Greek Tragedy*, p. 159. See also S. Goldhill, *Love, Sex and Tragedy: How the Ancient World Shapes Our Lives*, Chicago, IL: University of Chicago Press, 2004 and O. Taxidou, *Tragedy, Modernity and Mourning*, Edinburgh: Edinburgh University Press, 2004.
5. Carter, *The Politics of Greek Tragedy*, p. 90. See also pp. 7, 19. Adrian Poole has similarly noted that tragedy does not 'teach', it asks questions—questions, posed in blood, for which there appear no answers. See A. Poole, *Tragedy: Shakespeare and the Greek Example*, Oxford: Basil Blackwell, 1987, p. 3.

6. A number of key scholars agree on this point: Taxidou sees 'the concept of mourning as central to the tragic form'; Critchley notes that 'the emotion of grief and the phenomenon of lamentation [sit] at the centre of so many tragedies, from Aeschylus's *The Persians* onward'; and Honig describes tragedy as 'the genre of devastating loss'. See S. Critchley, *Tragedy, the Greeks and Us*, London: Profile Books, 2019, p. 9; Taxidou, *Tragedy, Modernity and Mourning*, p. 8; B. Honig, *Antigone Interrupted*, Cambridge: Cambridge University Press, 2013, p. 102.
7. It is important to note that this entry of the feminine into civic discourse was hardly unequivocal. As Loraux notes in *Tragic Ways of Killing a Woman*, the boldness of tragedy in its presentation of women 'turns out to be less than one had supposed'. Taxidou, more damningly, claims that the negation of the female 'is structural and formative of tragedy itself'. Since, in tragedy, it is men who perform and men who watch mourning, it is really an aesthetic vehicle for the appropriation of the female role. Taxidou is persuasive, but her point is hard to fully reconcile with Plato's critique—does tragedy turn men into women or women into men? One could also note here Eva Keuls' claim that 'the emotions purged by drama must have been primarily those ensuing from the alienation of the sexes'. See Loraux, *Tragic Ways of Killing a Woman*, p. 62; E. Keuls, *The Reign of the Phallus: Sexual Politics in Ancient Athens*, Berkeley, CA: University of California Press, 1993, p. 348.
8. Carter, *The Politics of Greek Tragedy*, p. 141.
9. A. Poole, *Tragedy: A Very Short Introduction*, Oxford: Oxford University Press, 2005, p. 35.
10. Poole, *Tragedy: A Very Short Introduction*, pp. 35–36.
11. This is Antigone speaking with Ismene in the opening lines of the play. Sophocles, *The Three Theban Plays*, trans. by Robert Fagles, London: Penguin Books, 1984, l.1–2.
12. Loraux, *The Divided City*, p. 33.
13. As Carter notes, the Greeks did not like to be criticized directly, especially in the presence of other Greeks. Carter, *The Politics of Greek Tragedy*, p. 133.
14. Critchley, *Tragedy, the Greeks and Us*, p. 73.
15. Sophocles, *Oedipus Rex* in *The Three Theban Plays*, trans. by Fagles, l.1360–1361. Similarly, at the end of his study of the Vichy syndrome, Henri Rousso declares that his 'initial hypothesis—that internal quarrels left deeper scars than either the defeat or the German occupation—seems to have been largely confirmed'. Rousso, *The Vichy Syndrome*, p. 297.
16. Goldhill, *Love, Sex and Tragedy*, p. 228.
17. See P. Euben, *The Tragedy of Political Theory: The Road Not Taken*, Princeton, NJ: Princeton University Press, 1990, p. 51; C. Meier, *The Political Art of Greek Tragedy*, trans. by Andrew Webber, Cambridge: Polity Press, 1993, pp. 1–7; Goldhill, *Love, Sex and Tragedy*, pp. 216, 228.
18. As Michael Humphrey has noted, 'while global witnessing may have extended the reach and complexity of the politics of atrocity the primary social and spatial context for witnessing remains the nation-state'. M. Humphrey, *The Politics of Atrocity and Reconciliation: From Terror to Trauma*, London: Routledge, 2002, p. 105.
19. In a curious way, as Goldhill notes in relation to a production of *Electra* in Northern Ireland, Greek tragedy has become one of the instruments by which 'divided societies' now show their wounds to themselves. Far from rendering it irrelevant, he notes, it is the distant nature of ancient drama that allows modern audiences to understand their

self-inflicted trauma. However, the tendency for modern productions of tragedy to foreground their contemporary relevance (as, for instance, when Creon is dressed as Hitler) shows the extent to which direct confrontation is now privileged above veiled allusion as a way of moving the audience. See Goldhill, *Love, Sex and Tragedy*, p. 215.
20. S. Levinson, *Written in Stone: Public Monuments in Changing Societies*, Durham, NC: Duke University Press, 1998.
21. Martine Walser quoted in A. Lewis, 'Germany's Metamorphosis: Memory and the Holocaust in the Berlin Republic', *Cultural Studies Review*, 9(2), 2003, p. 107.
22. The following statement from Habermas, recorded in his remarks on the Memorial to the Murdered Jews of Europe, is indicative of the common view: 'The divided past will continue to hinder the cooperation of citizens in the present unless the one side takes a credible stand for conditions which make a shared life possible, even bearable, for the other side'. J. Habermas, 'The Finger of Blame: The Germans and Their Memorial', in J. Habermas, *Time of Transitions*, ed. and trans. by Ciaran Cronin and Max Pensky, Cambridge: Polity, 2006, p. 412.
23. The origins of this idea could perhaps be traced back to the work of Jaspers and Arendt. See K. Jaspers, *The Question of German Guilt*; H. Arendt, 'Collective Responsibility' in J.W. Bernauer (ed.), *Amor Mundi: Explorations in the Faith and Thought of Hannah Arendt*, Boston, MA: Martinus Nijhoff Publishers, 1987, pp. 43–50; and H. Arendt, *Eichmann in Jerusalem: A Report on the Banality of Evil*, London: Penguin, 1994, p. 298.
24. J. Thompson, *Taking Responsibility for the Past: Reparation and Historical Injustice*; R. Vernon, *Historical Redress: Must We Pay for the Past?*, London: Continuum, 2012.
25. In his analysis of the memorialization of 11 September 2001, Bradford Vivian has made some important strides in this regard. 'In our so-called society of the spectacle', he writes, 'public events—including political conventions and campaigns, state ceremonies and cultural festivals, and national and international sporting competitions—increasingly are organized to unite an otherwise fractured citizenry in a dynamic affective experience. The symbolic rituals of mass mediated spectacle offer an affective idiom that appears to engender a common civic identity from public displays of sentiment during an era of widespread political polarities, conflicting moral paradigms, and heterogeneous cultural traditions'. The analysis presented here agrees with Vivian's to the extent that it understands rituals of reconciliation as de-politicized events that play on intimacy. However, my biopolitical approach places considerably less emphasis upon symbolic integration under conditions of neoliberal fragmentation and considerably more upon therapeutic intervention into basic psychological processes of mourning and melancholia as a way of managing trauma. B. Vivian, *Public Forgetting*, p. 81.
26. G. Debord, *The Society of the Spectacle*, Detroit, MI: Black and Red, 1983, p. 5.
27. This definition draws on Schmidt's entire chapter on Aristotle, but see in particular pp. 53–61. D. Schmidt, *On Germans and Other Greeks: Tragedy and Ethical Life*, Bloomington, IN: Indiana University Press, 2001.
28. Schmidt, *On Germans and Other Greeks*, p. 54. As Aristotle noted, far from spreading itself out, tragedy tends 'to confine itself to a single revolution of the sun, or but slightly to exceed this limit'. Aristotle, 1449b13. On this point, see also Taxidou, *Tragedy, Modernity and Mourning*, pp. 111–112.
29. Schmidt, *On Germans and Other Greeks*, pp. 54–55.
30. Schmidt, *On Germans and Other Greeks*, p. 55.

31. Schmidt, *On Germans and Other Greeks*, pp. 54–55. As Schmidt later notes, 'We experience the *katharsis* when a light is shined upon the operations of *hamartia*, and we learn something about how we need to understand beings capable of such profound suffering' (p. 60).
32. Schmidt, *On Germans and Other Greeks*, pp. 55–56.
33. Schmidt, *On Germans and Other Greeks*, p. 57.
34. According to Charles Segal, tragedy allows us to access 'the knowledge that the conscious mind is unwilling or unable to face'. In a similar vein, Simon Critchley has suggested that 'the experience of tragedy allows us to look, just for a moment, or perhaps for a sustained series of moments, at what is beyond or behind the mind's eye. Beneath the back-and-forth of speech and counter speech, the play of conflictual reasoning that we hear in drama, some uncontainable and vast dimension of life flickers and flares up, something that we would rather keep out of view but that presses in upon us with an unbearable insistence'. See C. Segal, 'Greek Tragedy and Society: A Structuralist Perspective' in P. Euben (ed.), *Greek Tragedy and Political Theory*, Berkeley, CA: University of California Press, 1986, p. 45 and Critchley, *Tragedy, the Greeks and Us*, p. 218.
35. Taxidou, *Tragedy, Modernity and Mourning*, p. 112.
36. Taxidou, *Tragedy, Modernity and Mourning*, pp. 112–117.
37. See Critchley, *Tragedy, the Greeks and Us*, p. 212.
38. This accords with David Carter's view that the 'central political player in Greek tragedy … is the Greek city-state'. Carter, *The Politics of Greek Tragedy*, p. 6.
39. Critchley, *Tragedy, the Greeks and Us*, p. 45.
40. Thus Segal will refer to tragedy as 'A festival at the very heart of the city [that] shows the social and ritual order of the city inverted and turned against itself in conflict and division'. In a similar vein, Goldhill has suggested tragic drama (and comedy too) shows 'a world ripped apart, civic foundations shattered and the noble values of citizenship turned against themselves in violence, confusion, despair and horror'. See Segal, 'Greek Tragedy and Society', p. 69 and Goldhill, *Love, Sex and Tragedy*, p. 227.
41. Critchley, *Tragedy, the Greeks and Us*, p. 217.
42. As Froma Zeitlin puts it, Oedipus is 'the crystallization in purest form of the city of Thebes itself'. See F. Zeitlin, 'Thebes: Theatre of Self and Society in Athenian Drama' in Euben (ed.), *Greek Tragedy and Political Theory*, p. 105.
43. Sophocles, *Oedipus the King* in *The Three Theban Plays*, trans. by Fagles, l.1504.
44. Sophocles, *Oedipus the King*, ll.1512, 1516.
45. Sophocles, *Oedipus the King*, ll.1516–1517.
46. Sophocles, *Oedipus the King*, ll.1561–1566.
47. T. Eagleton, 'Tragedy and Revolution' in C. Davis, J. Milbank and S. Zizeck (eds.), *Theology and the Political: The New Debate*, Durham: Duke University Press, 2005, p. 8.
48. In tragedy, according to Segal, 'confused intermingling, inversions, troubling identifications replace reassuring demarcation or differentiation. The original structures are suspended, forcing the mind to reach beyond those structures in the painful search for other principles of order or in the even more painful admission that there are no principles of order'. Segal, 'Greek Tragedy and Society', p. 48.
49. Sophocles, *Oedipus the King* in *The Three Theban Plays*, trans. by Fagles, ll.1356–1357.
50. Critchley, *Tragedy, the Greeks and Us*, p. 212.

51. In Aristotle, instructively, the pathos of tragedy hinges on the fact that the destructive act takes place among friends rather than enemies. For him, as Salkever notes, events only arouse pity and fear because they produce 'an unexpected break in a relationship of *philia*'; that is, a blood friendship, not a civic friendship. Salkever takes this as evidence that the tragedians had a certain audience in mind: 'the moderate democrats' for whom 'the most important goods are those connected with their homes and families'. However, this seems to unnecessarily restrict the metaphorical exchange between the two orders of *philia*, family and city, fratricidal conflict and civil war. S. Salkever, 'Tragedy and the Education of the *Demos*: Aristotle's Response to Plato' in P. Euben, *Greek Tragedy and Political Theory*, p. 298.
52. As Loraux points out, tragic purification 'surely purges the citizen more than the private individual, because it purges emotions that should be unknown to the ideal of the good citizen'. Loraux, *Tragic Ways of Killing a Woman*, p. 65.
53. By arguing in this way I am, in effect, suggesting that the institution of tragedy does precisely what Honig claims Creon and Pericles do (the latter in his famous 'Funeral Oration') and which Sophocles' *Antigone* appears to question and contest; namely, 'collectivizes lament, and presses grief into the service of the city'. However, on my reading, the way in which it does so is rather different. As a space of critical reflection, tragedy collectivizes lament without at the same time instrumentalizing it. See Honig, *Antigone Interrupted*, p. 109 and note 58, p. 249.
54. See Taxidou, *Tragedy, Modernity and Mourning*, pp. 159–160.
55. P. Cartledge, '"Deep Plays": Theatre as Process in Greek Civic Life' in P.E. Easterling (ed.), *The Cambridge Companion to Greek Tragedy*, Cambridge: Cambridge University Press, 2007, p. 32.
56. Zeitlin, 'Thebes: Theatre of Self and Society in Athenian Drama', p. 117.
57. Zeitlin, 'Thebes: Theatre of Self and Society in Athenian Drama', p. 121.
58. Honig, *Antigone Interrupted*, p. 118.
59. Honig, *Antigone Interrupted*, p. 116.
60. Honig poses the question of *Antigone* for the city in these terms: 'When it ends with Creon's code-defying grief, does it softly suggest that no economy of mourning and membership, and no institution of exception, is up to the task of voicing and managing the grief we seek in our politics to express, contain, or channel, that the *différance* of Creon's grief undoes them all?'. Honig, *Antigone Interrupted*, p. 117.
61. Doubtless some plays came dangerously close. As is often noted, Euripides' *The Trojan Women*, presented in the spring of 415 BCE, seemed explicitly calculated to reflect the violence perpetrated upon the women and children of Melos in the previous year back to the Athenian audience. Even in this instance, however, the buffer of myth remains. As Eva Keuls points out, 'like many an artist since then, trying to deal with controversial policies or to challenge a cultural presupposition, Euripides chose a subject parallel to the current events but set safely in the distant past—much as a soviet artist might have alluded to Stalin through the figure of Ivan the Terrible'. Honig herself seems to concede the point when she notes that the ban placed upon *The Capture of Miletus* 'puts some pressure on the common notion that Athenians shed tears at the theatre that they were not allowed to shed elsewhere. Instead, the episode suggests, tragic theatre was a relatively safe venue that allowed and even occasioned emotions like, but not the same as, the emotions once solicited by female mourners, some of whom were "professionals", not unlike the actors

A Different Catharsis? 293

who performed in dramas'. See Keuls, *The Reign of the Phallus*, p. 21; Honig, *Antigone Interrupted*, p. 103.
62. Schmidt, *On Germans and Other Greeks*, p. 70.
63. As Carter has noted, 'while tragic drama could ask questions of the shared values of the Greek poleis, it was far less likely to confront the state head-on: that ideal of political theatre is more typically encouraged in a modern, liberal democracy'. Carter, *The Politics of Greek Tragedy*, p. 145.
64. Nussbaum, *Political Emotions*, p. 264.
65. As Paul Cartledge has noted, in being 'absolutely contemporary', the *Capture of Miletus* 'proved all too successfully affecting'. Cartledge, '"Deep Plays"' in Easterling (ed.), *The Cambridge Companion to Greek Tragedy*, p. 24.
66. Goldhill, *Love, Sex and Tragedy*, p. 232.
67. Nussbaum herself hints in this direction when she writes: 'Large modern nations cannot precisely replicate the dramatic festivals of ancient Athens, but they can try to understand their political role and find their own analogues—using political rhetoric, publicly sponsored visual art, the design of public parks and monuments, public book discussions, and the choice and content of public holidays and celebrations'. Nussbaum, *Political Emotions*, p. 261.
68. Ash, 'The Truth about Dictatorship', *The New York Review of Books*, February 1998, pp. 11–12. A similar connection between the TRC and 'a type of Aristotelian catharsis' is drawn by Sonali Chakravarti, though she is critical of the capacity of any such catharsis to return individuals and societies to a more 'healthy' status quo. See Chakravarti, *Sing the Rage: Listening to Anger after Mass Violence*, Chicago, IL: University of Chicago Press, 2014, p. 71. My own attempt to utilize Greek tragedy for understanding rituals of reconciliation related specifically to the way in which they appeared to be deploying a concept of responsibility that did not take its bearings from the intentionality of the agent. As in tragedy, I noted, the citizen-spectators at these ritual events seem to be at once detached and involved. As the history they (or their ancestors) made as actors is played back to them as spectators, they are given an opportunity to see themselves as responsible agents who, regardless of good intentions, have a duty to make amends for the injustices of the past. In retrospect (and in light of research conducted for this book), I have come to believe that I exaggerated the aspect of detachment. What distinguishes the rituals of reconciliation from the Great Dionysia is precisely the fact that citizens are not allowed to assume a position of detachment. Everything is about being brought 'face to face' with the past. See P. Muldoon, 'Thinking Responsibility Differently: Reconciliation and the Tragedy of Colonisation', *Journal of Intercultural Studies*, 26(3), 2005, pp. 237–255.
69. Thus Michael Ignatieff suggests Willy Brandt's gesture of going down on his knees had a 'cathartic effect'; Paul Ricoeur suggests the recounting of suffering in the South African TRC 'gave rise to a shared *katharsis*'; and Emma Hutchinson claims the TRC can 'be seen as operating as a type of cathartic space'. See M. Ignatieff, 'Articles of Faith', *Index on Censorship*, 5, 1996, p. 122; Ricoeur, *Memory, History, Forgetting*, Chicago, IL: University of Chicago Press, 2004, p. 484; Hutchinson, *Affective Communities in World Politics*, Cambridge: Cambridge University Press, 2016, p. 252.
70. Cartledge, '"Deep Plays"' in Easterling (ed.), *The Cambridge Companion to Greek Tragedy*, p. 19.

71. This is particularly so in relation to those tragedies, like Euripides' *The Trojan Women*, that invite the audience to re-appraise earlier actions—in this case, the decision to kill all the men, and enslave the women and children, of the colony of Melos. For a discussion of this relation, see Nussbaum, *Political Emotions*, p. 260.
72. Segal, *Interpreting Greek Tragedy*, pp. 80–81.
73. 'Through the many voices that [were] allowed to speak in public', claimed Chakravarti, the TRC made it possible for the audience to 'see relationships between private identity and public experience that [had] not been recognised before'. Chakravarti, *Sing the Rage*, p. 84.
74. As Marc Galanter notes, official efforts at repair are often the result of the fact that a 'new judgement' is passed on 'old acts'. Sometimes this is because new facts come to light and sometimes it is because there is a 'reversal in the moral valance of the original acts so that what was viewed as good is now seen as bad'. See M. Galanter, 'Righting Old Wrongs' in Nancy L. Rosenblum (ed.), *Breaking the Cycles of Hatred: Memory, Law and Repair*, Princeton, NJ: Princeton University Press, 2003, p. 117.
75. The spokesperson here is Tiresias. Sophocles, *Oedipus the King* in *The Three Theban Plays*, trans. by Fagles, ll.359–360.
76. Thus Habermas will speak of the Memorial to the Murdered Jews as a 'permanent source of disquiet and admonition'—it is less a *Denkmal* than a *Mahnmal*. Habermas, 'The Finger of Blame', p. 41.
77. It is not without interest in this regard that the corpses of the Republican disappeared are not accepted as criminal proof in Spanish courts. See A. González-Ruibal, 'Excavating Memory, Burying History, Lessons from the Spanish Civil War' in K.P. Hofmann, R. Bernbeck, and U. Sommer (eds.), *Between Memory Sites and Memory Networks*, Berlin Studies of the Ancient World 45, Berlin: De Gruyter, p. 292.
78. As Habermas notes, the return of the past as a result of more or less contingent events—'scandals and court cases, sensitive legal matters, historical narratives, films, television series'—often sparks 'controversies over the image the citizens have of their own country, of who they are and who they want to be'. Habermas, 'The Finger of Blame', pp. 39–40.
79. As Eagleton writes: 'There are none so blind as those who see only themselves'. Eagleton, 'Tragedy and Revolution' in Davis, Milbank, and Zizeck (eds.), *Theology and the Political*, p. 14.
80. Q. Stevens, 'Nothing More Than Feelings: Abstract Memorials', *Architectural Theory Review*, 14(2), pp. 156–172.
81. Thus one of Chakravarti's primary criticisms of the victims' hearings of the South Africa TRC was that the commissioners simultaneously elicited emotional outpourings while ignoring their political implications. Chakravarti, *Sing the Rage*, p. 71.
82. Honig, *Antione Interrupted*, p. 119.
83. Goldhill, *Love, Sex and Tragedy*, pp. 228–229. The ethical view of *katharsis* also receives support from Stephen Salkever. See Salkever, 'Tragedy and the Education of the *Demos*' in Euben, *Greek Tragedy and Political Theory*, pp. 274–303.
84. See Critchley, *The Greeks, Tragedy and Us*, p. 258.
85. Eagleton, 'Tragedy and Revolution', p. 16.
86. Before his discussion of Aristotle, for instance, Critchley defines tragedy as 'the theatrical presentation of the tragic flaw, or *hamartia*, and its *catharsis* in the name of a rethinking of praxis, or action'. Critchley, *Tragedy, the Greeks and Us*, p. 85.

87. Poole, *Tragedy: Shakespeare and the Greek Example*, p. 11.
88. As Taxidou notes, tragedy does not offer 'an antidote to suffering and pain through an all-encompassing reconciliation'. Instead, it offers 'a radical form of critique that interrogates the basic assumptions and foundations of western democracy'. Taxidou, *Tragedy, Mourning and Modernity*, p. 2.
89. Critchley, *Tragedy, the Greeks and Us*, p. 16.

Conclusion

Remorseless Penance—Exposure, Falling, and Healing

> I haven't changed my way of life; I continue to love myself and to make use of others. Only, the confession of my crimes allows me to begin again lighter in heart and to taste a double enjoyment, first of my nature and secondly of a charming repentance.[1]

In his last complete work of fiction, *The Fall*, Albert Camus puts the following words into the mouth of his enigmatic protagonist, Jean-Baptiste Clamence: 'we should like, at the same time, to cease being guilty and yet not make the effort of cleansing ourselves'.[2] It is an unsettling remark, not, as might initially be expected, because the 'we' it invokes is presumptuous but, on the contrary, because it does, in fact, ring painfully, perhaps even axiomatically, true. Innocent by dint of powerlessness, by virtue of being a victim oneself, by the grace of late birth or, if worst comes to worst, by means of general fault (since, as Arendt noted, 'where all are guilty, nobody is')[3]—these are just some of the justifications to which 'we' have stubbornly clung to avoid the effort of cleansing ourselves. In *The Fall*, it is Clamence and his 'innocence' that is ostensibly in focus. But with characteristic brilliance, Camus uses the backdrop of Amsterdam to implicate his reader in those wider, more profound historical crimes about which 'we' are all still desperate to cease being guilty.[4] 'I live in the Jewish quarter', Clamence tells the stranger he meets in a dockside bar called 'Mexico City' (and to whom he starts to confess all), 'or what was called so until our Hitlerian brethren spaced it out a bit. What a clean-up! Seventy-five thousand Jews deported or assassinated; that's real vacuum-cleaning ... I am living on the site of one of the greatest crimes in history.'[5] Later in the novel he brings attention to another of those greatest crimes in history by pointing out a shop-sign containing the heads of two Negro slaves. 'Oh', he says, 'they weren't squeamish in those days! They were self-assured; they announced: "You see, I'm a man of substance, I'm in the slave-trade; I deal in black flesh".'[6] The point is not simply that this too was

The Penitent State. Paul Muldoon, Oxford University Press. © Paul Muldoon (2023).
DOI: 10.1093/oso/9780198831624.003.0008

one of the dark places of the earth, but that no one is innocent: one way or another 'we' are all implicated in the great crimes of history.[7]

Not making the effort of cleansing ourselves is what we now call avoidance or denial—but like all seemingly universal phenomena, this one too has its exceptions, the protagonist of *The Fall* included. Like Nietzsche's sovereign man and Schmitt's sovereign state, 'shielded equally from judgement as from penalty' because of their elevation above the 'human ants', Camus' Clamence relies upon his 'extraordinary ability to forget' to secure himself against troubling memories, until the misdeeds of the past—in his case, a failure to save a young woman from drowning in the Seine—can no longer be denied.[8] Returned, by degrees, to his memory, he is tortured by a sense of shame that grants him 'little ease' and which makes all the praise he continues to receive utterly intolerable. The problem is not that he falls in the estimation of others but that he falls in his estimation of himself.[9] He is not the 'complete man' he imagined and the belated recognition is devastating. An unravelling begins. Now without the shield of forgetfulness that has protected him against injury and allowed him to appear magnanimous, Clamence is suddenly vulnerable to all the slings and arrows that have rained down upon him over the years. The truth of them finally strikes home, completely depriving him of his health and vitality: 'I received all the wounds at the same time and lost my strength all at once.'[10]

Whether Camus had any historical parallels in mind when he developed the character of Clamence is unclear. Published only two years before his *Algerian Chronicles*, *The Fall* might easily be a veiled indictment of France for the colony it exploited (and then left to drown). That too was a failure that turned into a torture—not least of all for Camus.[11] Whatever the case, the debilitating condition he ascribes to Clamence is one with which we are by now all-too-familiar: with the return of memory comes the loss of self-esteem (and the desperate need to recover it).[12] No longer hidden from the truth about himself, Clamence's former manner of 'living aloft', seen and hailed by all, becomes unbearable because he knows (even if no one else does) that it is founded on a lie. As he informs his would-be confessor, a sense of shame 'has never left me since the adventure I found at the heart of my memory'.[13] But what is to be done? Clamence, like many a wrongdoer seeking release, wishes only that he could go back, that the young woman would throw herself into the water again so that he might, 'a second time', have a chance of saving them both. But he knows full well this is impossible. Time cannot be willed backwards: 'it's too late now'.[14] If he is to avoid a life of melancholia, an endless grieving for an unrecoverable honour, he needs another way out.

Conclusion 299

In his confession to the barfly stranger, Clamence acknowledges that the first 'solution' he arrived at was excessive. Since the praise of others now grates against his own sense of self, he found himself wanting to 'break open the handsome wax-figure [he] presented everywhere' and 'reveal to all eyes what he was made of'.[15] He dreams of jostling the blind on the street, puncturing the tyres of wheelchairs, smacking infants in the subway, and shouting 'lousy proletarians' at the workers toiling away on the scaffolding—all in order 'to destroy that flattering reputation'.[16] Then, when his tentative attempts to reveal himself as a reprobate do no more than disconcert opinion, he embarks upon a similarly unhelpful life of debauchery, finding in alcohol and women 'the only solace of which [he] was worthy'.[17] It is only when he discovers, in a state of exhaustion and despair, that memory is not erased by sensual satisfaction, but rather sits dormant, patiently waiting the moment of its devastating return, that he is finally forced to embrace the life of the penitent. 'I had to submit and admit my guilt', he says. 'I had to live in the little ease'.[18] The decision, inevitably, is life changing.

As Clamence informs the stranger, the 'little ease' was the name assigned to an ingenious dungeon cell of the Middle Ages which was not high enough to let its inmate stand up or wide enough to let him lie down. Forced to live out his life 'on the diagonal', the condemned man learned, in an appropriately embodied way, precisely what it meant to be guilty: to remain forever bowed, forever crooked; to never again stretch out joyously in the carefree manner of the innocent. And who could fault it? Cruel and excessive as it first appears, the 'little ease' stakes its own claim to being the model of proportionality the criminal justice system has always sought. Should not those who diminish the lives of others themselves lead a diminished life? Repentance, Camus reveals by means of this arresting metaphor of 'the little ease', is a true moral discipline because it grants one no relief and leaves one no place to hide. Unlike shame, which arises when someone discovers us in a disgraceful act, and which generally has us diving for cover, repentance is the uncovering of oneself—a stripping bare of the sin that leaves one exposed to the gaze, the judgement, and the condemnation of others.

Surely all the more reason, then, to cherish those rare moments when the guilty sovereign makes the decision, however belated, to uncover *itself* and 'take the fall'. As a member of a perpetrating community, historically implicated in crimes against humanity, I see great merit, ethically and politically, in committing to the fall and living on the diagonal. One reason why, arguably the primary reason why, the image of Brandt's *Kniefall* remains so powerful is that it represents a voluntary submission. Unlike the monuments of past oppression currently being defaced and smashed by protestors, Brandt didn't have to be pushed over. He committed himself (and implicitly the German nation) to the life of little ease and in so doing testified to precisely that consciousness of the damage done by state racism that campaigns like 'Rhodes Must Fall' in South Africa and 'Cook Must Fall' in Australia seek to elicit from a reluctant (or perhaps simply oblivious) public. But can it be assumed that our efforts at cleansing ourselves are an unalloyed good, especially when they are taken up by sovereign states out of an interest in healing the wounds of the past? As I have tried to show throughout this book, the healing of nations is a murky business carried out through institutions that are difficult to assess in moral terms and whose biopolitical role as stimulants to mourning raises troubling questions about the value of that 'life-changing decision' to admit to guilt. The fact that such acts appear, in principle, to be morally desirable (if not, in fact, morally *required*) does not vitiate the need to ask difficult questions about the way they function as healing operations: precisely whose life is changed and in what ways by the decision to repent?

It is, to be sure, difficult to read Foucault's pioneering work on biopower without becoming suspicious of any and every attempt, even the seemingly well-intentioned ones, to use power to change life. As the counterpart of the disciplinary power exercised over the body that renders it, at once, docile and productive (anatomo-power), the regulatory power exercised over the population (biopower) appears similarly insidious. Exercised over subjects insofar as they are members of a species, as opposed to citizens of a polity, biopower carries disturbing resonances of animal husbandry. In the same way that disciplinary power takes up the techniques of dressage and applies them to human bodies, biopower takes up the principles of pastoral management and applies them to national populations.[19] Inherently invested in growing and improving 'the stock' (in this case, the productive capacity of 'the population' being governed), biopower preserves an uncomfortable, if increasingly tenuous, connection with the 'science' of eugenics and its 'racial' discriminations. Indeed, since biopower, as Foucault puts it, always addresses itself to 'the random element inherent in biological processes'—the accident or deficiency that either reduces the efficacy of life or places it at risk—it cannot but 'break up' the biological continuum of the 'race' (that is, the human race). As he goes on to underline, this 'dividing practice'—the practice that, as it were, creates many 'races' out of the single human race—is less an exceptional procedure than 'a mechanism that allows biopower to work.'[20] Without it there is simply no way the biological anomaly can be isolated and exposed to 'treatment'.

It is, without doubt, in relation to these racial divisions that the dangers of biopower become fully manifest. In his late work, as was previously noted,

Foucault insisted that the biopolitical regulation of populations belonged to a new economy of power, whose procedures, techniques, and instruments were completely foreign to the form of sovereignty based around the right to take life. The only time, on his reckoning, that sovereign power, with its ancient right to kill, made an appearance in the biopolitical apparatus focused on protecting, managing, and multiplying life was when a break between superior and inferior, healthy and diseased, 'races' was introduced (in this case for pseudo-scientific, pseudo-ideological reasons) into the biological continuum of the population. Racial discrimination was, in his words, 'primarily a way of introducing a break within the domain of life that is under power's control: the break between what must live and what must die'.[21] In *Society Must Be Defended*, Foucault identifies the Nazi state as the exemplary, terrifying instance of what is possible when sovereign power is repurposed within a biopolitical governmentality. With the advent of state racism, biopolitics turns into thanato-politics—a politics in which some life (the diseased race) is destroyed so that other life (the healthy race) can flourish. For Foucault, and this applies even more so to Agamben, it is the sovereign decision on 'the life unworthy of life', the life that is deemed either not fit for living or a danger to the living, which exposes the dark potential of biopolitics.[22]

But exactly how much store deserves to be placed in this single, exceptional example? As Milchman and Rosenberg (among many others) have suggested, it is not clear the Foucault's 'unalterably bleak' judgement of biopower is fully warranted. 'Such a categorical judgement', they note, 'seems to us to overlook the possibilities contained in technologies that make life proliferate'.[23] As the history of plagues (remote and recent) shows us, the 'discriminations' biopolitics makes within the human race need not follow pre-existing 'racial' lines in the way that is characteristic of state racisms like Nazi Germany. Not only can distinctions between 'the healthy' and 'the diseased' be purely clinical (fully indiscriminate with regards to race), the sovereign's power of the exception can also be mobilized in ways that seek not to eliminate from life but to restore to life. In recent years, the incomplete and somewhat ambiguous nature of Foucault's analyses of biopower has opened a space for the concept of 'affirmative biopolitics' in which power is not so much exercised over life as *for* life. Roberto Esposito has, for instance, suggested that there is nothing *inherently* wrong with biopower since all communities need immunity from biological (and other) threats and dangers. The trouble only starts when the immune response goes into overdrive as a result of the creation of faux enemies and the body politic starts to attack itself in the same way that the body biological does in the case of autoimmune diseases. Esposito characterizes these kinds of self-defeating (self-annihilating) responses to the threat of the racial other as 'excess immunity' and seeks to overcome them by displacing substantive conceptions of community based on unities of 'blood and soil' for more formal conceptions of community based upon an idea of 'being in common'. The political challenge, as he sees it, is to create a more porous and more plural sense of community—one in which the friend enemy antagonism is abated—without completely sacrificing immunity.[24]

Arguably, whatever claim sovereign acts of repentance and redress make as manifestations of an affirmative biopolitics rests upon the way they respond to that political challenge by using public memory to care for those formerly treated as internal enemies. One does not need much assistance from the psychoanalysts to recognize just how well sovereign acts of denial chime with what Esposito calls the 'bivalent character of the immune dispositif'.[25] In line with the idea that biopolitics creates a zone of indistinction between the juridical and the medical, the concept of denial does double work in this context as an expression of a refusal on the part of the sovereign body to sacrifice its immunity not just from legal prosecution but from mass melancholia. Intent only on defending itself, it refuses traumatic memory in the same way it refuses criminal liability: no loss was suffered and no wrong was done. The cost of this denial, of this 'excess immunity', is, however, the turning of the body politic against itself in a life-sapping defence against the past. Not only does sovereign denial exclude the wronged from the community of 'grievable life', effectively condemning them to the half-life of radical alienation, it also condemns the body politic to the over-life of a paralysing shame. By contrast, confession milks the symbolic power of the repentant sovereign to produce a restorative, life-regenerating effect. By admitting to, and apologizing for, the wrong, the sovereign body alters the emotional climate, giving the victims a chance to resolve their impacted grief and itself an opportunity to overcome its wounded pride. Repentance, one might say, both re-values the life of the other, releasing it from alienation, and restores the self, freeing it from paralysis. Put simply, by sacrificing a degree of immunity, community—'a being in common'—is created in which life, that of the victims and the perpetrators alike, can flourish.

Although surprisingly few attempts have been made to look at the restorative justice paradigm through this biopolitical lens, the belief that sovereign acts of repentance have the power to 'heal through truth' is by no means uncommon. As should by now be clear, support for such acts (provided, of course, they meet the sincerity test) is widespread and continues to be stoked by the ever-more intimate connection forged in the field of restorative justice between two discourses of 'healing': the first psychological, centred on the concept of mourning, the second theological, centred on the concept

Conclusion 303

of reconciliation. Despite their philosophical incompatibility (with the first being a physical and the second a metaphysical system of thought), these two discourses are forever being entwined in ways that lend efforts at the repair of damaged life through the telling of ugly truths an air of the psychologically necessary and the politically meritorious. As Claire Moon puts it, 'healing, and reconciliation appear, now, to be self-evidently right'.[26] For the victims, truth telling is the public acknowledgement they need to come to terms with their (traumatic) loss of trust in others; for the perpetrators, it is the public atonement they need to come to terms with their (equally traumatic) loss of pride in themselves. Although a kind of affirmation for the one, and a kind of penance for the other, in other words, acts of sovereign repentance drive the healing process for both parties, giving them the opportunity to reconcile with their losses and, by that means, to reconcile with each other.[27]

As is often the case, however, it is the things that seem self-evidently right that stand most in need of our critical attention. My primary aim in this book has been to complicate this (overly rosy?) picture by introducing another 'dispositif'—one which is, once again, intrinsically connected to the exercise of biopower and which consequently has a bivalent (part-legal, part-medical) character: 'exposure'. As we noted in the Introduction, 'exposure to death' in the state of exception has been the fate of those deemed unworthy of life and is the ultimate source of that sense of betrayal that sits at the heart of trauma. Assuming Judith Lewis Herman is a reliable guide, psychic life suffers the most insidious form of damage when 'the caretaker' (parent, sovereign, god) either fails to shield the subject from or, worse still, wilfully exposes them to violence. Such an experience is truly indigestible or unassimilable because it is the experience of 'bare life'; the experience, that is, of finding oneself not simply in the wild, unprotected by law, but exposed *by means of the law* to the wildness or savagery of the sovereign. The reason betrayal *by* the caretaker is inclined to function, at the same time, as a betrayal *of* the caretaker (that is, as a revelation of its true character) is because it uncovers its constitutional ambiguity as a figure who lives both inside and outside the law. Inevitably it is those abandoned by the law and exposed to death in the state of exception that are best placed to recognize the sovereign person for what he really is: a figure who straddles the boundary between beast and man.[28]

Ideally speaking, acts of sovereign repentance make amends for this reduction to bare life by turning the experience of exposure back upon the state. In apology, at least in principle, the sovereign 'breaks open the handsome wax-figure' it has hitherto presented and 'reveals to all eyes what it is made of'. And, as in *The Fall*, this too is a life-changing decision—both for those to whom it issues the apology and for itself as an apologizer. For the survivor, it is a question of 'receiving recognition' (and the juridical-psychological work such recognition does). Exposure emerges here as the best part of justice because it serves, at one and the same time, as a revaluation of denigrated life and as a means of overcoming radical alienation. When the sovereign says sorry to its victims, it both affirms their dignity and confirms their story, simultaneously turning outcasts into citizens and trauma into mourning. For the sovereign, it is a question of 'honest self-understanding' (and, once again, the juridical-psychological work such honest self-understanding does). Exposed in the violence of its deeds, the sovereign body gives up the illusion of innocence and places itself at the mercy of those it abused, awaiting a forgiveness that might never arrive, but which, through its very contingency, is suggestive of a willingness to remained forever bowed and live on the diagonal. By its acts of repentance and redress, the sovereign simultaneously renounces its right to abuse and announces itself as an agent of care, willing to dwell in memory for the sake of the other, regardless of whether this return to the past condemns it to a life of little ease.

Whether we really are 'all Germans now' is, perhaps, a moot point. Even so, we are not wanting for examples of penitent states. The Memorial to the Murdered Jews in Germany, the apology to the Stolen Generations in Australia, and the Truth and Reconciliation Commission in South Africa would all, in their own way, appear to be acts of recognition and honest self-understanding. Each functions as an acknowledgement of the harm done to those once designated as internal enemies and each points to a willingness on the part of the perpetrating community to live in the little ease. Now forever written into the story of their respective nations, they deny the citizen-spectator the luxury of 'looking away'. In them one sees (or seems to see) precisely that remorseful acceptance of responsibility and determination to make amends which Murphy takes as the mark of the true penitent. Resentment in the face of such expressions of sovereign penance may well, as Habermas suggests, be something 'we', as perpetrators, ultimately wish to overcome; for, while it has some justification as a response to injustice, resentment among wrongdoers is really nothing but the weeping of a narcissistic wound. In the meantime, though, it retains a certain value as a sign of a necessary discomfort; of a frustration among the perpetrators at being unable to stretch out in the carefree manner of the innocent. As it turns out, one can erect a monument to one's own shame; one just can't do it without having to live forever after on the diagonal.

Things that appear one way can, however, work in an entirely different way and, as we have seen throughout this study, the exposure of the sovereign in its crimes does not always have the effect one might expect or desire of it.

We can, once again, thank the brilliance of Camus for shining a light on the problem that we have encountered again and again in this book and which casts a shadow over all sovereign acts of repentance: the problem of doubling. 'My profession', Clamence tells the stranger 'is double'; for as well as being a penitent, he is also a judge: a 'judge-penitent', as he describes himself, who 'practice[s] the profession of the penitent to be able to end up as a judge'.[29] The technique, revealed only at the end of the long confession he makes to the stranger, is as simple as it is ingenious. By virtue of his charm, Clamence is able to indulge in public confession, accusing himself 'up hill and down dale' before everyone he meets, though not, he adds, 'crudely'. Rather than simply beat his breast, he adapts his words to his listener, mingling together what concerns him and what concerns others, until he has managed to 'construct a portrait which is the image of all and of no one'. When the portrait is finished, he shows it with great sorrow, saying, 'this, alas is what I am', knowing all the while that it is also a mirror for his confessor. As they, inevitably, recognize themselves in the portrait and begin along the path of self-accusation, Clamence regains his position of superiority and switches roles from penitent to judge. 'Once more', he says, 'I have found a height to which I am the only one to climb and from which I can judge everybody.'[30]

Clamence's life-changing decision thus turns out to not be so life changing after all or, at least, not in the way one might first assume. Although not exactly insincere, none of his public confessing changes the way he relates to others because it does not actually involve a change in his 'way of life'—as he says, 'I continue to love myself and make use of others.' All it does (though this is hardly an insignificant effect) is change his own enjoyment of life by allowing him to 'begin again lighter in heart'. Every time one of his confessors collapses under the weight of his own guilt and starts to accuse himself, Clamence rises in jubilation and stretches out again: 'Then I grow taller, *tres cher*, I grow taller, I breathe freely.'[31] In short, as confession morphs into representation, Clamence is able to disassociate himself from wrongdoing. The image he confronts 'face to face' is not a reflection in the mirror, but a portrait that has been painted—a spectacle of himself *as other*. It is then all too easy to make the switch from penitent to judge and regain that 'ease', that sense of sovereign superiority and freedom, which the dungeon of shame denies:

> How intoxicating to feel like God the Father and to hand out definitive testimonials of bad character and habits. I sit enthroned among my bad angels at the summit of the Dutch heaven and I watch ascending towards me, as they issue from the fogs and the water, the multitude of the Last Judgment.[32]

In his final conversation with the stranger, Clamence admits that his 'solution' to the problem of agonizing memory is not ideal. 'When you don't like your own life', he says, 'you must change lives.' But that kind of change is exceedingly difficult. 'What can one do to become another?' he asks. 'Impossible. One would have to cease being anyone, forget oneself for someone else, at least once. But how?' For all his confessing, in other words, Clamence is unable to undergo the kenosis, the emptying out and submission to, required of the true penitent. He simply cannot (or will not?) become another. Hence he must content himself with the easing made possible through doubling: by making a representation of himself in confession, he gives himself an opportunity to stand in judgement, as if that representation had nothing to do with him at all.

Although 'doubling' is not the sole technique utilized in the modern institution of exception, it is certainly one of the most important ones. Regardless of how widespread they become, such institutions remain exceptional as historical moments in which the state makes a 'negative'—which is to say, a brutally truthful—representation of itself. Effectively a stage for the return of memory, the exceptional institution pierces the shield of forgetfulness, dramatically exposing the sovereign man for who he truly is and thus (like Oedipus) to the judgement and penalty he has hitherto avoided. As in Greek tragedy, this drama of recognition always ends with a fall and an intimation of the life of 'little ease' to come. Or that, at least, would be the result were it not for the fact that this truthful portrait, a product of the art and the act of representation, allows the sovereign man to be both 'there' and 'not there'. Put into the position of witness-spectator, the sovereign body is given licence to stand in judgement upon itself and say 'that is us, but not us', 'that is who we were, but not who we are'. Like Clamence, in other words, this sovereign man is something of a 'play-actor' who exists independently of the character he is currently performing and is thus able to switch roles from penitent to judge with relative ease. The point is not that the portrait is dishonest or insincere, that it is simply a mask or a deception, but that it enables disassociation. Although it is but observing itself in the mirror, the sovereign body can say: 'thank god we are no longer like that' and breathe freely again. Like Clamence, it finds healing by splitting or doubling, by instantiating itself as the judge of its penitent self.

While there is no doubt, then, that our modern institutions of exception are 'exposure sites', the sovereign body (and its crimes) may not ultimately be the thing that is most brutally exposed by them. That 'honour', dubious as it is, could well go to those who are required to testify to those crimes by telling the truth of their own damaged lives. Faith in what Martha Minow, following

Herman, has called the 'restorative power of truth-telling',[33] appears to have done much to cement the impression that the victims are the principal beneficiaries of this kind of disclosure. And yet, it is by no means clear that the sharing of private pain in a public way has the healing power frequently assigned to it. As truth-tellers *for* the political community, required to narrate the story of their damaged life, the survivors of sovereign violence are ever at risk of becoming the object, rather than the beneficiary, of the catharsis they inspire. Exposed, as it were, all over again, this time in the agony of their loss, they are forever at risk of being returned to the condition of bare life where human speech and animal cries enter into a zone of indistinction. Finally rendered visible, but principally as an object of trauma, the truth-tellers are the ones who are subject to judgement, their inner life put on display so that the wrongdoer can have a second chance at compassionate identification and save them both. Theirs is, once again, the life divided from the biological continuum, the life that is torn away and put on display so that the social body can be alleviated of its shame, so it can 'grow taller' and 'breathe freely'.

The critical issue, then, may not be whether the sovereign is sincere or insincere in its decision to repent but rather whose life that decision really changes. In this book I have tried to reveal sovereign repentance in its connection with psychological healing and the costs and benefits associated with it. States, I have argued, undertake repentance not simply (and perhaps not even primarily) because they fear the moral sanction of the international community but because they are cognizant of social trauma as a threat to or, at the very least, a drag upon individual and collective life. Conceived as a melancholic complex that can be belated in its effects, social trauma has come to be understood as the emergency yet to come—the emergency, as it were, lying in wait—that necessitates operations upon memory that produce cathartic effects. The suggestion that the state wants the world to remain exactly the same after its act of repentance would thus seem to be only half right. For while it does seek to continue its way of life, it is also quite earnest in wanting to stimulate the flow of emotions and transform the emotional climate. As I have shown through my examination of three of the most prominent institutions of state repentance—the public memorial, the political apology, and the truth commission—cathartic release is less the incidental by-product of official expressions of repentance than one of their fully intended and most coveted effects. Indeed, while sovereign repentance is often conceived (and, by turns, celebrated and criticized) in terms of the elevation of victimhood and the moralization of politics, the most important beneficiary, psychologically speaking, could very well be the perpetrating community. By means of its negative representation of itself, the sovereign body does not so much commit to living in the 'little ease' as disassociate itself from its troubling memories and slough off its shame.

The perversion Camus ascribes to his 'judge-penitent' seems, in this context, remarkably sage. Is it possible that what lies at the root of all our acts of repentance is a mourning for lost innocence? Do we have any higher objective than to breathe freely again? Generalizing across national contexts is, of course, an inherently fraught exercise and it would be wrong to underestimate the significant attempts that have been (and are being) made to correct 'constitutional wrongness', particularly in Germany and South Africa, but also in Australia. Each of these countries has, through legal and constitutional reform, sought to change the moral grammar of the political community and, as Clamence puts it, 'become another'. Yet, there remains a sense in which the penitent states examined in this book haven't fully succeeded in changing their way of life. If the confession of their crimes has brought the victims some of the recognition (and some of the relief) they sought, it has also allowed the sovereign body to begin again lighter in heart, reinvigorated by its charming repentance, but no more insightful about the structures of exclusion that inhere in the nation-state form. The problem of the friend-enemy distinction, and its potential application to struggles internal the state, remains.

Admittedly, after so many years of forgetfulness, critique of singular acts of sovereign repentance is inclined to sound ethically perverse. Who would recommend a return to a life of endless denial or, at the other end of the scale, a life of perpetual penance?[34] That sense of perversity ought not, however, deter us from interrogating the biopolitical implications of our attempts to cleanse ourselves through the confession of our crimes. Indicative not just (not even?) of a new ethical sensibility but of the extension of power over life, these public exercises in shared mourning speak of a politics that is not only highly invasive in the way it drags emotional life into its orbit but highly evasive in the way it blinds us to the abuse of sovereign right. Thanks to the emergence of the penitent state, the suffering of victims (or at least some of them) will no longer go unrecognized. But that is not to say that attempts at healing through remorseful acceptance do not come at a cost. With truth telling comes exposure not simply of the body politic to the wrong but of the inner life of the victims to a public assembled as witness. Exactly who is being shamed and who is being healed is by no means self-evident here. Incorporated in the cathartic event as spectators to the feast of pain, the sovereign body seems to be all too easily alleviated of its sense of shame without being seriously challenged in its political vision.

It is because our modern institutions of exception work at these two levels—the ethico-political and the biopolitical—simultaneously that they have proved so difficult to evaluate. As we have seen throughout this study, acts of sovereign repentance have a strange, hybrid character. At the same time that they signify a willingness to take responsibility and make amends, they prescribe behavioural norms and catalyse biological processes. What this means in essence is that the function of truth telling in the exceptional institution is always doubled. At once the sign by which a society expresses its willingness to confront a difficult past and the means by which it stimulates the mourning process, truth telling intersects (and indeed renders indistinguishable) the legitimacy-creating and the life-enhancing dimensions of state repentance. In the practice of truth telling, contrition and catharsis merge, defeating even our best attempts to disentangle the question of legitimacy from the question of life. Caring for life has become a means of legitimation and legitimation a means of caring for life. Regardless of the institutional form it takes, therefore, state repentance is aligned with goals that are always in excess (and thus potentially destructive) of that of restoring dignity to victims. Indeed, as attempts to govern trauma through cathartic spectacle, they persistently blur the very distinction between organic life and political life that the concept of dignity enshrines and, as it were, helps police.

Straw men can, of course, function just as well as props as they do as targets. But if it is possible to extract a 'lesson' from tragic drama without reducing it to a caricature of a good exceptional institution, it would be that catharsis and critique must remain conjoined. Forcing the political collective to return to memory and face the traumas of the past is by no means an inherently bad thing to do. Citizens in modern democracies are offered few opportunities to see themselves in the mirror and reflect on the nation-state as an institutionalized expression of a life-destroying, community-breaking, friend–enemy antagonism. But unless the traumas inflicted upon internal enemies are staged in a way that facilitates critical reflection on the nation-state form and delivers insight into 'going wrong' in politics, attempts to represent the political community back to itself will incline towards pure spectacle. Disassociation with the past through the representation of the self as other allows citizens to engage solely at the level of feelings, to enjoy the pleasures of the emotional purge without taking on the burden of ethical responsibility. The fact that contrition in a perpetrator is no longer the rare miracle it once was may not, then, be a cause for unequivocal celebration. To the extent that the exceptional institutions examined in this study create a stage not just for the performance of repentance but for an operation upon memory, they are but another manifestation of that fateful turn in modern politics by which the biological is brought under state control. Although ostensibly a sign of the waning of sovereign power, they would seem, on closer inspection, to be a disturbing extension of those apparatuses of security that regulate populations. Through its dramatic, symbolically fecund, acts of repentance, the sovereign has been able to solicit, corral, and discipline affects like sorrow and grief in order to overcome blockages and restore the flow of life that is the wellspring of its own power.

Notes

1. A. Camus, *The Fall*, Harmondsworth: Penguin, 1975, p. 104.
2. Camus, *The Fall*, p. 62.
3. H. Arendt, 'Collective Responsibility' in J.W. Bernauer (ed.), *Amor Mundi: Explorations in the Faith and Thought of Hannah Arendt*, Boston, MA: Martinus Nijhoff Publishers, 1987, p. 43. See also H. Arendt, 'Organised Guilt and Universal Responsibility' in H. Arendt, *Essays in Understanding 1930–1954: Formation, Exile, and Totalitarianism*, ed. by Jerome Kohn, New York: Schocken Books, 1994, p. 126.
4. 'The idea', says Clamence, 'that comes most naturally to man, as if from his very nature, is the idea of his innocence.' Camus, *The Fall*, p. 60.
5. Camus, *The Fall*, p. 10.
6. Camus, *The Fall*, p. 34.
7. By setting the action in the red-light district, Camus could be interpreted as making reference to yet one more of the greatest crimes in history: the exploitation of women as sex workers. If so, however, the allusion is sufficiently veiled to arouse the suspicion that this exploitation had not yet entered his consciousness as a 'crime'.
8. As Clamence says, 'Everything slid off—yes, just rolled off me.' It is hard to imagine Camus did not have Nietzsche's *ubermensch* in mind when he has Clamence declare 'I looked upon myself as something of a superman.' Camus, *The Fall*, pp. 20–23, 38.
9. As Clamence says, 'I didn't want their esteem because it wasn't general, and how could it be general when I couldn't share in it?' Camus, *The Fall*, p. 69.
10. Camus, *The Fall*, p. 60.
11. It is worth noting here that the term Camus uses to chastise the Frenchmen who wanted to offer up the French of Algeria as expiatory victims for the colonial system is the very same one he assigns to Clamence: 'judge-penitent'. Camus leaves his readers in little doubt that this kind of transference of responsibility is not something he can abide: 'The idea of acknowledging guilt as our judges-penitent do, by beating the breasts of others, revolts me'. See A. Camus, *Algerian Chronicles*, ed. by Alice Kaplan trans. by Arthur Goldhammer, Cambridge, Mass: Belknap Press, 2014, p. 31.
12. Instructively, Clamence does not say that his memory returned to him but rather that he returned to his memory. Without this element of choice, this decision to retrace one's steps and go back over what one has done, atonement would lose its moral value. Camus, *The Fall*, p. 39.
13. Camus, *The Fall*, p. 51.
14. Camus, *The Fall*, p. 108.
15. Camus, *The Fall*, p. 69.
16. Camus, *The Fall*, pp. 67–69.

Conclusion   311

17. Camus, *The Fall*, p. 76.
18. Camus, *The Fall*, p. 80.
19. Thus, in a lecture given at Stanford University, Foucault would associate biopolitics with 'a kind of animalization of man'. M. Foucault quoted in H. Dreyfus and P. Rabinow, *Michel Foucault: Beyond Structuralism and Hermeneutics*, Chicago, IL: University of Chicago Press, 1983, p. 138.
20. Foucault, *Society Must Be Defended: Lectures at the Collège de France 1973-1976*, trans. by David Macey, London: Penguin Books, 2004, p. 258.
21. Foucault, *Society Must Be Defended*, p. 254.
22. Foucault, *Society Must Be Defended*, pp. 258-263. Although Foucault is often criticized for using the extreme case to reveal the dangers inherent in biopower, he is by no means alone in characterizing Nazism as a diabolical assertion of power over the biological. As Arendt had already recognized, the signature feature of the totalitarian regime was its treatment of men not as human beings qua rights-bearing individuals but as human beings qua members of the species. According to her analysis, the central objective of totalitarian rule (and the inspiration for its signature form of terror) was to realize the 'destiny of the species' in its absolute perfection and vitality, weeding out, along the way, all those 'parasitic' or 'unhealthy' humans that put that imagined 'destiny' at risk. So it was that the Jews and many, many others designated as parasitic or unhealthy were abandoned by the law and murdered with impunity, regardless of the fact they were absolutely innocent of any crime. In a way, however, Arendt's critique goes deeper than Foucault's because it sees the exercise of power over life as a fundamental assault on both individuality *and* politics. In order to exercise absolute domination, she suggested, totalitarian regimes aimed to reduce all 'men' to 'a specimen of the animal species man'; each one identical to every other one and thus infinitely replaceable and disposable. On her reading of things, politics disappears at the same time as individuality because deliberation, the exchange of opinions and perspectives, becomes redundant when there is only one man. See H. Arendt, 'On the Nature of Totalitarianism: An Essay in Understanding' in H. Arendt, *Essays in Understanding*, pp. 340-341; and H. Arendt, *The Origins of Totalitarianism*, New York: Harvest, 1976, p. 457.
23. A. Milchman and A. Rosenberg, 'Review Essay: Michel Foucault—Crises and Problemizations', *Review of Politics*, 67(2), 2005, p. 341. See also D. Fassin, 'Another Politics of Life Is Possible', *Theory, Culture and Society*, 26(5), 2009, pp. 44-60; and D. Macey, 'Rethinking Biopolitics, Race and Power in the Wake of Foucault', *Theory, Culture, and Society*, 26(6), 2009, pp. 186-205.
24. R. Esposito, 'Community, Immunity, Biopolitcs', *Angelaki: Journal of Theoretical Humanitics*, 18(3), 2013, passim.
25. Esposito, 'Community, Immunity, Biopolitics', p. 86.
26. C. Moon, 'Healing Past Violence: Traumatic Assumptions and Therapeutic Interventions in War and Reconciliation', *Journal of Human Rights*, 8(1), 2009, p. 72.
27. According to Herman, for instance, there can be no successful mourning of loss (and hence no reconnection between individual and community) until the survivor is able to break through the 'barriers of amnesia'. In her account, '[t]he fundamental premise of the psychotherapeutic work is a belief in the restorative power of truth-telling'. This, predominantly Freudian, view does not, however, appear to exclude Christian themes of healing. Testimony, Herman tells us, conjoins a private dimension, 'which is confessional

and spiritual', with a public dimension, 'which is political and juridical', in such a way as to create a 'ritual of healing'. In a similar vein, but with an inverse focus, Mark Amstutz treats public recognition as indispensable to the theological idea of communal healing through repentance and forgiveness. 'If deep political cleavages of society are to be healed and if enemies are to move towards reconciliation', he notes, 'the injuries, crimes, and injustices of the past will have to be confronted through truth telling and acknowledgment.' Like Herman, however, he is not opposed to appealing to an altogether different discourse of healing to bolster the imperative of recognition. 'One of the accepted canons in psychotherapy', he suggests, 'is that mental health requires people to "come to terms" with the past.' 'This', he goes on, 'cannot be achieved by denial, repression, or neglect but only by directly confronting past injuries so that they cease to control the present.' J.L. Herman, *Trauma and Recovery*, New York: Basic Books, 1992, pp. 181–184; and M. Amstutz, *The Healing of Nations: The Promise and Limits of Political Forgiveness*, Lanham, MD: Rowman and Littlefield, 2005, pp. 24, 221. See also G. Schwan, 'The "Healing" Value of Truth-Telling: Chances and Social Conditions in a Secularized World', *Social Research*, 65(4), 1998, pp. 725–740.
28. G. Agamben, *Homo Sacer: Sovereign Power and Bare Life*, Stanford, CA: Stanford University Press, 1998, pp. 104–111.
29. Camus, *The Fall*, p. 101.
30. Camus, *The Fall*, pp. 100–104. After concluding this study, I stumbled across Bernhard Forchtner's *Lessons from the Past?*, which devotes a very illuminating chapter to the idea of the judge-penitent. My reading differs somewhat from his, however, because it does not link the subject position of the judge-penitent to having worked through the past and thereby acquired the right to provide moral guidance to others. On my reading, Camus' judge-penitent is a much less resolved character. Far from claiming that he has worked through the past and undergone a transformation, he admits to being the same person as he always was: a narcissist who represents himself in particular ways in public (who, in effect, becomes double) as a means of regaining a sense of sovereign elevation. In effect, he is less a figure of mourning, which implies a genuine process of 'working through', than of disassociation—the point of his endless confession is not to exercise judgement upon an externalized other but to get free of the past by externalizing himself as other. See B. Forchtner, *Lessons from the Past?*, London: Palgrave Macmillan, 2016, pp. 151–186.
31. Camus, *The Fall*, pp. 102–104.
32. Camus, *The Fall*, pp. 104–105.
33. M. Minow, *Between Vengeance and Forgiveness*, Boston, MA: Beacon Press, 1998, p. 66.
34. Camus' reflections on Algeria are instructive of his own hesitations about the life of 'little ease': 'It is good for a nation to be strong enough in its traditions and honorable enough to find the courage to denounce its own errors, but it must not forget the reasons it may still have to think well of itself. It is in any case dangerous to ask it to confess sole responsibility and resign itself to perpetual penance. I believe in a policy of reparations for Algeria, not a policy of expiation'. Camus, *Algerian Chronicles*, p. 31.

Bibliography

Adam, Herbert and Adam, Kanya. 'The Politics of Memory in Divided Societies' in W. James and L. Van De Vijver (eds.), *After the TRC: Reflections on Truth and Reconciliation in South Africa*, Athens, OH: Ohio University Press, 2001: 32–51.
Adorno, Theodor. 'What Does Coming to Terms with the Past Mean?' in G. Hartman (ed.), *Bitburg in Moral and Political Perspective*, Bloomington, IN: Indiana University Press, 1986: 114–130.
Agamben, Giorgio. *Homo Sacer: Sovereign Power and Bare Life*, Stanford, CA: Stanford University Press, 1998.
Agamben, Giorgio. *State of Exception*, Chicago, IL: University of Chicago Press, 2005.
Agamben, Giorgio. *Stasis: Civil War as Political Paradigm*, Stanford, CA: Stanford University Press. 2015.
Aguilar, Paloma. 'Justice, Politics and Memory in the Spanish Transition' in A. Barahona de Brito, C. Enriquez, and P. Aguilar (eds.), *The Politics of Memory: Transitional Justice in Democratising Societies*, Oxford: Oxford University Press, 2001: 92–118.
Aguilar, Paloma. *Memory and Amnesia: The Role of the Spanish Civil War in the Transition to Democracy*, trans. by Mark Oakley, New York: Berghahn Books, 2002.
Aldana, Raquel. 'A Victim-Centered Reflection on Truth Commissions and Prosecutions as a Response to Mass Atrocities', *Journal of Human Rights*, 5(1), 2006: 107–126.
Allan, Alfred. 'Truth and Reconciliation: A Psycholegal Perspective', *Ethnicity and Health*, 5(3–4), 2000: 191–204.
Amstutz, Mark. *The Healing of Nations: The Promise and Limits of Political Forgiveness*, Lanham, MD: Rowman and Littlefield, 2005.
Andrieu. Kora. '"Sorry for the Genocide": How Public Apologies Can Help Promote National Reconciliation', *Millennium: Journal of International Studies*, 38(3), 2009: 3–23.
Arendt, Hannah. *The Human Condition*, Chicago, IL: University of Chicago Press, 1958.
Arendt, Hannah. 'Totalitarian Imperialism: Reflections on the Hungarian Revolution', *The Journal of Politics*, 20(1), 1958: 5–43.
Arendt, Hannah. *The Origins of Totalitarianism*, San Diego, CA: Harcourt Brace, 1976.
Arendt, Hannah. 'Collective Responsibility' in J.W. Bernauer (ed.), *Amor Mundi: Explorations in the Faith and Thought of Hannah Arendt*, Boston, MA: Martinus Nijhoff Publishers, 1987: 43–50.
Arendt, Hannah. *Essays in Understanding*, New York: Schocken Books, 2005.
Arendt, Hannah. *The Promise of Politics*, New York: Schocken Books, 2005.
Aristotle, *The Politics and the Constitution of Athens*, edited by S. Everson, Cambridge: Cambridge University Press, 1996.
Aristotle/Horace/Longinus, *Classical Literary Criticism*, edited by T.S. Dorsch, Harmondsworth: Penguin, 1986.
Ash, Timothy Garton. 'The Truth about Dictatorship', *The New York Review of Books*, February 1998: 3–5.
Ash, Timothy Garton. *History of the Present: Essays, Sketches and Dispatches from Europe in the 1990s*, London: Allen Lane, 1999.
Assman, Jan. 'Collective Memory and Cultural Identity', *New German Critique*, 65, 1995: 125–133.
Azanian Peoples Organization (AZAPO) and others v. President of the Republic of South Africa and others, Constitutional Court of South Africa, Case No. CCT 117/96 (25 July 1996).
Bach, Jonathan and Nienass, Benjamin, 'Introduction: Innocence and the Politics of Memory', *German Politics and Society*, 39(1), 2021: 1–12.

Bibliography

Baptist, Karen, 'Shades of Grey: The Role of the Sublime in the Memorial to the Murdered Jews of Europe', *Landscape Review*, 14(2), 2012.

Barkan, Elazar. *The Guilt of Nations: Restitution and Negotiating Historical Injustices*. Baltimore, MD: Johns Hopkins University Press, 2000.

Barta, Tony. 'Sorry and Not Sorry, in Australia: How the Apology to the Stolen Generations Buried a History of Genocide', *Journal of Genocide Research*, 10(2), 2008: 201–214.

Behrendt, Larissa. 'Genocide: The Distance Between Law and Life', *Aboriginal History*, 25, 2001.

Bell, Duncan. 'Introduction' in D. Bell (ed.), *Memory, Trauma and World Politics: Reflections on the Relationship Between Past and Present*, London: Palgrave Macmillan, 2006: 1–29.

Benjamin, Andrew. 'Now Still Absent: Eisenman's Memorial to the Murdered Jews of Europe', *Architectural Theory Review*, 8(1), 2003: 57–62.

Bentley, Tom. 'The Sorrow of Empire', *Review of International Studies*, 41(3), 2015: 623–645.

Bentley, Tom. 'Settler State Apologies and the Elusiveness of Forgiveness: The Purification Ritual That Does Not Purify', *Contemporary Political Theory*, 19(3), 2019: 381–403.

Biggar, Nigel (ed.). *Burying the Past: Making Peace and Doing Justice after Civil Conflict*, Washington, DC: Georgetown University Press, 2003.

Booth, W. James. 'Communities of Memory: On Identity, Memory, and Debt', *American Political Science Review*, 93(2), 1999: 249–263.

Booth, W. James. 'The Unforgotten: Memories of Justice', *American Political Science Review*, 95(4), 2001: 777–791.

Booth, W. James. 'Kashmir Road: Some Reflections on Memory and Violence', *Millennium: Journal of International Studies*, 38(2), 2009: 361–377.

Boraine, Alex. 'Truth and Reconciliation in South Africa: The Third Way', in R.I. Rotberg and D.F. Thompson (eds.), *Truth v. Justice: The Morality of Truth Commissions*, Princeton, NJ: Princeton University Press, 2000: 141–158.

Borneman, John. 'Can Public Apologies Contribute to Peace? An Argument for Retribution', *Anthropology of East Europe Review*, 17(1), 1999: 7–20.

Borneman, John. 'Political Apologies as Performative Redress', *SAIS Review*, 25(2), 2005: 53–66.

Brasset, James and Vaughan-Williams, Nick. 'Governing Traumatic Events', *Alternatives: Global, Local, Political*, 37(3), 2012: 183–187.

Brody, Richard. 'The Inadequacy of Berlin's "Memorial to the Murdered Jews of Europe"', *The New Yorker*, 12 July 2012.

Brooks, Roy. L. *When Sorry Isn't Enough: The Controversy over Apologies and Reparations for Human Injustice*, New York: New York University Press, 1999.

Brooks, Roy L. 'Reflections on Reparations' in J. Torpey (ed.), *Politics and the Past: On Repairing Historical Injustices*, Lanham, MD: Rowman and Littlefield, 2003: 103–114.

Brounéus, Karen. 'The Trauma of Truth Telling: Effects of Witnessing in Rwandan Gacaca Courts on Psychological Health', *Journal of Conflict Resolution*, 54(3), 2010: 408–437.

Brown, Wendy. *States of Injury: Power and Freedom in Late Modernity*, Princeton, NJ: Princeton University Press, 1995.

Bruckner, Pascal. *The Tyranny of Guilt: An Essay on Western Masochism*, Princeton, NJ: Princeton University Press, 2010.

Brudholm, Thomas. *Resentment's Virtue: Jena Amery and the Refusal to Forgive*, Philadelphia, PA: Temple University Press, 2008.

Brudholm, Thomas and Cushman, Thomas (eds.). *The Religious in Responses to Mass Atrocity*, Cambridge: Cambridge University Press, 2009.

Buckley-Zistel, Susanne. 'Tracing the Politics of Aesthetics: From Imposing, via Counter to Affirmative Memorials to Violence', *Memory Studies*, 14(4), 2021: 781–796.

Bundy, Colin. 'The Beast of the Past: History and the TRC' in W. James and L. Van de Vijver (eds.), *After the TRC: Reflections on Truth and Reconciliation in South Africa*, Athens, OH: Ohio University Press, 2001: 9–21.

Buruma, Ian. *The Wages of Guilt: Memories of War in Germany and Japan*, London: Atlantic Books, 2009.

Bibliography 315

Butler, Judith. *The Psychic Life of Power:* Theories in Subjection, Stanford, CA: Stanford University Press, 1997.
Butler, Judith. *Precarious Life: The Powers of Mourning and Violence*, London: Verso, 2006.
Cairns, Alan. 'Coming to Terms with the Past' in J. Torpey (ed.), *Politics and the Past: On Repairing Historical Injustices*, Lanham, MD: Rowman and Littlefield, 2003: 63–90.
Callaghan, Mark. *Empathetic Memorials: The Other Designs for the Berlin Holocaust Memorial*, London: Palgrave Macmillan, 2020.
Camus, Albert. *The Fall*, Harmondsworth: Penguin, 1975.
Camus, Albert. *Algerian Chronicles*, ed by A. Kaplan, trans by A. Goldhammer, Cambridge, Mass: Belknap Press, 2014.
Carson, Anne. *Grief Lessons: Four Plays by Euripides*, New York: New York Review of Books, 2006.
Carter, David. *The Politics of Greek Tragedy*. Exeter: Bristol Phoenix Press, 2007.
Cartledge, Paul. '"Deep Plays": Theatre as Process in Greek Civic Life' in P.E. Easterling (ed.), *The Cambridge Companion to Greek Tragedy*, Cambridge: Cambridge University Press, 2007.
Celermajer, Danielle. 'The Apology in Australia: Re-Covenanting the National Imaginary' in E. Barkan and A. Karn (eds.), *Taking Wrongs Seriously: Apologies and Reconciliation*, Stanford, CA: Stanford University Press, 2006, pp. 153–184.
Celermajer, Danielle. 'Apology and the Possibility of Ethical Politics', *JCRT*, 9(1), winter 2008: 14–34.
Celermajer, Danielle. *The Sins of the Nation and the Ritual of Apologies*, Cambridge: Cambridge University Press, 2009.
Cels, Sanderijn. 'Interpreting Political Apologies: The Neglected Role of Performance', *Political Psychology*, 36(3), 2015: 351–360.
Chakravarti, Sonali. *Sing the Rage: Listening to Anger after Mass Violence*, Chicago, IL: University of Chicago Press, 2014.
Chaudhuri, Amit. 'The Real Meaning of Rhodes Must Fall', *The Guardian*, 16 March 2016.
Cohen, David. 'The Rhetoric of Justice: Strategies of Reconciliation and Revenge in the Restoration of Athenian Democracy in 403 BC', *European Journal of Sociology*, 42(2), 2001: 335–356.
Coicaud, Jean-Marc and Jonsson, Jibecke. 'Elements of a Road Map for a Politics of Apology' in M. Gibney, R.E. Howard-Hassman, J. Coicaud, and N. Steiner (eds.), *The Age of Apology: Facing Up to the Past*, Philadelphia, PA: University of Pennsylvania Press, 2008.
Colaiaco, James. *Socrates against Athens: Philosophy on Trial*, New York: Routledge, 2001.
Comay, Rebecca. 'Resistance and Repetition: Freud and Hegel', *Research in Phenomenology*, 45, 2015: 237–266.
Critchley, Simon. *Tragedy, the Greeks and Us*, London: Profile Books, 2019.
Cunningham, Michael. 'Saying Sorry: The Politics of Apology', *The Political Quarterly*, 70(3), 1999: 285–293.
Danto, Arthur C. 'The Vietnam Veterans Memorial', *The Nation*, 31 August 1985: 152–155.
Davis, Madeleine. 'Is Spain Recovering Its Memory? Breaking the *Pacto del Olvido*', *Human Rights Quarterly*, 27(3), 2005: 858–880.
Debord, Guy. *The Society of the Spectacle*, Detroit, MI: Black and Red, 1983.
De Mata, Ignacio Fernández. 'Sin Carries the Penance: The Spanish Civil War's Conflicts of Guilt and Justice' in K. Chainoglou, B. Collins, M. Phillips, and J. Strawson (eds.), *Injustice, Memory and Faith in Human Rights*, London: Routledge, 2018.
De Rivera, Joseph and Páez, Dario. 'Emotional Climate, Human Security, and Cultures of Peace', *Journal of Social Issues*, 63(2), 2007: 233–253.
Derrida, Jacques. *On Cosmopolitanism and Forgiveness*, London: Routledge, 2001.
Derrida, Jacques. *Rogues: Two Essays on Reason*, Stanford, CA: Stanford University Press, 2005.
Dolan, Emma. 'The Gendered Politics of Recognition and Recognizability through Political Apology', *Journal of Human Rights*, 20(5), 2021: 614–629.
Dreyfus, Herbert and Rabinow, Paul. *Michel Foucault: Beyond Structuralism and Hermeneutics*, Chicago, IL: University of Chicago Press, 1982.
Eagleton, Terry. 'Tragedy and Revolution' in C. Davis, J. Milbank and S. Zizeck (eds), *Theology and the Political: The New Debate*, Durham: Duke University Press, 2005.

Edkins, Jenny. *Trauma and the Memory of Politics*, Cambridge: Cambridge University Press, 2003.
Elster, Jon. *Closing the Books*, Cambridge: Cambridge University Press, 2004.
Erikson, Kai. 'Notes on Trauma and Community', *American Imago*, 48(4), 1991: 455–472.
Erikson, Kai. *A New Species of Trouble: Explorations in Disaster, Trauma, and Community*. New York: W.W. Norton and Co., 1994.
Escobedo, Andrew. 'On Sincere Apologies: Saying "Sorry" in *Hamlet*', *Philosophy and Literature*, 41(1A), 2017: 155–177.
Esposito, Robert. 'Community, Immunity, Biopolitics', *Angelaki: Journal of Theoretical Humanities*, 18(3), 2013: 83–90.
Euben, Peter. *The Tragedy of Political Theory: The Road Not Taken*, Princeton, NJ: Princeton University Press, 1990.
Fagenblat, Michael. 'The Apology, the Secular and the Theologico-Political', *Dialogue*, 27(2), 2008: 16–32.
Fassin, Didier. 'Another Politics of Life is Possible', *Theory, Culture and Society*, 26(5), 2009: 44–60.
Finley, M.I. 'Athenian Demagogues', *Past and Present*, 21, 1962: 3–24.
Forchtner, Bernhard. *Lessons from the Past? Memory, Narrativity and Subjectivity*, London: Palgrave Macmillan, 2016.
Foucault, Michel. *Power/Knowledge: Selected Interviews and Writings 1972–1977*, ed. by Colin Gordon, New York: Pantheon Books, 1980.
Foucault, Michel. 'Space, Knowledge, and Power' in P. Rabinow (ed.), *The Foucault Reader*, Harmondsworth: Penguin Books, 1987, pp. 239–258.
Foucault, Michel. *The History of Sexuality: An Introduction*, Harmondsworth: Penguin, 1987.
Foucault, Michel. *Discipline and Punish: The Birth of the Prison*, London: Penguin, 1991.
Foucault, Michel. 'Governmentality' in G. Burchell, C. Gordon, and P. Miller (eds.), *The Foucault Effect: Studies in Governmentality*, London: Harvester Wheatsheaf, 1991, pp. 87–104.
Foucault, Michel. *Society Must Be Defended: Lectures at the Collège de France 1975–76*, trans. by David Macey, London: Penguin Books, 2004.
Foucault, Michel. *Security, Territory, Population: Lectures at the Collège de France 1977–1978*, New York: Picador, 2007.
Freud, Sigmund. *Introductory Lectures on Psychoanalysis 1*, trans. by J. Strachey, Harmondsworth: Penguin Books, 1981.
Freud, Sigmund. 'Mourning and Melancholia' in *On Metapsychology: The Theory of Psychoanalysis*, Pelican Freud Library, volume 11, Harmondsworth: Penguin, 1987.
Galanter, Marc. 'Righting Old Wrongs' in Nancy L. Rosenblum (ed.), *Breaking the Cycles of Hatred: Memory, Law and Repair*, Princeton, NJ: Princeton University Press, 2003.
Gayland, Susan. 'Machiavelli's Medical *Mandragola*: Knowledge, Food, and Feces', *Renaissance Quarterly*, 74, 2021: 59–93.
Gemes, Juno. 'Witnessing the Apology', *Australian Aboriginal Studies*, 1, 2008: 115–123.
Ghandi, Leela. *Postcolonial Theory*, St Leonards: Allen and Unwin, 1998.
Gibney, Mark. 'Introduction to a Symposium on Political Apologies', *Journal of Human Rights*, 20(5), 2021: 580–581.
Gibney, Mark and Roxstrom, Erik. 'The Status of State Apologies', *Human Rights Quarterly*, 23, 2001: 911–939.
Gobodo-Madikizela, Pumla. 'Remorse, Forgiveness and Rehumanisation: Stories from South Africa', *Journal of Humanistic Psychology*, 42(1), 2002: 7–32.
Goldhill, Simon. *Love, Sex and Tragedy: How the Ancient World Shapes Our Lives*, Chicago, IL: University of Chicago Press, 2004.
González-Ruibal, Alfredo. 'Excavating Memory, Burying History: Lessons from the Spanish Civil War' in K.P. Hofmann, R. Bernbeck, and U. Sommer (eds.), *Between Memory Sites and Memory Networks*, Berlin Studies of the Ancient World 45: 279–302.
Gook, Ben. *Divided Subjects, Invisible Borders: Re-unified Germany after 1989*, London: Rowman and Littlefield, 2015.

Gordon, Colin. 'Governmental Rationality: An Introduction' in G. Burchill, C. Gordon, and P. Miller (eds.), *The Foucault Effect: Studies in Governmentality*. Chicago, IL: University of Chicago Press, 1991.

Govier, Trudy. *Forgiveness and Revenge*, London: Routledge, 2002.

Govier, Trudy and Verwoerd, Wilhelm. 'Taking Wrongs Seriously: A Qualified Defence of Public Apologies', *Saskatchewan Law Review*, 65, 2002: 139–162.

Govier, Trudy and Verwoerd, Wilhelm. 'The Promise and Pitfalls of Apology', *Journal of Social Philosophy*, 33(1), 2002: 67–82.

Grass, Günther. *The Tin Drum*, London: Penguin, 2010.

Graybill, Lyn. 'South Africa's Truth and Reconciliation Commission: Ethical and Theological Perspectives', *Ethics and International Affairs*, 12, 1998: 43–62.

Greenawalt, Kent. 'Amnesty's Justice' in R. Rotberg and D. Thompson, *Truth v. Justice: The Morality of Truth Commissions*, Princeton, NJ: Princeton University Press, 2000: 189–211.

Greer, Germaine. *Shakespeare*, Oxford: Oxford University Press, 1996.

Grenzer, Elke. 'The Topographies of Memory in Berlin: The Neue Wache and the Memorial for the Murdered Jews of Europe', *Canadian Journal of Urban Research*, 11(1), 2002: 93–110.

Griswold, Charles. *Forgiveness: A Philosophical Exploration*, Cambridge: Cambridge University Press, 2007.

Gross, Daniel. *The Secret History of Emotion: From Aristotle's Rhetoric to Modern Brain Science*, Chicago, IL: University of Chicago Press, 2007.

Gutmann, Amy and Thompson, Dennis. 'The Moral Foundations of Truth Commissions' in R. Rotberg and D. Thompson (eds.), *Truth v. Justice: The Morality of Truth Commissions*, Princeton, NJ: Princeton University Press, 2000: 22–45.

Habermas, Jürgen. 'Defusing the Past: A Politico-Cultural Tract' in G. Hartmann (ed.), *Bitburg in Moral and Political Perspective*, Bloomington, IN: Indiana University Press, 1986: 43–52.

Habermas, Jürgen. 'A Kind of Settlement of Damages', *New German Critique*, 44, 1988: 25–40.

Habermas, Jürgen. 'Concerning the Public Use of History', *New German Critique*, 44, 1988: 40–51.

Habermas, Jürgen. *A Berlin Republic: Writings on Germany*, trans. by Steven Rendall, Cambridge: Polity Press, 1998.

Habermas, Jürgen. *Time of Transitions*, ed. and trans. by Ciaran Cronin and Max Pensky, Cambridge: Polity, 2006.

Hacking, Ian. 'Memoro-Politics, Trauma and the Soul', *History of the Human Sciences*, 7(2), 1994: 29–52.

Halbwachs, Maurice. *On Collective Memory*, Chicago, IL: University of Chicago Press, 1992.

Hamber, Brandon and Wilson, Richard. 'Symbolic Closure through Memory, Reparation and Revenge in Post-Conflict Societies', *Journal of Human Rights*, 1(1), 2002: 35–53.

Hampsher-Monk, Ian. *A History of Modern Political Thought: Major Political Thinkers from Hobbes to Marx*, Oxford: Blackwell, 1992.

Hayner, Priscilla. 'Fifteen Truth Commissions—1974 to 1994: A Comparative Study', *Human Rights Quarterly*, 16(4), 1994: 597–655.

Hayner, Priscilla. 'Same Species, Different Animal: How South Africa Compares to Truth Commissions Worldwide' in C. Villa-Vincencio and W. Verwoerd (eds.), *Looking Back, Reaching Forward: Reflections on the Truth and Reconciliation Commission of South Africa*, London: Zed Books, 2000: 32–42.

Hazan, Pierre. *Judging War, Judging History: Behind Truth and Reconciliation*, Stanford, CA: Stanford University Press, 2010.

Henry, Yazir. 'Where Healing Begins' in C. Villa-Vincencio and W. Verwoerd (eds.), *Looking Back, Reaching Forward: Reflections on the Truth and Reconciliation Commission of South Africa*, Cape Town: University of Cape town Press, 2000: 166–173.

Herman, Judith Lewis. *Trauma and Recovery*, New York: Basic Books, 1992.

Hobbes, Thomas. *Leviathan*, Oxford: Oxford University Press, 1998.

Hoenselaars, Ton. 'Shakespeare's English History Plays' in M. de Grazia and S. Wells (eds.), *The New Cambridge Companion to Shakespeare*, Cambridge: Cambridge University Press, 2010: 137–153.

Holmes, Brooke. *Gender: Antiquity and Its Legacy*, Oxford: Oxford University Press, 2012.
Holst-Warhaft, Gail. *Dangerous Voices: Women's Laments in Greek Literature*, Florence: Taylor and Francis, 1992.
Holub, Robert C. *Jurgen Habermas: Critic in the Public Sphere*, London: Routledge, 1991.
Honig, Bonnie. *Antigone Interrupted*, Cambridge: Cambridge University Press, 2013.
Humphrey, Michael. *The Politics of Atrocity and Reconciliation: From Terror to Trauma*, London: Routledge, 2002.
Hutchinson, Emma. *Affective Communities in World Politics*, Cambridge: Cambridge University Press, 2016.
James, Matt. 'Wrestling with the Past: Apologies, Quasi-Apologies and Non-Apologies in Canada' in M. Gibney, R.E. Howard-Hassman, J. Coicaud, and N. Steiner (eds.), *The Age of Apology: Facing Up to the Past*, Philadelphia, PA: University of Pennsylvania Press, 2008.
Jankélévitch, Vladimir. 'Should We Pardon Them?', *Critical Inquiry*, 22, spring 1996: 552–572.
Joyce, Richard. 'Apologising', *Public Affairs Quarterly*, 13(2), 1999: 159–173.
Junker, William. 'Past's Weight, Future's Promise: Reading *Electra*', *Philosophy and Literature*, 27(2), 2003: 402–414.
Kampf, Zophar and Löwenheim, Nava. 'Rituals of Apology in the Global Arena', *Security Dialogue*, 43(1), 2012: 43–60.
Kant, Immanuel. 'Perpetual Peace: A Philosophical Sketch' in F. Reiss (ed.), *Kant: Political Writings*, Cambridge: Cambridge University Press, 1991.
Kantorowicz, Ernest. *The King's Two Bodies: A Study in Medieval Political Theology*, Princeton, NJ: Princeton University Press, 1957.
Keuls, Eva. *The Reign of the Phallus: Sexual Politics in Ancient Athens*, Berkeley, CA: University of California Press, 1993.
Kinnval, Catarina. 'Globalization and Religious Nationalism: Self, Identity and the Search for Ontological Security', *Political Psychology*, 25(5), 2004: 741–767.
Kiss, Elizabeth. 'Moral Ambition within and beyond Political Constraints: Reflections on Restorative Justice' in R.I. Rotberg and D. Thompson (eds.), *Truth v. Justice: The Morality of Truth Commissions*, Princeton, NJ: Princeton University Press, 2000: 68–99.
Klep, Katrien. 'Tracing Collective Memory: Chilean Truth Commissions and Memorial Sites', *Memory Studies*, 5(3), 2012: 259–269.
Klosko, George. *History of Political Theory*, vol. 2, Belmont, CA: Thompson Wadsworth, 1995.
Kovach, Thomas A. and Walser, Martin. *The Burden of the Past: Martin Walser on Modern German Identity—Texts, Contexts, Commentary*, Camden: Boydell & Brewer, 2008.
Krog, Antjie. *Country of My Skull*, London: Vintage, 1999.
La Capra, Dominic. *Writing History, Writing Trauma*, Baltimore, MD: The Johns Hopkins University Press, 2001.
Laub, Dori. 'Truth and Testimony: The Process and the Struggle', *American Imago*, 48(1), 1991: 75–91.
Lazare, Aron. *On Apology*, Oxford: Oxford University Press, 2004.
Lear, Jonathon. *Open-Minded: Working Out the Logic of the Soul*, Cambridge, MA: Harvard University Press, 1998.
Leebaw, Bronwyn. 'Legitimation or Judgement? South Africa's Restorative Approach to Transitional Justice', *Polity*, 36(1), 2003: 23–51.
Leebaw, Bronwyn, 'The Irreconcilable Goals of Transitional Justice', *Human Rights Quarterly*, 30(1), 2008: 95–118.
Leebaw, Bronwyn. 'Mobilizing Emotions: Shame, Victimhood and Agency' in M.N. Barnett (ed.), *Humanitarianism and Human Rights*, Cambridge: Cambridge University Press, 2020, pp. 140–159.
Levi, Primo. *The Drowned and the Saved*, London: Penguin Books, 1988.
Levi, Primo. *Survival in Auschwitz: The Nazi Assault on Humanity*, New York: Touchstone, 1996.
Levinson, Sanford. *Written in Stone: Public Monuments in Changing Societies*, Durham, NC: Duke University Press, 1998.

Lewis, Alison. 'Germany's Metamorphosis: Memory and the Holocaust in the Berlin Republic', *Cultural Studies Review*, 9(2), 2003: 102–122.
Lind, Jennifer. *Sorry States: Apologies in International Politics*. Ithaca, NY: Cornell University Press, 2008.
Lindstrom, Randall. 'Berlin's Kenotic Triad of Architecture', *Academia Letters*, August 2021, Article 3407: 1–6.
Little, David. 'A Different Kind of Justice: Dealing with Human Rights Violations in Transitional Societies', *Ethics and International Affairs*, 13, 1999: 65–80.
Lloyd, Genevieve. *The Man of Reason: 'Male' and 'Female' in Western Philosophy*, London: Routledge, 1984.
Locke, John. *The Two Treatises of Government*, ed. by Peter Laslett, Cambridge: Cambridge University Press, 1988.
Loraux, Nicole. *Tragic Ways of Killing a Woman*, trans. by Anthony Forster, Cambridge, MA: Harvard University Press, 1991.
Loraux, Nicole. *Mothers in Mourning*, Ithaca, NY: Cornell University Press, 1998.
Loraux, Nicole. *The Divided City: On Memory and Forgetting in Ancient Athens*, New York: Zone Books, 2006.
Lorde, Audre. *The Collected Poems of Audre Lorde*, New York: WW Norton, 1997.
Lotta, Maria-Sibylla. 'The Art of Apology: On the True and the Phony in Political Apology' in M. Buschmeier and K. von Kellenback (eds.), *Guilt: A Force of Cultural Transformation*, Oxford: Oxford University Press, 2021.
Lund, Guiliana. '"Healing the Nation": Medicolonial Discourse and the State of Emergency from Apartheid to Truth and Reconciliation', *Cultural Critique*, 54, 2003: 88–119.
Macey, David. 'Rethinking Biopolitics, Race and Power in the Wake of Foucault', *Theory, Culture, and Society*, 26(6), 2009: 186–205.
Maddison, Sarah. 'Why the Statues Must Fall', *The Sydney Morning Herald*, 12 June 2020.
Mahlum, Lisa. 'The Similarities of Difference: A Comparative Analysis of the New England Holocaust Memorial in Boston and the Memorial to the Murdered Jews of Europe in Berlin', *Intersections*, 10(1), 2009: 279–308.
Maier, Charles. *The Unmasterable Past: History, Holocaust, and German National Identity*, Cambridge, MA: Harvard University Press, 1988.
Maier, Charles. 'A Surfeit of Memory? Reflections on History, Melancholy and Denial', *History and Memory*, 5(2), 1993: 136–151.
Mamdani, Mahmood. 'Amnesty or Impunity? A Preliminary Critique of the Report of the Truth and Reconciliation Commission of South Africa', *Diacritics*, 32(3/4), 2002: 32–59.
Manne, Robert. *In Denial: The Stolen Generations and the Right*, The Australian Quarterly Essay, April 2001.
Manne, Robert. 'Sorry Business', *The Monthly*, March 2008, no. 32.
Maxwell, Krista. 'Settler Humanitarianism: Healing the Indigenous Child Victim', *Comparative Studies in Society and History*, 59(4), 2017: 974–1007.
McAlinden, Anne-Marie. 'Apologies as "Shame Management": The Politics of Remorse in the Aftermath of Historical Institutional Abuse', *Legal Studies*, 1, 2021: 1–22.
McGregor, Russell. 'Governance, Not Genocide: Aboriginal Assimilation in the Postwar Era' in A.D. Moses (ed.), *Genocide and Settler Society*, New York: Berghahn Books, 2005: 290–312.
Meier, Christian. *The Political Art of Greek Tragedy*, trans. by Andrew Webber, Cambridge: Polity Press, 1993.
Mendeloff, David. 'Truth-Seeking, Truth-Telling, and Postconflict Peacebuilding: Curb the Enthusiasm?', *International Studies Review*, 6(3), 2004: 355–380.
Mihai, Mihaela. 'When the State Says "Sorry": State Apologies as Exemplary Political Judgements', *The Journal of Political Philosophy*, 21(2), 2013: 200–220.
Mihai, Mihaela. *Negative Emotions and Transition Justice*, Columbia, MO: Columbia University Press, 2016.

Milchman. Alan and Rosenberg, Alan. 'Michel Foucault: Crises and Problemizations', *The Review of Politics*, 67(2), 2005: 335–351.
Million, Dian. *Therapeutic Nations: Healing in an Age of Indigenous Human Rights*, Tucson, AZ: University of Arizona Press, 2013.
Minow, Martha. *Between Vengeance and Forgiveness*, Boston, MA: Beacon Press, 1998.
Minow, Martha. 'The Hope for Healing: What Can Truth Commissions Do?' in R. Rotberg and D. Thompson (eds.), *Truth v. Justice: The Morality of Truth Commissions*, Princeton, NJ: Princeton University Press, 2000: 235–261.
Mitscherlich, Alexander and Margarete. *The Inability to Mourn*, trans. by B.R. Placzek, New York: Grove Press, 1975.
Moon, Claire. 'Healing Past Violence: Traumatic Assumptions and Therapeutic Interventions in War and Reconciliation', *Journal of Human Rights*, 8(1), 2009: 71–91.
Mouffe, Chantal. *On the Political*, London: Routledge, 2005.
Msimang, Sisonke. 'All Is Not Forgiven: South Africa and the Scars of Apartheid', *Foreign Affairs*, 97(1), 2018: 28–34.
Muldoon, Paul. 'Thinking Responsibility Differently: Reconciliation and the Tragedy of Colonisation', *Journal of Intercultural Studies*, 26(3), 2005: 237–255.
Muldoon, Paul. 'After Apology: The Remains of the Past', *Australian Humanities Review*, 61, 2017: 129–144.
Muldoon, Paul. 'A Reconciliation Most Desirable: Shame, Narcissism, Apology and Justice', *International Political Science Review*, 38(2), 2017: 213–227.
Muldoon, Paul. 'The Power of Forgetting: Ressentiment, Guilt and Transformative Politics', *Political Psychology*, 38(4), 2017: 669–683.
Murphy, Jeffrey. *Getting Even: Forgiveness and Its Limits*, Oxford: Oxford University Press, 2003.
Nagy, Rosemary. 'The Ambiguities of Reconciliation and Responsibility in South Africa', *Political Studies*, 52, 2004: 709–727.
Neill, Michael. 'Shakespeare's Tragedies' in M. de Grazia and S. Wells (eds.), *The New Cambridge Companion to Shakespeare*, Cambridge: Cambridge University Press, 2010: 121–137.
Nietzsche, Frederick. *On the Genealogy of Morals*, trans. by W. Kaufmann and R.J. Hollingdale, New York: Vintage, 1997.
Nietzsche, Frederick. *Untimely Meditations*, Cambridge: Cambridge University Press, 1997.
Nobles, Melissa. *The Politics of Official Apologies*, Cambridge: Cambridge University Press, 2008.
Ntsebeza, Dumisa. 'The Uses of Truth Commissions: Lessons for the World', in R. Rotberg and D. Thompson (eds.), *Truth v. Justice: The Morality of Truth Commissions*, Princeton, NJ: Princeton University Press, 2000: 158–170.
Nussbaum, Martha. *Upheaval of Thought: The Intelligence of the Emotions*, Cambridge, MA: Harvard University Press, 2001.
Nussbaum, Martha. *Political Emotions: Why Love Matters for Justice*, Cambridge, MA: The Belknap Press, 2013.
Nussbaum, Martha. *Anger and Forgiveness: Resentment, Generosity, Justice*, Oxford: Oxford University Press, 2016.
Oakeshott, Michael. *Hobbes: On Civil Association*, Oxford: Basil Blackwell, 1975.
Olick, Jeffrey. 'What Does It Mean to Normalise the Past?', *Social Science History*, 22(4), 1998: 547–568.
Olick, Jeffrey. 'Collective Memory: The Two Cultures', *Sociological Theory*, 17(3), 1999: 333–348.
Olubas, Brigitta and Greenwell, Lisa. 'Re-membering and Taking Up an Ethics of Listening: A Response to Loss and the Maternal in "the Stolen Children"', *Australian Humanities Review*, 15 October 1999.
Omar, Dullah. 'Introduction' to Promotion of National Unity and Reconciliation Act. www.justice.gov.za/trc/legal/justice.html.
Orr, Wendy. 'Reparation Delayed Is Healing Retarded' in C. Villa-Vincencio and W. Verwoerd (eds.), *Looking Back, Reaching Forward: Reflections on the Truth and Reconciliation Commission of South Africa*, London: Zed Books, 2000: 239–250.

Osiel, Mark. 'Why Prosecute? Critics of Punishment for Mass Atrocity', *Human Rights Quarterly*, 22(1), 2000: 118–147.
Páez, Darío. 'Official or Political Apologies and Improvement of Intergroup Relations: A Neo-Durkheimian Approach to Official Apologies as Rituals', *Revista de Psicologia Social*, 25(1), 2010: 1–15.
Philipose, Liz. 'The Politics of Pain and the End of Empire', *International Feminist Journal of Politics*, 9(1), 2007: 60–81.
Philpott, Daniel. 'Beyond Politics as Usual' in D. Philpott (ed.), *The Politics of Past Evil: Religion, Reconciliation and the Dilemmas of Transitional Justice*, Notre Dame, IN: University of Notre Dame Press, 2006: 11–42.
Pickford, Henry. 'Dialectical Reflections on Peter Eisenman's Memorial for the Murdered Jews of Europe', *Architectural Theory Review*, 17(2–3), 2012: 419–439.
Plato. *The Republic*, trans. by Robin Waterfield, Oxford: Oxford University Press, 1998.
Poole, Adrian. *Tragedy: Shakespeare and the Greek Example*, Oxford: Basil Blackwell, 1987.
Poole, Adrian. *Tragedy: A Very Short Introduction*, Oxford: Oxford University Press, 2005.
Pupavac, Vanessa. 'War on the Couch: The Emotionology of the New International Security Paradigm', *European Journal of Social Theory*, 7(2), 2004: 149–170.
Radstone, Susannah. 'The War of the Fathers: Trauma, Fantasy and September 11', *Signs: Journal of Women in Culture and Society*, 28(1), 2002: 457–459.
Rassool, Ciraj, Witz, Leslie, and Minkley, Gary. 'Burying and Memorialising the Body of Truth: The TRC and National Heritage' in W. James and L. Van de Vijver, *After the TRC: Reflections on Truth and Reconciliation in South Africa*, Cape Town: David Phillip Publishers, 2000: 115–127.
Read, Peter. *A Rape of the Soul So Profound: The Return of the Stolen Generation*, London: Routledge, 1999.
Reilly, Alex. 'Sovereign Apologies' in J. Evans, A. Reilly, and P. Wolfe (eds.), *Sovereignty: Frontiers of Possibility*, Honolulu, HI: University of Hawaii Press, 2013.
Ricoeur, Paul. *Figuring the Sacred: Religion, Narrative, Imagination*, Minneapolis, MN: Fortress Press, 1995.
Ricoeur, Paul. *Memory, History, Forgetting*, Chicago, IL: University of Chicago Press, 2004.
Rieff, David. *Against Remembrance*, Carlton: Melbourne University Press, 2011.
Rieff, David. *In Praise of Forgetting: Historical Memory and Its Ironies*, New Haven, CT: Yale University Press, 2016.
Rieff, Philip. *The Triumph of the Therapeutic: Uses of Faith after Freud*, New York: Harper and Row, 1966.
Rorty, Richard. *Achieving Our Country: Leftist Thought in Twentieth-Century America*, Cambridge, MA: Harvard University Press, 1997.
Rosenberg, Tina. *The Haunted Land: Facing Europe's Ghosts after Communism*, New York: Random House, 1995.
Rousso, Henri. *The Vichy Syndrome: History and Memory in France since 1944*, Cambridge, MA: Harvard University Press, 1991.
Rousso, Henri. *The Haunting Past: History, Memory, and Justice in Contemporary France*, Philadelphia, PA: University of Pennsylvanian Press, 1998.
Sachs, Albie. 'His Name Was Henry' in W. James and L. Van De Vijver (eds.), *After the TRC: Reflections on Truth and Reconciliation in South Africa*, Athens, OH: Ohio University Press, 2001: 94–101.
Salkever, Stephen. 'Tragedy and the Education of the *Demos*: Aristotle's Response to Plato' in P. Euben (ed.), *Greek Tragedy and Political Theory*, Princeton, NJ: Princeton University Press, 1990: 274–303.
Sanders, Mark. 'Ambiguities of Mourning: Law, Custom and Women before South Africa's Truth and Reconciliation Commission', *Law, Text, Culture*, 4(2), 1998: 105–151.
Sanders, Mark. *Complicities: The Intellectual and Apartheid*, Durham, NC: Duke University Press, 2002.
Sanders, Mark. 'Remembering Apartheid', *Diacritics*, 32(3/4), 2002: 60–80.

Schaap, Andrew. *Political Reconciliation*, London: Routledge, 2005.
Schmidt, Dennis. *On Germans and Other Greeks: Tragedy and Ethical Life*, Bloomington, IN: Indiana University Press, 2001.
Schmitt, Carl. *Political Theology*, Chicago, IL: University of Chicago Press, 2005.
Schmitt, Carl. *The Concept of the Political*, Chicago, IL: University of Chicago Press, 2007.
Schwan, Gesine. 'The "Healing" Value of Truth-Telling: Chances and Social Conditions in a Secularized World', *Social Research*, 65(4), 1988: 725–740.
Scott, David. *Omens of Adversity: Tragedy, Time, Memory, Justice*, Lanham, MD: Duke University Press, 2014.
Segal, Charles. *Euripides and the Poetics of Sorrow: Art, Gender and Commemoration in Alcestis, Hippolytus and Hecuba*, Durham, NC: Duke University Press, 1993.
Shakespeare, William. *Richard II*, ed. by C. Watts, Hertfordshire: Wordsworth, 2012.
Shakespeare, William. *Richard III*, ed. by J. Jowett, Oxford: Oxford University Press, 2000.
Shklar, Judith. *The Faces of Injustice*, New Haven, CT: Yale University Press, 1990.
Short, Damien. 'When Sorry Isn't Good Enough: Official Remembrance and Reconciliation in Australia', *Memory Studies*, 5(3), 2012: 293–304.
Shriver, Donald. 'Where and When in Political Life Is Justice Served by Forgiveness?' in N. Biggar (ed.), *Burying the Past: Making Peace and Doing Justice after Civil Conflict*, Washington, DC: Georgetown University Press, 2003: 25–45.
Shriver, Donald. *Honest Patriots: Loving a Country Enough to Remember Its Misdeeds*, Oxford: Oxford University Press, 2005.
Skinner, Quentin. 'Hobbes and the Purely Artificial Person of the State', *The Journal of Political Philosophy*, 7(1), 1999: 1–29.
Slye, R.C. 'Amnesty, Truth, and Reconciliation' in R. Rotberg and D. Thompson (eds.), *Truth v. Justice: The Morality of Truth Commissions*, Princeton, NJ: Princeton University Press, 2000: 170–188.
Smits, Katherine. 'Deliberation and Past Injustice: Recognition and the Reasonableness of Apology in the Australian Case', *Constellations*, 15(2), 2008: 236–248.
Sophocles. *Electra and Other Plays*, trans. by E.F. Watling, London: Penguin Books, 1953.
Sophocles. *The Three Theban Plays*, trans. by Robert Fagles, London: Penguin Books, 1984.
Spragens, Thomas. *Understanding Political Theory*, New York: St Martin's Press, 1976.
Sriram, Chandra. 'Transitional Justice Comes of Age: Enduring Lessons and Challenges', *Berkeley Journal of International Law*, 23(2), 2005: 101–118.
Staten, Henry. *Eros in Mourning: Homer to Lacan*, Baltimore, MD: Johns Hopkins University Press, 1995.
Stevens, Q. 'Nothing More Than Feelings: Abstract Memorials', *Architectural Theory Review*, 14(2), 2009: 156–172.
Stevens, Q. 'Visitor Responses at Berlin's Holocaust Memorial: Contrary to Conventions, Expectations and Rules', *Public Art Dialogue*, 2(1), 2012: 34–59.
Stevenson, Lisa. *Life Beside Itself: Imagining Care in the Canadian Arctic*, Oakland, CA: University of California Press, 2014.
Strong, Tracy B. 'Foreword' in C. Schmitt, *Political Theology*, Chicago, IL: University of Chicago Press, 2005.
Subotić, Jelena. 'Narrative, Ontological Security, and Foreign Policy Change', *Foreign Policy Analysis*, 12, 2016: 610–627.
Sztompka, Piotr. 'Cultural Trauma: The Other Face of Cultural Change', *European Journal of Social Theory*, 3(4), 2000: 449–466.
Tarlton, Charles. 'The Despotical Doctrine of Hobbes, Part II', *History of Political Thought*, 23(12), 2002: 63.
Tatum, James. *The Mourner's Song: War and Remembrance from the Iliad to Vietnam*, Chicago, IL: The University of Chicago Press, 2003.
Tavuchis, Nicholas. *Mea Culpa: A Sociology of Apology and Reconciliation*, Stanford, CA: Stanford University Press, 1991.

Taxidou, Olga. *Tragedy, Modernity and Mourning*, Edinburgh: Edinburgh University Press, 2004.
Taylor, Charles. 'The Politics of Recognition', in A. Gutmann (ed.), *Multiculturalism: Examining the Politics of Recognition*, Princeton: Princeton University Press, 1994: 25-73.
Thaler, Matthias. 'Just Pretending: Political Apologies for Historical Injustice and Vice's Tribute to Virtue', *Critical Review of International Social and Political Philosophy*, 15(3), 2012: 259-278.
Thompson, Janna. *Taking Responsibility for the Past*, Cambridge: Polity, 2002.
Thompson, Janna. 'Apology, Justice and Respect: A Critical Defense of Political Apology' in M. Gibney, R.E. Howard-Hassman, J.-M. Coicaud, and N. Steiner (eds.), *The Age of Apology*, Philadelphia, PA: University of Pennsylvania Press, 2008: 31-44.
Thucydides. *History of the Peloponnesian War*, London: Penguin Books, 1972.
Tillyard, E.M.W. *Shakespeare's History Plays*, London: Penguin Books, 1991.
Todorov, Tzvetan. *Hope and Memory*, London: Atlantic Books, 2005.
Torpey, John. '"Making Whole What Has Been Smashed": Reflections on Reparations', *Journal of Modern History*, 73(2), 2001: 333-358.
Torpey, John. 'Introduction: Politics and the Past' in J. Torpey (ed.), *Politics and the Past: On Repairing Historical Injustices*. Lanham, MD: Rowman and Littlefield, 2003.
Torpey, John. *Making Whole What Has Been Smashed: On Reparations Politics*, Cambridge, MA: Harvard University Press, 2006.
Trouillot, Michel-Rolph. 'Abortive Rituals: Historical Apologies in the Global Era', *Interventions: International Journal of Postcolonial Studies*, 2(2), 2000: 171-186.
Truth and Reconciliation Commission of South Africa Report.
Tutu, Desmond. 'Foreword' in H. Russell Botman and Robin Petersen (eds.), *To Remember and to Heal: Theological and Psychological Reflections on Truth and Reconciliation*, Cape Town: Human & Rousseau, 1996.
Tutu, Desmond. 'Interview', *Index on Censorship* 5, 1996.
Tutu, Desmond. *No Future without Forgiveness*, London: Rider/Random House, 1999.
VanAntwerpen, Jonathon. 'Reconciliation Reconceived: Religion, Secularism, and the Language of Transition' in W. Kymlicka and B. Bashir (eds.), *The Politics of Reconciliation in Multicultural Societies*, Oxford: Oxford University Press, 2010: 25-47.
Van Zyl Slabbert, F. 'Truth without Reconciliation, Reconciliation with Truth' in W. James and L. Van De Vijver, *After the TRC: Reflections on Truth and Reconciliation in South Africa*, Athens, OH: Ohio University Press, 2001: 62-73.
Verdeja, Ernesto. 'Official Apologies in the Aftermath of Political Violence', *Metaphilosophy*, 41(4), 2010: 563-581.
Verdoolaege, Annalies. 'Managing Reconciliation at the Human Rights Violations Hearings of the South African TRC', *Journal of Human Rights*, 5(1), 2006: 61-80.
Vernant, Jean-Pierre. *The Origins of Greek Thought*, Ithaca, NY: Cornell University Press, 1982.
Vernon, Richard. *Historical Redress: Must We Pay for the Past?*, London: Continuum, 2012.
Verwoerd, Wilhelm. 'Towards the Recognition of our Past Injustices' in C. Villa-Vincencio and W. Verwoerd (eds.), *Looking Back, Reaching Forward: Reflections on the Truth and Reconciliation Commission of South Africa*, Cape Town: University of Cape Town Press, 2000: 155-166.
Villa Vincencio, Charles. 'The Reek of Cruelty and the Quest for Healing: Where Retributive and Restorative Justice Meet', *Journal of Law and Religion*, 14(1), 1999-2000: 165-187.
Villa-Vincencio, Charles. 'Getting on with Life: A Move Towards Reconciliation' in C. Villa-Vincencio and W. Verwoerd (eds.), *Looking Back, Reaching Forward: Reflections on the Truth and Reconciliation Commission of South Africa*, Cape Town: University of Cape Town Press, 2000: 199-210.
Villa-Vincencio, Charles. 'On the Limitations of Academic History: The Quest for Truth Demands Both More and Less' in *After the TRC: Reflections on Truth and Reconciliation in South Africa*, Athens, OH: Ohio University Press, 2001: 21-32.
Vivian, Bradford. *Public Forgetting: The Rhetoric and Politics of Beginning Again*, University Park, PA: Pennsylvania State University Press, 2010.

Bibliography

Walaza, N. 'Insufficient Healing and Reparation' in C. Villa-Vincencio and W. Verwoerd (eds.), *Looking Back, Reaching Forward: Reflections on the Truth and Reconciliation Commission of South Africa*, Cape Town: University of Cape Town Press, 2000: 250–258.

Wale, Kim. 'Knotted Memories of a Betrayed Sacrifice: Rethinking Trauma and Hope in South Africa', *Memory Studies*, 2022: 1–15.

Watson, Nicole. 'The Northern Territory Emergency Response: The More Things Change the More They Stay the Same', *Alberta Law Review*, 48(4), 2011.

Wedgewood, C.V. *History and Hope: The Collected Essays of C.V. Wedgewood*, London: Fontana Press, 1987.

Weissbrodt, D. and Fraser, P.W. 'Report of the Chilean National Commission on Truth and Reconciliation', *Human Rights Quarterly*, 14(4), 1992: 601–622.

Weyneth, Robert. 'The Power of Apology and the Process of Historical Reconciliation', *The Public Historian*, 23(3), 2001: 9–38.

Williams, Bernard. *Shame and Necessity*, Berkeley, CA: University of California Press, 1993.

Wilson, Richard. *The Politics of Truth and Reconciliation in South Africa*, Cambridge: Cambridge University Press, 2009.

Winter, Stephen. 'Theorising the Political Apology', *The Journal of Political Philosophy*, 23(3), 2015: 261–281.

Wolfe, Patrick. 'Settler Colonialism and the Elimination of the Native', *Journal of Genocide Research*, 8(4), 2006: 387–409.

Yamamoto, Eric and Serrano, S.K. 'Healing Racial Wounds?' in R.L. Brooks (ed.), *When Sorry Isn't Enough: The Controversy over Apologies and Reparations for Human Injustice*, New York: New York University Press, 1999: 492–500.

Zehfuss, Maja. *Wounds of Memory: The Politics of War in Germany*, Cambridge: Cambridge University Press, 2007.

Index

For the benefit of digital users, indexed terms that span two pages (e.g., 52–53) may, on occasion, appear on only one of those pages.

A

Achilles, 90–91, 95–98
Agamben, Giorgio, 8–10, 15, 16–20, 43–44, 69, 98, 248–249, 300–301
Aguilar, Paloma, 102
Amnesty
  Athenian 403 BCE, 87–89, 93, 94–96, 98–99
  Institution of 25–26, 86, 101–102, 105–109, 213–217, 221, 229, 235, 236–237, 243, 244–246
Amstutz, Mark, 7, 123n132, 124n147, 162n1, 217–218, 311n27
anamnestic solidarity, 104–105, 155, 160–161
Antigone, 91–92, 95–99, 266–268, 279–280, 283
Apartheid, 7, 15, 27, 83–84, 111–112, 213–214, 221–222, 224–225, 228, 230–231, 233, 237–238, 240, 241, 243–247, 250–251
apology
  age of, 3–5, 8–10, 16–23, 26–28, 37–38, 40–41, 169, 270, 283
  sincerity in, 169–170, 178–181
  act of sovereignty, 169–170, 181–192
  abortive ritual, 170
  to the Stolen Generations, 171–172, 174, 175–178, 194–196, 198–203, 285, 304
Arendt, Hannah, 16, 91, 93, 104, 111–112, 157–158, 161–162, 247–249, 297–298
Aristotle, 105, 118n64, 271–281, 286–287

B

bare life, 15–20, 153, 158–160, 303–304, 306–307
Barkan, Elazar, 5–8, 64–65, 178–179
Benjamin, Walter, 104–105, 136

Brandt, William
  Kniefall, 1–4, 18, 61–62, 135, 194, 299–300
Brooks, Roy, 5–7, 15
Buruma, Ian, 41–43, 59
Butler, Judith, 20–21, 111–112, 160–161

C

Camus, Albert, 297–300, 304–306, 308
catharsis, 19–21, 47, 69, 107, 109–112, 140–141, 145, 148–153, 198–199, 217–218, 234–243, 271–272-281
Celermajer, Danielle, 190–191, 194–195
cosmopolitanism, 131–133, 135, 140–141, 160
Critchley, Simon, 91, 96, 268, 275, 277–278, 286–288

D

damaged life, 22–26, 40–44, 51–53, 64–65, 79, 110–111, 222, 224–225, 234–235, 251–252, 282, 284–285, 287–288, 302–303, 306–307
Derrida, Jacques, 190–191, 194, 200–201, 216–217, 230–231
Dodson, Patrick, 200–201, 203

E

Edkins, Jenny, 111–112, 124n137, 141–147, 149, 150–151, 153, 279
Electra, 90–92, 95–98, 104
Esposito, Roberto, 16–17, 301–302
Erikson, Kai, 43–45, 48–54, 63–64, 66–67
exhumation, 107, 223, 275–276, 282–283

F

Fagenblat, Michael, 26–27, 171–174, 187–192
falling, 1–2, 127–129, 194, 272–273, 298–306

Index

Foucault, Michel, 8–16, 18–20, 27, 48–49, 65–66, 68–69, 110–111, 218, 220–223, 226, 300–302
Freud, Sigmund, 7–8, 12–14, 24–25, 41, 43, 45–46, 54–55, 57, 66–68, 83–84, 98–99, 108, 110–112, 217, 243, 247

G

Greek Tragedy, 23, 28, 81–82, 89–93, 95–97, 112–113, 142–143, 151, 265–282–288, 306, 309–310
Great Dionysia, 28, 99, 265–268, 277, 278–284, 286–287
grievable life, 20–21, 159, 160–161, 200, 302
Goldhill, Simon, 266, 268–269, 281, 286–287

H

Habermas, Jürgen 26, 104–105, 131–140, 143, 147–149, 151, 158–162, 281–282, 304
Herman, Judith Lewis, 43–49, 51–53, 63–67, 128–129, 149, 156–157, 218–219, 238–239, 303, 306–307
Hobbes, Thomas 3, 9, 17–18, 170, 181–183, 283
Holst-Warhaft, Gail, 96–97, 120n91
Honig, Bonnie, 117n54, 121n94, 279–280, 285–286, 292n53
Hutchinson, Emma, 112–114, 217–218

I

Indigenous Peoples, 175, 184–185, 201
internal enemies, 9–10, 15, 16, 18, 20–21, 133–136, 157–158, 190–191, 302, 304, 309–310
institution of exception, 8–10, 13, 22–23, 28, 37, 42–43, 64–65, 87–88, 109, 110–111, 218–219, 265–285

J

justice
  distributive, 5–6
  retributive, 5–6, 214–215, 226–227, 233, 236–237
  restorative, 5–7, 9, 10, 21, 38–40, 86, 128–129, 175, 178–179, 214–216, 226–233, 243–244, 270, 302–303

K

Kenosis, 18, 145–146, 173, 192–196, 222, 306

L

Legitimacy, 8–9, 22, 39–40, 56, 131–133, 138–139, 184–185, 188–189, 195, 197, 202–203, 275–277, 308–309
  Crisis of, 37–41, 56–57
Levi, Primo, 1–2, 122n118, 143–144, 158, 160–161
Locke, John, 9, 181–183
Loraux, Nicole 25–26, 87–96, 98–99, 101–102, 111–113, 143, 265, 267–269, 282

M

Machiavelli, 79–80, 84, 86, 110–111, 179
Memorial
  identity, recognition, and injury 1–2, 7, 28, 127–129
  biopolitical dimension 95, 100, 109, 136, 157
  counter, 146–147
  Vietnam Veterans, 26, 52, 53, 142–144, 147–149-153–154
  to the Murdered Jews of Europe, 26, 86–87, 99–100, 129–141, 143–149, 154–162, 269–270, 281–282, 285, 287, 304
Memory
  collective, 53–54, 81–85, 105, 110-113–114, 127, 131–132, 140
  traumatic, 102, 302
Minow, Martha, 5–7, 22–23, 193–194, 217–218, 223, 238–240, 243, 247, 306–307
Mitscherlich, Alexander and Margarete, 43–44, 53–68, 100, 108–109, 138

N

narcissism, 55–56, 61–62, 104–105, 128, 137–138, 195
nation-state, 23–24, 26, 28, 69–70, 79–80, 111–112, 141–143, 150–151, 153–154, 160, 161–162, 192–193, 267–269, 282, 283–288, 308, 309–310
negative nationalism, 131

Nietzsche, Fredrich, 103–104, 135–137, 191, 233, 298
Nussbaum, Martha, 111–112, 149–151, 153–154, 157–158, 231, 232, 280

O
Oedipus, 265–269, 272–277, 279, 282, 287–288, 306

P
pastoral power, 27, 218, 220–223, 226, 227–234, 242–243
Plato, 96–97, 271–274
political theology 8–10, 171–174, 183, 192
psychoanalysis, 25, 65–68, 217–218

R
raison d'état, 4, 22, 24–25, 39–40, 112–113, 202
Reilly, Alex, 171–172, 183–188, 194
Rousso, Henri, 101–102, 106–107, 112–113

S
Schmitt, Carl, 8–11, 15, 17–18, 26–27, 37, 57, 65, 171–174, 183–185, 187, 189, 298
Shakespeare, William, 1, 79–82, 84, 86–87
Shoah, 1–2, 13, 15–16, 26, 46–47, 53–54, 84–85, 104–105, 130–132, 135–140, 143–144, 153–162
spectacle, 18–19, 28, 112–113, 169, 218, 238, 239–240, 250–251, 271, 272–273, 277, 283–285, 308–310

state racism, 9–10, 15, 16–17, 19–21, 23–24, 111–112, 161–162, 175–176, 230–231, 283–286, 299–302
Stolen Generations, 15, 26–27, 171–172, 174, 175–178, 180, 184–187, 190–192, 195–196, 198–199, 281–282, 285, 304

T
Taxidou, Olga, 266, 274
Thompson, Janna, 5–6, 179, 185–186, 246
Torpey, John, 3–4, 6–8, 37–38, 83–84
truth telling, 20–23, 25–26, 62, 64–65, 99, 102–103, 107, 108–113, 177, 215–219, 224–226, 228–229, 236–243, 247–252, 267–268, 282–284, 287, 302–303, 306–309

U
unconscious, 51, 54, 57–60, 104, 138–139, 155–157, 277

V
Verdeja, Ernesto, 170–171, 182, 190–191, 197

W
witnessing, 202–203, 213, 218, 222–223, 225–228, 234, 236–243, 247, 250–252, 269–270, 282–285, 306, 308